STOLEN GRACE

A Memoir:
How God Rescued Me from the Jaws and Claws
of the United Methodist Church

Rev. Dr. Errol E. Leslie

Published in the United States of America

ISBN 978-1-963379-06-8 (SC)
ISBN 979-8-89395-885-0 (HC)

Errol Leslie Publishing
222 West 6th Street
Suite 400, San Pedro, CA, 90731
errollesliepublishing@gmail.com
321 614 1546

Order Information and Rights Permission:

Quantity sales. Special discounts might be available on quantity purchases by corporations, associations, and others. For details, contact the publisher at the address above.

For Book Rights Adaptation and other Rights Permission.
Call us at toll-free 1-888-945-8513 or send us an email at
admin@stellarliterary.com.

Acknowledgment

To Rev. Dr. William "Scott" Campbell, who spent countless hours reviewing my case and made every effort to help me retain my status as a United Methodist Church pastor.

To Rev. Dr. Larry Lake, who played a strong supportive role as the assistant counsel for the defense.

To Rev. Dr. Sydney Sadio, who held my hand and walked with me through the very early part of the process and who first helped me to understand that the bishop could not force me to surrender my credentials.

To the several ministerial colleagues --Methodist and non-Methodist -- who kept assuring me of their prayers and support throughout the process and who encouraged me to stay strong.

To the many persons in the Palm Bay Community and beyond throughout the western world who also encouraged me and showed very strong support through this ordeal.

Dear Scott, Larry, and Sydney,

Words are not enough for me to express my thanks to you for the amount of time, energy, and emotion that you invested into standing up for fairness, truth and justice on my behalf. As a result of your efforts, I learned so much about the laws of the church. Without that knowledge, I would not have been able to write now with such confidence. Scott, you went way beyond what I had ever dreamed, and that untiring commitment helped me to retain my sanity. May God continue to bless all of you, your respective families, and your respective ministries

During the period between the start of this narrative and the completion leading to this publication, three persons who were referenced have passed on. This includes Bishop F Herbert Skeete who gave me my first appointment in the United Methodist Church in July 1995. Bishop Skeete was extremely supportive throughout the process, constantly encouraged me and remained in my corner until the end. I use this medium to posthumously pay tribute to him and would also dedicate this work to his memory. I also acknowledge the passing of two more persons who were referenced and who also dedicated their lives to serving God albeit at different levels of the church.

ON GOD'S WORD, I PROMISE TO SHARE THE TRUTH, THE WHOLE TRUTH, AND NOTHING BUT THE TRUTH.

Title: Stolen Grace: **A Memoir: How God Rescued Me from the Jaws and Claws of the United Methodist Church**

Author: **Rev Errol E. Leslie**

Genre: **Christian Church Leadership / Christian Family & Relationships**

Reviewed by: **Jack Chambers**

One of the hardest realizations a person can come to in this life is to realize that we are human, and as such are prone to imperfection, no matter how much we strive to be otherwise. The moment comes in our lives when we make a decision that turns out to be the wrong one, and that begins the path to redemption. Acknowledging our faults and knowing the need to make things right makes us human, and as Brendan Fraser once said, "I guess darkness serves a purpose: to show us that there is redemption through chaos. I believe in that. I think that's the basis of Greek mythology."

In author Rev Errol E. Leslie's Stolen Grace: A Memoir: How God Rescued Me from the Jaws and Claws of the United Methodist Church, the author shares a heartfelt and personal story of his own redemption after a mistake in his personal life turned into a personal and professional nightmare. After a mistake on his part, the Reverend's ministry is put into question and his status as a leader within the church is removed as a result of a false accusation, the author must go on a journey to learn the laws of the church and fight for the truth as he makes amends for the mistake that began this nightmare and forces the truth out of the darkness and into the light.

The author did a fantastic job of crafting the perfect balance of faith and religion-based discussion with personal experience within the Methodist church and the legal system as a whole. The painful and intimate way the author examines his own precluding actions and acknowledges his mistakes was a refreshing change of pace for a narrative of this stature, as the author was able to separate the wrongs done to him while still owning up to his decisions to enter into a relationship outside his marriage that led to these complaints with the church.

This is the perfect read for those who enjoy non-fiction memoirs with a hint of religious and spiritual text, and personal stories of fighting for truth and justice. One thing which really stood out was the way the author was able to incorporate documentation and legal discoveries regarding the rights of those within the inner structures of the United Methodist Church. The way the author was able to give so much detail regarding the experiences he had within this process showcased the rarely seen behind-the-scenes stories of organized religions and the politics that go on behind closed doors.

Thoughtful, engaging, and haunting in its delivery, author Rev Errol E. Leslie's Stolen Grace: A Memoir: How God Rescued Me from the Jaws and Claws of the United Methodist Church is a must-read book. The themes of redemption, forgiveness, and moving forward were well explored throughout this book, as was the concept of justice and the need to free the truth to really get a handle on how life is behind the scenes of an organization such as this. The author's painful struggles and willingness to open up and share the mistakes and strives towards forgiveness they made while also fighting for his rights in the process made this such a powerful story to read!

Post by Judith Chepkombet » 02 Jun 2022, 09:01

[Following is a volunteer review of "Stolen Grace" by Rev Errol E Leslie.]

4 out of 4 stars

The author narrates a memoir of his life odyssey. He shares his life ordeal in the parsonage, and which is more of betrayal and pain than glory. The author who was born in a small village in Westmoreland on the island of Jamaica grew up and discovered his passion in the church which he termed a calling from God.

In this memoir, *Stolen Grace* by Rev. Errol E. Leslie, he narrated how he was 'persecuted' in the hands of the United Methodist Church where he served as a Reverend in Palm Bay Florida. The author uses interesting quotes from the bible to relate and describe his situation at the "ruthless" hands of the united Methodist authority that punished him for a mistake humanly erred by himself.

I would equate the plight of the author to have landed in the hands of 'Jezebel' from the biblical scriptures. The author reconnected to an old girlfriend from the past and opines this to have been the beginning of his problems. The lady who at the time lived in Georgia had undergone a divorce and was struggling in another relationship. She sought counseling help from Rev. Leslie and someone to share her troubles. Unfortunately, her second relationship ended as well but by then their relationship with the reverend had started growing to be more intimate. The reverend was having a hard time with his family and the growing intimacy was becoming more of a temptation to his faith and moral precepts.

The author kept my curiosity at par in suspense as he began the book with his plight and revealed how he erred in the later chapters of the book. I also enjoyed how the author related his story to the scriptures going further to even liken some of the characters in his story to characters from the bible. First, he relates his temptation and fall to that of David from the Bible and narrates how he expected the church to handle his issue with grace. However, this was never the case. Secondly, he related some of the heads of the clergy handling his trial with a hardened and ruthless heart to the pharaoh in the time of Moses, Pilate in the persecution of Jesus. He also likened the bishops to the priest and the Levite in the parable of the Good Samaritan who showed no care or mercy to a fallen human being.

I didn't encounter any typos or grammatical errors and the book was exceptionally well-edited.

The book had direct quotes and references from the bible and is one that will entertain most readers who love reading good memoirs. I will rate the book 4 out of 4 stars, for the book was entertaining and the reading experience was not much of a bother to deduct a star.

4 out of 4 stars

Review by ThankGod Onyishi | 06 Jun 2022, 11:05

There is a high possibility that every one of us will experience problems that will shake us or negatively affect us, no matter how small or big. These could come from financial problems, emotional problems, health problems, or even relationship problems. How do we deal with these problems when we are faced with them? If we make mistakes in the course of dealing with these problems, are these mistakes ones that we can easily be dug out of?

In *Stolen Grace: How God Rescued Me from the Jaws and Claws of the United Methodist Church*, Rev. Errol E. Leslie recounts his experiences with the United Methodist Church. The author is confident that his call to ministry is a genuine call from God as he uses a story recorded in the Acts of the Apostles, Chapter 5, to explain. However, does a genuine call from God assure a smooth road? Rev. Leslie is put to the test. Does he succumb to temptation?

I honestly enjoyed every single thing about this book. Even though it was a non-fiction book and one that dealt with hearings in a church, I felt at certain times that I was the judge, going through the evidence, reading documents presented before me, and wondering what the author deserved. This was the effect that the author's inclusion of these documents had on me. I liked how the documents and reports contained dates, especially those of the Reverend's wife. It helped display the credibility of the story, and testimonies from individuals helped to show that the author was not just trying to clear his name but that, indeed, he was telling the truth.

The book talked about a wide range of things, which was pleasant. It discussed struggles in marriages and the importance of communication and change in marriages. By reading this book, I learned that partners should be able to not only listen to the complaints of one another but effect changes in the necessary areas to maintain relationships. I was saddened by the fact that the injustice the author faced was done by people who were called to serve God and in a place that should supposedly be the home of forgiveness, love, and a nonjudgmental space. It was so painful to see how the author suffered based on false accusations by a woman and a church unwilling to carry out necessary investigations. His fate had already been decided before a trial even commenced. I love the author's persistence and how he maintains his call even after all the struggles. This quality is worthy of emulation and one that would be helpful in our lives. There were also different stories or testimonies in the book that house strong themes like physical and sexual abuse. The author's mistakes teach us to seek solutions in better places, and I appreciate that he acknowledges his mistakes.

The thing I liked least about this book was the fact that it seemed we were hearing from just one of the parties. Although the book seems packed with evidence corroborating the author's side of the story, for fairness, I would have appreciated hearing more from the other party too. Nevertheless, I rate this book **four out of four stars** because, first, there were no errors in the book; it was exceptionally well edited. Also, I could write a short book about what I liked about this book, and I applaud the author for that.

I recommend this book to people who enjoy memoirs and people going through struggles in their lives. This book houses a lot of lessons and provides reassurance that you are indeed loved.

ONLINE
Book
CLUB

[Following is a volunteer review of "Stolen Grace" by Rev Errol E Leslie.]

4 out of 4 stars

Review by Walter R

In Stolen Grace: A Memoir: How God Rescued Me from the Jaws and Claws of the United Methodist Church, Rev Errol E. Leslie tells the story of his call to ministry and how his work in the United Methodist Church was disrupted by a mistake which the leaders of the church decided to punish him so harshly for. The book begins with the author's note on a genuine call to ministry, in which he states, supporting with Bible passages, that a simple call to serve God will survive all threats.

This book has a lot of positive aspects. It follows a true story, and it is very relatable. Recently, we have had several women speak up against the harsh treatments they received from men; this has made society move towards getting justice for women who have been allegedly maltreated. However, as in all claims, there is always another side of the story that should be heard before blind support is given to a claimant. This crucifixion before getting to the root of a matter is what the author suffers in this book.

It was painful to see how the author's career got destroyed due to an accusation that stemmed from a weave of lies and a half-truth. Rev Errol was judged without being allowed to defend himself properly, and this goes a long way in reiterating the principle of "hear both sides." The book provides reassurance that we all experience life issues at some point. It examines the strong possibility that certain actions of individuals are responses to issues they have gone through or are going through. The author strongly speaks against being judgmental and seeks to understand people better. The book contains story-like testimonies that drive home enshrined messages, images, and texts supporting the author's claims. The author provides several examples to illustrate his disgust at the actions of a set of people who sought to punish him unjustly and offers hope while passing his message across.

I did not find any negative aspects of this book. I also did not find any errors in the book. It was exceptionally well edited.

I rate this book **four out of four stars** because it was a fantastic read, and there was nothing to dislike about it. Although I believe Christians would appreciate the book better due to the use of certain Bible passages by the author to drive home his point, I would also recommend this book to lovers of memoirs, human rights activists, and people in search of the truth.

ONLINE

B**ook**

C L U B

Post by **Walter R** » 07 Feb 2022, 09:35
Yes, it is indeed sad that the church has also become a symbol of corruption. Great review.

Post by **mnyazi dzuya** » 07 Feb 2022, 11:54
I love reading memoirs. Stolen Grace is one of the books I would like to read through. How the author gets rescued by God; and how he made it through the painful journey of his career is intriguing. I would like to see the positive aspects and the painful journey of his career. I love how this book has been well-reviewed.

I love memoir like this as there are several takeaways from it. I so eager to know what Rev. Errol was punished for.

The church is one place that is supposed to feel safe, unfortunately it doesn't. Nice review!

Post by **bhattuc** » 07 Feb 2022, 18:31
The review is evoking interest in me for going for more details by going through the book maybe at a later time. Thanks for the excellent review.

Post by **Joseph Kasapo** » 08 Feb 2022, 01:05
Great review. It is sad how the church is becoming weak when it comes to such issues.

Post by **Blison-+** » 08 Feb 2022, 07:55
How God Rescued the author from the jaws and claws from the UMC, And how painful to see his career got destroyed. Good review!

Post by **Fine Brand** » 08 Feb 2022, 09:38
This book talks about real life experiences and I can relate. Great review.

Post by **eniola matthew** » 08 Feb 2022, 11:40
hmm true life story 😨 and experience, I can relate. Nice 😊 review

Post by **Sarah Dogbatse** » 11 Feb 2022, 17:59
The book talks a lot about how our churches are being destroyed with corruption. It's painful how Rev Errol E Leslie's job got destroyed. But in all God was with him and rescued him from the UMC. Great review

Post by **Walter R** » 13 Feb 2022, 07:54
Have never really been a great fan of memoirs. Great review.

Post by **LOAM** » 13 Feb 2022, 21:00
Great review. It is sad how the church is becoming weak when it comes to such issues. Great review

Post by **Raymond N** » 16 Feb 2022, 01:12
Sad to know that we are really quick to criticize and punish people without hearing the full story. Thank you for the review.

Post by **Segunjohn** » 04 Apr 2022, 11:21
Thank you for a well detailed and honest review. I've always loved nonfiction books and this sounds like one I'll definitely love to have for myself.

CONTENTS

PREFACE

I would never be able to verbalize how this particular memoir was given birth. I never sat down and designed any plans to write. All I remember is that I woke up and on one day I kept hearing from God that I must tell my story to the world. Once I started writing, I could not stop and never felt that I could experience total peace and fulfillment until this story was told. While growing up and even after I started pastoral ministry, I never ever thought that I would be publishing any literary works. The experience of preparing this draft has led me to the thought that even though I am a little older, I should be continuing to write Bible study material and even publish some of my sermons and other works later.

For this publication, there are some persons who will read it who are already somewhat familiar with the story and I hope that they will hear it from another perspective and see the proverbial "other side of the story." The truth is that, as we will see later on, I felt muzzled by the church and experienced the ongoing pain of watching them telling and publicly sharing a one-sided story and one from their perspective. I am hoping that there are some pastors who never heard it but may read this and determine that they will never fall in the trap into which I fell. It has been a long and painful road and it does come with regrets but through it, I have experienced God walking beside me day by day and also continuing to lead me on in ministry. Hopefully this story will also be encouraging to any pastor/s who may have felt discarded by human beings within the church. We should embrace the fundamental biblical teaching that God never leaves us nor forsake us but that He is with us always—even unto the end of the age. I urge that regardless of the circumstances you should never ever give up on your call to Christian ministry as long as you are continuing to sense that call from God.

Please create a way to share Christ with others. I am also hoping that from reading this, bishops and leaders within the Methodist church and other Christian denominations will recognize the need to find a way to gently minister to and counsel pastors who have succumbed to temptation. You will never know what background circumstances could trigger such actions. Pastors can have domestic problems and do have emotions too! There are times when we could use the Bible instead of a human "rule book" or use a soft brush instead of a hammer!

I recently preached a sermon on forgiveness and emphasized how much we need to prepare for this giant of temptation day after day. When I faced the temptation to which I succumbed, I wished that my thoughts and actions were alongside that of Joseph when he was tempted by Potiphar's wife. In that situation, Joseph responded by stating how much faith and confidence Potiphar had placed in him so he could not do what she wanted him to do. The most important rationale which Joseph gave though was that he could not carry out her wishes "and sin against God." I had neither prepared myself for the temptation nor did I handle it as Joseph did. As a result, some persons have expressed the gamut of emotions—shock, anger, disappointment, and at times I have even felt snubbed. One of the most gut-wrenching experiences which I had, related to a time when I was trying to rent a space for my newly formed congregation to meet. I was negotiating with the pastor of another mainline denomination with whom I had had a great relationship. She made me go through the routine process of filling out the paperwork and getting testimonials about me (even though she had known me for six years). At the end of the process, she called me and told me that her church board had declined my application. When I asked her what the basis of their decision was, she said in a stern voice. "The Methodist Church took away your credentials, didn't they?" That was a tough one for me to swallow.

I remember when I was growing up as a teenager and people in my community learned that I was offering for the ministry, everyone was so thrilled. That piece of information won me even higher and greater respect from the community than I had already achieved on my own.

I was the first from my small village to go into the pastoral ministry of a mainline denomination, and by extension, I was also the first from my church. Many of the persons who cheered me on have now passed on, and that would include my own parents. They probably wept from heaven as they saw that I had also let them down. I wish that I could express my apologies to their faces, but they must know how penitent and remorseful I have been. I should hope that from the telling of this story, all my family, friends, and acquaintances who were disappointed in me would also know how sincerely sorry I am.

Among the things which I learned is that it is also okay for pastors to go for counseling or do therapy. For every other session of counseling in which I was involved, I would sit in the counselor's chair. This time, I found myself doing therapy on three separate occasions and sat in the counselee's chair. Once in Connecticut and twice in Florida. I really could not see myself in any other field but in pastoral ministry, so I definitely needed help in dealing with that potential reality. However, it was the shocking and unexpected response of the church hierarchy which mainly drove me to seek therapy. This response was brutal, unethical, and inhumane and after several months of expressed pain, I listened to the advice of some of my supporters and sought professional help.

While I experienced a very painful period in my life, it was refreshing to get several unsolicited pieces of communication from persons voluntarily telling me that they still loved and respected me. From all appearances and feedback which I would receive, I seemed to have been involved in an effective ministry and many were blessed and still being blessed by my ministry. While I am absolutely confident about the call which I received from God, I equally realized that I was not faithful to that call. Here though, is the one thing I do know, God continues to love me. I have total assurance that He has forgiven me and I am hundred percent confident that He can use me and will continue to use me as one of His chosen and called servants to lead and give spiritual guidance to those whom He may choose to place under my pastoral care.

I had hoped that the same act of grace and forgiveness which God lavished on me would also have been demonstrated by the hierarchy of the United Methodist Church, but surprisingly—or perhaps not so surprisingly—I was denied that as a result of which, I felt cheated and robbed of the gift of grace which God Himself offered to me freely. It felt like there was an attempt to have my grace stolen, but praise God, it could not be intercepted when God continued to pour it on me. In situations such as the one in which I was involved, I do expect that the hierarchy of the church is going to investigate, follow its discipline, and discharge its responsibilities. However, one would also expect these leaders to take on and use a Christian approach in the way that they would carry out this responsibility. As if to throw salt into the wound, the process which played out within the church did not quite represent the most ethical approach either.

There is, however, another side to this coin. From time to time, people both inside and outside of the church are still trying to figure out how it is that over the years; some pastors and leaders in high offices within the church continue to display such blatant contradictions between what they preach and what they practice. These leaders do not seem to realize how much they behave like the Pharisees—the group that Jesus criticized so often for hypocrisy. As such, we have seen abuse, injustice, deception, lies, dishonesty, and other unethical behavior coming from representatives of the church and this at every level. This behavioral pattern is often brushed aside and seen as okay. Rightly or wrongly, many persons have become disillusioned with the church when they observe this kind of behavior. At the same time, when persons become involved in "perceived stronger acts of sinfulness" the same church leaders cave in on them with knives, swords, gunshots, and the like. Very often, fellow sinners throw other sinners under the bus and into the fiery furnace. Often, these acts of reprimand give the leaders in the church a sense of fulfillment because, in their minds, they are acting on behalf of God.

All over the Bible and especially in the New Testament, there are references to God's unconditional love, forgiveness, mercy, and grace.

Elementary theology also teaches that God's forgiveness does not just happen once but that it is ongoing and always available. Guilty persons just have to ask. Not only are we assured of God's forgiveness but He has also promised that He will remember our sins no more. The psalmist mentions that as far as the east is from the west, that is how far He will separate our sins from us. Paul the apostle made some references to what he regarded as a sense of spiritual hopelessness outside of the power of God's love, mercy, and grace. For example, his discourse recorded in Romans 7:14–25 speaks volumes about his own personal concerns.

> We know that the law is spiritual; but I am unspiritual, sold as a slave to sin. I do not understand what I do. For what I want to do I do not do, but what I hate I do. And if I do what I do not want to do, I agree that the law is good. As it is, it is no longer I myself who do it, but it is sin living in me. For I know that good itself does not dwell in me, that is, in my sinful nature. For I have the desire to do what is good, but I cannot carry it out. For I do not do the good I want to do, but the evil I do not want to do—this I keep on doing. Now if I do what I do not want to do, it is no longer I who do it, but it is sin living in me that does it.
>
> So I find this law at work: Although I want to do good, evil is right there with me. For in my inner being I delight in God's law; but I see another law at work in me, waging war against the law of my mind and making me a prisoner of the law of sin at work within me. What a wretched man I am! Who will rescue me from this body that is subject to death? Thanks be to God, who delivers me through Jesus Christ our Lord! So then, I myself in my mind am a slave to God's law, but in my sinful nature a slave to the law of sin.

There is a real connection between the referenced passage above and two other separate passages written to the church at Corinth.

Firstly here is a passage from 1 Corinthians 9:24:

> Don't you realize that in a race everyone runs, but only one person gets the prize? So run to win! All athletes are disciplined in their training. They do it to win a

prize that will fade away, but we do it for an eternal prize. So I run with purpose in every step. I am not just shadowboxing. I discipline my body like an athlete, training it to do what it should. Otherwise, I fear that after preaching to others I myself might be disqualified.

Secondly, a passage from 2 Corinthians 12:7–9 about the Thorn in the Flesh:

> Because of the surpassing greatness of the revelations, for this reason, to keep me from exalting myself, there was given me a thorn in the flesh, a messenger of Satan to torment me—to keep me from exalting myself! Concerning this I implored the Lord three times that it might leave me. And He has said to me, "My grace is sufficient for you, for power is perfected in weakness." Most gladly, therefore, I will rather boast about my weaknesses, so that the power of Christ may dwell in me.

There is every appearance that Paul had his own struggles with doing the right things. There have been several theories which have been put forward by scholars who have tried to identify specifically what that thorn was. Regardless of the correct theory—whatever that may turn out to be, it caused Paul to struggle and stumble. At the same time, he wanted to be a good example to those to whom he preached so he disciplined himself (1 Corinthians 9:27) so that he would not be disqualified from the prize. Paul was deeply aware of the struggle with sin, but he was equally conscious that he had to fight all the internal and external forces which threatened his walk with God.

Therefore inasmuch as we emphasize the assurance of God's forgiveness, we are also mindful of Paul's reminder in Romans chapter 6 and verse 1 that we should not continue to sin just because we know that God's grace is available in great abundance. As followers of Christ, we should all heed Paul's caution in this verse. However, even after all that, we are always reassured as we still learn in the first verse of Romans chapter 8 that *"There is therefore now no condemnation to them that are in Christ Jesus."* We also learn in the last few verses of that same chapter that there is nothing in all creation that can separate us from the Love of God. Like Paul, we too give thanks to God for the victory which is always ours through Jesus Christ who, by His death and resurrection, has made us into "joint heirs with Him." I trust that this discourse would help to change the approach of a few persons who seem to enjoy pointing out the speck in the eye of others while some big logs are blocking their own view.

There are many other Bible references to substantiate the thoughts expressed above, but we will just reference a few below.

> Therefore, since we have been justified through faith, we have peace with God through our Lord Jesus Christ. (Romans 5:1)

> In Him, we have redemption through His Blood, the forgiveness of our trespasses, according to the riches of His grace which he lavished upon us. (Ephesians 1:7)

> That in the ages to come, he might shew the exceeding riches of His grace in his kindness toward us through Jesus Christ. (Ephesians 2:7)

> But Where sin abounded, grace much more abound. (Romans 5:20)

CHAPTER 1

A Strong, Genuine and Convincing Call from God

There is a very powerful and moving story recorded in the book of the Acts of the Apostles chapter 5. The apostles are being interrogated by the Pharisees and Sadducees who are jealous because they continue to witness the miracles being done through these apostles.

However a Pharisee in the council named Gamaliel cautioned his colleagues and asked them to hold back on their rush to punishment. Gamaliel's argument references two previous situations where persons had started religious movements and initially received a great following, but in both instances the respective movements failed and folded up. Firstly, Gamaliel mentioned Thaddeus who *"rose up, claiming to be somebody and a number of men, about four hundred joined him but he was killed and all who followed him were dispersed and disappeared."* Gamaliel went on to share about the second man named Judas, the Galilean who rose up at the time of the census and got people to follow him, but he also perished and all who followed him scattered. Based on those two experiences, Gamaliel urged the religious leaders to keep away from these men (the apostles) and leave them alone for if their plan or undertaking be of human origin it will fail. But if it be of God, *"You will not be able to overthrow them—in which case you May even be found fighting against God."* In essence this professor, who had students like Paul the apostle studying under him, suggested that any movement approved by God would bear plenty of fruit while any not approved by God would wither and fail.

This warning bore the marks of Jesus's words to Peter at Caesarea Philippi recorded in Matthew chapter 16, where Jesus assures Peter that he was Peter, the rock, and on this rock, *"I will build my church and the gates of hell will not prevail against it."* Jesus went on to remind Peter that He (Jesus) would give him the keys of the kingdom of heaven, and *"whatever you bind on earth will be bound in heaven and whatever you loose on earth will be loosed in heaven."* This statement by Jesus was a mark or stamp of authority on Peter's ministry. Peter like the other apostles, graciously and humbly accepted that authority given to them while recognizing, as Jesus stated in another conversation, that Jesus was the vine and they were merely the branches. As such, they needed to keep abiding in Him if they wanted to bear fruit. *"Apart from me,"* said Jesus, *"you can do nothing."*

There have been millions of pastors/ministers who have expressed a desire to serve God since that time. This service would be based on a perceived call from God to be part of the team on whom His authority would be placed. One can imagine that some of these might have been like Thaddeus and Judas referenced above and whose ministry did not last a long time for one reason or another. It would be reasonable to conclude that the vast majority of pastors who have received a genuine call from God would have completed their ministry on earth having overcome a multiplicity of hurdles and obstacles—some of their own making and others placed upon them by outside forces.

Personally, I expect that I will be one of those described above in the latter category as I know that I am going to be a pastor until the day I die. At some point I may grow older and not physically able to carry on active ministry but I have no doubt that I will be doing all I can even in physical retirement to proclaim the name of Jesus and tell others about His goodness. My call to ministry has remained strong since age thirteen, and I know that it came from God who knew me and had His eyes on me from I was in my mother's womb. Since I know that God placed his hands and stamp of approval on me, I am encouraged by Paul's words recorded in Philippians 1:6.

> Being confident of this, that he who began a good
> work in you will carry it on to completion until the day
> of Christ Jesus.

Growing up in a small village in Haddo, Westmoreland, in the island of Jamaica, I was raised in a church that had about twenty-five members overall and with an average attendance of fifteen persons. As such, it may not be surprising that I was called to teach Sunday school at the age of thirteen. By age sixteen, I was the leader of the church's youth group and at age eighteen I was a co-youth director for an entire circuit of Methodist churches. Both levels of leadership meant that I was motivating and encouraging young people and not merely being the "senior" youth in a given situation. It is the kind of responsibility which would normally have been given to someone in their mid to late twenties and even thirties or forties. I sensed that this leadership position was preparing me for the larger call which God was placing on me for pastoral leadership. I had started preparing to serve my church as a lay preacher at the same age of sixteen while I was leading the youth group, and at age eighteen, I had started my serious quest and candidature for a ministry within the Methodist Church in the Caribbean and the Americas. However, there was one serious dilemma which I faced. All along, while I was a part of the Methodist Church, I also spent a lot of time at the neighboring Salvation Army. Essentially, I would attend the Methodist Sunday school at 9:00 a.m. and then stayed for the worship service at 11:00 a.m. Following the worship service, there was a weekly prayer meeting, which would run for one hour or more. Even as kids, we would leave church around 2:30 p.m. and had a quick cooked lunch at home. Enthusiastically, I would then go to Sunday school at the Salvation Army at 4:00 p.m. and back to their evening service at 7:00 p.m. If we include the after-church prayer service at the Methodist Church, it meant that I was doing church five times on a Sunday. As I pondered candidature for the Methodist ministry, I was also being encouraged to offer as an officer for the Salvation Army. My dilemma was in trying to discern whether God wanted me in the Methodist church or in the Salvation Army. However, I had absolutely no doubt that I felt a sincere and authentic call from God for ministry. I was not coerced, coaxed, pushed, forced, or anything which could suggest that I was doubtful or that it was not my own decision in responding to God hundred percent. I remember voluntarily sharing the information with my pastor at the time, and he helped me to understand the process. Interestingly, within a few days after I told him, I went to church one Sunday, and my then elementary school principal, who was also a leader of the church informed me that at a meeting which he attended, he had given my name to the superintendent minister as one who should be pursued and encouraged to offer for the ministry. He was pleasantly surprised when I informed him that the thought was already in my head. My call to ministry was very strong such that my older sister told me that it was because I was baptized/christened as a child twice—once in the Salvation Army and once in the Methodist Church. I was also told that at the service at the Salvation Army, the officer held me up as a baby and prayed this prayer among others. "Lord have mercy on poor little Errol." God really did have mercy and placed me as one of His messengers.

In addition to the Methodist Church and the Salvation Army, I had also made connections with other Christian bodies. For example, there was a Wesleyan Holiness Church that was about half of one hour's walk from my home. I would also connect with that church and attended nightly services there during the week. It was from that experience that I became passionate for Evangelism, and I would go to the altar just about every time that there was an invitation or an appeal so to do. Outside of the immediate church environment, I also gained great spiritual fulfillment and growth from my active participation in the interschools Christian fellowship during my high school years as well as the Jamaica youth for Christ during my young adult years. My Christian foundation was well laid and strong. For this I will be eternally grateful to my parents, Sunday school teachers, pastors, as well as several adult residents from the little village in which I grew up, who would give unfailing support and encouragement throughout my preparation and candidature. I remember clearly that at age sixteen, I preached my first sermon, and interestingly enough, it was at one of the evening services at the Salvation Army. That same year, I would continue to preach as a lay speaker at several Methodist churches within a twelve-mile radius from where I grew up, and two years later, I started preparing as a candidate for the ministry of the Methodist church. I entered seminary in September of 1974 and graduated in June of 1978. Thankfully, I enjoyed some very fulfilling years of ministry serving the Methodist Church in Jamaica before I immigrated to the USA in 1995. My goal then was to pursue a ministry in music. While that specific dream was not realized, I was still able to experience the joys of fulfilling my call and serving Christ through pastoral ministry. Within a year after I immigrated, my clergy membership was transferred from the Methodist Church in the Caribbean and the Americas to the New England Conference of the United Methodist Church.

After nearly forty years of ministry, I made a choice which marked the beginning of the end of my ministry within the United Methodist Church. I alluded to this in the preface and have described the specific sequence of events in the upcoming pages. Suffice it to say that while my ordination and other credentials remain in place to this day, my pastoral services within the United Methodist Church were terminated, and I was never given another appointment. This all came about because I, unfortunately, had crossed moral boundaries and was given what some pastors tend to describe as the "ecclesiastical death penalty." Translated, I was no longer considered a member of the clergy within the United Methodist Church.

That was a very devastating time in my life as I never really saw it coming. Because my call to ministry, as described above, was still very strong, I sought counseling from a variety of persons, prayed continuously to God, and poured out my heart to Him as David did after his encounter with Bathsheba and subsequent murder of her husband Uriah. I was truly repentant and contrite before God. I had hoped that since David committed two sinful acts, back-to-back, and was still forgiven by God, who later described him as "a man after my own heart," I might have been given a chance to redeem myself from that bad choice on my part. I spent time reading, digesting, and processing Psalm 51 several times and was as sincerely contrite as I thought that David was at the time of his bad choices. Within that specific psalm, I focused on the words *"Create in me a clean heart Oh God and restore me unto the joy of Thy Salvation."* While I am not claiming to be at the same level as David was, I cannot help but observing that David received his call from God as I also did at a young age and so may not have been able to stand the thought of not being able to serve Him fully in spite of his deeds. David was not going to be intimidated by the size of Goliath and even with Saul and others trying to dissuade him, he decided that he was going to fight the battles in the name of God. In fact, he removed the armpit and other military gear which Saul had given to him because they did not feel right on him. David told Goliath, "You come to me with spears and sword, but I come in the name of the Lord." As David was determined to overcome his challenge, so I was determined to overcome the anticipated struggles as a pastor chosen and called by God. Humanly speaking, it was hard, but I decided that I was going to have God fight the battles for me.

With that fear of not having the opportunity to serve in a pastoral capacity while still sensing a strong sense of call, I did not immediately resign as some other persons in the same situation have done or even as some persons suggested, I should do. After all the prayers and counsel received, I decided to plea with the bishop and other leaders in the church for forgiveness.

I not only expressed my deep regrets and contrition to God, but I also shared it several times with those human forces that sought to make a judgment on my character and to determine my pastoral destiny. As I describe in the pages to follow, my pleas went unheeded even though I made a decision not to give in to the pressures nor bribes from the administration of the church. So when the Florida Conference offered me $25,000 in exchange for my resignation and termination of my ministerial credentials, I considered that an insult. I was neither going to sell Jesus nor my call to ministry for thirty pieces of silver and in so doing trade my call for cash. Neither was I going to sell what I considered to be my birthright. I decided to make my plea all the way not because I thought that I was innocent but because my call was so strong. My case ended up in the form of a church trial, and in January of 2016, by a vote of 9–4, a jury of my peers determined that my pastoral appointment within the United Methodist Church should end. Because of what I perceived as an unethical approach as well as the many flaws and deception during the entire process, I appealed the decision at both the regional and the national level. Notwithstanding my own failure, it was clear that the playing field was not level during the process and the goal posts were moved a few times. I was absolutely convinced that one of the higher church courts was going to reverse the decision, but to my disappointment, that hope was not realized either. At the beginning of the process and also at my suggestion, my defense team decided not to challenge the charge but instead to seek a lesser penalty than what the hierarchy of the church suggested in the first place. My defense team proposed several resolutions instead of the ecclesiastical death penalty, but it was all to no avail. No other suggestion would be entertained by the leaders of the church.

One such proposal was that I be taken out of appointment for one full year during which time counseling services would be sought at my own expense. Associated with that proposal was that I would also have to meet intermittently during that period with select pastors so that I could give an account or updates on the program. That proposal received thumbs down from the church hierarchy.

Another proposal was that I would be given an opportunity to take an early retirement. That proposal would not have been my first choice, but the process would at least have ended amicably. The reasoning behind this proposal was that I was, at the time, less than two years from being eligible for full retirement benefits and pension. However, this proposal also received thumbs down. This was now beginning to feel like the message which the prophet Nathan gave to David as he told him that parable. The church is getting ready to slaughter and sell my "one sheep," which grew up with me from I was a child and which I had cuddled over and over. There was no concern about my sentimental or my spiritual attachment to this very important part of my life. There seemed to have been no care about my spiritual state or my financial state or my social state. In their minds it was okay to kick a servant of God to the curb and send him into obscurity regardless of whether he is run over by a truck or eaten by a crocodile.

One member of my defense team asked the counsel (prosecutor) for the church if he did not have any concern about my having a young family with daughters in college and high school respectively and that among other things I would lose a lot of income and also my retirement benefits. He further challenged the counsel for the church to consider the fact that I had, at the time, given thirty-eight years of service to the Methodist Church, which was split between the Methodist Church in the Caribbean and the Americas and the United Methodist Church. To this suggestion, the counsel responded, "I don't care." All this negotiation was taking place ahead of the formal church trial, so it was not difficult to figure out how this case was going to turn out once it got to a trial. It was becoming more and more clear that the church was about to go through the routine formalities of a church trial, but the result was a foregone conclusion.

The level of disrespect and indignity which I experienced from the leaders of the church is almost beyond description. In fact, when I watch cop shows on television, I am usually very impressed with the gentle manner in which some cops deal with alleged criminals. For the most part, they have been very polite even when an arrest is going to be made. I had the exact opposite experience. Beginning with the district superintendent who would continuously talk down to me in a condescending manner and continuing with the bishop who communicated with me during the supervisory session, I was yelled at, told to "stop talking," and scenes like that—which made me realize that murder suspects or other high-crime suspects received far more respect and dignity from the police than I received from the hierarchy of the church. As it turned out, I was given one week to pack up and leave the parsonage even before the judicial process had properly begun. It was a most inhumane action and happened right in the heart of the Christmas season. Interestingly, and by the church's own admission, they had acted inappropriately and improperly when they asked me to vacate the parsonage. It was clearly an illegal and incorrect piece of action on their part. The associated letter from the bishop's office to me is referenced later in this memoir.

When the church insisted on moving forward with a trial, my defense team also requested that it would be a closed trial as opposed to an open trial. A closed trial would mean that nothing about the trial would go public but even with the anticipated verdict and penalty; the information would be kept within the confines of the administrative wing of the United Methodist Church. On the other hand, an open trial would mean that everything about the trial including documents, decisions taken, recommendations made, would be made public and be in the public domain. For reasons which I still am not able to figure out, the church insisted that it was going to have an open trial. My defense team thought that they decided to do that in order to further add to my pain by humiliating and embarrass me publicly and in front of the entire world. Needless to say, that is exactly what the church tried to do as the morning after the trial; the news was on the Internet through *United Methodist News* and carried in every Methodist as well as a few local newspapers. The news had literally gone viral so anyone who needed to get the information just needed to Google my name and the story would pop up.

As a result, on that same day following the trial, I received several telephone calls, texts, and emails aimed at trying to get a response from me. On the following Sunday, the bishop in New England where I had gone back to serve during the judiciary process requested that copies be made of the news article which was posted online and that the copies be distributed to every attendee in the two churches that I was serving when the church trial took place.

With all this happening, there are several ways that I could have responded. Some persons suggested and expected me to move out of the community in order to avoid shame, embarrassment and more name calling. Others thought that this unfortunate incident signaled an abrupt and disgraceful end to my ministry. Some even wondered if I was going to pack my bags and head back to the Caribbean with the hopes of getting a pastoral appointment there. A few friends suggested that I should seek to find another church which would use me as their pastor. In fact, one friend identified a church which at the time was trying to find a pastor. This last suggestion came closest to something I would have considered, but the Florida Methodist Conference made sure that they did enough damage to my character and reputation such that no other church—regardless of how desperate they were—would ever consider me to be their pastor. In one instance, a pastor from another denomination but with whom I had enjoyed great collegiality refused to let me use a room in their building to start an independent fellowship. This was on the incorrect assumption that the bishop had removed my ministerial credentials. While this perception was inaccurate, it bothered me that I had another door shut in my face as I tried to get back into pastoral ministry.

Even then, I knew that God was not done with me and I continued to feel the urge to help to lead and pastor the people of God. That emotion certainly put into perspective Jeremiah's concern expressed in Jeremiah 20:9 when he said,

But if I say I'll never mention the LORD or speak in
his name, his word burns in my heart like a fire. It's like
a fire in my bones! I am worn out trying to hold it in! I
can't do it!

I knew that I had messed up but knew even more that God had not
condemned me. I knew that He would never condemn me so long as I was
genuinely contrite and repentant—which I was!

I continued to remember how many references were made in the
Scriptures to the need which all persons have for grace. I thought of people
like John Wesley who, after he saw the drunk walking below his window,
exclaimed, "There go I but for the grace of God. I thought of the powerful
message in the lyrics of a song written by Bill Gaither, "I'm just a sinner
saved by grace." I thought of the message from the very popular song
"Amazing grace, how sweet the sound that saved a wretch like me; I once
was lost but now I am found was blind but now I see."

The entire book of Romans kept going through my mind, but
especially chapters 5 and 8. How reassuring it was to be reminded from
Romans 8:1 that there is therefore now no condemnation to them that are
in Christ Jesus. How reassuring it was to be reminded that nothing could
separate me from the love of God. Not my sin, not the condemnation of
the church, not the removal from pastoring congregations that I loved and
who loved me, not the criticism nor scorn from a few persons in the
community, not the gossiping and backbiting among some within the
community. None of the above or anything else could separate me from
God's love. I remembered, read, and reread this passage from Romans 8,
which was appropriately subtitled "More Than Conquerors":

What, then, shall we say in response to these things? If
God is for us, who can be against us? He who did not
spare his own Son, but gave him up for us all— how
will he not also, along with him, graciously give us all
things? Who will bring any charge against those whom
God has chosen? It is God who justifies. Who then is
the one who condemns? No one. Christ Jesus who

died—more than that, who was raised to life—is at the right hand of God and is also interceding for us. Who shall separate us from the love of Christ? Shall trouble or hardship or persecution or famine or nakedness or danger or sword? As it is written: "For your sake we face death all day long; we are considered as sheep to be slaughtered." No, in all these things we are more than conquerors through him who loved us. For I am convinced that neither death nor life, neither angels nor demons, neither the present nor the future, nor any powers, neither height nor depth, nor anything else in all creation, will be able to separate us from the love of God that is in Christ Jesus our Lord.

Truthfully, this unconditional love of God was shown more through several members of the wider community who were made aware of what happened and most certainly through the parishioners associated with the last three churches which I served. Interestingly, almost ten years after the fact, some ex-parishioners are still angry with the leaders of the Methodist Church for the action which they took. With all those reassuring thoughts, I figured that this may have been my Damascus Road experience where God decided to give me a wake-up call. I felt the strong urge to continue ministry rather than succumbing to the frail judgment of human beings.

Through all this, I was reminded of the poem by Maya Angelou and took some encouragement and inspiration from the message as shared below.

When I say "I am a Christian," I am not shouting that "I am clean living," I am whispering that "I was lost but now I am found and forgiven."

When I say "I am a Christian," I don't speak of this with pride, I'm confessing that I tumble and need Christ to be my guide.

When I say "I am a Christian" I'm not trying to be strong, I'm professing that I am weak and need His strength to carry on.

When I say "I am a Christian," I'm not bragging of success, I'm admitting I have failed and need God to clean up my mess.

When I say "I am a Christian," I'm not claiming to be perfect. My flaws are too visible but God believes I am worth it.

When I say "I am a Christian," I still feel the sting of pain. I have my share of heartaches but I call upon his name.

When I say "I am a Christian" I'm not holier than thou, I'm just a simple sinner who received God's grace somehow.

One of the lessons that Jesus taught in the parable of the prodigal son is that we should not give up on someone when we may never know what some people are struggling with. Someone may appear to have everything going right for them but at home, their marriage is falling apart, and their mind is going crazy. Sometimes people need compassion and understanding as harsh judgment merely rubs salt into the wound. In fact, most of the heroes of faith described in Hebrews chapter 11 had some serious flaws in their lives at one point.

After prayer and discussion with my wife, we decided to start a nondenominational congregation. Like so many other institutions, there were lots of hiccups, anxiety and even fear as we ventured on this project. We had nine persons attend our first service. One of the biggest obstacles was that we did not have an established place to meet and at one point we were even meeting in our private residence. At the time of writing this memoir, we have upwards of sixty persons associated with the ministry and we have an average attendance of thirty-five on a given Sunday. Within the context of larger congregations, this might seem like a small number; but we are thankful to God for the great family Spirit, the number of ministries in which we have been involved, the number of community projects and programs in which we have shared, and most of all, the spiritual impact and growth which the attendees have been experiencing. It has been so encouraging that I cannot help but thinking about Joseph telling his brothers as recorded in Genesis 50:20 that what they did to him was meant to them for evil, but God meant it for good.

> You intended to harm me, but God intended it all for good. He brought me to this position so I could save the lives of many people.

We have participated in several hurricane relief efforts and just went to the Bahamas (twice) on our first overseas mission trip where we helped with a toy drive and other ministries to the children of Grand Bahama. We just completed our anniversary celebration services, which took on an evangelistic or revival slant. On our final Sunday, we had sixty-four persons in attendance.

Now we have expanded to start a music school, recording studio as well as podcast streaming. God has blessed the congregation with a multiplicity of personnel gifts and talents, and within a congregation which averages thirty five in attendances, I am able to call on any one of five persons to bring or share the message if I am unavailable. As we seek to continue in ministry, we rejoice that we have had as many as fifteen teenagers and kids at church on the same Sunday. We rejoice that we have had as much as seventeen at our weekly Wednesday Bible study. We rejoice that we have had as many as eleven at our weekly Friday prayer service. We rejoice that we have been able to participate in food pantry programs. We rejoice that we now have our own gospel choir that practices every Thursday and minister in song every Sunday during worship. We rejoice that we are now in the process of building our youth connections for Saturdays. For a small congregation, we have been extraordinarily busy, and for this we can only say, "To God be the glory, great things He hath done." Hence, in the words of Charles Wesley, we praise God for all that is past and trust Him for all that's to come.

CHAPTER 2

A Trying Period in My Life and Ministry

It was the last night before the day when we would all head back home from a three-day clergy conference of the Florida Annual Conference of the United Methodist Church held in Leesburg, Florida. I did not really want to have gone to the conference in the first place, but in the end, I am glad that I did. There was a very moving worship experience on that last night, and after a number of personal testimonies, the assigned preacher for the occasion wrapped it up by making an appeal for pastors to come forward to the altar to pray or to be prayed for.

The call was not the typical call like an evangelist would make for first time Christians. Instead, he suggested that we should search our hearts to see if we were carrying any burdens and reminded us that Christ would take our burdens. He reminded us how several pastors had quit ministry because they became overwhelmed with burdens and that there were a few who had even committed suicide. "Wow," I thought to myself. I was carrying some real heavy burdens and had done so for a long time. Ministry had become challenging, and I was not experiencing the joy which I once had. It was almost a routine exercise. I reluctantly swallowed my pride and went to the altar because that was what I would encourage persons to do whenever I would make an evangelistic-type altar call. I had forced it because in my heart I knew that I had been carrying heavy burdens. As I prayed with the music and singing in the background, I felt a pair of hands rubbing my shoulders, and that touch made me feel that there was someone who cared and who might even have been praying silently for me. They felt like the hands of my district superintendent, Dr. Gary

Spencer. "What a nice gesture," I thought to myself. I hoped that he would have followed up on it within the next few days with even a telephone call, but it never happened.

My burden was heavy, and even after having gone to the altar, it remained on my shoulders and kept getting heavier every day. I experienced silent depression as I did not always feel appreciated at home. It was not long before I started feeling alone, isolated and in my own mind, kind of discarded.

For years, I tried to express my concerns verbally, but the situation never changed, and it did not seem to get any better. Perhaps these concerns were just ignored. We had talked about it over and over in several different forums, in different ways. We had even prayed about it, but it seemed like the enemy did not want to let go. I had been going to church every Sunday and preaching at two services.

I had been carrying out all my pastoral duties and responsibilities as best as I could. I attended meetings, did funerals and weddings, shared with the youth, did Bible studies and leading prayer services, etc. All throughout these times, I was smiling on the outside but crying on the inside. I enjoyed a great relationship with my parishioners and the vast majority of the parishioners welcomed and appreciated my ministry. I utilized both my musical as well as my culinary gifts to help enhance the church's ministry.

However, I was also doing a great job of covering up my emotional pain. I was really not happy in my marriage. I had been giving everything but my life for my family but I was sensing a lot of disrespect and disregard. I did not feel appreciated and it was not long before I started feeling alone, isolated and in my own mind, kind of discarded. However, in spite of isolation and my consistent appeal to my family, no one seemed to care and they just kept inflicting the pain on me. It was not for lack of talking, begging, yelling, screaming, crying, and asking nicely.

"Please stop and consider the pain you are inflicting on me because it is hard". My cries fell on deafened ears.

So, life did not turn out the way I had dreamed about when I was a teenager, and it certainly was not the same as how some of my ministerial colleagues' lives appeared to be. Over the years, I have gotten to know some other pastors who were also quite depressed, so it was not abnormal for me to try to cover up mine—maybe out of pride or embarrassment. Some of these pastors also tried to cover it up and some decided to live on with the pain. In my years of doing marriage counseling, I have heard of so many instances where one spouse would respond to unhappiness by becoming involved in areas of life that they never would have thought of if things were normal in their marriage.

I still remember when a nonsmoking lady told me how her situation caused her to go out and buy a pack of cigarettes which she just kept on smoking one behind the other like a chain smoker would. I also know of several women who were the victims of physical and verbal abuse who have looked for happiness outside of the home because it is so badly lacking in their own home.

I was personally very close to a situation where a spouse was so verbally and otherwise abused that he would go away from home as many evenings as was practical. Rather than staying in the comfort of his home with his wife, he would go to the bar/pub and hang out with his friends on a regular basis. Very often, he would drink until he got drunk. When I first heard of him getting drunk as often as he did, I became judgmental like other persons in the community were.

It took a little while before I was privy to the circumstances which pushed him away from home and once I had that information, I was able to understand even better how spouses who experience physical, verbal, or any form of emotional abuse can cope for so much longer and no more. Because I am not personally fond of alcohol, I would never be found in a bar regardless of the situation, but it is a reasonable psychological theory that persons will seek different ways of coping when they are faced with certain situations. As such, while I would not condone the actions of someone who continuously drinks and gets drunk, I would suggest that in those circumstances, persons on the outside may want to work with the root cause of that kind of addiction.

Recently, former Florida Gubernatorial candidate Andrew Gillum faced a socioethical situation which forced him to make an acknowledgment as well as an explanation as to how he got himself into that situation. On the surface, the former mayor and candidate has great intentions for his life of service, but beneath that surface is a human being with lots of emotions. According to the police report, he was unresponsive when approached in his hotel room where investigators found baggies of suspected crystal methamphetamine.

He then announced that he would enter rehab and step back from politics for the time being.

Mr. Gillum stated that he had had conversations with his family and decided to seek help, guidance, and enter into a rehabilitation facility. He continued to share that the incident was a "wake-up call" for him and that he had fallen into a state of deep depression after his race for governor ended. He had witnessed his father suffer from alcoholism, and therefore came to know the damaging effects it could have on persons if left untreated. He regarded alcoholism as a symptom of deeper struggles. This experience caused the former mayor to also commit to take some time and fully heal before showing back up in the world as a "more complete person." In apologizing to his family and all the people of Florida who had supported him and put their faith in him over the years, Mr. Gillum decided to step down from all "public-facing roles for the foreseeable future" and focused on his family and himself.

In the same vein, former president Bill Clinton rationalized his indiscretion of the 1990s by stating that he did it to relieve the stress, which he was experiencing as he governed the country. I would dare to say that there are several more Andrew Gillums and Bill Clintons in the country and in this world who have indulged in unimaginable behavior which they regret as they reflect on the situation. This once more brings home the point that sometimes wrong behavior is not so much driven by poor characteristic traits but by background circumstances.

When my congregation held its recently concluded celebration services, we heard some very powerful testimonies which were shared by a variety of persons. One very compelling testimony made reference to a situation where the person who shared confessed that she was so abused and experienced so many bad things in life that she ended up doing and participating in areas of life that were brought about by the circumstances in her life. With her permission, I have shared the full script of that testimony below.

Jeremiah 1:5 says, "Before I formed you in the womb, I knew you, and before you were born, I set you apart," says the Lord. I cannot recall exactly what age I was when I first came across this passage, all I knew was that it pierced my soul as I read every word. It brought me comfort knowing how special I am to God, but on the other hand, my life experiences made me feel anything but special. As a young girl, I remembered asking God, "Why am I here?" "Is this all there is to my life?" No one loves me! I walked around feeling confused and downright sad. I hated who I was and believed I was better off dead. At that time, I knew of God, but I did not know who he truly was and what I meant to him. All I knew was, I felt alone, forgotten, and that I was a big mistake.

Hebrews 13:5 says, "I will never leave you nor forsake you" says the Lord. But my question to the Lord at that time was, "Where were you lord when my Father was beating my pregnant mother?" "Where were you Lord when that monster of a stepfather molested me at the age of 7?" "Where were you Lord when my mother and great grandmother introduced me to the Ouija board?" "Where were you Lord when my mother repeatedly told me that I was never going to be anything in life?" "Why didn't you stop them all from hurting me?" But God had a plan for this girl's life. She just did not know it. Jeremiah 29:11 says, "For I know the plans I have for you declares the Lord; plans to prosper you and not to harm you, plans to give you hope and a future." Nothing made sense to me, as I was getting older.

My life was filled with tremendous pain and confusion. I needed answers. I needed the pain to go away. Everyone in my family pretended like nothing happened, but for me "LIFE" happened. All the adults that were supposed to protect me, had hurt and disappointed me. I needed to know why my hands shook so much even when I was not nervous, who my father was, and why didn't he love me. Well, the day finally arrived, and little did I know that what I was about to hear would make me hurt even more.

One day I remembered, I could not take it anymore and decided to confront my mom about my father. She proceeded to tell me what transpired and as I was listening, I could hear the pain and anger in her voice. I needed to know!

She and my dad had run away to California from Belize at the age of 19. Apparently, she got pregnant right away. According to her, things went south very quickly. She became a victim of physical abuse at the hands of my father. He was a womanizer and an alcoholic. He was rarely ever around to take care of her according to my mom. Her eyes began to get glossy as she was telling me how my father would beat her down the stairs and leaving her with nothing to eat. Mind you now, my grandmother was living in Los Angeles at that time but wanted nothing to do with my mom because she chose to be with father. As a result, my mother gave birth to me with no one by her side. She further stated that she nearly died in the hospital due to hemorrhaging.

And if you think it could not get any worse, well it did. Upon leaving the hospital, my mom said she had nowhere to go and made the decision to go and see if my grandmother would accommodate her. My grandmother did not want us in the house and told my mom that she could stay in the garage. Wow! She refused to clean it and it was her husband at that time that tried to give the garage a little cleaning so my mom and I could stay in there. My heart was breaking as I listened. Well three months later, my mom took me to Belize and that was where I had to cross my biggest hurdle.

Mark 9:42 says, "And whosoever shall offend one [these] little ones that believe in me, it is better for him that a millstone was hanged about his neck, and he was cast into the sea." Things seemed relatively okay for me up until the age of 7. I did normal things little girls did at that age. I was a happy child enjoying life like I was supposed to. I remembered my mom marrying my stepfather when I was maybe about 5–6. I was too small to care about who she got married to. From my vantage point, everyone looked happy and I was gaining a father, so I thought!

Satan had found his dwelling. One day I recalled getting into trouble and got spanked or scolded for it. I ran to my stepfather to be coaxed as most kids do when they got into trouble. He began telling me it was ok and told me to come with him. I am not sure where everyone else was, but he took me to the bedroom and started taking advantage me. That was the moment my life got turned upside down. I was never the same again.

My innocence was stolen! He molested me for nearly 6 years straight. He had exposed me to so many vile and disgusting things as a child that many of those things stayed with me as I grew older. My body was doing things I could not understand. I was embarrassed and ashamed to tell anyone what I was feeling. He told me it was our little secret and to keep it between us. The older I got, nothing made sense to me. I wanted to run away but I had nowhere to go. To escape the pain, I lived in my head. That was my safe place. As years went by, I functioned like everything was normal, but my insides were completely numb. I was a dead woman walking! At the age of 22, I finally developed the courage to tell my mom that I got molested by her ex-husband and her response blew my mind. She proceeded to say that it was my fault. I was so hurt that I moved out of my mom's house and went to stay with my cousin. Psalm 46:1 says, "God is our refuge and strength, an ever-present help in trouble." Brothers and sisters, I must tell you that my life did not get any better after I was molested but God was making his presence known to me, a little bit at a time.

I was depressed, But God...

I was turning to men to soothe the pain, But God...

I was self-medicating, But God...

I was a people pleaser, But God...

I was homeless twice, But God...

I was trying to fit in anywhere I could, But God...

I hated who I was, But God...

I took so many detours in my life, but God said, "I am here daughter." He sent many people, he gave me dreams, and he even whispered to me, "It's time." Fast forward to the present, I can boldly say, I am no longer a slave to sin or fear because I am a child of God. I serve a God that never left me when many people did. He has prepared me for a time such as this. I was marked before I entered this world, marked by Satan to destroy, but chosen by God to be his shining light. I am fearfully and wonderfully made. I am the apple of God's eye. Nothing or no one can ever come between me and my God. The Lord says, "No weapon formed against me shall prosper."

To each of you, we live in a fallen world. Problems will still be there, but we do not fight alone. Instead of telling God how big our problems are, we must tell our problems how big our God is. No more playing with the enemy! He stole many years of my life and I had to tell him no more! If he can take this girl from Belize out of her deep, dark pit, he can deliver you from yours. I don't know about you, but I serve an awesome God! Please let God be the center of your life. Don't just talk about him, be about him. Hallelujah!!

She was not a pastor, but her testimony definitely represents how life's circumstances can sometimes drastically alter one's behavioral pattern. As human beings, we tend to seek for peace, joy, happiness, and contentment if they seem to be eluding us in the places where we expect to find them. I would even concede that pastors are specially called servants and, by the nature of their role, are expected to be stronger in their response to life's challenges. However, as was the case in my situation, one human being can persevere and endure for so long, but there comes a time when even with the best effort, things could fall apart.

This was emotionally and psychologically hard as I still clearly remember the day when at age ten, the younger of my two daughters came up to me, looked at me and said, "I would like my husband to be like my daddy." This was a very flattering compliment which was unsolicited. I remember the many nights when I would sit with them as they were going to bed and I would hug them both and sing "Twinkle Twinkle Little Star." I would always say good night by reminding them that they were my two main stars.

In the healthy marriages which I have experienced, when one spouse expresses a concern about a situation at home, the person receiving the "complaint" may decide to make some adjustments or even promise to try and act against his/her natural innate instincts in order to create an atmosphere of peace. At least this is what I would have expected and hoped for in my own marriage. As a pastor and marriage officer, I have always counseled couples about the importance of compromise in a marriage for it to be successful. To a large degree, I felt that my cries were hopeless, and my instinctive response was to be silent and noncommunicative, which just led to a worsening situation.

This was now becoming emotionally draining where I felt out of place in my own home, and I did not feel like I belonged. I was extremely unhappy and felt emotionally lonely, and the peace and comfort that I sought continued to elude me.

I had not grown up in a dirty house and not accustomed to hurdling over boxes and plastic bags spread all over the floor. On the contrary, I remember helping my mother to clean our family home every Friday night and sometimes on Saturdays. I remember my mother had us in the kitchen helping to clean and wash dishes from time to time. As such, I was not accustomed to having dirty dishes piled up in the kitchen sink for days upon days until they made their way on to the kitchen counter and then over to the kitchen table. I was not accustomed to wanting a meal and not having enough space on the dining table or on the kitchen table to put down a plate of food because everywhere was packed with dirty dishes. I would try and clean the kitchen as often as I could but within days it would get back to the seemingly preferred state- at least from the perspective of my wife and daughters. Similarly, the floors were filled with plastic bags and boxes to the point where there was hardly any room to push a vacuum cleaner. It was painful that I would make several pleas indicating that we were living in a very unhealthy environment but was ignored and was virtually told to "live with it". I did not too mind the fact that I had to be doing my own laundry but I became frustrated because the laundry room in and of itself was a total mess and I could hardly find anywhere to walk because the floor was plastered with….. You guessed it plastic bags, boxes and clothing of all sorts! I remember so many times when I wanted to change a towel for a shower and could not find a clean towel with which to replace it. When I would try to sleep at nights, I had to try to wiggle my way around bundles of clothing, papers and files which were sprawled out on the bed. Somehow, my wife had perfected the art of twisting her body into an 'S' but for me, that was very uncomfortable. This was a situation which was totally grossing me out and I indicated as much to my wife and daughters. In fact, this situation had started from the time we lived in Massachusetts. Persons would come to the house and I would be extremely embarrassed. I remember one person taking a stab at me at a church meeting for keeping a messy and untidy parsonage. I shared this information with my wife but it did not make any difference to her.

When we were about to move to Florida in 2008, we visited the parsonage where we would be living and I observed how neat and clean it was. In the nicest way I could, I mentioned this to my family and asked if we could make an effort to maintain the parsonage this way. This way, we would be able to leave the reputation of keeping an untidy house back in New England and make a clean start once we got to Florida. This request went unheeded as it did not take a long time before I was reliving the old filthy and untidy house.

I remember several months or maybe a year after we had moved in, the house was again in bad shape. We were fortunate to have found a lady who was willing to clean and tidy it for us. When she was finished cleaning under the beds and moving plastic bags and boxes from off the floor, the house looked and felt fresh and nice and inviting. That very night, I met with my family in my office and begged them to try and maintain the house the way it was but that also went unheeded. The same unnecessary pain and embarrassment which I experienced in New England, was continuing here and it was really depressing as I had nowhere to go. It was shameful for me when one day I observed my wife entertaining a guest for upwards of half an hour outside the front door without inviting her inside.

As if that was not bad enough, my sleep had to compete with the television glaring loudly and or the overhead lights being on because reading and television provided the entertainment for my wife. My repeated requests for that entertainment to take place in the living room since there was a television set as well as lights out there went unheeded. I also had to "live with that too". It was painful to go into the refrigerator to take out and warm a meal only to find out that it was old and tasted badly so I had to throw it out. In time, I was not able to decipher between freshly cooked food and stale food that had been placed in the refrigerator for weeks.

In normal circumstances, when one spouse expresses a concern about a situation at home, the person receiving the "complaint' may decide to make some adjustments or even promise to try and act against his/her natural innate instincts in order to create an atmosphere of peace. However, when the person with the concerns is repeatedly told to "live with it' or asked "what's the big deal?" that is a sure recipe for a disastrous marriage. That attitude demonstrates a lack of care, regard, concern, love and respect.

I had talked about this issue for the previous twelve years but I was able to exercise my patience even amidst great shame and embarrassment when my parishioners would unexpectedly drop in at the house. Things came to a head one night during the month of July 2009. It was the summer holidays and one of my daughters was home while the other was out at her friend's home. I had gone home from the church office hoping to have some lunch. Needless to say, the kitchen was in its usual state of mess while my daughter was lying in her bedroom which was just as messy and watching television. I knew that her friend was going to come and visit her that day and so like a normal parent would, I reminded her that she needed to clean her room and the kitchen so that the atmosphere would be a little more "inviting" after her friend showed up. I did not expect that such a normal request of a father to a fourteen year old would result in my being castigated and made to feel like a miserable and grumpy old man........... But it did!!!!! My fourteen-year-old threw a fit and decided that she was not going to do anything and decided to 'report me' to her mom when she got home from work that night.

So, in the presence of both my fourteen-year-old and my eleven year-old, my wife chose to curse me out, gave me a tongue lashing and lambasted me for daring to ask her daughter to clean her room and the kitchen while she waited for her friend to visit. I could not believe it when in that same interaction, my fourteen-year-old daughter who by now was fueled by the support of her mother looked at me and asked "why don't you clean it?" I reached over to use physical discipline and my wife went and stood between us. To this day, she never questioned why a fourteen-year-old was able to talk to her own father in that defiant way and with that tone of voice. It got worse because on the following day, I called my cell phone provider and asked them to suspend my daughter's line. That was my way of disciplining her for being defiant and disrespectful. However, that did not work because my wife chose to let my daughter use her own phone so she could continue to stay in touch with her friends. That night was the beginning of a life of isolation for me because it was the night my daughters learnt their first lesson in disrespect to me from their mom. From that time forth, any act of discipline which I would try to instill in my daughters as they grew up, would be overruled or vetoed by my wife.

There was one occasion when my older daughter carried out an extremely selfish act in relation to her little sister. This happened just before her sixteenth birthday so when she asked us to throw a party for her sixteenth birthday, I emphatically told her "No" as a way of disciplining her and to teach her how to think of others and not only of herself. My wife knew that I was angry and wanted to carry out the disciplinary action in that way. Needless to say, after that older daughter appealed to my wife, without any consultation or discussion with me, my wife chose not only to plan the birthday party but also to have a member of the church plan it with her. It was an embarrassment to me that my daughter's birthday party was being planned with some other parent involved even though I stated that it was for disciplinary reasons why I did not want to give her that party.

As such the burden became much bigger than a mere filthy house. It was now a mental issue where I felt out of place in my own home and I did not feel like I belonged. I was extremely unhappy and felt emotionally lonely but no one in my family could be bothered by this. My wife would causally dismiss every concern which I would raise with her. I found it extremely frustrating to communicate any concerns I had to my wife as she would get extremely defensive and/or would try to rationalize any expression or an action with the most irrational kind of reasoning imaginable. She had a very combative spirit and this made it hard to sit down and have a peaceful discussion as normal and mature persons would.

With all the stress I was experiencing, I started having health problems and my blood pressure went through the roof and seemingly uncontrollable. After a while my consistently high blood pressure resulted in my being diagnosed with an irregular heartbeat (Atrial fibrillation). Of course, I was placed on even more medication after I was hospitalized for three days. I had remembered when my doctor asked if there was something happening in my life which was causing my blood pressure to be that uncontrollable and I mentioned the unbearable situation which I was experiencing at home. I had hoped that that situation would turn out to be a wakeup call for my wife but ironically while she was driving me home from the hospital on the day I was discharged, the only reference which she made to my hospital stay was that I needed to be in better control of my emotions so that I would not have to go through this experience again. Wow! Okay. "Thank you, my wife!! "I said to myself.

Among many other things, there was one other issue which was tearing me apart. As a teenager growing up in the church, I played the guitar, the accordion, as well as the harmonica. I played in a community band and in a school band, but most importantly, I led my church's youth group as we sang in a wide variety of situations ranging from annual Christmas caroling to singing at national events.

Once I graduated seminary, I used every opportunity to start or help with gospel music groups as it seemed that music was in my DNA.

As an adult, I learned to play some additional instruments for I had developed an insatiable appetite for playing musical instruments.

From my teenage days, I had visions of growing up, getting married, and establishing a family music ministry. The potential for this to develop became strong after I met my wife and realized that she was a singer and a piano player. Shortly after we got married, we started Karol Music Ministries, and as a duo, we would do concerts all over our home country of Jamaica. This is something we had talked about during our days of dating, and we both felt committed to this ministry. Once we migrated to the United States, we continued the ministry, and as the children grew a little older and mature, they became a part of the ministry. We would travel to different parts of the state and eventually out of state. It was a nice feeling as my teenage dream was being realized. When we introduced the concept of a dinner and a concert to Brevard County in Florida, it turned out to be a huge success, and the following year, persons kept asking for the repeat date. I tried to get my family to start preparing for the next one, but for some reason, which I have not heard to this day, we could not get it together. In fact, we had set aside a Saturday night to be our regular weekly night for family devotions and practice for our music ministry, but for many nights, my daughters and I would be sitting in the office and waiting for the better part of one hour or more before we even got started. Eventually, the girls lost interest, and before we knew it, we were neither having weekly family devotions nor family music ministry practice. I tried begging to see if we could reestablish our music ministry because without it, I had lost a big part of my life. Unfortunately, it did not happen. If there was one thing which was holding things together and helped to ease my pain and retain my sanity, it was the music ministry. After investing a lot of money, time, and emotions to see my teenage dreams realized, I saw it go up in flames, and that was very hard to swallow.

There are several other issues which bothered me and which I could share, but there may not be a need to give unnecessary details at this point. Primarily, I wanted to use the opportunity to share how emotionally difficult my life was at that point. Because of the feeling of isolation as well as the happiness at home being taken from me, I did not communicate much because I just could not. It was hard when the friends of my daughters would come to the house to visit and while I interacted with and was social with them, I could not laugh and talk and make jokes because my spirit was so broken. This also made me feel empty as throughout my ministry, I always had a passion for working with and becoming friendly with younger folk.

Suffice it to say, my life was painful.

CHAPTER 3

An Unwise Choice of Coping Mechanisms

I can imagine that the situation which I described above may not come across as unbearable for everyone as it turned to be for me. I am confident that there are several—maybe many—persons who would have been able to ward this off and just go with the flow. However, it is a given that in the same way that we all have different pain thresholds, so we are made with differing tolerance levels. After twelve years, I just did not have the tolerance level to persevere any further. The happiness which I had sought and hoped for in marriage with a family eluded me, and while I was not physically lonely, I was emotionally lonely, and that for a long time.

It was into this situation of loneliness, depression, and frustration that a former school mate walked. If there was ever a situation that fits the description of the perfect storm, this was it. It had been just over forty years since I graduated high school, and out of nowhere, I received an e-mail from this schoolmate telling me where she was and asking me to call her. I remembered her very well. She was smart, physically attractive, and a Christian. I was extremely naive, and I welcomed the gesture as an opportunity to renew acquaintances and catch up on our respective family situations and all that had transpired since high school graduation. So we continued our e-mail communication, and before long, we were talking on the phone. I considered this relationship to be safe because she was in New York and I was in Florida. It was great to be catching up on many years of time that had elapsed. From all appearances, she had made contact with several other schoolmates such that she was able to give me updates on them as well. I found this to be very refreshing and helpful.

One of the first personal things that she shared was that she was divorced from her husband, who just happened to have been a past student of the same school we attended, so there was a lot of familiarity there. As is almost always the case, she went on to lambaste her former husband and mentioned what a terrible life she had had. According to her, he was physically abusive, he had cheated on her multiple times, and he would often go away on trips and leave her alone at home to take care of the children. She even described him as a womanizer. We continued the conversations, and I was determined that I was going to deal with this situation pastorally in spite of all I described previously. So the conversations went on and on, and after a few months, she indicated that she was going to move to Georgia. Once she got to Georgia, our communication continued, and one of the things she shared was that she was in touch with still another former schoolmate from the sixties and that he was going to fly to Georgia and spend some time visiting. I became a little curious but refused to be judgmental. As the days went by, she would give me updates on the visit and what was supposed to be a one-week visit for that third schoolmate turned into three weeks and then into six weeks, and before I knew it, I was asked if I would be willing to officiate at their wedding. I felt quite honored that she would bypass so many other pastors and ask me—ask a schoolmate—to perform the ceremony. Of course, I was also able to see it from the sentimental side. I started to become very concerned when she would share deeply private issues that were supposed to be intimate about that relationship and I would hear about everything that he was doing wrong or what he did not have. I still naively saw myself as the pastoral counselor, so I would make time to have these telephone conversations with her.

One day I received a telephone call from her, and she told me that this second schoolmate with whom an intimate relationship had seemingly developed decided that he was going back to Florida. Apparently, he was also having domestic issues at home, so he must have seen a relationship with my friend to be an easy way to escape. It might have been in that context that she sought to encourage him to divorce his wife and marry her. Whatever might have transpired as they tried to make this illegitimate relationship work, this guy decided at some point that he had had enough and told her, "I am going back home to my wife."

At that point, the average person in my situation would begin to think that my former female schoolmate had a mental problem and would seek to stay away from her. So I started convincing myself that clearly I was not normal, and as such, I continued "counseling" her over the telephone. With all her sad stories about her life, I gave her no indication that I was going through a rough patch in my own marriage as well. It turned out that her mom lived in Florida, and the next thing I heard was that she was thinking of coming to visit and spend some time with her mom, who happened to live as close as one hour's drive from me. Suddenly my thoughts were not totally pastoral. I was beginning to ask myself if there was something in this for me. She shared confidential information from her short-lived relationship with my other schoolmate; she lured him into leaving his wife in Florida and coming to be with her in Georgia. She shared negative information repeatedly about him to me, but I was still asking what might be in this for me. My thoughts went between being pastoral and pursuing a potential relationship. I was not good at concealing what seemed to be developing into a personal pursuit, and once she recognized that weakness, she decided to exploit it to the maximum. After we got on the same page, and I started to express my reservations, she played the victim game by reminding me about how horrible her ex-husband was to her and how she had had some real bad experiences with subsequent relationships. She would tell me pity stories, and I would buy them. I felt sorry for her. The heartbreaking point for me was when she expressed the concern that she might never experience true love again for the rest of her life. Among the thoughts which came into my head at about that time was the one which caused me to think that maybe God was putting us in each other's path. She was going to provide all the happiness which was so painfully lacking in my marriage, and I was going to make her the happiest wife that ever lived.

It was not too long before she solidified her plans to come to visit her mom in Florida. She was going to rent a car to drive down to Florida but would make a stop in Palm Bay for a few days so she could get to see and spend some time with me before continuing her journey to Port St. Lucie.

It was exciting for me too until she mentioned a "oneway rental." I asked myself the obvious question. Why would she only do a one-way rental? Then I also thought, if she was visiting her mom, would she not have any plans to return to Georgia? Anyway, she made her plans, and I helped her with them. Because of my familiarity with the town, I was able to make suggestions for hotels that she could stay at before she continued on to see her mom. By this time, I was becoming torn in my heart as I faced what was definitely a moral dilemma.

I made plans to meet her at the hotel on the night of her arrival, and it was a long embrace as we greeted each other. Neither of us had to verbalize anything as it was obvious that we had a mutual interest in pursuing a possible marital relationship. I remember stopping to buy supper for her on my way, but we had a long talk before she even started to eat. I remember that while I was there, my daughter called me and asked me to do something for her on the road, so I invited my friend to go for the drive with me. The night was over, and I went home feeling extremely excited and could not wait for the next day when I would go back and visit at the hotel. Once more we talked, and this time we both verbalized our mutual hope for the future. I became very uncomfortable when she started making references to the natural instincts of the human body, and as nicely as I could, I asked her to slow down a bit. By the time I left that morning, I started to realize that I was in trouble. For the rest of that weekend, there was a lot of talking over the phone, and of course, I got there when I was able. We found ourselves talking and holding hands, and I had determined that there was no way that we were going to get carried away within a few short days. I invited her to church on Sunday, and I could not help but observe that she did not socialize much with the parishioners. I went to visit on Sunday afternoon after church and that was when we both lost it. Inasmuch as she was a strong Christian, neither of us seemed able to help the other and from a moral standpoint; everything went downhill from there.

At this point, I was already beginning to feel guilty as my thoughts were racing and not in the right direction. "Errol, you have got to do better than this. It is not right," I said to myself. Her move to her mother's house and then into her own house, both of which were one hour away, did not change anything morally. I realized that I had gotten myself into one big mess and tried to figure out how I would get out of it. I heard more of her pity stories as we started making plans to get married, so now my conscience would not allow me to say how suddenly uncomfortable I was beginning to feel. She was persistent, aggressive, and very demanding. I allowed myself to fall into the virtual trap referenced by the writer of the book of Proverbs in chapter 7:15–27.

> So, I came out to meet you; I looked for you and have found you! I have covered my bed with colored linens from Egypt. I have perfumed my bed with myrrh, aloes and cinnamon. Come, let's drink deeply of love till morning; let's enjoy ourselves with love! My husband is not at home; he has gone on a long journey. He took his purse filled with money and will not be home till full moon. With persuasive words she led him astray; she seduced him with her smooth talk. All at once he followed her like an ox going to the slaughter, like a deer stepping into a noose till an arrow pierces his liver, like a bird darting into a snare, little knowing it will cost him his life. Now then, my sons, listen to me; pay attention to what I say. Do not let your heart turn to her way or stray into her paths. Many are the victims she has brought down; her slain are a mighty throng. Her house is a highway to the grave, leading down to the chambers of death.

I will acknowledge that while she was aggressive, I had also needed to remind myself that I am a called servant of God. Instead, I got caught up in the moment and allowed my emotions to get the better of me. I look back at that now, and I keep hearing the words of Jesus recorded in the Gospels: "What shall it profit a man if he shall gain the whole world and lose his soul and what can a man give in exchange for his soul?" I wanted to continue being a pastor because that is my calling, but here I am now giving in to a moment or moments of weakness. How would I be able to counsel persons in my congregation who may be facing similar issues? How would I be able to counsel couples who may have one partner cheating on the other? Elementary Christian principles teach that any kind of sexual activity should be reserved for marriage. In my head, my hope at the time was really that we were going to get married anyway. As it turned out, I recognized that I was really getting way ahead of myself. It was a real spiritual disaster that I was creating for myself.

I soon realized that I had to share my situation with another human being, and after long and careful thought, I chose my pastoral colleague in New Jersey. She suggested that I was to first indicate to my daughters and then to my wife that I needed a divorce in order to "free my conscience" and legitimize a relationship that was now blazing hot, even if extremely immature and premature. I was happy that both my daughters expressed understanding about the need for divorce, but my wife would have none of it when I started the discussion with her. So now I was facing a real dilemma since neither of the two women was willing to let go. For better or for worse, I chose to continue my illegitimate relationship because really and truly, this was where I was going to find the happiness which was so absent from my home. She was offering everything which I felt was lacking at home, and I thought that there would have to be a way to get out of my then misery and start to enjoy a life of bliss.

She strongly suggested that I did not need my wife's permission to walk away from her and suggested that I should just do it as soon as I could and marry her. Of course, it was not as easy as she suggested since I not only saw the need to have a "smooth" departure from my family, but I also had a church family that would be devastated if I just walked away especially in the circumstances as they would turn out to be. I asked her to give me some time for me to work things out in my mind, and my first thought was that I was going to mention the negative issues in my marriage to my district superintendent with the hope that he would guide me in terms of getting a divorce while still actively serving a local congregation. Regrettably, while I was trying to figure out the appropriate timing to share with my superintendent, I was still knowingly engaging in immoral activities as I spent more and more time at her home. In looking back at this, it was not only sad but disrespectful of my God. It would have been nice if I had taken some time away from the church, but instead, I chose to still lead worship services and preach sermons while being involved immorally. Even with the knowledge of God's undying love and unlimited grace, I now look back and feel that I was not only being unfaithful but also unfair and unwise.

However, if the truth is to be told, I was also feeling some amount of pressure from this young lady as well. The pressure was such that even if I did not want to go and visit for one reason or another, her aggressive nature would cause her to place demands on my time, and so I would feel an obligation to visit more than I normally would have wanted to.

On one particular night, I had just finished a meeting at church. It was very late, and I was very tired. I called her and mentioned that I was too physically tired to take the drive down that night as I had promised so asked that I be "excused." She went on a tirade, threw a fit, and told me that I was going to see some other woman, so I was just using physical tiredness as an excuse. We had our first real fight that night, but I purposed in my mind that I was not going to cower because the reason given was honest. I spent another half an hour or so before I went home. Shortly after I got home, my wife was able to tell me that my friend had called and told her all about our relationship. I could not believe what I was hearing. I felt so betrayed and wondered how she could have done that to me. However, I also thought that this might have been an indication that God was stopping me in my tracks by giving me this wake-up call. I could not have denied this to my wife so now I not only needed to seek God's forgiveness; I needed to seek my wife's forgiveness. Here is how my wife described the call she received that night.

TIMELINE OF COMMUNICATION WITH COMPLAINANT—1
By Kaye Leslie

First Telephone contact—Early week of June 16th (probably Monday—16th or Tuesday— 17th, continuing to Wednesday—18th because my cell phone died) the complainant called me.

The complainant demanded to know if my husband, the respondent, had asked me for a divorce to marry her. She said she had told him if he did not do so she was going to come to the church (Palm Bay UMC) one Sunday and tell the congregation of their relationship because men thought they could get away with anything, just like her ex-husband.

The complainant said she did not mean to get involved with the respondent but he was an old friend from high school who she had reconnected with and over time she encouraged him to share more and more about his personal life and found out we were having some problems and offered to help. She further said she was counseling him as one old friend to another about his daughters and the situation at home (as she had done with many others before) and the "relationship" just happened. She said she had not planned it but sometimes these things happen. When I mentioned I had no intention to divorce my husband she told me not to make the kids get in the way because "the girls are old enough to deal with it."

She alleged he had had numerous relationships with other women, and named several women, most of whom are church members and all of whom are known to me. I was confident that none of these relationships existed. I tried telling her that she did not have all the details and was misguided but she would have none of it and said he was laughing at me because he was lying to me, having affairs right under my nose and I had no clue. I told her she was delusional if she thought so and if in fact he led her to believe this then they were both delusional. She said he boasted that he had spent my money as he wanted and was laughing with her about it. She made many more inflammatory claims and seemed more and more upset when I did not rant and rave and threaten to divorce the respondent. At this point she mentioned my writing desk that he allowed the thrift shop to erroneously sell her and claimed he knew it was mine and did not care. She told me she did not need furniture because she had more than enough of her own and she would be returning it. She still had not done so at the time of this written record.

The complainant also suggested that the difficulties my younger daughter was having at school were typical of girls who had been sexually abused by their fathers and suggested that this was the case. I was and am certain that neither of my two girls was sexually or physically abused by their father in any way and told her so. She mentioned that she had tried to get my younger daughter's father (referring to the respondent) to send her off to a boarding college that she (the complainant) knew would be good for my daughter, because she (the complainant) had dealt with many matters of this nature because "It was her job!"

Again, the complainant spoke of her relationship with my husband, the respondent, and told me of the cruise they took together, their trip to Georgia and the fact that "the injections work," her way of implying an intimate relationship.

Over the last few years the respondent has had a few health issues and in November of last year was hospitalized for observation, tests and treatment. In late April/early May he made a trip to the emergency room because of similar symptoms. Interestingly enough, the complainant discounted his health issues in this cell phone conversation and claimed there was nothing wrong with him and his so called trip to the emergency room was at her insistence to ensure it was safe for him to go on the cruise. (As it turns out the emergency room visit was post cruise.)

Before hanging up the complainant told me the respondent could not be trusted and again mentioned that she had told him several times that she was "coming to the church to tell the congregation what he was doing.

Please note how she carved up these allegations about me in relation to my own daughters. My wife had the presence of mind to recognize that there was something about her stories which did not add up. However, the leaders in the Florida Conference did not seem to get that at all. They believed every story that she could make up.

In fact, she would not only accuse me to my face, but she would also indicate to the leaders in the conference that I was having an affair with every female name with whom I had any kind of association. Even then, as I mentioned before, the conference leaders just kept believing her such that ladies in the church and in the wider Palm Bay community were feeling very upset and angry about their names being spilled all over the community. That negative situation meant nothing to the hierarchy of the church.

As one would imagine, my wife was very upset after that telephone conversation and shared with me in detail most of what is contained in the statement above. As she ranted and raved, I acknowledged that I had the relationship, but outside of that general truth, everything else was false. As I reflected on what my wife had shared with me from the telephone conversation, I realized that I was trapped. My newfound friend was way beyond being a liar. I started associating her with being evil as only someone with evil intent could make up stories like the ones she shared with my wife and then pass them on as facts.

Now I knew that the relationship which seemed to have had such promise and was blazing with fire was about to go up in smoke. My dilemma was huge. I did not want to continue a relationship with someone who was capable of exaggerating the truth in order to destroy someone whom they claimed to care for. However, I also knew that because of her strong demands, she would carry out her threat to "expose" me openly in front of my congregation. Somehow I was now remembering her saying that she had attempted to do that in relation to her ex-husband, who also happened to be a pastor as well. Now I was remembering her saying that she was planning to do that to a separate pastor whom she claimed had done her wrong. I remembered her saying those two things very clearly, but I did not allow that to cause me to hold back. All things considered, at the time she would share about what "other pastors" had done to her, in my mind, I thought that I was going to be different from—in fact better than—all the other men in her life. I was genuine in my desire to make her happy. I was going to show her affection to the point where she would be healed of all the wounds and scars, which she claimed that she had had from previous relationships.

What did I get myself into? I felt totally trapped, and now I had to find a way to get out. I figured that now would be a good time to tell my friend how upset I was about what she had done, but because of all the pain I was experiencing in my marriage, I wanted our illegitimate relationship to continue. I never thought that any pain that she might cause me could turn out to be worse than the pain I had been experiencing in marriage. As such, I had no thoughts of turning back but wanted to continue pursuing her. Needless to say, I acknowledged my wife's concern but callously told her that I still had plans to divorce her and marry my friend. However, as we continued in the relationship, I became more and more concerned about how demanding she was. If she wanted me to come to see her at a time and that was inconvenient for me, it did not matter, for she would get angry and upset if I thought that I was too tired or I had issues to take care of in the church. I also realized that she was extremely jealous so that if I was on the phone and talking with someone in her presence, she demanded to know who it was. If it happened to be a female, I had to give an explanation as to what kind of relationship we had, and if it turned out to be a female at the other end of the line, she would insist that I was having a sexual relationship with that person. It was miserable. She would then move from the personal to the general and make a sweeping statement that all pastors were immoral and were using their robes to cover up their sins.

At this point, I was beginning to feel the ropes of my trap tighten and started to wonder again if she had mental issues.

While all this was happening, I was still waiting for the right opportunity to set up a meeting with my district superintendent and unburden myself. She was even pushing me to go talk with my district superintendent because she wanted to get married immediately. I was in the most confused state of mind. Now the words from Psalm 119:65 to 72 were beginning to ring in my ears.

> You have dealt well with your servant, O Lord, according to Your word. Teach me good judgment and knowledge, for I believe your commandments. Before I was afflicted I went astray, but now I keep Your word. You are good, and do good; Teach me Your statutes. The proud have forged[a] a lie against me, But I will keep Your precepts with my whole heart. Their heart is as fat as grease, But I delight in Your law. It is good for me that I have been afflicted, That I may learn Your statutes. The law of Your mouth is better to me Than thousands of coins of gold and silver.

Yet in her mind, I was operating too slowly, so she makes a second telephone call to my wife. This is how my wife recalled that second telephone conversation below.

TIMELINE OF COMMUNICATION WITH
COMPLAINANT—2
By Kaye Leslie

The second set of communications took place on Thursday (July 24) when the complainant called me. Due to poor reception the call got disconnected and I did the polite if unwise thing to do and called her back.

The complainant called to let me know the reason the respondent had withheld our family mechanics name and address from me was because the mechanic was her son and his garage was at her home. Yes, the mechanic is her son but he operates from his home at a different address. She went on and on about the respondents relationship with her son and the fact that he would take him food that he did not need. At this point she threatened to return my car that was in the possession of her son.

In this conversation she made sure to tell me the respondent had bought her a car and they had a bank account together. Early in March, before the relationship started, the respondent and I lent the complainant our older daughter's car because our daughter was away at college. This is something we have done for other persons who needed a shortterm vehicle. Although not wealthy, the respondent and I had discussed buying two used cars since we were having problems with our cars and looked at the possibility of lending the complainant one. We had also looked at lending her the money to help to buy a car (since she claimed she had a "settlement coming soon") if we decided against the second car, which we eventually did. Not knowing this she went on about his buying her a car that she did not need because she can buy her own car. I told her if she felt that way about it to sell the car and give me the money or sell me the car for a dollar since she did not need it. She brought up my writing desk which he had sold her and I told her to feel free to return it as she had said she would before since she did not need it (she never did).

The complainant told me she had done his laundry and she was going to throw his clothes out. She also said he had laundry to be done in his car and will probably try to sneak it into the house while I was at work. The ranting and raving continued as she criticized the respondent and repeated many of the old claims. She spoke again of the many women he had in the church and that he had invited her up for the Caribbean Minister's weekend and she went on and on.

At this point I had had enough and very nicely told her she was no better than he was if they were both pursuing a relationship knowing it was wrong in God's sight. I asked her how she rationalized having an affair, worse an affair with a married man while continuing to "serve" God as if all was well (something the respondent and I had just discussed). I asked her why not just end the relationship and walk away? She said she knows it is wrong but she loved him and was not willing to give him up. I told her unfortunately I loved him too and when I took my marriage vows they were before God and for better or worse, and definitely for life. I further told her the respondent and I would work out our marriage, take care of our family, seek God's face and prayerfully work with our church family. She went silent and I told her I had to go.

After this second telephone call, I thought that I could not continue in a relationship with someone who was so deceptive and who was turning out to be a pathological liar. It occurred to me that she was intent on upsetting my wife to the point where she would voluntarily leave me, which would make it much easier for me to get a divorce. Clearly, my wife was not going to fall into that trap, and while I was conscious that I had done wrong, I did not want my wife to be going through that kind of abuse and annoyance. It was time for me to force myself out of the trap—cost it what it would. I decided that I was going to put a "hold" on visiting Port St. Lucie and would restrict my communication to telephone conversations. I paid a high price for making that decision. Within two days after that, my friend had gone ahead and written a formal complaint to my district superintendent accusing me of sexual abuse, among other things. Just like the two times when she telephoned my wife, in her complaint she made up unimaginable stories about me and exaggerated the truth to the point that I was now totally convinced that I was jumping out of the proverbial frying pan and into the fire. The original complaint in its entirety is below:

Port St Lucie
Fl 34 987
July 28, 2014

Dear Dr. Spencer

    I contacted Dr Errol Leslie
to help me with a situation where
my daughter just disclosed that she
was raped at age 6 years by a
Pastor friend of the family.

    My daughter just got married
and told her new husband. I was
and still devasted by the action
of this minister as he knew
I was trying to get over my
divorce after twenty five years
of marriage to a Pastor.
    Dr. Leslie started to tell me
his own family problems and
used this situation to sexually

abuse me when I went to him
for spiritual guidance & support.

Dr. Leslie told me about his
own abuse of women and even
getting two of these woman
pregnant. He is worse than the
Pastor that raped my six year
old daughter.

He is on line meeting women
and arranging meetings all over
the U.S. He went to Miami to
meet one and when she found
out he was a Pastor she just
stayed at the Hotel and talk
to him.

He had sex with a number
of his current church ▬▬▬ wh
chaperone the young people t
Disney for Night of Joy.

③

Dr. Leslie makes friends with their women and then control them by giving them some position in the church after sexually abusing them.

He controls them by paying their light bill, car payment or rent. Dr. Leslie 'services' the women in his church by telling them not to blame God for his weaknesses.

Dr. Leslie comes over for "Prayer and Bible Study" and uses this time for oral sex. After getting his best friends wife pregnant, who just happens to also be a Pastor. He forces her to have an abortion

(4)

Dr. Leslie then gets a member of the church board pregnant in Massachusetts. This woman just happens to be white and married. He then insists on her having an abortion because she could not explain to her white husband why she is having a black baby boy.

He "feeds" the homeless and gives them grocery from the food pantry in exchange for Oral Sex. He takes these women to a motel Suburban and use his Pastoral position + Counsellin skills to control them.

More than half of the women setting in church while he continue to preach have been destroyed by his sexual behavior.

Dr. Leslie needs help and should never have the opportunity to Pastor any church in the world. His wife is aware of his sexual activities with these emotionally broken women and usually ask them to stop coming to church.

His church will never grow as Dr. Leslie kills the wounded women who come to the church for healing and help.

His wife Kay is a hoarder and she will not even take a bathe because Dr. Leslies abuse of her and his two girls. No Pastor should control women in this way using the name of God and God's house at a

(6)

place to meet this broken women and then abuse them sexually again. Many of these women are prostitutes and women that have used drugs and have been physically beaten by the people who claim they love them.

Pastor Leslie uses his position and the church building to abuse these women and totally destroy them.

He did this to me and then gets one of his female Pastors to try and 'help' me. I spoke twice to Dr. Althea Spencer - Miller at his request.

I explained to her what he did to me and she was shocked Dr. Leslie would use

(7)

his power of the church to control and destroy lives. Dr. Leslie has tried to bribe me by buying a car for me, going on a five day cruise to Mexico, by telling me he will marry me, going to my daughter's graduation using the church's time by saying he is doing a wedding in Georgia.

Dr. Leslie has destroyed hundreds of lives in all the places he has pastored and someone needs to stop him.

He tells his wife he has a wedding in Mexico or Jamaica and she can't leave the church to go with him as she is needed to run the church while he is out of the country.

Kay Leslie obeys him because she will not dare to go against his wishes and get fired as the church secretary.

I have counselled drug abuse patients and never had this experience of someone out of control + no one having the back bone to stand up to Dr. Leslie.

He is a manipulator and a danger to himself and others

Veda V. Hendrich

P.S. Since march 4th to present Dr. Leslie has been having sex with me in my house in PSL. and Suburban Hotel
Ved. V Hendrh

I ask you to observe how many times the complainant made a reference to pastors in this complaint. Her ex-husband is a pastor; the person who she claims raped her daughter is a pastor; the friend whose wife I allegedly got pregnant is a pastor. She had it in for pastors as she would constantly be picking on pastors throughout several conversations which I would have with her. It may not help to spell out some of the details, which she would share from time to time; suffice it to say that her perception of all pastors (her words) was very negative and held in low esteem. This was her opportunity to nail one to the cross as she had tried to do with some others and the hierarchy of the United Methodist Church aided and abetted her in this effort. Note also (as I pointed out to Bishop Carter) that there are actually twenty-seven allegations in the eight-page complaint. Notwithstanding, even with all the ridiculously out-of-line allegations, the church refused to acknowledge that there may have been good reason to look into her state of mind as she penned that complaint. In her opening, she accused me of taking advantage of a vulnerable situation and sexually abusing her. The counsel for the church originally included that (sexual abuse) as one of the four charges against me which, in and of itself, indicated that he was not prepared to look at any possible truths coming from my response. In fact, he referred to the interview which he had with the complainant in which she stated that I was her pastor and that I had power over her. He included that in the original charging documents as referenced below. He bought whatever she wrote as well as other things she shared with him verbally and accepted it as much as he believed the gospels. Of course, he never thought that it would be useful in any way to interview me since my word could not be trusted. During the referenced interview, he would have gotten all the needed information from the complainant on which he could establish the charges.

In his appeal to the Committee on Appeals of the South East Jurisdiction, my defense counsel mentioned that the counsel for the church had not questioned or interviewed me before bringing his charges. The committee's response to this was that there was nowhere in the Discipline where it was required for the counsel/investigator to interview me. Please note again the fact that this committee comprised several professionally trained attorneys. To say that they knew better than what they were asserting in that response would be an understatement. In any culture anywhere in the world, the accused always has an opportunity to tell his/her side of the story. In the secular court system in any culture, an investigating police officer would not only interview the accuser/complainant, he/she would also interview the accused and any potential witnesses. In so doing, the system would at least give the appearance of fairness and balance. However, in this instance the counsel for the church would not even pretend to be taking a fair or balanced approach. Here is an excerpt from the charges which he sent to the committee on investigation.

> Reverend Leslie was pastor to Ms. Hendricks—a position of authority and power in the Complainant's life. Ms. Hendricks, in an interview with the Counsel for the Church, stated that Rev. Leslie had power over her, was a manipulator, and an expert at "fooling women."

I definitely was not pastor to the complainant, but she chose to build that narrative as she did the twenty-seven allegations contained in the complaint. As I keep saying, her statements were just accepted without question. Thankfully, after the case got to the Committee on Investigation, that body was objective enough to realize that this charge of sexual abuse needed to be dropped.

From the perspective of the church, the reader will also understand why the counsel for the church, in tandem with the presiding officer, refused to allow the trial court comprising my pastoral colleagues to see a copy of the original complaint which the Book of Discipline mandates. That formal complaint which has been reproduced in its original format (above) is what started off the proceedings but was only used conveniently after that when it was in the interest of the church to do so.

CHAPTER 4

A Fall into a Den of Lions

I got home from a church meeting on Tuesday (August 29, 2014) at approximately 6:00 p.m., and I received a call from my district superintendent, Dr. Gary Spencer, requesting that I meet him at his office on the following day at 1:00 p.m. I inquired as to what the issue was, and his response was that he could not disclose that. Because of what had transpired as described above, I had my suspicions as to what this meeting was going to be about. I was so sure that my assumption was correct that I immediately went online to find out from the Book of Discipline what would be the implications for a complaint about sexual misconduct. I was not as familiar with the United Methodist Book of Discipline, and this fact turned out to be costly on my part. When I arrived at the office of the district superintendent on the requested day, I realized that the conference assistant to the bishop, Rev. David Dodge, from the conference office was also going to be at the meeting.

The meeting got started at approximately 1:05 p.m. Dr. Spencer opened with a short prayer and then proceeded to inform me that a formal complaint had been filed against me for sexual misconduct and that because of the nature of the complaint the conference had to act quickly and decisively in responding. He also told me that they had documentary evidence which made the complaint believable. Reverend Dodge then gave me an indication of how the process would go for the investigation. I was told that I was going to be on immediate suspension and that, following the meeting, they were both going to meet with representatives of the Staff Parish Relations Committee of the Palm Bay United Methodist Church in order to share the information in a meeting which was already prearranged from the previous night. An arrangement had already been made for a substitute pastor to preach the sermon at church on that following Sunday (August 3). The next step was that they would go the church on the Sunday following (August 3) in order to make the announcement that I was on suspension and that the reason was because of the complaint referenced above. He also suggested that I had the choice of surrendering my credentials then and there. If I voluntarily surrendered my credentials, the nature of the announcement would be different and would make no reference to sexual misconduct. He also said that the process would then just end "abruptly." If I did not surrender my credentials then and there, the bishop would engage in a "supervisory session" on a date to be arranged. At this supervisory session, he would first meet with the complainant and then with me in trying to come to a just resolution. However, they both made it clear that because of the charges, the bishop will have no alternative but to ask me to surrender my credentials. When I protested that "harsh" projection, Reverend Dodge used an illustration and mentioned that when he was a child and did something which his mother had warned him not to do, he had to face the consequences for being disobedient. I considered that illustration extraordinarily immature and ridiculous because mothers respond in different ways and often show mercy and offer forgiveness to a disobedient child. In addition, it also showed that there was no indication that there was going to be a fair process which would look at all the factors and circumstances in consideration of the clause from the *Book of Discipline*—paragraph 361.2 on page 312 (2016 *Book of Discipline*) I was also told that if we could not arrive at a just resolution, it would then go to a trial. At the same time, I was reminded that if it got to the stage of a trial, it would become a public event and, as such, there was an attempt to discourage any effort to get it to that "distance." Reverend Dodge mentioned that he knew of similar cases where the respondent would just voluntarily surrender credentials rather than going through the painful process of a church trial. Dr. Spencer then suggested that I should plan on going back to the church and clear my office as much as possible on that same day and prepare to hand over all my keys. I was to stay away from the church and should have no contact with anyone from the church. He indicated again that they had documents as evidence. He suggested that I should clear my office that same afternoon and after telling him how impractical that was, he suggested that it needed to be done by Friday morning. He also asked me to surrender any church check books which I may have had at that point. Again I reiterated how harsh I thought the projection was and used the opportunity to remind them of the (then) recent case where a bishop in the Greater New Jersey Annual Conference had a charge brought against him by his wife for having being involved in an extramarital affair with a female district superintendent and essentially got a "slap on the wrist" as a consequence. He was asked to step down as bishop but remained in good standing and was asked to serve as pastor for a regular congregation. He still had his ministerial credentials intact even though my crossing of the moral line was not any different from his. The female district superintendent with whom he had the affair for a good while also got away scotch free and did not even receive as much as the proverbial slap on the wrist. I found it interesting that neither of them responded to this statement. Even though they did not respond to the statement, I also thought of the married female pastor in the New England Conference who, in the early 2000s, was engaged in a sexual affair with a male parishioner and the consequences she faced was a mere suspension from pastoral ministry for two or three years. There were several other known cases of sexual misconduct which had taken place among Methodist clergy involving pastors who are still serving but the two referenced ones were at the time, only the most recent. With all that knowledge and my taking the opportunity to remind them, their only response was that I was given a second opportunity to surrender my credentials, but I declined to do so.

When I finally had a chance to speak, but without seeing the written complaint, I told them that I was not in a position to deny the allegations. I did acknowledge that I had been involved in an inappropriate relationship over a three-month period and also tried to explain the circumstances as well as the dynamics which led to that situation. I apologized profusely and truly expressed my regret and remorse as strongly and as sincerely as I could. I also indicated to them that my wife and I had been agonizing over this issue for the past six weeks, and their body language expressed surprise. In fact, Dr. Spencer asked me to repeat what I had said. The point that I was trying to get across to them was that I was aware that I was being unfaithful for a short while and that, rightly or wrongly, I was so angry that I was pushing back at my wife when she started to voice her suspicions and question my inappropriate relationship. As that first meeting came to a close, I remember walking up to both Dr. Spencer and Reverend Dodge individually. I sincerely hugged them both and told them again how sorry I was for what I had done and also for the fact that through my behavior, I had let down so many persons in my life.

On that same afternoon and while I was still at the district office, I gave Dr. Spencer the checkbook for the pastor's discretionary fund, and when they got to the church a little later, I gave him all the additional checkbooks. I left the district office that afternoon without seeing a copy of the written complaint. In the meantime, I called my wife before I started driving in order to give her the information. Within a short while after I got to the church, both Reverend Dodge as well as Dr. Spencer were at the church to pick up the checkbooks and to share that they had been in touch with the Bishop of New England. They shared that at some point I would have the option of having the case heard in Florida or in New England since my clergy membership was with the New England Conference. On that same evening, July 30, in the presence of both Rev. Dodge and Dr. Spencer, my wife asked me if I had been given a copy of the complaint or seen the complaint. I responded "no" as I had neither seen nor received a copy of the complaint. On Friday, August 1, 2014, during a telephone call to Reverend Dodge my wife asked about us receiving a copy of the written complaint, and she was told that I would receive a copy in due time. My wife then asked him to explain how an action as significant as a "suspension" could take place with a pending announcement in church the following Sunday, and "her husband" had not seen a copy of the complaint. Reverend Dodge did not respond to that enquiry either.

On Thursday (July 31) while driving, I received a telephone call from Dr. Spencer in which he suggested that I meet him at a convenient point in order to sign the statement waiving my right to have the case heard in the New England Conference. I indicated that my schedule would not allow me to sign that evening, and even though he stressed the urgency of signing it, I did not follow through on signing that evening. As a "compromise," he suggested that I meet him at 9:00 a.m. on Friday to sign it because it had to be signed by noontime on that Friday or the "trial" would automatically default to the New England Conference. (See "Committee on Investigation" transcript, page 120 and 121.) He asked me about the possibility of meeting at the parsonage, but I told him that it would not be a good place to meet since both my mother in law as well as one of my two teenage daughters would have been there. At that time, my mother-in-law was not aware of the charges. I was a little curious about the seeming urgency to "rush" the process, and I felt extremely pressured at the thought of having to drop everything else that I had to do in order to facilitate this "rush" and fit into the schedule of others. On Friday, August 1, I met Dr. Spencer in order to sign the statement to have the case heard in the Florida Conference. When he handed me the document, he mentioned that I was signing it in order to indicate that I was not being coerced into having the hearing happen in the Florida Conference. At the time of signing, I did not know that there were no such time restraints or limitations for signing the document. He was merely taking advantage of my obvious ignorance relating to the process because he had a reason for wanting the case to be heard in Florida. (He also capitalized on my ignorance when he started the initial conversation and got me to respond without showing me the official copy of the complaint as he should have done.) On top of all that, my state of mind was not even allowing me to think clearly anyway. After I signed the document, which was composed by someone else but required my signature, I asked Dr. Spencer if I could have one of the unsigned copies of the document which I had signed for my records, and his response was that I was not allowed to keep a copy. I found it strange that I had been asked to sign a document waiving my own rights but was not allowed to keep a copy. This document was prepared by Rev. David Dodge, and I never had a chance to review it. However, as mentioned, because of my state of mind at that time, I did not mention that concern to Dr. Spencer. I want to emphasize that I barely had a chance to scan the document and even less of an opportunity to process the information in the document which I was asked to sign but could not keep a copy of. A copy of the document is below.

Paragraph 2719 Agreement

1. Rev Errol Leslie is a member of the New England Conference of The United Methodist Church. Rev Leslie is currently appointed in the Florida Conference of the United Methodist Church.

2. On July 28, 2014, a complaint against Rev Leslie was received by Bishop Ken Carter of the Florida Conference and Bishop Sudarshana Devadhar of the New England Conference.

3. Paragraph 2719 of the 2012 Book of Discipline provides that "[a]ny clergy member residing beyond the bounds of the conference in which membership is held shall be subject to the procedures of ¶¶ 2701 - 2718 exercised by the appropriate officers of the conference in which he or she is a member, unless the presiding bishops of the two annual conferences and the clergy member subject to the procedures agree that fairness will be better served by having the procedures carried out by the appropriate officers of the annual conference in which he or she is serving under appointment, or if retired, currently residing."

4. After consideration of the complaint and the provisions of ¶ 2719, Rev Leslie has agreed, freely and voluntarily without coercion, that fairness will be better served by having the procedures of ¶¶ 2701 - 2718 carried out by the appropriate officers of the Florida Annual Conference.

5. Bishops Carter and Devadhar agree that the appropriate officers of the Florida Annual Conference should carry out the procedures of ¶¶ 2701 - 2718.

6. The parties to this agreement further agree that any decisions concerning suspension required under ¶¶ 363(a) or 2704.2(c) upon the recommendation of the bishop of the Florida Conference shall be made by the Executive Committees of the Boards of Ministry of both the Florida Conference and the New England Conference

DATED this _____ day of _____ 201_

Rev. Errol Leslie

Bishop Sudarshana Devadhar

Bishop Ken Carter

Shortly after, I was told verbally that the supervisory session was scheduled for September 12. I was also told that the board of ordained ministries for both the New England Conference as well as the Florida Conference had met and had agreed that I be placed on suspension. At that same meeting, I was given a third opportunity to surrender my credentials with the reminder that such action would change the nature of the announcement which was to be made in church on that Sunday. If I surrendered my credentials then and there, the pending announcement would not make any reference to sexual misconduct. Once more I declined to surrender my ministerial credentials. I indicated to him that I still felt called to the ministry and so would not want to surrender my credentials. Reverend Spencer's response was that I could still be a pastor; I just could not be a United Methodist Church pastor. He also made a slight reference to the process that was to follow and ended by saying that he could not think as to why I would let it go to a trial if I was admitting to the charges. Once more I thought of the cases which I previously mentioned and about which he knew both in the Greater New Jersey and New England Conferences respectively. I wondered why he would single me out but would not comment on those two separate situations with three pastors including a bishop involved. At that point I still had not even seen the written complaint. I correctly assumed who had filed the complaint but definitely had not seen it. Dr. Spencer and I both spent a short time talking about the implication of the charges. I asked Dr. Spencer to pray for me before he left, and he did.

As instructed, I did not go to church on Sunday, August 3, but had word from my family that the announcement was made in both services. On the evening of August 3, I received a telephone call from the complainant. I answered the phone, and she wanted to know how I was doing and if I had gone to church that morning. I did not answer the question, but the question did lead me to wonder how much research she had done about the United Methodist Church process or whether she was being coached by anyone in the UMC both with regards to the composition of the letter and also with regards to the process. I thought it strange that she would ask a pastor if he had gone to church on a Sunday morning. In the meantime, Reverend Dodge had sent the following e-mail to his counterpart in the New England Conference.

Well friends, it has been a long, but fruitful day. Gary Spencer and I met with Errol Leslie for an hour and a half this afternoon. We explained to him the nature of the complaint and he shared that the complaint is accurate in regards to his involvement with the complainant. It is Gary's and my expectation that Rev. Leslie will surrender his credentials but he asked for some time to consider his options and to determine how to handle his financial obligations. Thus, I told him we would move forward on determining a date for the supervisory response. If he does surrender credentials before the selected date we would then cancel the supervisory response. Gary explained to Rev. Leslie that he is not to initiate any contact with church members and he is to clear out his office in a timely manner.

Gary will continue to monitor that progress. We determined that neither Rev. Leslie, nor his wife, Kaye, who is the church secretary, are signers for the church's checking account. He does have a pastor's discretionary fund for which only he signs. He turned over that checkbook to Gary.

Rev. Leslie was very cooperative throughout our conversation and repeatedly expressed his remorse over this situation.

I have notified our Director of Clergy Excellence who has conferred with the chair of our Board of Ordained Ministry. A conference call is scheduled for 10:00 Thursday morning to act on the request for suspension. I also notified our communications director, Gretchen Hastings. She is expecting a call from the communications director of the New England Conference so that statements can be prepared that will be in harmony with one another. Gary and I also met with the SPRC. They were very surprised and shocked. It is apparent that they have a lot of appreciation for both Rev. and Mrs. Leslie. Plans are in place for Gary and I to be at the two services on Sunday to make the announcement regarding the complaint and the suspension. Gary will do the early service. He is unavailable for the 11:00 service due to a charge conference scheduled at another church that morning. So, I will make the announcement at the conclusion of that service. Gary will return to the church as soon as his charge conference is completed so that he can be present with me following the service as we seek to provide a safe place for people to deal with their emotional responses to the announcement. Tomorrow I will construct the letters that will go to Rev. Leslie and to Ms. Hendricks and will explain the process. I will send copies to Bishop Devadhar and Rev. Robinson-Johnson. As soon as a date is established for the supervisory response 1 will notify you of that, also.

Thank you, Erica, for the sample letter to use with Rev. Leslie regarding Para. 2719.1 will correct the names and email that to Gary for Rev. Leslie's signature.

I believe that captures the activities of the day. Please let me know if there any questions or any further suggestions.

Blessings,
Rev. David A. Dodge
Assistant to Bishop Kenneth H. Carter, Jr.
Florida Conference of
The United Methodist Church

By now, I was waiting to wake up from what I hoped was a bad dream. I had many friends and family all over the world and in this age of technology, information like what I just described could go viral in just hours—and it did. I started reading the Bible more. I prayed like I never prayed before. I was listening to more gospel music from YouTube. Suddenly the lyrics and message from the songs meant more to me than they ever did. I continued to read Psalm 51 and read that over and over. I still tried to put myself in David's shoe and waited for God to tell me that he was still my God and that I was still His child. In my state of emotional and spiritual distraught, I reached out to a lady in the community whose level of spirituality I had found to be very impressive.

She was as strong and as committed a Christian as one could be. I met with her twice per week for prayer and "counseling." She was not a trained counselor or pastor, but I had observed her over the years and had full confidence that she would be the one to help restore the peace I was seeking from God. I knew that God was not going to forsake me, but in the moment, everything felt and looked scary.

On the evening of Monday, August 4, my wife got a telephone call from Dr. Spencer informing her that he had arranged a church council meeting for 6:00 p.m. that evening which would be in the form of a Staff Parish Relations Committee (SPRC) meeting. For persons who are not familiar with Methodist structure, this committee would correspond to the human resources or personnel committee in the regular working world. He suggested that Kaye should not attend that meeting (my wife was secretary for the church council), and she complied. We subsequently heard that following that impromptu church council meeting, an SPRC meeting was also held.

On Tuesday (August 5), I received a voice mail from Dr. Spencer telling me that he was checking up on me to see how I was doing and that, while there was no special agenda, I could call him if I wanted to do so. That same evening, I sent him a text acknowledging and saying thanks for the voice mail. On Wednesday (August 06), I mailed a letter to Rev. David Dodge with copies to Bishops Ken Carter and Sudarshana Devadhar as well as to Dr. Spencer and Rev. Evelyn Robinson-Johnson. In this letter, I requested a copy of the written complaint as well as the supporting evidentiary documents as per Judicial Council ruling number 974 (October 2003). On Thursday afternoon (August 7), I received a call from Dr. Spencer indicating that he had a copy of the written complaint and that he could get it to me at a mutually convenient time. He said that with Bishop Carter being out of the country, Bishop Devadhar had given permission for me to receive the copy of the complaint. I subsequently found out that Dr. Spencer had blatantly lied (again) when he told me that Bishop Devadhar had given permission for me to receive a copy of the document since this was mandated by the above mentioned Judicial Council ruling. The ruling is clear that the respondent must receive a copy of the written complaint in order for him/her to make an adequate response. Once more he sought to take full advantage of a perceived ignorance on my part and pretended that he was waiting for permission in order to give me a copy of the complaint.

After I observed the deceptive and misleading practices of Reverend Spencer, I realized the big debt of gratitude which I owed to Rev. Sydney Sadio. He was the first clergy person with whom I made contact after the complaint was filed. I told him that my biggest concern was that the bishop was going to take away my ministerial credentials. It really was a big concern because, in my ignorance relating to the Book of Discipline, I thought that the bishop really had the authority to unilaterally take my credentials away. Both Reverend Spencer and Reverend Dodge fed into that perceived ignorance and at no time did either of them tell me that the bishop could not unilaterally take my credentials away. They just inferred that that was going to happen and that I would have no choice. However, during my first conversation with Reverend Sadio, he shared that very valuable piece of information. I am convinced that if he had not done so, I would have acted in ignorance and signed the document which they kept insisting that I should sign. Even at the supervisory response session when I met with Bishop Carter, he asked me to sign and communicated that request in a way which made it appear that I would have had no choice. However, because Reverend Sadio had told me otherwise, I could confidently tell the bishop that I would not sign.

As it turned out, Both Dr. Spencer and Reverend Dodge had put several things in place before I could see and adequately respond to the complaint. As mentioned, they were even trying to get me to surrender my credentials without showing me a complaint which they must have known was grossly exaggerated. However, for these leaders in the Florida Conference of the United Methodist Church, the most important thing was to have gotten my signature saying I was surrendering my credentials; basic and elementary Christian ethics was not given any consideration at all. Dr. Spencer had also lied about the need for me to sign the document waiving my rights for the trial to take place in the New England Conference within a three-day time frame. They both must have realized that I was not very familiar with the system and so they sought to explore this weakness to the maximum. As it turned out, there was no rushed time frame within which such document needed to be signed. As the process continued, it became obvious that they wanted to control the process in Florida in order to ensure that I receive the maximum penalty. Once more, Christian Ethics seemed lacking in several decisions that were made.

There was a third effort to deceive because I asked Dr. Spencer about the supporting documents and evidence and he responded that the complaint is the "evidence." I used the opportunity to remind him that the Judicial Council ruling makes a very clear distinction between the written complaints on the one hand and the supporting documents on the other hand. Having explained that to Dr. Spencer, about an hour or so later, he called me to indicate that he had both documents and could meet me at a mutually convenient time and place in order to hand them to me. We set up that time and at that meeting he asked me if I was planning to meet with the bishop on September 12. My response was that I am just taking it one day at a time.

The first time I had anything close to a pleasant conversation was on Monday August 11 at around 3:30 p.m. when I received a call from Bishop Carter. In this call, he assured me that he was not my "adversary" and that he was praying for me as well. He asked me if I had any questions for him and I told him that my head was still spinning and I had no questions at that time. I also informed him that there was a letter in the mail to Rev. David Dodge which was copied to him as well. The bishop said that he was looking forward to receiving the letter. At just about the time that I spoke with the bishop, my wife had mailed a letter to Reverend Dodge in which I informed him that I would respect the expected confidentiality with regards to communication but also mentioned in the letter that the complainant had kept in touch with me through texts as well as attempted telephone calls. As of the date (August 19, 2014), I received a mixture of both regular and hateful text messages from the complainant. She had also attempted to call several times, but I did not pick up the phone on any of the occasions.

It really became very frustrating for me as I continued to receive these unwanted telephone calls and hundreds of texts from the complainant. The texts were overwhelming, but she never relented even though I did not respond to any of them.

On Wednesday, August 13, while I was in the office of my cardiologist, I received four telephone calls from the emergency room of the Port St. Lucie hospital. When I finally had a chance to answer on the fourth attempt, I realized that the person at the other end of the line was the complainant who wanted to know if I do not want to speak with her and also indicated that she was there for a procedure. I wished her all the best and also told her that I was not allowed to speak with her but that I would pray for her. She ended the conversation by telling me "I love you." I did not respond to that comment. We then hung up.

In response to a message I had left for him, on the day of August 22, I received a call back from Reverend Dodge, and I asked him if it was okay to follow through on a commitment, which I had made to do the invocation for a public community event which was scheduled for Saturday August 30. He said that he would check back with the bishop and then get back to me. Within fifteen minutes of that call Reverend Dodge called back to say that the bishop had indicated that it would have been fine for me to do the invocation but was mindful that I could run into parishioners from PBUMC. He also asked me if I was aware of an e-mail, which one of my youth had sent to the bishop requesting that I be allowed to accompany the youth group on their annual trip to the Disney night of joy event. I told him that I was aware of the e-mail because both my daughters are members of the youth group.

The pressure and stress started again as on Tuesday, August 26, at 12:43 p.m., I received a call from Dr. Gary Spencer inquiring if I had cleaned the stuff from my office. I told him that I had done what I could but reminded him that he had said that I could leave some things there. He specifically asked me to take the instruments out and my response was that since the status was "suspension" and my case was still active, I think that any such action would be a little premature. As such, I also asked Dr. Spencer if there had been a conclusion to my case and he said no. I then again questioned why I would need to be cleaning out my office if the case had not been concluded. Again I asked him if there was something he knew which I did not know. I asked those questions because by this time I had been speaking with colleagues and doing my own research and recognized that the church was moving too fast and was also over aggressive. I did not see or feel any sense of "due process" being allowed to guide how the leadership of the church was behaving. It became clear to me again that they were not about to balance the information which I wanted to share with the information they had received from the complainant. It was hard for me to figure out how they could not have realized how grossly exaggerated the complaint was. Even with that thought, however, I did indicate that if I had anything in the office which was getting in the way of the interim pastor, I would have been happy to remove those. In response to any personal files in the desk drawers I reminded Dr. Spencer that the majority of the files were church files. At the end of the conversation, I asked him to put his instructions in writing. His response was that he had already done that so I told him that the only written communication that I received from anyone had been signed by Rev. David Dodge. He then said that he had already given me those instructions but that he would now put it in writing. Needless to say, I did not receive any such communication in writing, but I had been deceived and lied to by the district superintendent before.

At approximately 3:44 p.m. on the same day, another call came in from Dr. Spencer, but it went to voice mail since I was not able to take the call. When I listened to the voice mail, he stated that he was okay with me leaving some things in the office, but he wanted to make sure that the interim pastor would be able to use the desk. He also commented on my own comment in the previous conversation and stated that he did not know anything that I do not know. In the voice mail he reiterated that the charge was sexual misconduct and that I had admitted to that so he was not quite sure what kind of outcome I would be expecting on September 12. That statement again was very telling. The implication was clear that there was one goal and conclusion to the case which was in his mind and that was to see my pastoral ministry be terminated. He did end his voice mail by saying that if I had any questions, I could call him. Once more, I am continuing to see that my fate was a foregone conclusion and now the church was just going to be routinely doing what was required by the Book of Discipline.

In the meantime, while the church is making plans to hang me, I continued to receive many text messages as well as several telephone calls from the complainant. I did not respond to any of them, but it was beyond frustration that she continued to be aggressive while the church leaders who were getting ready to hang me did not seem to care.

The supervisory session with the bishop was set for September 12. As I prepared for it, I had mixed feelings of hope and despair. The bishop could listen to the events which led to my temptations and which caused me to go astray and arrive at a just resolution or he could be as aggressive as the district superintendent was and throw me under the bus. I thought about the only conversation I had had with him and felt encouraged that he did not see himself as my adversary. However, I was not sure how much an aggressive district superintendent may have influenced the bishop. By now the leadership in the church must have realized that they did not come remotely close to following the Book of Discipline as they launched the process. As you will see later, both Reverend Spencer and Reverend Dodge expected me to surrender my credentials without a "fight." The majority of the parishioners had expressed support for me in one way or another and they were extremely unhappy and upset because of the inhumane way that they perceived the hierarchy of church to be dealing with me. The anger and wrath of the congregation was shown to the district superintendent at just about every meeting that he attempted to have with them. It was not because they thought that I was innocent why they were angry, and it certainly was not because they condoned anything which I had done. It was because they were able to see what they deemed to be unfair practice by the hierarchy of the church and chose to let their feelings be known. Separate and apart from the church family, the wider Palm Bay community also expressed their anger which bordered on protest. The fact is that many had regarded me as a community pastor and as such many persons in the wider community vowed never to support any activities at the church. I was the pastor asked to do the invocation at most community events. I was the pastor who had initiated and started a food-sharing ministry that fed upwards of eight hundred persons every week. I was the pastor that had hosted several gospel concerts, including weekend gospel festivals by bringing in singers from all over the state and even outside of the state of Florida. The church had developed a reputation and came to be known as the gospel concert church. It meant even more to the community that my family used to participate in these gospel events. The leadership of the Florida Conference of the United Methodist Church was now at a point where they had to decide on what options they had since I had not voluntarily surrendered my credentials. I waited anxiously for the supervisory session as did the congregation of the Palm Bay United Methodist Church.

All along I had wondered if the reason for the church's aggression had anything to do with a fear of any legal action from the complainant. She had two daughters who were both practicing attorneys in Florida. Even though she never had a good relationship with any of her children, she had a habit of walking around and bragging about her "attorney daughters" and used this as a weapon or indirect threat to other parties with the hope that this would help her to have things go her way.

On Friday, September 12, as I walked into the lobby area of the conference office in Lakeland, Florida, for the supervisory session, I received two texts from the complainant indicating, respectively, that (1) she can hear my voice and (2) she is nearby.

On that day, I met with Bishop Ken Carter, Dr. Gary Spencer, and the district superintendent of the south central district, Rev. Walter Monroe, as part of the supervisory session. Rev. Dr. Sydney Sadio, whom I had invited to attend as my "advocate," was also present. Other than shaking his hand and saying "Good morning," I observed that the bishop did not acknowledge Dr. Sadio's presence; neither did he seek to have him introduce himself or find out who he was. The other three persons referenced had met with the complainant just prior to that. Bishop Carter opened the meeting with a prayer. It was noteworthy that his opening words of the prayer included "that the truth will be told." In hindsight, I can understand why his opening prayer would make a reference to the truth being told because the complainant, whom I already described as a pathological liar, had accused me all along of telling lies. She knew that she had exaggerated the story to such an extent that she had to preempt my response and seek to discredit me by telling the bishop that I was going to be telling lots of lies.

Her strategy worked hundred percent because after the bishop finished his opening prayer, he glared at me repeatedly. I was able to see the fire in his eyes, and before he said one word, I could tell that I was doomed. We could have ended the session without him starting it. I knew what it felt like for a prey to wake up and see a lion or a tiger standing over it. I felt like a zebra staring into the eyes of a growling lion. He then proceeded to ask me if I had had sex with the complainant and if I could affirm that I had told that to the district superintendent. I was taken off guard with that being the opening question, so I tried to make a speech without giving a straight "Yes" or "No" answer. I must confess that my answer was kind of vague. He then told me that there could not be any ambiguity when it came to the concept of sexual intercourse. Immediately, I could tell that I was in a trial and not in a supervisory session, which the Book of Discipline describes as needing to be pastoral and administrative. My sense from the tone and style of the bishop was that there was no inclination to have a fair hearing. Instead of asking me to make a statement in response to the allegations, I was bombarded with several questions. As I attempted to answer them, I could hear a lot of sarcastic "sighs" and "groans" from the bishop. After I asked for an opportunity to make a statement, I started to present my case. Within the first minute of my presentation, the bishop asked me to stop talking and indicated that he was not interested in details. He refused to look at any documentary evidence which I had to prove that the complaint was full of blatant lies, and he just kept insisting that he wanted justice for her and for all the other women whom I had abused. Again—and for emphasis—I was not about to deny that I had the affair, but I was not going to allow this complaint to stand with all those additional claims about my character.

At one point, I told the bishop that there is a total of twenty-seven allegations in the complaint, which should bring into question the state of mind of the complainant, but he brushed it aside, saying that he was only focusing on the allegation involving sex. It turned out that the bishop also mentioned that there was an issue "involving money," which the complainant had mentioned during the prior meeting with all three church officials. I became very curious as to what that issue was, but I was so aware of the complainant's gift of convincing unsuspecting persons that all her made-up stories are real. I just wished that I had been given a chance to have this "money issue" clarified. That situation helped me to understand why a conference appointed auditor was sent to the church to audit the books later on in the process. It also explained why Dr. Spencer had asked me on day 1 to surrender any checkbooks which I had in my possession. Neither the district superintendent nor the bishop took any time to wonder if these were truthful allegations—or perhaps they did and determined that they were true. Now I was also being falsely accused of impropriety on top of the one allegation, which I knew was really true. The issue of money was not one of the twentyseven allegations which were made in the signed complaint, but the complainant, recognizing that she had them all in the palm of her hands, used the opportunity to drive in a few more nails during the meeting.

Mentally and emotionally, it was hard to believe that my wife and I had spent so much time helping the church with fundraisers and the thanks and appreciation we got for our efforts amounted to a suspicion that we were taking money from the church. Prior to the complaint being filed, I would use my day off on a Friday to go shopping and then later to prepare the meals, which we would sell every Friday a as part of our weekly fundraiser fish fry. I was taking time on a Saturday to go and work in the newly established thrift shop because we did not have enough volunteers. We would utilize our musical talents by putting on concerts from which the church would earn income. This we did on a regular basis. Hence, it was more than painful when, after all this effort in going the extra mile, a financial audit was ordered as a result of a vindictive person making up stories.

As happened at the beginning of the process, during this supervisory session, both the bishop as well as Dr. Spencer suggested that I should surrender my credentials, and I refused to do so. As mentioned, from the day I met with Dr. Spencer and Reverend Dodge, they had led me to believe that the bishop had the sole authority to revoke my credentials regardless of how I felt about it. Fortunately, I had spoken with my colleague, Rev. Sydney Sadio, who indicated very clearly that no bishop had the right or power to revoke my credentials. However, when Bishop Carter told me to sign the document, he said it in a way which would suggest that it was not my choice. Thanks to my newfound knowledge, I did not give in because with that level of determination on their part, there was no way they would have allowed me to recant. I made it clear to the bishop that if I surrendered my credentials, it would indicate that I was pleading guilty to all the other false accusations which were included in the original complaint. As such, my reasoning was that I would like to have a fair hearing at a trial. When Dr. Sadio inquired if there was any other possible resolution other than having me surrender my credentials, the bishop said that he would only change from that position if the complainant recanted her complaint. I decided that I was not going to surrender my ministerial credentials on the basis of a complaint which was based on concoctions. I was beginning to think that they were convinced that I was "the scum of the earth," and since I knew otherwise, I was not going to cower. The bishop as well as District Superintendent Spencer both hinted at the negative implications of a public trial, but I was still prepared to go along and wait for the trial. The bishop reminded me that all the evidence submitted would be used at the public hearing while Dr. Spencer reiterated that by saying there would also be television cameras present. Here went Dr. Spencer again in his fourth attempt to deceive by lying about television cameras being in the church trial courtroom. This was obviously an effort to intimidate me because he thought that I would cower about this situation going public. Bishop Carter mentioned that he would not feel comfortable if he were to have coerced me into signing a document surrendering my credentials. While I did not respond verbally, in my heart I thought that that was exactly what he had been trying to do! My reasoning and thought at the time was that at this public trial, I would hope to finally receive a fair hearing and my documentary evidence would not be ignored. I felt that there was a very one-sided and biased approach by the bishop in carrying out what was supposed to have been a balanced hearing.

At a few points during the session, Dr. Sadio tried to get a word in with either a question or a comment, and while the bishop allowed it, there was no indication that he was listening to what Dr. Sadio was saying with an open mind. Dr. Sadio referenced nationally known pastors who in the past had been involved with extramarital relations, including Jimmy Swaggart of TV "fame" and Bishop Long in Atlanta; both of whom were forgiven and welcomed back by their respective congregations. In that regard, Dr. Sadio asked if there was no place for forgiveness and the demonstration of the grace of God. The bishop's response was that his concern was for justice for "all these women." He mentioned to me that I was "blaming the accuser" and not taking any responsibility. In mentioning to him that I was taking responsibility for my role in the situation, he said that I should take responsibility by surrendering my credentials and by going to the SPRC meeting, which was scheduled for the following day, and admitting to them that I had had extramarital sex. He was really yelling and screaming at the top of his voice like some parents would yell at a kid. At that point, I was tempted to mention again the case of the bishop in the Greater New Jersey Conference who was involved in the sexual affair with a female district superintendent, and they were both happily continuing their ministry because nothing of any significance came of the case. However, I held my tongue because I was in such a state of shock and disappointment over the bishop's attitude. In my mind, I was thinking, "Bishop, think about your fellow bishop up in New Jersey. This was someone who served the church at the same level that you are now serving. He is human too, why don't you go yell at him to show him how disgusted and infuriated you are?" Of course, this was only in my thoughts, so the bishop went on to mention at that time that a member of my church's youth group had written to him and asked him to allow me to attend the Disney night of joy event with the youth group. His follow-up question was whether or not he could tell that youth group member that I had had sex with one of the chaperones. Even though I knew that it was a false statement, I told him that he had my permission to do so. At that point, Dr. Spencer asked me if I would be willing to attend the SPRC meeting scheduled for the following day and make an admission. The bishop did not give me any opportunity to respond to that "invitation" because he moved on to another subject.

It seemed to me that the bishop was visibly upset when I insisted that we take the process to a trial since we were not able to arrive at a just resolution. At one point during that session, he even mentioned that he was "infuriated." And I was thinking again, "How infuriated are you at the guy in New Jersey?" At another point the bishop commented that no one could think that the conference was acting along racial lines because the complainant was actually Black. I was not quite sure as to why the bishop would initiate the issue of race in the process because it was not something that I had brought up even if I wondered about it. However, having mentioned it, I wondered if the presence of District Superintendent Monroe (African American) was his way of convincing himself that there might not have been an element of race which directly or indirectly guided the approach which they were all taking. In frustration, the bishop then suggested that he was going to refer the trial back to the New England Conference since he did not see why the Florida Conference should invest money and time into this public trial. He thought that this money could be better spent in providing food for hungry persons.

My interpretation of that comment was that he did not think that I was worth the "investment." I needed to be "thrown under the bus" with or without a proper hearing. He also indicated that at some point, I would receive a letter from him as far as the remainder of the process goes. Frustratingly, he also hinted that I could win the trial because peers do not normally like to "condemn" fellow peers. He seemed extremely disappointed at the prospect of my winning at the trial. His second hint was that if I really did win the trial, they would not want be back in the Florida Conference and reminded me that I was only a guest in the Florida Conference. "Wow," I thought to myself, "how caring and pastoral is that? Is there any place where he could try to squeeze a little of what the scripture teaches about grace?" Ironically, while I had taken some comfort in and had some hope from the bishop's earlier telephone call on August 11 telling me that he was not my adversary, I interpreted his demeanor during the conduct of the session as been extremely meanspirited, harsh, and adversarial. I was treated with extreme disrespect, and my dignity was flattened. I thought again about a few cop shows on TV depicting a variety of real criminal actions, and I always observed how respectful the cops have been to the persons who are arrested or who are about to be arrested. The session ended without a resolution as the bishop would not look at any other punitive option other than for me to surrender my credentials. I guess that we all hoped that the process would come to an end on that day, but we all walked away with disappointment on both sides.

CHAPTER 5

Ongoing Negotiations with the Florida Conference

When I left the meeting with the bishop, I felt totally and completely and comprehensively hundred percent humiliated. It had never happened to me before—neither in my home from my parents or in elementary school or in high school or in college. I was truly distraught when I left the conference office. I felt so humiliated from the indignity with which I was treated. I had never experienced that in my entire life, and now I was age sixty. In the epistle of James, there is some guidance about the use of the tongue, and it would behoove Bishop Carter and District Superintendent Spencer to read and process this passage. They both used the same tongue that preached sermons about forgiveness and love to belittle me without any care for my emotions. This they did in spite of Paul saying that "when one is overtaken with a fault, you who are wise should restore such a one gently." I had to ask myself, "Did I commit an unpardonable sin?" Was there any pastoral care that could be offered to me or my family even if they continued to pursue the extreme punitive measures? I was also thinking of the person who penned the statement that *"the church is not a museum for saints but a hospital for sinners."*

I remember hearing a member of another church expressing her disgust to a pastor who had welcomed and embraced a gentleman who had been in prison for several years because he allegedly committed murder. This person expressed that there should be no place in the church for such a person. As she continued to rant and express her anger, another pastor asked her in a nice calm voice, "If someone like that who is broken should not come to the church for refuge, tell me, where should he go?" That is the kind of question I would have loved to ask Bishop Carter and the two district superintendents who were both treating me just like that lady wanted that ex-prisoner who was now a part of her church to be treated.

Notwithstanding the fact that the push to a feeling of isolation helped to drive me into this very sinful period of my life, my family gave me full support. It was hard to believe that there was such a treatment of disrespect and indignity coming from the church. In the church and even in the secular world, there has been a movement toward restorative justice. I commend all the lawmakers who recognize that it makes better psychological sense to try and restore persons who have done wrong instead of being punitive. It is the foundation of Christian teaching, yet somehow, the church seems to be staying clear of this form of response to those who have done wrong. In fact, my defense team jumped through hoops to try and get this play into the picture, but the church would have none of it. I read the following quote in a recent devotional and thought that it was quite appropriate for my situation.

> Most people know we're messed up. Instead of lectures, they need a hope for redemption. Stern faces or sharp words can block their view of that hope… Followers of Jesus must become the face of grace in these life-changing encounters with others… A Christian's grace-filled actions can smooth someone's path to the savior's presence.

I thought also of the quotation from Galatians 6:1–2.

> If a man be overtaken in any trespass, you who are spiritual restore such a one in a spirit of gentleness, considering yourself lest ye also be tempted. Bear one another's burdens and so fulfill the law of Christ

Very shortly after I got home, I penned a letter to the bishop; but after thinking about it, I decided not to put it in the mail. I am including it in through this medium as it captures my thoughts at the time.

Bishop Kenneth Carter,

Dear Bishop Carter,

When I received a telephone call from you on August 11th indicating that you were praying for me and that you were not "my adversary," it was very reassuring. In that spirit, I attended the supervisory session on Friday September 12th, 2014 in relation to the complaint that has been filed against me. It did not take a long time for me to realize that the mood in the room was anything but what the book of discipline intended in paragraph 363.1 (B) about the supervisory session being pastoral and administrative. While you mentioned occasionally that the session was not a judicial one, I was made to feel that I was going through a second trial before the real trial began. I did not get a sense of the response being "pastoral and administrative." In fact, contrary to what you suggested in that telephone conversation, the tone was quite adversarial and at one point during the session you even verbalized that you were "infuriated."

As such, I was disappointed that when you eventually allowed me an opportunity to give a narrative in the development of a relationship, from my perspective, you cut me off within the first minute telling me that you were not interested in details. On several other occasions, as I tried to speak, you would shut me down or cut me off and at one point you actually verbalized "stop talking." I was disappointed that you were not willing to look at any documents which I had to show to you which may have contradicted any information which the complainant either had in her written complaint or may have shared with you when you met with her prior to meeting with me. At one point during the session, you mentioned that one of my youths had requested permission for me to accompany the youth group to the annual Disney Night of Joy event. You then looked me straight in the eye and asked me if you had my permission for you to respond to that youth by telling him or her that I had had sex with one of the chaperones. I thought that question was very telling. You obviously just bought and swallowed wholesale all the damaging lies which the complainant created.

I considered your sarcastic 'oohs' and 'aahs' to be very disruptive and disrespectful. I was hoping that, in spite of the allegations, I would have been treated with a little respect since we are still at the point where allegations are being investigated.

Respectfully, I would like to submit that I do not think that I received a fair hearing in keeping with the book of discipline 362.2. In answer to a question asked by my advocate, Dr. Sydney Sadio, you indicated that your main concern "right now" is for justice for "all these women" named in the complaint. With that in mind, I am enclosing in this communication a list of all the women that I know of through texts sent to me by the complainant even after the complaint was filed. You may already have some of these on your list but I want to make sure that you have them all. I trust that, this time, you or your designee will take some time to look at the list and submit it to the appropriate person(s) who will take the matter from here to the next level. Any other enclosed texts included in this communication will speak for themselves and I seek to mention them numerically for easy reference...

As I indicated, I penned but did not submit the letter referenced above. I thought that "my hand was already in the lion's mouth," so I needed to be careful not to aggravate him further. On Tuesday, September 16, at approximately 5:30 p.m., I received another call from the district superintendent. He indicated that he had received a call from Mrs. Hendricks in which she indicated that a Jean Fenton had called and threatened her (Mrs. Hendricks). Dr. Spencer used the opportunity to remind me that I was not to be in touch with any members of my church. I told him that Jean was not a member of my church and that, in any case, Mrs. Hendricks was the one who first called Jean and was lambasting me and berating my character. Jean's call to her was in response to something which Mrs. Hendricks initiated. I also answered his question confirming that Jean did not attend the Palm Bay United Methodist Church (PBUMC) either. Here is another case where the complainant, who was by no means an angel, continued to play the victim game at my expense. She would do research on my activities in Palm Bay and try to "report" anything which she thought could effectively rub salt into a wound which was already painfully stinging. Following that discussion, he reminded me that I need to clear my office so that the appointed pastor could have the use of the office. I needed to remove the pictures from off the wall and take my instruments from behind the curtain. I mentioned again that for me to do that would be somewhat premature since I was still appointed to the church. His response was that I was on suspension, and I then indicated that "suspension" was temporary and not permanent. At that point, he threatened to come himself and put the things from my office out on the sidewalk, and I suggested to him that he could go ahead and do that. He expressed concern as to why I was resisting, and I mentioned that I was waiting for the process to play out and would remove my belongings if and whenever there was official and final word that I was no longer appointed to the church. Dr. Spencer then said that more than likely, I would not be appointed back to the church and that Joe Moxley would be appointed there. I reiterated that I would respond to whatever official communication I received telling me that I was no longer appointed there. His response was that he would exercise his authority as district superintendent and put it in writing for me to remove my personal belongings from the office. I told him that I would await that piece of written communication.

It seemed that there would be no end to the bullying and pressure tactics from Dr. Spencer as on Wednesday, September 24, at approximately 3:45 p.m., I received a voice mail from him stating that the complainant had called the bishop's office and requested that I do not make any contacts with her son. The voice mail suggested that it was okay if he contacted me but that I should not make any contacts. I did not respond to the voice mail. The son referred to was a grown man in his forties who just so happened to be my automechanic and who, like his siblings, did not have a good relationship with his mom. In fact, he was very upset about what she had done to me, especially as he knew her history of being involved in several inappropriate relationships before and after the divorce from her ex-husband.

On Wednesday, October 1, I was informed by my wife that the interim pastor was in the process of packing a box with the personal stuff which I had on my desk. I suggested to her that she should not comment nor respond to any comments about the box being packed.

On Friday, October 17, while I was in Jamaica, I received an e-mail from Patti Moxley, the administrative assistant to the district superintendent. The e-mail indicated that Dr. Spencer had sent me a letter and left two voice mails for me regarding a meeting he wanted me to attend and which he had scheduled for October 16. I had not received the referenced letter or the voice mails before I left for Jamaica on October 13. At the end of the e-mail, it was suggested that since they did not have any responses from me, they would assume that I was going to be present at the meeting. Of course, the date was already past at the time I first saw the e-mail. I telephoned the district office from Jamaica and left a voice mail for Patti indicating that I was in Jamaica and that I had not received the communication in any form. When I called back about two hours later, I was able to speak with Patti and gave her the same information which I had left on the voice mail. She told me that they would schedule the meeting for October 23, which was the day after I was scheduled to return to the United States. I used the opportunity to ask her if she could tell me the nature of the meeting, and she shared that the bishop had some follow-up questions for me, and it sounded like they wanted to get the matter behind them. She also said that I would be welcome to take my advocate with me to the meeting. I called Dr. Sadio from Jamaica and put him on standby for this upcoming meeting. When I arrived home on October 22, I heard the two voice mails which Dr. Spencer had left for me but did not receive any letters.

On Thursday, October 23, Dr. Sadio and I arrived at the district office for the meeting. Linda, a member of the office staff, was also present at the meeting, and we were told that she was there in order to take notes. Dr. Spencer opened the meeting with a prayer and then indicated to me that he had a list of follow-up questions which the bishop had requested that he asked me. He wanted to know if I had any questions before he started, and I asked him to tell me where we were in the process. I indicated that I had spent over an hour in one meeting with Reverend David Dodge and himself and a similar time frame with the bishop in the supervisory session. I mentioned that in spite of those two meetings, I still did not get a chance to give a narrative of the development of a relationship from my perspective. I told him that I was desirous of having that opportunity. His response was essentially to acknowledge my comment but then proceeded to ask the questions from a prepared list which I assumed was sent to him from the bishop's office. This was another area of disappointment for me. I had longed for an opportunity to tell my story truthfully from my perspective but was denied that opportunity over and over. I had longed for an opportunity to address the members—or at least the officers—of the church where I was serving. My plan was to be honest with them, tell them the truth, and seek their forgiveness. If that opportunity had been granted, I felt confident that I would have received the forgiveness of the congregation as I continued to receive positive feedback from the persons who really missed my ministry.

The questions seemed to have been based on both the written complaint which was filed as well as any verbal communication which the complainant may have had with the bishop. There were also indications that the complainant had continued to tell lies and I was taken aback when Dr. Spencer asked me if I had threatened the complainant with physical violence. All I could remember at that time was her telling me how her ex-husband had been physically violent to her during their marriage. I answered all the questions, and when I was asked if I had any other comments, I reiterated that I was never in a professional counseling relationship with the complainant at any time. Toward the end of the session, I was asked to provide any copies of text messages, e-mails, and telephone calls, which I had. The arrangement was for me to hand-deliver them to Dr. Spencer on Monday, October 27, at 9:30 a.m.

On Monday, October 27, I met Dr. Spencer at Panera Bread restaurant in West Melbourne and gave him copies of many texts which the complainant had sent me. He seemed surprised at the large volume and said half jokingly that it was more than he would want to read. We did not have much of a conversation, and then we parted company.

On Friday, October 31, at approximately 12:24 p.m., I received a telephone call from Bishop Carter. During this call he informed me that because we could not come to a just resolution in the ninety-day period and that it was then the ninetieth day; he had passed the matter and the associated materials on to the counsel for the church. The counsel for the church would review the material and then determine whether to dismiss the case or to move it forward to the judicial stage. In the meantime, he told me, they were moving toward a period of involuntary leave of absence for me. As such, he recommended that I read the appropriate section of the Book of Discipline which referenced that concept. In his words, he thought that the nature of the written complaint is such that the "involuntary leave of absence should at least apply." I asked him at what point the period of involuntary leave would begin, and his answer was so vague that I could not even put it in writing. At the end of the day, I was not enlightened in any way with any clear answer regarding the question of timing.

Bishop Carter also mentioned to me that he had e-mailed me the same information which we were discussing and that a more formal letter with the said information would have been coming from his office the following week. Following the telephone conversation, I went to the computer and read the associated e-mail which the bishop had said that he was going to send. The e-mail referenced "multiple attempts at a just resolution," and I thought to myself that there was one attempt at a just resolution. Why would he also exaggerate and use the term "multiple"? They wanted me to surrender my credentials, and I would not do so. They would not offer anything in between.

My understanding is that on November 5, 2014, Dr. Spencer indicated to the members who attended the charge conference of the church at PBUMC that the cabinet was definitely moving toward an involuntary leave of absence for me. On Monday, November 10, I received the formal letter from the bishop confirming his intended action. On Tuesday, November 18, I started receiving texts from the complainant again, but I did not respond to any of them. This happened to have been the first night after the joint meeting of the board of ordained ministry and the cabinet of the Florida Conference had met. On Saturday, November 22, while I was at the public library in Melbourne, I received several texts from the complainant. I communicated with my wife and asked her to check the mailbox in order to see if there was any communication from the conference office. As it turned out, we seemed to have missed a certified piece of mail from the bishop's office because the notice in the mailbox indicated that we needed to pick it up from the post office on the following Monday. The texts to me from the complainant prompted me to think that she might have had some information and so decided to begin texting and taunting me again. She had definitely kept abreast with all the developments because it gave her satisfaction that my life was being slowly and quietly destroyed. On the flip side, the conference had to assure her that they were following through with their plans because they did not want to have a lawsuit on their hands.

On Monday, November 24, I went to the local post office and signed for the certified letter from the bishop in which he indicated that the executive committee of the board of ordained ministry had agreed to his request for involuntary leave of absence for me. In this letter, he indicated that my salaries, benefits, and availability of the parsonage would end on November 30 and that it would be necessary for me to make the parsonage empty and available by December 1. It was very scary as I was staring down a path of no income within a month of that letter. The panic really set in after I received the letter from the bishop. I did not know if I was going to have to stand at a traffic light and hold up a sign and beg. I did not know if I was going to be standing in food pantry lines. I saw quite some irony in this because in my own ministry I had started so many food pantries. Now I was going to be at the other end of the line. The hierarchy of the church would not have known that either, and frankly, they did not seem to care.

The scare was that my family was also going to be homeless since we would have nowhere to go. We just had not planned on it. I was also going to be pressured to vacate the parsonage in one week. As would be seen later on, this was an illegal and unnecessary burden, which was being placed on me because the leadership of the Florida Conference had botched the process recommended by the Book of Discipline.

On Tuesday, November 25, Dr. Spencer left a voice mail in which he indicated that he realized that the time frame established for my family to move out of the parsonage was unreasonable. As such, he stated that he was willing to "negotiate" that time frame. We missed each other after a number of efforts to reconnect via telephone but finally did so on Wednesday, November 26. In that conversation, he indicated that he would grant one additional week for my family to move out of the parsonage. I told him that even with that extension, it would be impractical because we now needed to begin identifying somewhere to go. His response was that we had known about it since August so he could not understand why I did not begin to put something in place. That statement by Dr. Spencer reiterated that they had one goal in mind from the very outset. How could he have predetermined that I should have started to plan my departure from the parsonage based on the complaint alone? Where was the due process in all this? In their minds I should have been out before the process even got started, and so it was little wonder that they faked a fair process in order to satisfy the requirements of the Book of Discipline. I told Dr. Spencer that, at the time, I had faith in the justice system of the church, and as such, I was waiting to see how things would play out with my case. I also expressed to him that I would have hoped that there would be some sensitivity to the time of year and also the season into which we were entering. He continued to express disbelief that I did not have anything in place. I reiterated that I had given thought to it but did not take any decisive steps since, as far as I know, everything was still under investigation.

A few hours after the conversation, I received an e-mail from Dr. Spencer in which he indicated that the bishop and he had decided that my family could remain in the parsonage until the end of December because "the bishop and he 'felt' for my family during the season." I gathered later that a church council meeting was held at the church on Monday, December 1, in which the meeting was told what decisions were taken regarding my family moving out of the parsonage. It was at that meeting that Dr. Spencer was told how unreasonable and unconscionable it was for the church to expect my family to vacate the parsonage in one week.

On Thursday, December 4, I received a telephone call from the conference benefits specialist, Helen Mitchell. In her telephone call, she indicated that a letter had been sent out to me indicating that my benefits would end on November 30 but that it was extended to December 31. Essentially she was saying that while the benefits would still end; there was a one-month extension beyond the date indicated in the letter. In her conversation, she also told me that I had the option to continue in the plan for an additional two months, but I would have to pay the full premium of over $1,600 monthly for the family plan.

On the morning of Friday, December 5, I responded to a second voice mail from Ms. Mitchell. When I returned her call, she indicated that there was an update on my benefits plan and that the original end date of November 30 as indicated in the letter would stand. She apologized for the confusion, indicating that the conference did not have to deal with my situation regularly, so this accounted for the uncertainty. She also indicated that as she spoke, Dr. Spencer was in a meeting at the conference office and that he would communicate with me any updates from that meeting. On that same day, I received a second e-mail from Dr. Gary Spencer in which he was seeking to "clarify" his first e-mail. The clarification was to establish that I needed to have been out of the parsonage by December 31.

On Wednesday, December 17, I received another call from Dr. Gary Spencer. He indicated that the complainant had called him to indicate to him that she heard that I had gone to a Baptist church, got baptized, and had joined the church. He said that he was also told that I was working at the church and that, as a United Methodist Church minister, this should not be happening. I asked him to explain how that piece of information connected with the case and his response was that he had to treat this piece of information as if it came from anyone else. I then used the opportunity to remind him that she indicated to a retired pastor that her goal was to destroy me, and I then proceeded to ask him if her sharing of that information indicated anything about her. It would have been clear to any reasonable thinking person that this complainant was going to dig up every negative and then create what she could not find in order to set the leadership of the church totally against me. Her success in seeming to convince Dr. Spencer and the bishop with all these irrelevant and childlike additional complaints was an indication of either (a) how naive the district superintendent and bishop et al. were and/or (b) that they were going to use every additional complaint as a tool to help to dig my grave.

His response to my direct question was that he was not able to answer that question. I also indicated to him that she had continued to send me texts and left telephone voice mails for me. I asked him if he would be willing to request that she does not continue to stalk, haunt, or taunt me. He acknowledged that he recognized how annoying that must be for me but did not make any promises to communicate my request to her. Truthfully, I was attending a Baptist church regularly but was definitely not working on or with the staff. This was one of the mediums through which I was getting my spiritual fill.

In the same telephone conversation, Dr. Spencer reminded me about the need to move out of the parsonage by December 31, and I indicated to him that I had already started moving. On Tuesday, December 30, I sent a text to Dr. Spencer indicating that the home into which we were moving had some issues with mold and so it was going to take us a little longer to move in than we had anticipated. He acknowledged receipt of the text and then asked me if I was able to give him a date when I thought that I would be able to move. I indicated via text that I was hoping to move out by the end of the month (January). On Wednesday January 7, I received another text from Dr. Spencer in which he suggested that I need to be out of the parsonage by January 16 and that I needed to remove my personal belongings from the church office by January 14. He also indicated that the Moxley's were planning on moving into the parsonage on January 17. My response to him was that we had planned the final moving out of the parsonage on January 18 (Martin Luther King Day) since this was when my helpers would be available. Once I got home that night, I checked my e-mail and found that there was an e-mail from Dr. Spencer in which he reiterated the need for me to move out of the parsonage by the sixteenth and then added that since the Moxleys were moving in on the seventeenth, they would put anything that they might find in the parsonage outside. I decided that I was not going to respond to the e-mail. On Thursday, January 8, I received a text from Dr. Spencer indicating that the Moxleys had arranged a truck to move them in on January 17 and that I was to take a key for the parsonage to the church on that same day. Once more I decided that I was not going to respond to Dr. Spencer. The pressure for us to move out was so intense that my wife ended up tearing her rotator cuff and had to do surgery as a result. We were working round-the-clock to try and get things together—and that in the middle of the Christmas season. It was hard to believe the heartlessness that was spewing out from Dr. Spencer and wondered if he had any humane bones in him. With this kind of heartlessness, which was fueled by a seemingly evil complainant feeding him continuously with irrelevant but negative emotions, I give thanks to the Lord God Almighty that I was able to keep my sanity—as hard as it was—during that period.

This e-mail below is representative of the kind of pressure I was under as I was forced out of the parsonage prematurely and illegitimately. The pressure was relentless. It is strange how such barbaric behavior with associated threats that border on gangster-like actions can be considered to be statesmanlike or even a demonstration of great Christian leadership. The superintendent had made these same threats verbally several times over the phone as well.

From: DS-Atlantic Central
Sent: Wednesday, January 07, 2015, 12:33:11 PM
(UTC-05:00) Eastern Time (US and Canada)
To: Errol Leslie
Cc: David Dodge
Subject: Parsonage

Errol,

I sent you a text today about the need to move out of the parsonage and I am following up with this e-mail to confirm you have received the text.

I need you to be out of the parsonage by Friday, Jan. 16. This is 2 weeks beyond the deadline that we set for you to be out of the parsonage. I also need for you to remove your personal items from the office no later than Wednesday, Jan. 14. I have scheduled Rev. Moxley to move into the parsonage on Jan. 17. My hope is that your personal items in the parsonage will be gone by the 16, and if there are items there, we will set them outside so that the Moxley family can move in on the 17.

Gary

Dr. Gary Spencer

District Superintendent—Atlantic Central

9015 Americana Rd. #4

Vero Beach, FL. 32966

Office: 772-299-0255

This was my response to the e-mail below which I also penned but did not send.

Dear Dr. Spencer,

Contrary to the thoughts you expressed during our conversation earlier this evening (09/16) regarding the removal of items from my office at the church, I was neither trying to be difficult, adamant, nor uncooperative. I reiterate what I mentioned in our conversation, which I was able to confirm from the book of discipline that my suspension is from all clergy responsibilities but not from an appointment. Please refer to the book of discipline 363.1 (D). In that regard I am not required to remove my personal belongings from the office prematurely.

However, in the spirit of cooperation and Christian witness as mentioned in said telephone conversation, I would be willing to hear from the interim pastor which items in the office are a hindrance to him and his working comfortably from the office. I would then act accordingly.

I trust that this is acceptable to you and am not sure if you would still want to take your alternative action indicated during our telephone conversation to clear my office yourself and put my belongings out in the passage or by the curbside. Please let me know.

CHAPTER 6

Letters of Support from Clergy and Laity

Very early in the process, the chancellor for the Florida Conference entered into serious negotiations in an attempt to get me to surrender my credentials voluntarily. I felt grossly insulted by this and was really offended. What would cause him to think that I was so hungry that I was going to fall for a trailer load—in this case, a matchbox full of cash—in exchange for my divinely ordained call from God? For me, that would have been disrespectful to and dishonoring of the call of God on my life. To make it worse, he made it sound as if he was doing us a favor, so we needed to accept it quickly before we would lose the opportunity. How rude and condescending? As it turned out, the defense team was strong in rejecting the offer, and I did not even consider it for one moment when it was first brought to my attention.

In a message dated March 4, 2015, 7:23 a.m., Eastern Standard Time, butler.tampa@gmail.com writes,

Scott:

Thanks for getting back with me yesterday.

This email is a follow-up to our conversation and is intended to be a "take it for what it's worth" comment and not trying to tell you what to do.

Over my 39 years as an attorney I've learned not to get my insurance company clients too excited about the possibilities of a settlement until it happens. Too often they can get entrenched in their position and then get very defensive when an offer from the other side doesn't meet their expectation. That can produce a "Forget it, we'll see you in court" response and that's the end of the negotiations.

We may be at the end of the negotiations in the Leslie complaint matter. Or we may not be. However, as I reflect on what I think will be a response to your anticipated memo, I fear that a suggestion of Errol Leslie receiving salary and benefits beyond an anticipated trial date could very well be met with the response quoted above.

I don't fault Reverend Leslie, you and your Team for testing the waters or for putting a stake in the ground if that's your desire. But, I am alerting you to what I perceive to be the realities of the situation and I don't see it changing, or at least not much.

Bottom line, if the settlement negotiations are to continue and to be fruitful, my suggestion is that Reverend Leslie and the Team come back with a proposal that is at or close to what I suggested above.

Just trying to be helpful.

Paul

On March 4, 2015, at 9:51 a.m., Campbellwscott@aol.com wrote,

Hi Paul,

Thanks for your note.

I will have a more formal response to you by the end of the day, but I did want to just clarify the way Errol is viewing the situation. If the church were to simply pay him what it owes him for failing to follow Disciplinary processes, that's not really a settlement. It's an obligation that the church has incurred by not following its own rules. To merely provide what it owes him through the conclusion of the trial in exchange for the surrender of his orders saves the church an enormous amount of money and leaves Errol with only what the church is obligated to pay anyway. I was in touch with Tim Rogers in South Carolina yesterday regarding the cost of trials. He was the Director of Connectional Ministries during a year when the SC Conference had three trials that averaged $75,000 each.

From our point of view the Florida Conference would be asking Errol to surrender his orders, to renounce his calling and no longer to be a minister in exchange for what it is legally obligated to do anyway. That simply doesn't add up for us. It makes more sense for us to do everything we can to try to save his orders. There are dozens, if not hundreds, of pastors across the connection who have been where he is and who have retained their clergy orders. I can name a half dozen myself.

Please understand; I'm not talking here about becoming entrenched in a position that blinds us to other possibilities. It's a simple matter of fairness. The church is proposing that Errol give up everything, including the opportunity to clear his name from slanderous and libelous accusations, but if it is not willing to share the significant savings that will be gained by avoiding a trial, that is a seriously flawed equation from our point of view.

I hope we are not at the end of the conversation, but if we are, I am sorry for that. I believe that you are doing the best you can do to reach a fair end to this sad story as am I. I will be in touch later.

Blessings,
Scott

In a message dated March 4, 2015, 10:06 a.m., Eastern Standard Time, butler.tampa@gmail.com writes,

Thanks, Scott.

Just so we are both seeing the situation in the same way, or as best as possible, let me share my perspective.

Rev. Leslie is currently owed approximately $11,655 for back pay.

If Rev. Leslie is not placed on an Involuntary Leave of Absence, his salary and benefits will accrue at an approximate rate of $3,642 per month.

If Rev. Leslie is placed on an Involuntary Leave of Absence (done correctly!!), his salary and benefits will cease at that time until the outcome of the trial

If Rev. Leslie is found guilty and his credentials taken at trial, the salary would not continue under any circumstance.

As for the cost of the trial, it seems as if you are saying the $75,000 cost to the conference is something that the conference is bringing on itself. Let's keep in mind that there would be no complaint, no trial, and no expense but for the breach of Rev. Leslie's covenant under the Book of Discipline, thereby triggering the cost under the BOD. In a civil forum, it would not be uncommon for the person charged and found guilty to be assessed court costs. I'm thinking Rev. Leslie is not willing to escrow funds to pay those should he be found guilty is he?

We may be at the end of the conversation, but let's see. I simply want you and Rev. Leslie to assess the options as I see them. Should there not be a settlement at this time, I really think the window will close for the possibility of Rev. Leslie taking advantage of the additional compensation he would receive at $3,642 per month for the agreed amount of months in keeping with the reasoning above. Thanks for your continued efforts.

Paul

On March 4, 2015, at 3:39 PM, Campbellwscott@aol.com wrote,

Dear Paul,

Thanks for these clarifications. They help to make our decision clear. What I am given to understand is that if we do not accept the approach being proposed, the conference will, in all likelihood, attempt to once more seek the status of involuntary leave of absence for Rev. Leslie prior to the trial. With the notices that are required, I believe we will, at best, be looking at something in the neighborhood of a month from now before this process can be completed, perhaps slightly less. If the conference is successful in achieving this change in status, and if the trial gets underway within the next two months, we would be looking at a settlement amount covering a 4-or 5-week period at the rate you cite in order to avoid the ordeal and expense of a trial. If I am misreading this, please let me know.

And just to be clear, I am not saying that the conference is bringing on the cost of a trial itself. Our Constitution guarantees a fair hearing for every accused clergy person. The fact that the Florida Conference never provided a real opportunity for Rev. Leslie to be heard has helped to propel us in this direction, as has the perspective that only the ecclesiastical "death penalty" is an appropriate response to these circumstances. The bishop and the counsel for the church have options they have not chosen to exercise and those decisions are costly for everyone involved. The reality is that pastors are human beings and sometimes they stumble and fall. The question is how the church ought to respond to someone who has a single blemish in an otherwise stellar 39 year career in ministry. Someone once said that the church remains the only army that shoots its wounded. There is more than a little truth in that observation.

Forgive my little rant. All this is to say that if the church is unwilling to see that sparing the costs of a potential trial ought to be a part of the considerations in any plea agreement, then I think those of us on this side of the aisle need to do all we can do to try to save Rev. Leslie's orders.

I continue to appreciate your candid and forthright approach to all that is before us. Thank you for giving us the opportunity to have this dialogue.

Grace and Peace,

Scott

P.S. If we should choose not to pursue a comprehensive settlement, we will need to confer going forward about the calculation of the conference's back obligation to Rev. Leslie. If you could send me a breakdown of how you arrived at the monthly amount of $3,642 I would be grateful. Thanks.

From: "Paul B. Butler, Jr."
<butler.tampa@gmail.com>
Sent: Wednesday, March 4, 2015, 6:37 pm To:
Scott Campbell <Campbellwscott@aol.com>
CC:

Scott:

At least we tried. I would have felt bad had we not given it a shot.

And I take no offense at your self-described "rant."

In order to make certain our communication is not missing the mark in the "other direction" my take is that dollar amount at stake for Rev. Leslie is perhaps a bit more than you are suggesting. Please, please do not assume this is an offer. It is not. But, from my standpoint I've always thought in terms of a worst-case dollar scenario for the Florida Conference being an exposure for payment for salary, housing and benefits to Reverend Leslie through June. If you include the current back pay due, the total comes to around $25,700. Plus, a settlement now does two important things monetarily for Rev. Leslie. It prevents him from incurring the expenses associated with the trial itself, and preparation for same. But, more importantly, it takes him out of limbo and the earning potential for him from other sources kicks in months earlier. This earning potential for four months or so is not be an insignificant amount.

I'm going to pass on to the Others that the window appears to have closed based on my reading of where we are. If I'm wrong, please, please, please correct me almost immediately.

Thanks for exploring this. I think we did right in doing so.

While I was experiencing the badgering, pressure, and humiliation from the leaders in the Florida Conference, official letters of appeal were sent to the bishop from the church council, the wider Palm Bay community, and many individuals in the Palm Bay community pleading a case on my behalf and begging for forgiveness, pardon, and mercy in spite of my immoral actions. The bishop's response to these many letters reflected the same arrogance and disrespect which he showed to me during the supervisory session. He ignored all the letters, including the one from the members of the church council who were agonizing over the situation. He also ignored a letter from a retired bishop who happened to have been the bishop that first gave me an appointment in the New England Conference in 1995 and who had gotten to know me well. He did not respond to any except for one such letter which went to him from another retired pastor whose membership was associated with the church. I was truly touched by the many persons at both clergy and laity level who were writing to the bishop and pleading with him on my behalf for some relief. This was, in and of itself, an indication of the level of support which I was getting from the community at both the local and national level. I am including some of these letters at this point. This first referenced letter is from Bishop Herbert Skeete.

9/30/15

Dear Bishop Carter:

I write this letter as chaplain and spiritual advisor for the Caribbean Pastors association. Rev Leslie is an active member. I have prayed with him and his wife. He is very sorry for his error.

There are many victims related to this complaint. Errol has lost his appointment in Florida, and, while he was placed on involuntary leave he was forced to tap into his pension fund for his existence. This will cause harm for many years.

His family has suffered greatly; fortunately, his wife and daughters are still very supportive.

I would note that his accuser first contacted Errol and pursued a relationship. She knew that he was married and I would not doubt she was aware of his marital difficulty at that period. The Caribbean community is a closely-knit society where news spread very quickly. She bears some responsibility in this affair for her pursuit.

Errol takes responsibility for any harm which his actions may have caused during a difficult time in his relationship with his wife. He is penitent and deeply regrets his error. His pastoral record is clean; he has been an effective pastor for many years. Jesus' example with the woman caught in adultery should be a challenge for the church's rush to judgment. The church should make possible for healing to the broken when penitent and rise above the conscious or unconscious influence of an old stereotype. This is not Errol Leslie. I know Errol who was a pastor in New England when I appointed him. I strongly believe Errol can still be an asset to the UMC.

I am praying that this can be resolved in a constructive way to enable Errol and his family to move on in service to God and the church he loves and has given the best of his life.

Hopefully Yours,
F. Herbert Skeete
Bishop of UMC. Rtd.

The next letter is from Rev. Denzil Southwood-Smith—a retired pastor whose membership was associated with the congregation I was serving.

Rev. Denzil A. Southwood-Smith (Retired)
October 31, 2014
Bishop Kenneth H Carter, Jr.
Resident Bishop, Florida United Methodist
Conference
450 Martin Luther King, Jr. Avenue
Lakeland, FL 33815
Dear Bishop Carter:
Reference: Charges/inquiry—Rev. Dr. Errol Leslie

I am a retired United Methodist Minister. I am wheelchair bound, following a series of strokes in 2007, and now live in Palm Bay with my wife and elder son David who are my caregivers. We attend the Palm Bay United Methodist Church where Rev. Dr. Errol Leslie had been the pastor, until recent events removed him. pro tern from the position.

I was as shocked as all the members present, when the District Superintendent—Rev. Dr. Gary Spencer along with Rev. David Dodge as your representative attended services on the first Sunday in August of this year and informed the church that, due to certain charges against Rev. Leslie, he was being temporarily suspended from duty pending Discipline-Required investigation.

As I am unable to travel to Lakeland to present as an advocate for Pastor Leslie, I have spoken on the telephone with the D.S. who promised to pass on my concerns to yourself and the investigating committee, as and when the investigations continue.

Please allow me by, and in, this letter, to give some advocacy for Rev. Leslie.

I first met Pastor Leslie when he made a pastoral visit to me in the Melbourne Terrace Rehabilitation Center, bringing me the Sacrament. He continued to give me pastoral care while I remained a patient in this institution. Following my discharge, I have been attending the church regularly with my family; and have been as active as my medical condition has allowed... singing in the choir and sometimes solos. I have on more than one occasion preached a sermon. I have done most of these activities from my wheelchair.

On the Sunday following the official suspension of Pastor Leslie, on my arrival at church for the 11:00 a.m. service, I was approached at the window of my car by a lady I recognized as Ms. Veda Hendricks. I had met Ms. Hendricks during Lent of this year when, at Pastor Leslie's invitation, she, as had other Lay speakers, conducted one of our Wednesday afternoon Lenten services. Retired Pastor—Rev. Web Simpkins and I had also conducted some of these services. On this particular Sunday morning she apparently had attended the 8:30 service and I was arriving for the 11:00 a.m. service. After exchanging greetings, I asked her if she had heard what had happened to Rev. Errol Leslie, she replied "Yes, I am the person who did it." I then responded "Do you mean that you are the perpetrator?" She proudly answered "Yes, it was I; please call me..."— handing me a slip of paper with her telephone number written on it. She asked me to call her. She had apparently been busy giving out her telephone number to many of the congregants. On returning home after the service, I called her number and had to leave a message on her answering machine. She called me later and proceeded to make a lot of charges against Pastor Leslie, much to my shocked surprise. The things she said did not match up to the person I had come to know and respect. She said "He is a wicked man, and I want to destroy him."

This particularly puzzled me, because in Pastor's introduction of her in the Lenten service at which she spoke, he said she was an old friend as they had attended the same high school in Savannah-la-mar in Jamaica and had both been active in the Christian youth group.

I remember that she had said in the Lenten presentation that she had kept herself pristine and was a virgin when she married. She also told us that she and her husband—a Pentecostal pastor—had gone on a second honeymoon (after many years of marriage and having reared children, now grown) and on their return home, he shocked her by telling her that he was in love with someone else and was filing for divorce. In our telephone conversation, she also said that she was encouraging other people to also make charges against Pastor Leslie. She said she was very good at English, was a teacher of this subject, and could help others to write their charges properly or edit their letters.

Prior to entering the ministry, I had many years of experience in Personnel and Human Resource Management. As Ms. Hendricks continued speaking, I began to wonder even more why she was making these charges as well as encouraging others to do the same. Could it be that she was and is still having "tremors" from her failed marriage experience? It is my hope that she is not in danger of a breakdown. One question we always would ask in business in investigations is "Who gains"? I cannot for the life of me see who can or would gain in this character assassination campaign against Pastor Errol Leslie. It is my hope that these charges against him will be disproved and found to be spurious, as I know that his family is now suffering, as is the church which had been having excellent outreach particularly in the food sharing ministry and other areas including inter-church co-operation. Apparently Satan did not like this success.

Ms. Hendricks also told me that Pastor Errol said that he wanted to divorce his wife and marry her. This, to me, is nonsense, as Pastor Errol is uxorious and is very proud of his family—obviously a tightly knit family, judging not only from their constant ministry in the church but also from their many fine musical presentations of gospel music.

Thank you, Bishop, for allowing me to speak on behalf of Pastor Errol who I respect as a pastor, colleague and friend; I even call him "little brother." My wife and family join me in this petition for Pastor Errol and continue to give our prayerful support for you, the District Superintendent and all the parties involved in this investigation.

Yours in Christ,
Denzil A. Southwood-Smith

The church council chairperson of the Palm Bay United Methodist Church convened a meeting of the council to discuss the issue. At the end of the meeting, they agreed to send the following letter to Bishop Carter. They were essentially pleading for mercy on my behalf.

August 15, 2014
The Right Reverend Dr. Kenneth H. Carter, Jr.
450 Martin Luther King, Jr. Ave
Lakeland, FL 33815

Right Reverend Sir:

It is with faithful conviction that we, the members of The Palm Bay United Methodist Church, are writing to express our support for our pastor, the Reverend Dr. Errol Leslie. In recent weeks, Dr. Leslie was summarily suspended and relieved of his pastoral duties at our church. The suddenness with which this action occurred has proved to be highly disruptive, and it has caused much angst within our church community.

In particular, we are profoundly dismayed and disappointed with the manner in which our pastor was relieved of his duties. We feel that the announcement of his suspension to the entire congregation, with visitors and children present, including our pastor's two teenage daughters, was utterly inappropriate and inconsiderate.

Dr. Leslie has been our pastor for approximately six years. During his tenure, he has been an admired and respected leader of our church who tirelessly carried out his duties. He has worked cooperatively with ministers of other denominations with the goal of being an integral part of the entire Palm Bay community and its environs. To us, Pastor is truly a man of God; it grieves us immensely that he has been removed under these circumstances.

We cannot help but feel utterly disheartened by the recent sequence of events in our church.

However, in this extraordinarily difficult time we pray for fairness and justice in the adjudication of this matter. We also pray for wisdom, understanding and compassion in those who must make the critical and difficult decisions that are needed to bring this matter to resolution. Furthermore, we pray for patience and faithfulness in our fellow members and ourselves. Last, but not least, we pray for our pastor, that he may have the patience and strength to endure this ordeal.

Thank you for your time and consideration. We know you share our prayer that this matter will be resolved as soon as possible.

Sincerely,
The Congregation of the Palm Bay
United Methodist Church

However, callously and arrogantly, and as per usual, Bishop Carter ignored the letter—even this latest one from the church council. This action at best seemed to be very uncaring as somehow the bishop did not think that he had a responsibility to soothe the pain of one of his congregations. This action—or lack thereof—aggravated the entire congregation and then prompted actions which led to one member eventually writing a letter expressing his dissatisfaction over the Bishop's seeming lack of care.

This next letter was addressed to the members of the Palm Bay United Methodist Church Congregation.

February 8, 2015
Members Palm Bay United Methodist Church
2100 Port Malabar Blvd.

Dear Fellow Congregants,

Let me first thank those of you who have expressed concerns over not seeing me in church for the past couple of weeks. I am really flattered that you have taken such interest in my well-being and me. It means a lot to me and I am absolutely grateful.

I want you to know that my absence has nothing to do with my health. In fact, I am currently in a fairly good physical health, thank the Lord.

For almost a year now, I have been wrestling with the manner in which the hierarchy of the Church handled the case against Rev. Dr. Errol Leslie.

On the surface, there is, seemingly, a lack of due process. Dr. Leslie was suspended and subsequently terminated without even the semblance of any due process. We were promised a thorough investigation; but where and what are the findings?

It started when the District Superintend announced in church, before all and sundry, that Pastor Leslie will be suspended pending an investigation regarding some alleged sexual misconduct. This announcement set off a rumor mill. We are still awaiting the outcome of the investigation. We don't even know what this sexual misconduct is. Rumors are swirling regarding the nature and extent of this sexual misconduct. Without going into all its salacious, gory details; the superintendent ought to be a little more explicit.

As I see it, there are three categories that ought to be considered in the outcome of the investigation:

1.) Whether Dr. Leslie's misconduct is egregious enough to warrant the punishment meted out to him, and does the punishment fits the crime. Furthermore, Is this punishment consistent and equitably administered to all who is similarly charged and convicted.

2.) Whether the termination of the Pastor is designed to protect the members of the church and/or the community from a predator. We want to know who are the people being protected, and how.

3.) Whether the Pastor is so tarnished, weakened and so compromised that he is incapable of performing his pastoral duties. The assumption here is that, as with Adam of old, having allegedly fallen prey to the blandishments of a vicious, conniving and disgruntled viper, is indicative of his lack of the necessary moral fortitude to do God's work.

4.) Was there a fair process in which Dr. Leslie was given an opportunity to respond to the allegations with a statement and documentation of his own or was a determination made based on a one-sided presentation?

Yes, the above are some of the issues I am wrestling with. It is very difficult for me to believe in, and accept the teaching of, an administration that is so devoid of compassion, empathy and even a little probity. Even in the church, the appearance of justice should be apparent.

I want you, my friends, to know that my faith remains intact. It is unshakeable. But I refuse to listen to an administration, who, for personal reasons, chose to abdicate our basic Christian Principles that they, themselves, have sworn to uphold.

Some months ago, the Church Council wrote to the Bishop, pleading for justice and compassion in the adjudication of the matter involving Pastor Leslie. We were not even afforded the courtesy of a response, acknowledging the receipt of our letter. Are these the people I want to have dominion over my faith? Are they really Christians, whose leadership and behavior I would want to emulate?

Paul is my favorite apostle. I wonder if they think that their action meets the approbation of Paul.

Again, I thank you for your concerns about me. Let me trust, despite all the terrible things happening in the church, we can remain in fellowship one with the other.

God Bless,
Sincerely,
Winston L. Thompson

The ladies who were falsely accused also sent letters to Bishop Carter. Their stellar reputation was now being threatened by someone who seemed to have had a knack for making up and spreading rumors, so they saw the need to defend themselves.

From: Abbey C (Not her real name)

Subject: Report to PBUMC COUNCIL MEETING Tuesday, 10/21/

Date: Mon, Oct 20, 2014 7:34 p.m.

Report to PBUMC COUNCIL MEETING Tuesday, 10/ 21/ 14.

With reference to allegations of misconduct between Rev Leslie and myself as reported to Bishop Carter by Veda Hendricks.

At first this shocking allegation was a rumor. Although it pained me I had the support of close friends, my spiritual leader and family.

It became more than rumor when our District Superintendent, Gary Spencer, asked Rev. Dionne Hammond of 1st United Methodist to arrange to meet with me to discuss the allegation. In that regard, Rev. Dionne telephoned me for an appointment. She said that my name was on a "list," provided by the D S. After our conversation she concluded there was no need to meet with me.

Early in October when D S Gary Spencer Attended our church service I used the opportunity to engage him in a conversation regarding 1. His need to have my name on the list as given to his emissary Rev Dionne.

2. The damage to my character

3. The absolute fabrication of the allegation.

I repeatedly and categorically denied said allegation to the D S and I do so today in front of you. Any and all relationships with Pastor Leslie has been pastoral and respectful.

The D S also asked if I would tell him of any inappropriate advances Pastor Leslie made to me. I replied that I would be truthful to him and to Mrs. Leslie also. I stand before you as a member of this congregation and a member of God's family to repeat that all allegations are false, mischievous and harmful to my character. My family considers it slanderous and on all counts libelous. I will continue to pray for quick healing not only for myself but for the other innocent ladies on the "list." I am again appalled that the offices of the Bishop and D S had not found a more professional way of handling this life altering and character changing allegation against me. Thanks for your time.

Another letter from a second female parishioner:

Miriam N [Not her real name];'
Palm Bay UMC Church Council
October 20, 2014 at 11:56 p.m.

I, Miriam N, was made aware that my name was included on a "list" of women who have been linked to 'sleeping with the pastor of our church at Palm Bay

UMC/ Rev Leslie. And apparently, my daughters1 names, although may not be on a list, are also being tossed around too. Now, instead of me being sickened and upset from the previous call I received from Pastor Dionne Hammond, I am livid, as well as deeply saddened and hurt, that such nonsense is being rumored in church and also in the Palm Bay community. As a mother of two daughters, I have reason to be alarmed and concerned when I am being falsely accused of "sleeping with my pastor/ and equally alarmed when my daughters are also being slandered and falsely accused as well. Such libelous, slanderous and devastating accusations have literally hurt me and my family to the core.

This serious accusation is defaming my character as a woman, and as a mother, as well as defaming the characters of my daughters. I should not have to be defending my integrity and my morals, both as a woman and as a mother. Since hearing the nature of this accusation, I am tired of breaking down in tears, and I hope and pray that the leaders of The Florida United Methodist Church Conference, will conduct a thorough investigation of the source of these accusations, so that my name, as well as my daughters' names will be exonerated.

These false accusations are cruel and viscous, and have been carried out by an individual with ulterior motives and malicious intent.

My father, in all his infinite wisdom, taught me to speak up whenever I have been falsely accused or unjustly attacked. These false accusations have really taken a toll on my family! I have and will continue to categorically and emphatically deny these accusations. I am also deeply disappointed that the Bishop and the District Superintendent, who are the leaders of our Florida United Methodist. Church Conference, did not think I was worth the time of day, when I wanted to sit down with them, face to face, to discuss my concerns and the distress my family and I were going through. I do not appreciate being judged and treated like a disease to be avoided by the bishop and district superintendent.

Thank you for taking the time to listen to me, Miriam N; member of Palm Bay UMC.

Another letter from a third female parishioner:

Thursday, October 23, 2014 AOL:

Subject: Re: Council Meeting

I would like to go on record by addressing the outrageously false allegations leveled at me in regards to an inappropriate relationship with Pastor Errol Leslie. I have been truly burdened by this as it is a direct assault on my character. I have been thrown into "a pile of dung," and I have been trying to fathom this craziness! This is 100% false and is a defamation to my character. I have no other relationship with Pastor Leslie other than in a Pastoral capacity. The accusations are total fabrication and anyone that is capable of such fabrication is truly an instrument of the devil. This woman, whom I have never even met, has not only turned my life upside down, but various other women of the church.

I am greatly disappointed in the way the situation has been handled, because for someone to just be given "carte blanche" to spread lies with no consequences, is beyond me.

But one thing I know, God knows all, and He is in the details of our lives.

He Reigns!
Polly S [Not her real name]

Another letter from a fourth parishioner:

Palm Bay, FL 32909
October 7, 2014
The Right Reverend Dr. Kenneth H. Carter, Jr
FLUMC Episcopal Office
450 Martin Luther King, Jr. Avenue Lakeland, FL
33815

Right Reverend Sir:

I have been in deep meditation and deep prayers and have finally come to the decision to write you. My name is Bobbette S [Not her real name] and I am a member of The Palm Bay United Methodist Church in Palm Bay, Florida.

My concern relates to activities at The Palm Bay United Methodist Church in relation to the suspension of our Pastor, The Reverend Dr. Errol Leslie. I have been made aware that my name, Bobbette S has been placed on a list as being associated with Dr. Leslie's name as having an affair with him.

I consider this matter very serious as I am a married woman and this could have disastrous consequences on my almost 25 years' marriage. I emphatically and categorically deny this libelous statement.

I would therefore appreciate having an audience with you to discuss this more fully.

Thank you for your time.

Sincerely, Bobbette S (Mrs.)

c.c. Dr. Gary Spencer, District
Superintendent, FLUMC
(NB. This letter is also being sent to the e-mail
addresses—bishop@ flumc.org; ds-ac@flumc.org)

The accused ladies all sent letters to the bishop of the Florida Conference, but neither the bishop nor the district superintendent saw it fitting to take the time to respond to them and address the deep and painful feeling of hurt which these ladies experienced. The ladies who sent letters to the bishop were not the only ones accused. These specifically responded because they were interrogated by Rev. Dionne Hammond, who was copastor of the neighboring First United Church of Melbourne and was also named as assistant counsel of the church. There was a family that had three generations (eighty-three-year-old grandmother, sixty-year-old daughter, and thirty-two-year-old daughter/granddaughter). I was pretty close to this family and was also accused to my face by the complainant of having an affair with all three generations of ladies.

I remember when Dr. Campbell, my defense counsel, reminded the counsel for the church that all the ladies who were accused about having an affair with me had not only refuted the allegations, but they were all upset. The official finding of Reverend Dionne Hammond who investigated the ladies was that there was no sexual relationship with any of these ladies. Dr. Campbell inquired if all these denials did not mean anything to the counsel for the church and if he did not have a different perception after the official finding. His response was simply, "Rev. Leslie got to the heads of the women and made them deny it." I would never have thought that I had so much power, influence and charm that would have caused four mature adult women to deny these charges only because they wanted to protect me. It is a reasonable assumption that in the normal situation if someone is publicly accused as I was and other names are being swirled around as also having been involved, any ladies who, in that situation, may have felt that they were the victims of predatorial behavior would not hesitate to come forward and make that acknowledgment. However, in this instance, there was not one who would admit to that.

Even when Reverend Therrell tried to force this information out of a twenty-year-old, that certainly did not work for him or for the church.

One of the ladies accused also sent a copy of her letter via e-mail, and it got a response from Bishop Carter, which, on the surface, looked promising.

> Kenneth H. Carter, Jr. <Bishop@flumc.org> Tue, Oct 7, 2014 at 8:31 p.m.
>
> To: Bobbette S
>
> Cc: DS-Atlantic Central <ds-ac@flumc.org>
>
> Dear Ms. Bobbette S
>
> Thank you for this email. When we receive the letter I will respond more fully. Please understand that we have been seeking to discover the truth. We are certainly not making accusations but responding to persons in your community. I deeply respect your statement and it is most helpful. While I did not initiate any of these events, I apologize for the strain and stress this has caused and I join you in prayer.
>
> The peace of the Lord,
> +Ken Carter
> Resident Bishop

This lack of response from the bishop was just blatantly and shamefully arrogant. These ladies were hurting while absolutely no one from the leadership of the church reached out to them. It sounded quite hypocritical that the counsel for the church placed such great emphasis on how much "harm" I had done to so many persons but showed absolutely no consideration to the harm done to these ladies by the complainant and, by extension, the hierarchy of the church. The ladies were all questioned by different representatives of the bishop but yet no remorse was shown. The list of names given to the district superintendent included younger women in the church and community, and at no time did these leaders stop to wonder if the allegations were true or if they were fabricated—as indeed they were. Significantly, there was one young lady who was the same age of and a friend of my daughter who was also questioned. She reported to my daughter that she was so frightened and had no clue what Reverend Therrell (the counsel for the church) was talking about when he called and spoke with her. He even tried to put words into her mouth, trying to force her to say things which never happened.

On observing the lack of a caring response to these ladies by the bishop and the other leaders, I sent personal letters of apology to each one accused. I felt very guilty that because of my poor choice, innocent ladies from the church were being drawn into the drama.

October 20, 2014

Ms. Polly

Dear Polly

As you know, a written complaint was filed against me in July of this year. This complaint which was initially handed to District Superintendent, Dr. Gary Spencer and then passed on to the bishop's office alleges among other things that I engaged in inappropriate relationships with several women in the Palm Bay United Methodist Church. Unfortunately, your name was among several others mentioned in relation to this allegation. At no time did I even mention your name to anyone in that light. However, the complainant decided to pass on fictitious and speculative information as though it was factual.

I want you to know that I deeply regret that and apologize profusely for the fact that you were mentioned in such an extremely negative light. Even though the allegation is totally untrue, I know that it has the potential to mar your stellar character as it is perceived by some persons in the community. I have already indicated to the bishop as well as the district superintendent that the allegation is totally false. I trust that any hurt, pain or stress which this situation has caused you will disappear quickly even as I continue to try to "clear the air."

Once more, please accept my apology and thank you for your understanding. I trust that God will help us to put this situation behind us quickly and grant you comfort and peace until this is accomplished.

Every Blessing.
Yours respectfully,
Errol E. Leslie

October 20, 2014

Mrs. Bobbie

Dear Bobbie,

As you know, a written complaint was filed against me in July of this year. This complaint which was initially handed to District Superintendent, Dr. Gary Spencer and then passed on to the bishop's office alleges among other thing that I engaged in inappropriate relationships with several women in the Palm Bay United Methodist Church. Unfortunately, your name was among several others mentioned in relation to this allegation. At no time did I even mention your name to anyone in that light. However, the complainant decided to pass on fictitious and speculative information as though it was factual.

I want you to know that I deeply regret that and apologize profusely for the fact that you were mentioned in such an extremely negative light. Even though the allegation is totally untrue, I know that it has the potential to mar your stellar character as it is perceived by some persons in the community. I have already indicated to the bishop as well as the district superintendent that the allegation is totally false. I trust that any hurt, pain or stress which this situation has caused you will disappear quickly even as I continue to try to "clear the air."

Once more, please accept my apology and thank you for your understanding. I trust that God will help us to put this situation behind us quickly and grant you comfort and peace until this is accomplished.

Every Blessing.
Yours respectfully,
Errol E. Leslie

Mrs. Miriam

Dear Miriam,

As you know, a written complaint was filed against me in July of this year. This complaint which was initially handed to District Superintendent, Dr. Gary Spencer and then passed on to the bishop's office alleges among other thing that I have been engaged in inappropriate relationships with several women in the Palm Bay United Methodist Church. Unfortunately, your name was among several others mentioned in relation to this allegation. At no time did I even mention your name to anyone in that light. However, the complainant decided to pass on fictitious and speculative information as though it was factual.

I am even more disturbed that, as I understand it, your daughters, Jean and Jane (Not their real names) were also included on the list of persons referenced earlier. You would know that I have only seen these two lovely ladies through the eyes of a pastor and "father." They are both dear to me and so I would ask that you also convey to them my sadness and regret about the whole situation.

I want you to know that I deeply regret that and apologize profusely for the fact that you were mentioned in such an extremely negative light. Even though the allegation is totally untrue, I know that it has the potential to mar your stellar character as it is perceived by some persons in the community. I have already indicated to the bishop as well as the district superintendent that the allegation is totally false. I trust that any hurt, pain or stress which this situation has caused you will disappear quickly even as I continue to try to "clear the air."

Once more, please accept my apology and thank you for your understanding. I trust that God will help us to put this situation behind us quickly and grant you comfort and peace until this is accomplished. Every Blessing.

Yours respectfully,
Errol E. Leslie

CHAPTER 7

The Flaws of the Church Are Pointed Out

While all this was happening, Rev. Sydney Sadio was continuing to research my case and was utterly convinced that the bishop and the other leaders had acted incorrectly in placing me on involuntary leave of absence. As such, he himself penned a letter to Bishop Carter, and unlike me, who held on to my penned letter, he mailed his letter. Dr. Sadio had been very involved in the United Methodist Church at the administrative level and so was far more familiar with the system than I was. His letter below spelt out everything that was wrong with what the leaders of the Florida Conference had done.

Bishop Kenneth H. Carter Jr.
450 Martin Luther King Jr Blvd
Lakeland, Fl. 33815

1st December 2014

Dear Bishop Carter,

May the blessing of this holy Advent season be with you. I am writing to you in my capacity of accompanying elder for Rev. Errol Leslie.

Let me introduce myself. I am a retired elder of the Greater New Jersey Annual Conference and now residing in Wellington, Florida. I have been involved in the United Methodist Church at Local, District,

127

Annual Conference, Jurisdictional and General church levels. I have also been a delegate to several Jurisdictional and General Conferences. I have chaired the Annual Conference Board of Ordained Ministry, the Committee on Investigation, the Episcopacy Committee; I was a District Superintendent, and Dean of the Cabinet among other responsibilities. I say this not to boast but to let you know that I have great respect and admiration for the leaders of our Church. I am grateful to the Church for the opportunities it has afforded me to serve and if I had to live my life over I would take the same vocational path.

In my various church responsibilities I have studied the Book of Discipline carefully as well as the Administrative and Judicial Process Handbook of the General Council on Finance and Administration and I believe that there are some serious errors that have been made in addressing the matter before us regarding the complaint against Rev. Errol Leslie. It appears that categories that are distinctly separate in our disciplinary processes have been conflated resulting in an abrogation of Rev. Leslie's rights. Let me explain.

The Administrative and Judicial Process Handbook makes it clear in its opening paragraphs that there are two sets of fair process procedures in our polity—one for administrative matters and one for judicial matters. Since 2012 these procedures have been carefully separated in the Discipline. Each of these tracts has its distinctive elements which must be followed scrupulously to make certain that fair process is maintained. Judicial Council decision 1189 makes this very clear when it declares:

Officers of the church who are involved in the administration of disciplinary process with respect to the conduct of clergy that can result in

an adverse effect on the conference relations of a clergy member must strictly comply with disciplinary provisions. Said officers are guardians of a sacred trust to follow faithfully and adhere to disciplinary process. Important rights are in play and the clergy person as well as those who have grievance against them, must be treated with utmost fairness.

In the case of Rev. Leslie, a category of involuntary leave of absence has been improperly borrowed from the Administrative side of the equation and imposed without following proper procedures. A bishop may choose to request involuntary leave of absence from the Board of Ordained Ministry in the context of filing an administrative complaint. Detailed reasons for this request must be communicated in writing to both the Board and the individual being accused. The Board then must convene an administrative fair hearing under the auspices of the Conference Relations Committee. The accused is entitled to be present to defend himself at the hearing (See JC1189) The Conference Relations Committee then makes a recommendation to the full Board which may or may not support the Committee's recommendation. There are provisions to deal with this matter between sessions of the Annual Conference but eventually the whole matter must be approved by the Executive Session of the Annual

Conference. A bishop has no authority to impose involuntary leave of absence without every one of these steps being scrupulously followed.

All of this however begs the main question. It is apparent that you have chosen to pursue a judicial complaint against Rev. Leslie and not an administrative complaint (which under the 2012 Discipline is reserved exclusively for issues relating to performance in ministry). This is evidenced by the fact that you have received a written and signed complaint, entered into a supervisory process and appointed a counsel for the church all of which belongs exclusively in the judicial complaint process. Changes in membership status in administrative proceedings belong to the Board of Ordained Ministry while in judicial proceedings they belong to the Trial Court. In no case do they belong to the Episcopal Office.

Rev. Leslie, while remaining open throughout this process to proposals for a just resolution, respectfully requests that any incorrect interpretation of the Discipline to change his ministerial status should be revised and discontinued. He continues to claim his constitutional right to a trial by his peers. I must remind you Bishop that until the judicial process is complete Rev. Leslie is presumed innocent and remains a member in good standing of the annual conference and is thus entitled to an appointment. And, in the absence of an appointment JC 1189 makes it very clear that the annual conference is responsible to compensate him equitably throughout the process until such time as he may no longer be considered in good standing. The Book of Discipline Para 2704.2.c is an option here. Rev. Leslie further requests permission to remain in the parsonage of his present appointment at least until the completion of the judicial process.

Thank you for your careful attention in these important matters.

Grace and Peace

Rev. Dr. Sydney S. Sadio
Accompanying elder to Rev. Errol Leslie.
Copy: Dr. Gary Spencer

For once the bishop chose to respond to one of the many letters which were written to him on my behalf, but in his response no form of wrongdoing was acknowledged, and he was more inclined to defend the illegal action of the Florida Conference.

As such, Dr. Sadio penned a second letter.

Bishop Kenneth Carter Jr.
450 Martin Luther King Jr. Avenue
Lakeland, FL 33815-1522
December 9, 2014

Dear Bishop,

Greetings,

Thank you very much for your response to my letter and I applaud your intention of seeking justice for both the complainant and the respondent in the matter at hand. However, even though I am convinced that there is no malevolence on your part I beg to differ with you in your interpretation of the Discipline.

I am sure you have been a delegate to the General Conference and you must be aware that sometimes when changes are made in one part of the Discipline they sometimes leave certain other parts somewhat unclear, and that is why the GCFA Guidelines give us some clarity as to how we should interpret and proceed especially in these undertakings.

Section XVI of the Discipline deals with Administrative Fair Process, although I do not believe this is the proper section to deal with the matter at hand. And you are right in quoting para352.2.c. However, paragraph 363 deals specifically with complaint procedures and begins with the receipt of a formal complaint by the bishop and sets in motion the supervisory response And under 363.1.b the supervisory response is pastoral and ADMINISTRATIVE and not part of any JUDICIAL process. The respondent may choose ANOTHER PERSON (no qualification here) to accompany him with the right to voice. It is under this clause that I was present with Rev. Leslie at the meeting arranged by you.

Since there was no just resolution, you have referred the matter to the Counsel for the Church as a complaint. Now, paragraph 364 deals with the Disposition of Recommendations of Involuntary Status Change, and it is this paragraph which has not been scrupulously followed. Specifically, Rev. Leslie has not been given a fair process hearing. The Discipline requires that he be given the opportunity to address the recommendation (for involuntary leave of absence) in person, in writing, and with the assistance of a clergyperson who is a member in full connection with his annual Conference. No involuntary change of membership status can occur without such a hearing taking place. This may have been an oversight but it is still in error and is subject to challenge and an appeal. And since this procedure was not scrupulously followed, the involuntary leave of absence is invalid and must be called into question.

You must make a decision whether you are dealing with this as an administrative matter or a judicial matter. If it is administrative, it is up to the Board of Ordained Ministry to immediately follow proper procedures in response to your request for a change in Rev. Leslie's conference relationship. Further, if you are taking the administrative route then you must withdraw the judicial complaint and your appointment of a counsel for the church as the administrative process does not include these actions. I am aware that

I will not be permitted to represent Rev. Leslie at an administrative hearing, but we are prepared to have him accompanied by a member of his own conference.

If you have determined that this is a judicial process, then you must withdraw your request for involuntary leave of absence while the counsel for the church investigates the case. Since Rev. Leslie remains a member in good standing, he is still under appointment and the annual conference is responsible for providing him with salary and benefits. If you choose to remove him from his parsonage, the annual conference is responsible for providing him with suitable alternative housing in the meanwhile.

Since it appears that you are choosing to consider this to be a judicial matter, I would remind you that in judicial matters, according to paragraph 2708.7 there is no restriction on the conference membership of an advocate for the respondent. It is under this clause that I am representing Rev. Leslie.

Thank you very much for your timely and careful consideration of these matters and we await your kind response. We need to know at your earliest convenience the path you are choosing to follow in this matter, especially since you have ordered Rev. Leslie to leave the parsonage and have had all his benefits withdrawn.

A blessed and Holy Christmas to you and your family,

With grace and peace

Sydney S. Sadio

Counsel for Rev. Errol Leslie

Copy: Rev. Dr. Gary Spencer

Following this second letter, Bishop Carter returned to his arrogant behavior and totally ignored the points of clarification which Dr. Sadio had made. He did not respond to the second letter. However, Dr. Sadio never gave up and decided to consult with someone else who was very knowledgeable with the Book of Discipline and who would also try to persuade the bishop about all the wrongdoing of the Florida Conference. Dr. Sadio contacted Rev. Dr. William Campbell, popularly known as "Scott" Campbell of the New England Conference, and asked him if he would help with the case. Even though Scott was a member of the New England Conference where my clergy membership belonged, I had never met him, and he had not met me. As a result, I was a little nervous at first to call him even though Dr. Sadio had indicated to me that he (Scott) was definitely willing to work on my case as a defense counsel. However, after my first call to Scott, my mind was put at ease as he reassured me that he believed in grace, mercy, and forgiveness and also that there were so many loopholes in the process that the Florida Conference had adopted. As a result of him putting me at ease, I started sending him electronic versions of all the documents which I had acquired up to that point. One of the first things that Scott did was to write his own letter to Bishop Carter explaining to him why it was unconstitutional for the Florida Conference to have placed me on involuntary leave of absence.

In so doing, he reiterated Dr. Sadio's position.

This is the February 23 letter to Bishop Carter from Scott Campbell.

> Bishop Kenneth H. Carter, Jr.
> 450 Martin Luther King, Jr. Avenue
> Lakeland, FL 33815-1522
>
> February 23, 2015
>
> Dear Bishop Carter,
>
> Grace and Peace to you through our Lord Jesus Christ. Let me belatedly congratulate you on your election to the episcopacy. Our paths have not crossed since we were in Tampa together.
>
> I have, as you have heard from Bishop Devadhar, agreed to serve as the clergy counsel for the Rev. Errol Leslie. I am a full member of the New England

Conference. It is in that capacity that I am writing to you. After a careful review of the process that has been used to place Rev. Leslie on Involuntary Leave of Absence I am convinced that there are serious, and, indeed, fatal flaws in the path that was followed to place him in that category. Specifically, the violations of Disciplinary process include the following:

- Paragraph 355.1 specifies that the bishop and superintendent must give to the clergy member and the Board of Ordained Ministry a written statement of the specific reasons involuntary leave is being requested. No such document was ever provided to Rev. Leslie. Judicial Council decision 1189 underscores this point: The bishop and the district superintendent are required to give specific reasons for the request in writing to the member and the Board of Ordained Ministry.

- Paragraph 355.2 requires that the Board of Ordained Ministry hold a hearing that follows the fair process guidelines of The Discipline (2701). No such hearing ever took place. Judicial Council decision 1189 makes it clear that the bishop cannot approach the Board of Ordained Ministry to request involuntary leave without the presence of the member: Fair process requires that the member is entitled to hear all information considered by the Board. Fair process requires the bishop's point of view to be received in the presence of the member... and not in the absence of the member or in an ex parte manner. Rev. Leslie was not provided with a chance to be heard before any final action was taken (2701.2 a)), was not given notice of such a meeting (2701.2 b)), and was not represented by an advocate before the Board

(2701.2 c). The Judicial and Administrative Procedures Handbook of the General Council on Finance and Administration sheds further light on the procedures that must be followed by the Board, none of which were observed in the present case.

- The fact that 355.4 was cited in justifying the action taken by the Board does not excuse the conference from its responsibility to strictly adhere to the fair process provisions called for in 355.

- Again, JC 1189 speaks to this point: 355.4 is not a stand alone provision, but must be read and applied in its entirely. Even when pursued as an interim action between sessions of the Annual Conference, all provisions of 355 are applicable and must be observed.

The failure of the conference to follow Disciplinary procedures, even if done inadvertently, is a serious matter, rendering invalid the action that has been taken. Once more JC 1189 is clear: **Deviations from the Disciplinary process, even when undertaken in good faith or for the sake of convenience or efficiency, fall below acceptable standards of fair process.** You will note that in that case the Judicial Council ordered the member reinstated and compensated for the violations of fair process by the conference.

Therefore, on behalf of Rev. Leslie, I am requesting the following remedial actions by the Florida Annual Conference:

1. Rev. Leslie be immediately removed from the status of Involuntary Leave of Absence.
2. Rev. Leslie be reimbursed, retroactive to December 1, 2014 for all lost salary and benefits,

including the cost of his housing, by the Florida Annual Conference. Housing reimbursement should be commensurate with the fair rental value of the parsonage in which he was living, as established by local real estate professionals.

3. Rev. Leslie be continued as a member in good standing of the Florida Annual Conference until such time as the pending judicial processes are complete or a just resolution is achieved.

4. The above financial support be continued until the pending judicial processes are complete or a just resolution is achieved.

I thank you for your prompt and careful attention to these important matters. I know that you are a fair-minded person and that you will want to do the right thing in this case. A final word from JC 1189:

Officers of the church who are involved in the administration of disciplinary process with respect to the conduct of clergy that can result in an adverse effect on the conference relations of a clergy member must strictly comply with disciplinary provisions. Said officers are guardians of a sacred trust to follow faithfully and adhere to disciplinary process. Important rights are in play and the clergy person, as well as those who have grievance against them, must be treated with the utmost fairness.

In Christ,
Scott Campbell

At this point, serious negotiations have begun to take place between the Florida Conference chancellor and my new defense counsel. I was given several opportunities to surrender my credentials in exchange for a lump sum of money. At one point, I was offered a lump sum of $25,000 if I would voluntarily surrender my credentials. I had mixed emotions to this offer. Firstly, I felt insulted with the thought that I could denounce my calling to Christian ministry for money. This was like Jacob asking Esau to sell him his birthright. Of course, I declined to do so, and I began to think that the Florida Conference was now beginning to feel the pressure because I would not give in—certainly not for a monetary bribe. After a number of e-mail exchanges, Bishop Carter finally acknowledged that the Florida Conference had made a "mistake" in placing me on involuntary leave of absence and would seek to correct their mistake. Within a few days, I received a letter from Rev. David Dodge, which officially confirmed that the Florida Conference had erred and would seek to compensate me for the error. Here is a copy of the letter below.

The United Methodist Church
Florida + Episcopal Area
March 12, 2015
Rev. Errol Leslie

Dear Rev. Leslie:

I believe you are aware that we have discovered that the process of placing you on Involuntary Leave of Absence was to be the responsibility of the New England Conference rather than the Florida Conference. Due to this error on our part your clergy status is being returned to the active status and your appointment will show as being appointed to the Atlantic Central District office. In this relationship your direct line of accountability will be with Dr. Gary Spencer. Any activities of ministry should be shared with Dr. Spencer previous to the activity, and he will decide on the appropriateness of your involvement in such.

As a result of this correction, the Florida Conference will be restoring your salary back to December 1, the date on which you were placed

on Involuntary Leave of Absence and inclusive of interest on the funds calculated at 5% per annum. This also will include pension, which will be remitted to your account at the General Board of Pension and Health Benefits. The General Board will inform of us of any gains that would have occurred in these intervening days and that will also be restored to your account. We will also be remitting to you what the prevailing rate the church would have paid toward your family health insurance plan.

Regarding housing and utilities, we will be reimbursing you for the fair rental value of the parsonage and what the average monthly cost of the utilities have been. These will be prorated from the date that you eventually moved out of the parsonage.

We are in communication with Bishop Devadhar of the New England Annual Conference regarding your appointment status and our plan for restoring your salary and benefits. Any change that might take place in your status, previous to the completion of the judicial process, will be the responsibility of the New England Conference.

As soon as we have finished the computations of that which is owed to you, and there is agreement on this amount, a check will be forwarded to you. You will be responsible for any and all personal income tax and self-employment tax obligations that are a part of compensation received. I am including a summary sheet of what is projected.

Finally, we regret that this error in process took place and trust that you see that the Florida Conference is trying to rectify that by this payment. The payment will continue on a monthly basis until such time as you have either a change in your clergy status that negates future payments, or June 30, 2015, which will be the conclusion of your appointment in the Florida Conference, or whichever occurs first.

Please let me know if you have any additional questions or concerns. I will be glad to do anything I can to clarify this for you.

Assistant to Bishop Kenneth H. Carter, Jr.

Rev. Paul Butler

Enclosure: Summary of back pay

and future pay for Errol Leslie

I could not help but think to myself that this was not an error. This decision was arrived at following a number of meetings by several persons at the leadership level of the church. It was hard to believe that such a significant decision regarding the conference relations of a clergy person could pass through so many levels and not one person would have caught the error. Could it be that all these persons, including the bishop and several district superintendents, could be so ignorant? I hardly think so. This action was clearly taken out of their desperation to punish me even if it meant acting outside of the guidelines of the Book of Discipline. It may also have been a situation where they are continuing to capitalize on my ignorance in relation to the Book of Discipline. Both Reverend Spencer and Reverend Dodge had taken full advantage of that at the outset, and now they were trying it again—maybe not thinking that both Reverend Sadio and Reverend Campbell would have been coming into the picture and on my defense team. Here is where the words from Proverbs 4:24 apply:

Put away from you a deceitful mouth and put devious speech far from you. (New America Standard Version)

It has been said that *the most dangerous lies are those that resemble the truth. An honest man alters his ideas to fit the truth and a dishonest man alters the truth to fit his ideas.*

This is Bishop Carter's letter below, which indicates the emotional trauma which I was put through in order to satisfy this craving on the part of the leadership of the Florida Conference.

November 6, 2014

The Reverend Errol Leslie

2796 Rodeo, NE

Palm Bay, FL 32905

Dear Rev. Leslie:

As we shared with you last Friday, in conversation and by email, the Supervisory Response to Ms. Hendricks' formal complaint has not led to a just resolution. The Supervisory Response has included multiple face-to-face meetings, telephone conversations and correspondence during the ninety-day period.

Because the Supervisory Response (Book of Discipline, paragraph 363b) has not led to a Just Resolution, I will forward the complaint to the Counsel for the Church (Book of Discipline, 363e).

This is a step in the process toward a Judicial Complaint (Book of Discipline, 2704.2a).

In this period I am requesting an involuntary leave of absence (Book of Discipline, 355) from ordained ministry for Rev. Leslie. Both parties will have all of the rights to due process described in the Book of Discipline.

I will be in prayer for each of you during this season when the church seeks a way forward where we can "do justice, love mercy and walk humbly with God."

Resident Bishop, Florida Area
The United Methodist Church
450 MARTIN LUTHER KING, JR.
AVENUE, LAKELAND, FL 33815-1522
TELEPHONE: 1-863-688-4427
TOLL FREE: 1-800-282-8011, EXT.
154 facsimile: 1-863-687-0568
FLORIDA CONFERENCE
WEBSITE: WWW.FLUMC.ORG

As stated, one has to assume that nobody anticipated that I was going to have an expert in the laws of the church defend my case, so they decided to corrupt the system and impose this illegal punishment on me. I was not given a chance to go before any committees as the Book of Discipline required. I was also bothered by Bishop Carter's continuous use of the word *multiple* in reference to the number of attempts which the church supposedly used to arrive at a just resolution. There were not "multiple attempts." The church brought nothing to the table at any time but the surrender of my credentials. After the decision was reversed, and for the next four months or so, I received my regular salary plus a cash allowance for housing and health insurance. However, I was not compensated for all the money which I had spent on moving out of the parsonage and finding a home in which to live. Neither was I compensated for all the trauma which the leadership had caused me out of malice and vindictiveness. Here are some of the ways in which I was emotionally traumatized by the church which was supposed to be a community of healing and restoration.

1.) I was treated with disrespect, totally humiliated, and experienced tremendous indignity from the outset until the end. I was treated like the "scum of the earth." I was told to hand in all keys, checkbooks, pack up my office on the day I had the first meeting. I was later told to move out of the office; and if I did not, the district superintendent threatened to come and personally put things out on the curbside. In fact, I was also told by the district superintendent that I could not go back on to the campus of the church.

2.) The bishop indicated to me during the supervisory hearings that there was also a "money" issue involved. I happen to know that there was a financial audit done at the church, and that played into the perception that I was financially dishonest and that there was some kind of impropriety. It was a real heartbreaking thought. The interim pastor actually told a parishioner that I was not allowed to set foot back on the premises because there was misappropriation of funds while I was there. Needless to say, the audit did not reveal anything that would show even the remotest evidence of misappropriation of funds.

3.) I was kicked out of the parsonage with one week's notice, and then it was extended to one month. I was told repeatedly by the DS that if I did not get out on time, he would come and personally put my stuff outside. Thankfully, a friend offered us the use of his empty home. However, we had to spend quite a bit of money to repair the home and then only to find out that there was mold in the kitchen caused from a leaking pipe. There was also a problem with the septic, so it was really a very depressing time. When the mentioned problems were communicated to the district superintendent, there was no care shown. He merely and callously indicated that I needed to get out as he had instructed. So here is a household with two teenage girls and an eighty-eight-year-old grandmother, being kicked out of a parsonage prematurely, and as it turned out illegitimately, and there was not even the slightest concern shown relating to our well-being and comfort by the leadership of the people who are the top administrators of the church.

4.) A one-sided investigation with no one representing the church being willing to listen to me. To this day, the counsel for the church has not initiated any contacts with me outside of the questioning during the official trial.

5.) The complainant was able to write all those outrageous allegations about me while the leadership of the church bought it wholesale and swallowed it up like Gospel. Is that why I was treated with such disrespect? Is that why I was humiliated to the ground? She was also empowered to call whomsoever she wanted in the church and spread all kinds of stories about me way over and above the confession I have already made.

6.) The constant telephone calls from the district superintendent relating to communication which he had from the complainant turned out to be very annoying and exasperating. This was especially so because the superintendent himself knew that most of these complaints were trivial and had no bearing on the trial. One such complaint was that I had become a member of the Baptist church in Melbourne. Another was that I was calling her son too regularly. In the case of the latter, I had to indicate to the superintendent that the son of the complainant was my auto mechanic and that he was an adult over forty years of age. I also pointed out that this son, like his siblings did not care much for their mother because of how she had treated their father anyway.

7.) One of the issues which made most of the Palm Bay Community angry was what they deemed to be the unnecessary public announcement made at church in the presence of visitors and my two daughters. Regardless of how much love my daughters may have had for me, they will remember this announcement for life. It is a life sentence.

8.) For almost six months after the official complaint was filed, I experienced taunting as well as harassing texts and telephone voice mails from the complainant. Even after asking the district superintendent to intervene, this did not stop. Once more, I felt that I was a fish out of water. I wanted to reach out to the administration for spiritual and emotional help, but all I received were sticks and bullets as well as stones and rocks being thrown at me.

9.) A congregation was snatched away from me without notice, and I was not even given an opportunity to make a statement apologizing and attempting to indicate my remorse let alone to say goodbye. Equally, from the feedback which I received, the majority of the congregation was also very upset and would have done anything to receive me back as their pastor regardless of what they had now learned. That knowledge in and of itself pained my heart as I have always cared about every aspect of my parishioners' lives.

10.) I have had to go through years with my life in emotional turmoil and my family in anxiety and uncertain mode.

11.) When I was placed on involuntary leave of absence, I lost my health-care benefits, and so for three months, with the exception of one time when my daughter was seriously ill, we were not able to seek and receive medical attention. Eventually, we were able to get health insurance through the Affordable Care Act.

In this second letter below from Bishop Carter, we are not only seeing a blatant disregard and disobedience to the order and discipline of the United Methodist Church but was also a demonstration of a very cold and callous heart that did not seem to show any kind of care for a fellow human being—a human being who had served the Methodist Church faithfully and unblemished for thirty-nine years. It was not only illegitimate and unethical but calculatedly thoughtless. As such, the bishop really expected me to pack up and move my family out of the parsonage within the space of one calendar week right in the heart of the Christmas season.

Letter number two Florida Area Resident Bishop:

November 20, 2014
The Reverend Errol Leslie
2796 Rodeo, NE
Palm Bay, FL 32905
Certified, Return Receipt Requested

Dear Rev. Leslie:

I am taking this opportunity to apprise you of the process as it relates to the complaint that was filed against you by Ms. Veda Hendricks.

In that a just resolution could not be completed under the process outlined in 51363 of the 2012 Book of Discipline, I have only two options available to me. The first is dismiss the complaint, which I cannot do given the evidence that is provided. The second is to refer the matter to the counsel for the church, which I have done.

In that the time allowed for the suspension is concluded, I have requested that you be placed on Involuntary Leave of Absence. This action is taken through the direction of 51355.2a. That request has been approved by the Executive Committee of the Board of Ordained Ministry as required in 51355.4. Your salary, benefits and the availability of the parsonage will conclude at the end of November 2014. It will be necessary for you to make the parsonage available by December 1.

As this process moves forward you will have access to a clergyperson who may accompany you in the process. In alignment with 1]362.2c, that clergyperson must be a member in full connection of your annual conference. That would mean that the individual must be a clergyperson who is a member in full connection of the New England Annual Conference.

You will be advised by the counsel for the church of the next steps in the process and the time sequence.

For any questions about transition from the local ministry, please contact Dr. Gary Spencer. And for any questions related to the process, you are welcome to contact the episcopal office.

The peace of the Lord,
Kenneth H. Carter Jr.
C: Bishop Sudarshana Devadhar
Dr. Gary Spencer

From this illegitimate decision made by the Florida Conference, my pension was affected in three ways. I was forced to withdraw total of $28,000 from my accumulated pension fund. This was what I used to help to repair the house that we were going to be living in as well as for moving and other affiliated expenses. This withdrawal resulted in a loss of $5,820 (20 percent) in taxes to the IRS. The Florida Conference did not take this into consideration when they were calculating my refund, just as they did not think about how much it cost me for removal or for fixing the house where we were forced to stay. There were also monthly storage fees, which we had to be paying because the house into which we moved was so much smaller. As a result, much of our furniture and other belongings had to be placed in storage.

When I actively served at the church, I would send a monthly amount of $500 toward my pension. However, as most, if not all, Methodist clergy know, this had to be done by salary deduction. Once I was reinstated, I could not put in my personal contribution each month because it had to be remitted by the church treasurer. This took away from what would be available to me on a monthly basis from the personal investment plan for my pension. As such, my anticipated pension has been permanently affected.

With my checks coming from the conference, a good percentage of my salary which would normally be nontaxable would now be taxable for the year 2015. For example, part of it would go to pension fund referenced above: health, housing exclusion allowance, Medicare, etc. On the contrary, the amount which the conference is reimbursing me toward health care is merely designated "other earnings," which made it taxable.

Reverend Campbell was immediately able to see all the errors which worked to my disadvantage and sought to do two main things among others in trying to get a fair process.

1.) He tried to get the process to move from the Florida Conference to the New England Conference where my clergy membership belonged.

2.) He successfully attempted another effort at a just resolution by involving an organization called Just Peace, which was known for helping conferences arrive at peaceful resolutions in situations such as the one I faced.

I eventually learned that the constitution of the United Methodist Church made it abundantly clear—even with the document which I was tricked and coerced into signing prematurely, supposedly requesting that the process takes place in the Florida Conference—that any such process can only legitimately take place in the home conference of the accused. We need to remember that the district superintendent had tricked me into signing a document requesting that the process be carried out in the Florida Conference. From that point, in spite of the efforts of Reverend Campbell, the leadership of the Florida Conference—bishop, assistant to the bishop, counsel for the church, district superintendent—clung on to the process like it was their firstborn child and would not let it go. There was every indication that the extraordinary possessive behavior was spurred on by their determination to punish me to the maximum.

They were not willing to risk having another conference carry out the process in the event that I faced anything less than withdrawal of my ministerial credentials. Unfortunately, there was no help or cooperation from the bishop of the New England Conference, who unilaterally had the power to claim or demand that the trial of one of his "pastors" be held in that pastor's home conference. I happened to have been in touch with a retired bishop who shared how in a similar situation; he had instructed that the pastor in question be sent back to his home conference for the investigative process to take place. However, the request by my defense counsel to have the process be conducted in the New England Conference was made for reasons beyond what the constitution of the church dictated. It was also about fair process and objective analysis as indicated by this first letter below addressed to the presiding officer of the upcoming trial and composed by Reverend Campbell.

March 30, 2015

Dear Bishop Gwinn,

In the matter of the Rev. Errol Leslie, Respondent, I am officially requesting a change of venue for his trial under the provisions of 2708.4 of The 2012 Book of Discipline. It is the conviction of the defense that the respondent cannot receive a fair trial in the Florida Annual Conference. This belief is based upon a number of factors.

The Discipline is clear about the purpose of the supervisory response to a complaint. In 363.1.b we read: The response is pastoral and administrative and shall be directed toward a just resolution among all parties. This fundamental orientation towards healing and justice for all concerned was ignored from the very beginning of the supervisory process and culminated in Bishop Carter placing Rev. Leslie on an illegal "Involuntary Leave of Absence." (These violations are detailed in Appendix I) Throughout the complaint process, and continuing to the present moment, the Florida Conference has been concerned with one primary objective—compelling the surrender of Rev. Leslie's orders. Following are some of the actions of the officers of the Florida Conference that not only denied Rev. Leslie his fair process rights, but demeaned his human dignity as well.

- On July 30, 2014 the Rev. David Dodge and the Rev. Gary Spencer examined Rev. Leslie about matters alleged in the original complaint from Ms. Veda Hendricks without allowing him to see that complaint in direct violation of Judicial Council decision 974, which states:

The respondent has a right not only to examine but to possess the written complaint and any supporting material accompanying it at the initiation of the supervisory process. A respondent cannot make an adequate response to a complaint without being privy to the complaint in its totality. Fairness alone dictates access to such written complaints and their supporting documents.

The Superintendent refused to inform Rev. Leslie prior to the meeting about the subject matter that would be addressed even though Rev. Leslie asked directly why he was being summoned. It was an ambush. The Reverends Dodge and Spencer did not tell him that he was entitled to be accompanied by an elder of his choice. When he specifically asked to see the complaint, they denied his request. Yet, he was told at that meeting that he was being placed on suspension and that arrangements had already been made to notify his church of that fact. A substitute preacher had already been arranged at his church for the following Sunday. All this took place without ever having heard Rev. Leslie's side of the story. He was encouraged then and there to surrender his credentials in order to avoid a painful and embarrassing public spectacle.

Further, so-called "confessions" from this supervisory session have appeared as supporting documents in the Bill of Charges from the Counsel for the Church, even though The Discipline is clear in 363.1.b that the supervisory response is not a part of any judicial process. The use of this material subsequently in a judicial process is a direct violation of the letter and the spirit of The Discipline and of the rights of the Respondent. (See Item 2 in "List of Written Documents and Exhibits" in Judicial Complaint package)

On July 31, 2014, one day after Rev. Leslie learned that he had been suspended; Rev. Gary Spencer pressured Rev. Leslie into signing a document choosing between the complaint processes going forward in the New England Conference, where Rev. Leslie's membership resides, or in the Florida conference where he was serving. (See Item 4 in "List of Written Documents and Exhibits" in Judicial Complaint package.) Rev. Spencer told Rev. Leslie that the document had to be signed by noon time on that Friday or the "trial" would automatically default to the NEC. 2719 provides no such timeline or ultimatum. When Rev. Leslie asked for a copy of the document Rev. Spencer denied his request. Once again, these events transpired without Rev. Leslie having access to counsel or having seen the complaint against him. At this same meeting, Rev. Spencer once more encouraged Rev. Leslie to surrender his credentials, explaining that if he did, the pending announcement "would not make any reference to sexual misconduct." (Source: Rev. Leslie's notes after the meeting.)

On September 12, 2014 Rev. Leslie met with Bishop Carter and Rev. Gary Spencer and the District Superintendent of the South Central District, the Rev. Walter Monroe, for a supervisory session. This time Rev. Leslie was also accompanied by a retired elder from the Greater New Jersey Conference, the Rev. Dr. Sydney Sadio. Once again, there was little interest on the part of the officials of the conference in hearing Rev. Leslie's side of the story. In fact, there was an active effort not to hear his story. According to both Dr. Sadio and Rev. Leslie, Bishop Carter cut off Rev. Leslie's attempt to demonstrate that the complaint was filled with blatant lies by stating that he was interested in justice for the complainant and "all the other women whom (Rev. Leslie) had abused."

Rev. Leslie describes the following in his notes of the events of that day:

As happened at the beginning of the process, both the bishop as well as Dr. Spencer suggested that I should surrender my credentials and I refused to do so. My reasoning was that I would like to have a fair hearing at a trial. When Dr. Sadio enquired if there was any other possible resolution other than having me surrender my credentials, the bishop said that he would only change from that position if the complainant recanted her complaint. I decided that I was not going to surrender my ministerial credentials on the basis of a complaint which was based on concoctions. The bishop as well as District Superintendent Spencer both hinted at the negative implications of a public trial but I was still prepared to go along and wait for the trial. The bishop reminded me that all the evidence submitted would be used at the public hearing while Dr. Spencer reiterated that by saying there would also be television cameras present.

Rev. Leslie describes the following reactions from Bishop Carter during the supervisory session: (This description is confirmed by Dr. Sadio.)

It seemed to me that the bishop was visibly upset when I insisted that we take the process to a trial since we were not able to arrive at a just resolution. At one point during that session, he even mentioned that he was" infuriated." At one point the bishop commented that no one can think that the conference is acting along racial lines because the complainant is actually black. He suggested that he was going to refer the trial back to the New England Conference since he did not see why the Florida conference should invest money and time into this public trial. He thought that this money could be better spent in providing food for hungry persons.

On September 28, 2014 the Rev. Dionne Hammond completed an investigation on behalf of the Florida Conference in which she concluded that there was no evidence of other inappropriate relationships involving Rev. Leslie, despite the numerous allegations to that effect in the signed, written complaint. (See Item 5 in "List of Written Documents and Exhibits" in Judicial Complaint package) This information was never shared with the Respondent. To this day we have no written description of Rev. Dionne's investigation. The conference appears uninterested in any exculpatory evidence, despite the fact that at the point in the process when Rev. Dionne's investigation took place, the bishop was charged with administering a process that sought a just resolution for all parties. This passion to convict Rev. Leslie continues to be evident in a recent email from the Counsel for the Church that he will seek to exclude from evidence at the trial all material related to false allegations contained in the original complaint (See Appendix II).

On October 23, 2014 Rev. Leslie again met with Rev. Spencer. Rev. Leslie was asked to respond to a number of questions that, according to Rev. Spencer, had been prepared by Bishop Carter. All of these questions were ostensibly to assist the conference in investigating the veracity of the complaint against Rev. Leslie, but, in fact, were attempts to get him to incriminate himself. Despite the clear directive of The Discipline in 363.1.b that the supervisory process is to be "pastoral and administrative" in nature, and that it is not to be a part of any judicial process, and, further, that "At all supervisory meetings no verbatim record shall be made" Rev. Therrell has submitted to the court a partial verbatim record of that meeting, in direct violation of The Discipline and without concern for the Respondent's rights. The document is even entitled in Rev. Therrell's list of written documents as "Transcript of Questions for Rev. Errol Leslie to answer..." Rev. Therrell acknowledges in his description "Transcript was taken in a meeting held on Thursday, October 23, 2014 at 10 a.m." Further, the Judicial Complaint itself includes specifications that illegally reference these confidential conversations. (See Item 3 in "List of Written Documents and Exhibits" in Judicial Complaint package)

At the conclusion of the 90 day Supervisory Response period, Bishop Carter, in consultation with the cabinet and the executive committee of the Board of Ordained Ministry of the Florida Conference, placed Rev. Leslie in the status of "Involuntary Leave of Absence." His salary, his medical insurance and his pension contributions were terminated as of November 30, 2014. He was allowed to remain in the parsonage until mid-January. On February 23, 2015, acting on Rev. Leslie's behalf, I sent a letter to Bishop Carter outlining the Disciplinary violations which had occurred in this process. (See Appendix I) The Conference subsequently acknowledged that it had failed to follow appropriate processes and has taken financial responsibility for the damage that ensued. (See Appendix III) Nevertheless, the serious disregard for the fair process rights of Rev. Leslie has harmed him greatly. It is especially important that Rev. Leslie never had a chance to be heard before his ministerial colleagues on the Board of Ordained Ministry. The failure to follow The Discipline in this crucial matter demonstrates a continuing disregard for equal justice on the part of the leaders of the Florida Conference.

The respondent's chief concern at this point, insofar as it impacts his ability to receive a fair trial in the Florida Annual Conference, is that the very superintendents who were parties to the serious disregard for Disciplinary fair process involved in assigning Rev. Leslie to Involuntary Leave of Absence, and who serve at the pleasure of the bishop who coordinated this illegal action, will now be called upon to nominate those who will ultimately constitute the trial court and who will render judgment in his trial. The participation of the superintendents in this process is already tainted by their being parties to previous violations of The Discipline in this very case. The fate of the Respondent lies, in part, with those who have already deprived him of his rights.

In a telephone conversation with Rev. Therrell during the third week in February, as Counsel for the Respondent, I sought to ascertain whether the Church was open to a resolution that did not require Rev. Leslie to surrender his orders. He indicated he was not open to such alternatives. I pointed out to him that I personally knew a number of pastors who had stumbled in ways similar to the allegations made towards Rev. Leslie who had been restored to ordained ministry after going through appropriate processes of healing. Rev. Therrell replied "This is Florida. That may happen in other places, but it doesn't happen here." He went on to assure me that there were only two options for Rev. Leslie. He could surrender his orders voluntarily or they would be taken away by the trial court. He knew Florida and he was certain that a trial court would vote to convict.

While I recognize that there is a certain amount of pre-trial posturing that occurs in such conversations, Rev. Therrell's assurance to me that the outcome of the trial was a foregone conclusion in Florida is consistent with other attempts of the Conference officials to intimidate Rev. Leslie into surrendering his orders and to persuade him not to exercise his constitutional right to a trial. From the beginning, the goal has never been to find the truth and to administer justice equitably for all. The single-minded objective of the Florida Conference has been to drive Rev. Leslie from the ministry.

In a letter dated March 12, 2015 from Rev. David Dodge, Assistant to Bishop Carter, Rev. Leslie was informed that he would not be reappointed to serve in Florida. (See Appendix III) While the Bishop certainly has every right to make such a decision in relation to persons serving in cross-conference appointments, it is just one more indication that the leadership of this conference, including the cabinet members who will nominate the pool for the trial court, have already made up their minds about Rev. Leslie's guilt. This letter is also disingenuous in naming the real reasons for Florida's decision to reimburse Rev. Leslie. There is no requirement that Involuntary Leave must be administered from a member's home conference. The problem was Florida's disregard for Disciplinary processes.

The defense has recently been informed that within the last month Rev. Therrell has continued his investigation into allegations by the complainant that the Respondent was sexually involved with other persons. This questioning of a young woman, if true, was not related to the formal complaint that the Counsel for the Church has already submitted concerning the allegation that Rev. Leslie was involved in an affair with Ms. Hendricks. It provides further evidence of the attempts of the Florida Conference to denigrate and besmirch the character of Rev. Leslie. At the same time that Rev. Therrell is preparing to tell the court that such allegations are not relevant to the case (See Appendix II), it appears that he himself may have been engaged in trying to find corroboration for the complainant's many false allegations. This is not the way justice in the church ought to work.

Finally, Rev. Leslie is an outsider in the Florida Conference. This places him at a distinct disadvantage in that he neither knows many of his peers, nor is he known by them. The Counsel for the Church will have a distinct advantage in the voir dire process as a direct result of his membership in the conference over a period of years. While it may be argued that Rev. Leslie voluntarily renounced his right for the complaint process to go forward in his own conference, he was pressured into making that decision in an untimely fashion. Despite the clear direction of JC 974, he had not even been allowed to see the complaint against him, nor did he have the benefit of counsel when he was forced to make that decision the day after he learned of his suspension. And even more importantly, he was unaware that the Florida Conference would subsequently repeatedly disregard his fair process rights.

When Rev. Leslie asked me to represent him in January of 2015, one of the first things I did was to investigate the feasibility of revoking the agreement for the judicial process to go forward in Florida. The decision of the bishops involved (Bishop Devadhar and Bishop Carter) was that the case had moved too far, especially since a Counsel for the Church had already been appointed, to honor that request. While the Respondent understands that it is too late to move this trial back to his own conference, it is not too late to move the trial to a neutral site so that all participants will begin on level ground.

In the heat of concocted allegations by an untruthful complainant (as shown in the Church's own documents and demonstrated by the fact that the majority of the Complainant's allegations are not included in the Judicial Complaint), a false perception emerged that Rev. Leslie was a dangerous predator and that he must be removed from ministry. Those early false allegations have tainted every decision that has subsequently been made by officials related to the Florida Conference. Those fears have been used to justify an indifference to the fair process requirements of The Discipline on the part of those entrusted with administering its provisions. The Respondent is convinced that he cannot, in light of all that has transpired, receive a fair trial in the Florida Conference. He respectfully exercises his right under 2708.4 of The 2012 Book of Discipline to request a change of venue for his upcoming trial.

Grace and Peace,
Scott Campbell
Rev. Scott Campbell, Counsel for Rev. Leslie
Appendix I—February 23 Letter to
Bishop Carter from Scott Campbell
February 23, 2015

By sheer coincidence, there was a significant ruling from the Judicial Council right in the middle of the planning which altered or at least "slowed down" the process which was continuing to move forward.

Typically, a process like the one I am describing would move (at the bishop's discretion) from the bishop to a committee on investigation and then to a counsel for the church/prosecutor who would bring the charges. However, the general conference of the church had moved to eliminate the step that included the committee on investigation, and it was this latter model which was being followed in the Florida Conference dealing with my case. However, the Judicial Council later ruled generally, that the "Committee on Investigation" should be reestablished and placed back into the formula for any such cases. This change led to differences in interpretation among the parties involved, and so the process which began on February 18 in 2015, needed, of necessity, to begin again once this reversal took effect.

Once the process started over, it seemed that it was a matter of time before it would automatically be placed in the hands of the New England Conference. The Book of Discipline made it clear that the only situation in which another conference can carry out the proceedings for someone on trial is if (a) the person is living within the geographic confines of that other conference and (b) if that person is serving in that conference.

With the slowing down of the process, I was given an opportunity to go back and serve in the New England Conference as Bishop Carter and the Florida Conference made it clear that they did not want me back in the conference, and so he officially terminated my appointment effective June 30, 2015. This forced the hand of Bishop Devadhar to give me an appointment in New England, which is where my official conference membership resided. In spite of all of the above narrative, my status was still considered active especially with the aforementioned "lull" in the process, which was being aggressively and possessively undertaken by the Florida Conference.

Interestingly enough, the person who helped me to drive the truck to Connecticut and stayed for two days in order to help me unpack and set up the house was the son of the complainant. Not only had he become my auto mechanic, but he and I had developed a very close relationship. He was as happy for me that I had a chance to serve in pastoral ministry again as he was disgusted that his own mother could carry out that act of betrayal.

As such, it seemed like it was a no-brainer that the New England Conference was definitely going to be carrying out any judicial process based on the two criteria described immediately above. By July 1, 2015, I was officially serving two congregations in the Connecticut/Western Massachusetts district of the New England Conference. However, just to play it safe, Dr. Campbell wrote an official letter to the bishops of both conferences bringing the above two items to their attention and requesting that the discipline be observed so that the process would be taken over by the New England Conference. However, surprisingly— or maybe not so surprisingly—Bishop Devadhar of the New England Conference again declined the request.

Prior to the start of my appointment in the New England Conference, Dr. Campbell had also made a request of the appointed presiding officer—Bishop Alfred Gwinn—for the parties to try for a just resolution through a body called Just Peace. Just Peace is a body within The United Methodist Church which helps both the church and accused pastors/persons to arrive at a resolution which is satisfactory to both parties without going through the rigors and stress of a trial. In a sense, it compares to what is described as a "plea deal" in a regular criminal court. When my defense counsel requested to have a just resolution the counsel for the church agreed but with two conditions:

a.) That the complainant be allowed to attend and take part in the process.

b.) That I (the defendant) pay half of the cost for the process.

The representative from Just Peace stated that in her several years' experience; she had never heard of these conditions being made. As it turned out, it was just another way for the leaders of the Methodist Church to drive another sword into my side. We need to keep in mind again that from day 1, the church kept pressuring me to surrender my credentials. I kept on insisting that I still felt hundred percent called to the ministry and as such, I was requesting that some kind of mediation be exercised. On the day for the just resolution, the parties met, including the mediator from Just Peace and two representatives from the local church in Palm Bay where I was serving. As each person present was asked to share, I remember clearly the complainant sharing that she did not think that I should be allowed to pastor any churches anywhere in the world. Both the counsel for the church as well as his assistant insisted that I should surrender my credentials. Among the things which I said, I apologized to the two representatives from the local church and asked them to express my sincere remorse to the wider congregation. I made this request because I was truly and genuinely sorry, and I had not been given an opportunity to express this remorse directly to the congregation.

My defense counsel proposed a wide variety of ways to resolve this issue. One such proposal included suspending me from ministry for one full year and making me do counseling at my own expense. He also suggested early retirement as an option. Every suggestion which my defense counsel proposed was rejected by the counsel for the church, and the only resolution which was acceptable to them was for me to turn in and surrender my ministerial credentials. Needless to say, we ended a long and wasteful day without arriving at any agreement because the church would not move away from the one and only thing that they wanted from day 1. This was to have me surrender my credentials. As my defense counsel said, after the thousands of dollars spent, the result at the end was just as it was at the beginning. I must renounce my calling to be a pastor in the church of our Lord Jesus Christ. Later on, as you read the comments from both bishops relating to the result of the church trial, we will observe that Bishop Carter of the Florida Conference stated that the trial came about after "several failed attempts to arrive at a just resolution." This statement implied that they had offered several less punitive solutions/resolutions. How could Bishop Carter have made such a comment which he knew in his heart was not true? How could he have been so disingenuous? Of course, he had also mentioned in his letter to me that they were moving forward because of "several" failed attempts at a just resolution." What it really was is that there were several failed attempts to get me to voluntarily surrender my credentials. The truth of the matter is that they had offered nothing but asking for my credentials. To say that Bishop Carter was being dishonest in that comment as was the counsel for the church is a real understatement. This was just a part of a long list of unethical, unjust, and dishonest practices carried out by the church at every level and at every step.

CHAPTER 8

Second Forced Move Out of a Parsonage

By July of 2015, I was placed in an appointment in the Connecticut/ Western Massachusetts District of the New England Conference. Specifically, I was serving two half time appointments at the Wesley Memorial and Vernon United Methodist churches. Prior to the start of this appointment, I had to meet with the staff parish relations Committees in a joint meeting representing both congregations. Even though I had met with SPRC committees in this context before, this one turned out to be more of a challenging experience. The district superintendent indicated that at that meeting, I would need myself, to explain to the committees what was happening in Florida and what the implications were. I prayed about it and God enabled me to go through that meeting while comfortably sharing my story. Having done that, I waited patiently and anxiously in another room while the joint committee discussed whether or not they would have me serve after what I had told them in the presence of the New England district superintendent as well as the dean of the cabinet. Once we (dean of cabinet, district superintendent, and I) got back into the room, there was a unanimous decision that grace and mercy should prevail over judgment and condemnation, so they decided to accept me as their pastor. That was both a humbling and an encouraging experience, and I thanked God that I had another opportunity to lead congregations again. It was an exciting time for me when I arrived in New England to continue my ministry. It felt like Saul being renamed Paul and like David really receiving a clean heart and being restored into the joy of God's salvation. I was so grateful for this renewed opportunity and vowed that I would never ever go down that road again. I started feeling a level of security and safety since I was now back in my home conference. However, this excitement was short-lived as, within months, I started receiving communication from the bishop in the /Florida Conference. It was at about that time that Dr. Campbell wrote another letter to both Bishop Carter of Florida and Devadhar of the New England Conference suggesting that this was the appropriate time for the process to be transferred to New England. Needless to say, Bishop Devadhar Responded negatively while Bishop Carter, in his usual arrogant style, ignored the letter.

It was kind of puzzling for anyone to try and figure out Bishop Devadhar because his actions never matched his words. Let us keep in mind again that from the outset, he could have unilaterally determined that the Florida Conference did not have the legal right and authority to carry through with the process. Notwithstanding, as the process— which he refused to pursue—went on in Florida, he would call me at the appropriate times to wish me well and to tell me that he was praying for me. In fact, after the church trial that determined to terminate my appointment with the New England Conference, I went back to the parsonage of the churches that I had started to serve in New England. Both my new district superintendent (in New England) as well as my defense counsel begged Bishop Devadhar to allow me to continue serving in the church even at a "lower status" as a lay pastor or as a lay supply, but the bishop would have none of it. My defense counsel had done enough research which would establish to the bishop that in spite of the outcome of the trial, that there were pastoral options opened to me but that fell on deafened ears. When I got back to New England and was summoned to a telephone conference call with the bishop and my New England direct superintendent, I inquired if my defense counsel could be present on that call. However, I was told that that it would not be necessary because the call was going to be strictly pastoral. That was encouraging as I anticipated some words of encouragement from the bishop in New England which would help me to cope with and get over the devastating blow of being told by the Florida Conference that that my pastoral appointment in New England had ended. Instead of receiving pastoral counsel, I had a discussion with the bishop in which he told me that I needed to be out of the parsonage in thirty days. Like my defense counsel and district superintendent, I asked him over and over if there was an alternative form of ministry in which I could be involved, and he told me "no," claiming that if he did that then he himself could be brought up for ministerial charges. As he said that, I knew that he was just making up excuses, but I did not decide to fight that battle. That telephone conversation lasted over one hour and was one in which the bishop refused to acknowledge the blatant disobedience to the discipline of the United Methodist Church and further refused thereby to offer another form of ministry. It was ironic that at the end of the conversation, he asked, "Can I pray for you?" My instinct was to tell him no, but I decided to say yes. So for the second time within a twelve-month period, I saw myself abruptly packing up and leaving a parsonage into which I was comfortably settled. I had moved from Florida to Connecticut, in July of 2015 at my own expense but was so excited about getting back into ministry that the moving expenses did not bother me at all. However, after only six months, I was getting ready to pack for the return leg, and this time, I was more conscious of the monetary cost, and it certainly felt more burdensome.

So when Bishop Devadhar offered to pray for me after he refused to offer the help, which was hundred percent within his power to do, it was one of those times when it was difficult not to be judgmental because, as I said, my immediate instinct was to tell him no.

However, that was not the only time when Bishop Devadhar placed ecclesiastical status over caring and demonstrating God's grace through action. There was another occasion before the trial when I just started back serving in the New England Conference and attended a district meeting which was held in Connecticut. It was at that meeting where I first met Bishop Devadhar physically, and even prior to that I had only spoken with him twice on the phone. On both occasions when we spoke, it was in relation to the appointment which the conference was "forced" to give me because I was still considered to be in good standing while the Florida Conference was allowed to carry out their murder plot. I thought that this meeting would have presented a chance to meet and speak with the bishop. At the first opportunity—during a break—I went and introduced myself and also apologized for what I had done to him, my colleagues, the conference, and the wider Christian community. In the same breath, I asked for his forgiveness. All that went smoothly, but when I asked him if it would be okay for me to call his office in order to make an appointment to meet with him, he quickly told me that he was not allowed to discuss the case with me. So here is my episcopal and spiritual leader telling me that he is not in a position to discuss a case which had stressed me out for over a year and which he knew in his heart was technically flawed. That would compare with an injured person being taken to the hospital and the doctor telling him that he is not allowed to treat him so he can keep bleeding.

I was reminded of the priest and the Levite about whom Jesus spoke in the parable of the Good Samaritan. Bishop Devadhar saw someone who was spiritually and emotionally wounded, wounded from an unhappy marriage, wounded because of an overwhelming sense of guilt, wounded because I was betrayed by someone who I thought was going to bring me happiness for the rest of my life on earth, wounded because I was kicked about and kicked around by the hierarchy of the Florida Conference. The bishop saw in me one for whom Jesus had also died, one who was beaten up by a process which was everything but honest. However, he chose to pass by on the other side. In his mind, I am sure he thought that he was doing just what the bishop was expected to do by offering to pray for me as often as he did. However, I read somewhere in the Bible that Jesus had reached out to many persons who had fallen and gave them a helping hand to get back on their feet. In fact, I also read that King David of the Old Testament had exactly that experience and was still regarded as a man after God's own heart in spite of his double sin of adultery and murder. I also read somewhere in the epistle of James that we should be doers of the Word and not just hearers only. James also reminded us that we cannot speak of our faith without demonstrating our works. Of course, there was nothing in the Book of Discipline which supported his claim, but needless to say, after dismissing my request, he did what he does best and offered, as usual, to pray for me. I wonder if this is what James meant when he said that "faith without works is death."

165

I had to fly from the New England Conference to Florida at my own expense for the hearing with the Florida Committee on investigation. On the day of the hearing, I received a voice mail from Bishop Devadhar (who had just turned down another opportunity to deal directly with the process) that he was praying for me. It is worth noting that while Bishop Devadhar turned his back on me; I was up against a battery of legally trained attorneys at just about every level of the process. The chairperson of the Committee on Investigation for the Florida Conference was Judge Anthony Tatti, who was a Florida circuit court judge. He was one of many legally trained personnel who at one point or another worked through the process— and sometimes together worked against me. Before Judge Tatti, there was the chancellor to the bishop of the Florida Conference. After that, Rev. Jay Therrell, who was appointed to be the church's counsel for this case and who antagonized and harassed me brutally and mercilessly. Reverend Therrell was still also a member of the Florida bar, having been a prosecutor before he started pastoral ministry.

In fact, to this day, the only time Reverend Therrell and I had verbal exchange was at the Just Peace effort when I greeted him at the end of the proceedings by telling him thanks and told him that it was nice to meet him. Of course, he also cross-examined me at the church trial. Other than that, Reverend Therrell would walk past me at any hearing and would not even make eye contact as if I was the scum of the earth.

After the trial at which I was convicted and we made an appeal, the committee on appeal of the southeastern jurisdiction comprised mainly of professionally trained attorneys. At the annual conference of the New England Conference when Dr. Campbell requested a ruling from the bishop as to whether or not one annual conference can terminate the membership of a clergy member who belonged to a different annual conference, Bishop Devadhar consulted with his conference chancellor, who of course, was also a professionally trained attorney. Finally, when the Committee on Appeals of the southeastern jurisdiction upheld the decision of the Florida Trial Court, the defense appeal was made to the Judicial Council, which was also comprised of professional attorneys. When one considers all these attorneys working on behalf of the church and add in the biased approach of bishops Devadhar and Carter, one could say that the mouse had a greater chance against the lion (in the fable) than I had against that den of lions. It only takes one little cat to take down a mouse, but I found myself in the jaws and claws of several large lions. While this is so, the Book of Discipline was clear that as the respondent, I was not allowed to engage an attorney to represent me during the case. So here I was facing these highly respected and highly regarded set of attorneys, and the Book of Discipline of the United Methodist Church making it clear that I was not allowed to engage an attorney to act on my behalf. At best, I could have an attorney as my assistant counsel, but he/she would be without voice. Even then, there are not many pastors who could have afforded to retain an attorney for an ongoing issue, so this seesaw had me about ten thousand feet in the air within a second of the start of the game. If I attempted to have an attorney respond to the church, it would be considered "out of place," and I would be automatically disqualified from making an appeal if the verdict went against me—as it did. One by one and at every level, they routinely went through the motions of what turned out to be a mockery of a trial.

As if things were not bad enough with that battery of attorneys working against my defense counsel and my team—none of us having legal training—Bishop Carter appointed Bishop Alfred Gwinn to be the presiding officer for the trial. Bishop Gwinn was not particularly known for strong ethics in his role as a presiding officer or even when he served as bishop in the North Carolina Conference. In fact, there is documentation of a case where Bishop Gwinn (while he served actively in the referenced conference) twisted the truth sufficiently to cause a member of the clergy to turn in his credentials. After the fact, he never made any effort to correct the situation or make restitution with the brother whom he had irreparably harmed. Everyone is welcomed to do their own research on this particular case, but I will quote a snippet of a dissenting opinion from a member of the Judicial Council that considered the appeal of another unfortunate member of the clergy. The referenced Judicial Council decision is number 1055, and the dissenting opinion is below. First, let us note how the Judicial Council in that instance responded, in part, to an appeal against unethical, misleading, and deceptive behavior.

Complaint procedures delineated under 362 are available for clergy who choose to assert their fair process rights. We have reviewed all of the parties' submissions. Under the circumstances the Judicial Council would have to make findings of fact to respond to the questions posed. The Judicial Council is not a fact-finding body. There is no indication that there was any element of duress or intimidation that prompted the members' decision to tender his voluntary withdrawal. The questions posed were therefore moot and hypothetical in nature.

Decision

Withdrawal whether under complaint or voluntary is effective at the time it is received. October 27, 2006 Mary A. Daffin and Shamwange P. Kyungu were absent. Keith D. Boyette dissents.

So in the referenced case involving Bishop Gwinn, who turned out to be the presiding officer for my case, was also, at the time, the bishop involved in this referenced case. He was the person who deceived and lied to one of his clergy members resulting in a withdrawal of his ministerial credentials. When he served as a bishop of the North Carolina conference, he indicated to one clergy member of the conference that there was a complaint filed against him. That piece of information (a filed complaint) led the person in question to withdraw voluntarily. After his withdrawal was "sealed," he then realized that there was really no complaint, but the bishop ruled and the Judicial Council affirmed that he withdrew voluntarily so could not be reinstated. Again everyone is welcomed to research the case. Here, the bishop indicates to one of his clergy members that a formal complaint had been filed against him and that the case could potentially go to a church trial. Most of the trials within the Methodist Church are as public as any case in a secular court and so for this reason, several pastors who have been accused would rather surrender their credentials than face the humiliation and embarrassment of a trial. So when told that there was a complaint against him, the pastor in question withdrew his credentials for fear of putting himself and his family through the excruciating mental pain. However, after that pastor agonizingly surrendered his credentials based on the information which Bishop Gwinn had given, it was revealed that there was really no complaint. However, the process of withdrawal was made to be irreversible so that pastor was left out in the cold. Bishop Gwinn never offered an apology and did not help to see if the status could be reversed. Understandably, that pastor took his case to the Judicial Council, which claimed that once a withdrawal of one's ministerial credentials are initiated by the pastor, then that status is irreversible regardless of the circumstances or the reasons. That response reminded me of the Pharisees, who criticized Jesus for healing on the Sabbath. It is kind of amazing how the people of God would still allow law to triumph over truth and grace. If in those circumstances, the Judicial Council was spineless and ruled in favor of the church, what are the odds that they would recognize the blatant corrupted, immoral, and unethical methods which the Florida Conference in tandem with Bishop Devadhar used to steal the grace which Jesus freely offered to me?

I invite you to read the dissenting opinion of Keith Boyette thoroughly in order to see the gross injustice shown to the appellant in that instance. Keep in mind that the presiding bishop (at the time) referred to above is Bishop Alfred Gwinn, and he is now to be the presiding officer (judge) over my case.

Now let us look at why this one member of the Judicial Council dissented from the actions of both bishop Gwinn and his colleagues on the Judicial Council in the North Carolina case.

Dissenting Opinion

This matter turns on the issue of whether the withdrawal of a clergy person from the ordained ministry of the North Carolina Annual Conference was voluntary. The presiding bishop, among other things, ruled that the clergy person "voluntary withdrew from the ministerial office between sessions of the Annual

Conference" and that his "withdrawal was effective immediately and resulted in the forfeiture of his disciplinary right to fair process." In his ruling, the presiding bishop states that the clergy person withdrew from the ordained ministry on July 21, 2005. Initially, the presiding bishop concedes that the clergy person's withdrawal from the ordained ministry was classified by the bishop and the annual conference as a withdrawal under complaint pursuant to 361.3 of the 2004 Discipline. The presiding bishop, in his ruling then states:

After the bishop had deposited with the secretary of the Annual Conference [the clergy person's] letter surrendering his credentials, the bishop informed [the clergy person] by letter dated November 21, 2005 that he had decided to amend the record filed with the secretary to indicate that [the clergy person's] withdrawal was a voluntary withdrawal under 361.2 and 361.4 of The Book of Discipline and not a withdrawal under complaint.

The questions of law asked at the clergy session of the annual conference challenged this amendment of the record. It was the bishop who had originally characterized the clergy person's withdrawal as occurring under complaint. It is apparent from both the questions asked of the bishop and from the amendment of the records of the Annual Conference by the bishop that both the clergy person and the bishop believed that a complaint existed at the time of the clergy person's withdrawal on July 21, 2005. It is also apparent from both the questions asked of the bishop and from the amendment of the records of the Annual Conference by the bishop that it was later determined that no complaint existed on July 21, 2005, when the clergy person delivered his letter of withdrawal. The questions of law delivered to the presiding bishop raise this crucial issue: When a clergy person withdraws upon a representation that a complaint has been filed against him and it is later determined that no complaint existed, what is the impact of the non-existence of the complaint at the time of the withdrawal on the clergy person's withdrawal? The decision of my colleagues concludes that a withdrawal is a withdrawal and that it does not matter whether the clergy person understood that he was withdrawing in response to a complaint which in fact did not exist at the time of his withdrawal. I differ. Those officers of the church who are involved in the administration of the disciplinary process with respect to the conduct of a clergy person must act in good faith and through the communication of accurate information at every step of their supervision of the clergy person. Important rights are in play, and clergy persons as well as those who have grievances against them must be treated with the utmost fairness. The Judicial Council has held that when a clergy person withdraws under complaint, the withdrawal is effective immediately and the clergy person's disciplinary rights terminate immediately. Decisions 691 and 798. However, the Judicial Council has also held that when a withdrawal under complaint occurs under circumstances where the acts outlined in the complaint are barred by the statute of limitations, the withdrawal under complaint is null and void. Decisions 741 and 753. Importantly, the Judicial Council has not held that such withdrawal under complaint is thereby converted to a voluntary withdrawal because of the legal non-existence of the complaint. I see no reason to deviate from this principal where a person withdraws under complaint and then it is determined that no complaint in fact existed at the time of withdrawal as is the case here. Such a withdrawal is not then converted to a voluntary withdrawal. Rather, the withdrawal under complaint is null and void once it is determined that there was no complaint. The annual conference is then free to proceed against the clergy person in whatever way it deems appropriate within the provisions of the Discipline, including processing a complaint that might thereafter be filed. In arriving at this determination, I am not engaging in fact-finding on disputed facts. As I have indicated above, the ruling of the presiding bishop here provides the factual basis for the determination I have made. There is no question that the situation faced by the presiding bishop, the annual conference and the clergy person was fluid and ambiguous on or about July 21. There was nothing inherent in the circumstances presented that required the presiding bishop and the annual conference to act in the fashion it did in the face of such ambiguity. It is the bishop and the annual conference that has the responsibility of ensuring that disciplinary procedures and processes are faithfully followed. In my opinion, that was not done here and I would so hold, declaring the clergy person's withdrawal under complaint null and void, and not thereby converted to a voluntary withdrawal, since there was no complaint at the time of the "withdrawal" and permitting the annual conference to proceed as the Discipline would require under the facts that would then occur. Keith D. Boyette

As we read on about my specific case, we will see instances where Bishop Gwinn made some questionable rulings. As my defense counsel pointed out, his rulings always seemed to be prejudicial toward the church and biased against the defense. Whether it was a pretrial motion or an issue during the actual trial, Bishop Gwinn did not make one ruling in favor of the defense in relation to process or procedure. As such, there was some amount of anxiety among my defense team when he was appointed to be the presiding officer.

Again, it is interesting how there was such a battery of legally trained attorneys working on behalf of the church, while purporting to be neutral. In fact, there was another attorney from the church's end involved in my case. He was the chancellor to the council of bishops. This is the person with whom the council of bishops consult on any legal issues. He appeared unknown and unannounced to the defense on a pretrial conference call arranged by Bishop Gwynn, and his only role in that call was to listen. Other than announcing himself at the beginning, he never said a word. Technically, he was not a party to the case, but somehow the bishop overlooked elementary Christian ethics as well as the separation of powers clause and invited him on. This, of course, helped to make the weight of legal minds doing battle for the church even heavier. If one should therefore establish a figurative picture of the seesaw approach, it is clear that the picture was so unbalanced that the church's team would not just be merely on the floor with the defense going toward the heavens but the church's team would probably be putting a hole into the ground. Later on as the proceedings went by, my defense counsel would make a submission in the form of an appeal or a motion, and after two or three days, we would receive a legally worded response supposedly composed by this top-notch attorney. Once more, I must say that it felt a little flattering that someone of my lowly stature was able to pull out all the giant legal minds from the Methodist Church across the country to do battle against me.

Let us be reminded again that I was unable to bring a legally trained attorney to help me with the process because one of the clauses in the Book of Discipline suggested that this could not happen. So even without a case becoming active, it was clear that the system was set up to favor the church and work against the defense because the defense was just not allowed to utilize the services of an attorney in any way, shape, or form.

As we read further and observe an opinion from an absent member from the Judicial Council, who adjudicated over my own case, it would become clear that the members of the Judicial Council seemed not to have the backbone to be fair, objective, and honest. Somehow they seemed to think that they needed to do that which seemed to be politically correct and pander to the "higher-ups."

Having laid the foundation above, it should not be that difficult to see why it was an uphill climb to obtain fairness and justice in a system that is intrinsically biased. The bishop in Greater New Jersey Conference along with his female district superintendent as well as the female elder in the New England Conference were guilty of the same breach which I had made. Somehow, there was a different outcome and all three of them are still considered to be in good standing within the United Methodist Church. Every attempt which my defense counsel raised to show the breaches of discipline by the leaders of the church was thwarted by the presiding officer working in tandem with the church's counsel as well as the chancellor to the council of bishops who was referenced earlier. Here is one such request.

Below are some very compelling and persuasive arguments which were submitted to the presiding officer which requested him to consider balancing the scales and recognizing the concerns of the defense. However, these arguments did not seem to have borne any weight for him. Where appropriate, I will contextualize each argument as they are mentioned. These first two references illegal activities (knowingly or unknowingly) by the Florida Conference, which clearly established and demonstrated a one-sided investigation.

1.) The Florida Annual Conference later admitted that it acted improperly in placing Rev. Leslie on Involuntary Leave of Absence (See Appendix V), and, further, admitted that it allowed an illegal verbatim to be made of a supervisory session with Rev. Leslie (See Appendix VI). That verbatim was subsequently shared with the Counsel for the Church and the Presiding Officer.

The Bishop's office or the Superintendent's office illegally shared certain contents of Rev. Leslie's supervisory file with the Counsel for the Church. The Supervisory Response, mandated by

363.1, is to be "administrative and pastoral in nature" and "not to be a part of any judicial Motion to Refer the Complaint to The New England Annual Conference

My defense counsel gave the following reasons why the bill of charges brought by the Florida Conference should be set aside and the matter move forward in the New England Conference

In the Matter of the Rev. Errol Leslie

The Respondent hereby petitions the Presiding Officer to set aside the Bill of Charges forwarded by the Committee on Investigation of the Florida Annual Conference under the provisions of 2708.3 of the 2008 Discipline and direct the Complainant to pursue her concerns with the appropriate officials in the New England Annual Conference.

The Rationale
Jurisdictional Matters

1.) The Constitution of the United Methodist Church states unequivocally that the annual conference shall have reserved to it the right to vote on all matters relating to the character and conference relations of its clergy (33).

2.) 604.4 of The Discipline (2012) states that the annual conference shall have power to make inquiry into the moral and official conduct of its clergy members.

3.) 2719.1 states that a clergy member residing beyond the bounds of his or her own conference shall be subject to the procedures of 2701-2718 exercised by the appropriate officials of the conference in which he or she is a member.

4.) 2719.1 specifies that the only exception to this clear policy of The Discipline, requires that three specific conditions be met in order for an exception to be permitted, those requirements being that a clergy member must:

   a.) Reside within the bounds of another annual conference

   b.) Be under appointment or retired within the bounds of that other annual conference

   c.) Agree with the bishops of both conferences that fairness will be better served by carrying forward complaint procedures in that other annual conference

5.) The Rev. Errol Leslie no longer resides within the bounds of the Florida Annual Conference.

6.) Rev. Leslie, by the decision of the Bishop of the Florida Annual Conference and not by his own choice, is no longer serving under appointment within that conference.

7.) By announcing in a letter dated March 12, 2015 that as of June 30, 2015 the appointment of Rev. Leslie within the bounds of the Florida Annual Conference would be discontinued (See Appendix I), the Florida Conference abrogated the agreement that had obtained prior to that point under the terms of 2719.1, and it forfeited its right to adjudicate the subsequent judicial proceedings.

8.) Rev. Leslie notified Bishops Carter and Devadhar, Resident Bishop of the Florida and New England Annual Conferences respectively, in a letter dated September 3, 2015 (See Appendix II), well before the convening of a Committee on Investigation on September 23, 2015 by the Florida Annual

Conference, that he no longer agreed that fairness would be better served by having the complaint procedures go forward in Florida.

9.) The 2008 Discipline, under which the Florida Conference elected to conduct these proceedings, specifies in 2701 that judicial proceedings do not begin until a counsel for the church refers a matter as a judicial complaint to a committee on investigation.

10.) The counsel for the church referred this matter as a judicial complaint to the committee on investigation on August 5, 2015, at which time Rev. Leslie was already living and serving under appointment in the New England Conference. He no longer qualified for the 2719.1 exemption to the presumption that judicial matters must occur in a clergy member's own conference.

11.) Rev. Leslie is a member of the New England Annual Conference and continues to live and serve under appointment in that conference.

12.) Rev. Leslie originally signed a request for proceedings to go forward in Florida without having been permitted to see the complaint against him, despite his request to see it (see JC 974, which states: At the initiation of the supervisory process the respondent has a right not only to examine but to possess the written complaint and any supporting material accompanying it).

13.) The Rev. Gary Spencer, the District Superintendent who helped to draft and presented the document in question to Rev. Leslie for his signature, has testified before the Committee on Investigation that he set a deadline of 12:00 p.m. on August 1, 2014 for Rev. Leslie to choose where the complaint process was to go forward, compelling him to make that choice while still not sharing the signed written complaint against him.

14.) While Rev. Leslie was still without accompaniment by a clergy advocate, he did sign that document under this artificial time constraint, only two days after having been informed of the complaint against him and under pressure from the Superintendent to make up his mind quickly. Rev Leslie was barely able to scan through the document within a five minute meeting and was then deprived the opportunity to keep a copy even though he specifically asked for one.

15.) The actual written complaint was filled with allegations that have never been substantiated by the Church nor been included in the judicial complaint, accusations of which the Respondent was completely unaware at the time his choosing was compelled, and accusations that would have directly impacted his decision about where to pursue the complaint process (JC 974 further states: A respondent cannot make an adequate response to a complaint without being privy to the complaint in its totality).

Fair Process Issues

2.) The Bishop of the Florida Conference erroneously informed Rev. Leslie in a letter dated November 20, 2014 (See Appendix III) that he could only be represented by a member in full connection of the New England Annual Conference in the upcoming judicial process, thus, effectively depriving Rev. Leslie of counsel during a period when he had been illegally placed on Involuntary Leave of Absence by the Florida Annual Conference. No such limitation applies in judicial matters, only in administrative matters.

3.) Rev. Leslie was informed in that same letter from Bishop Carter that he had been placed on Involuntary Leave of Absence without any of the fair process guidelines of The Discipline being followed. (See Appendix IV)

4.) Conversations from the supervisory process and a partial verbatim transcript from a supervisory session, which, according to guidelines mandated by The Discipline, must be saved in Rev. Leslie's supervisory file, were subsequently shared with the counsel for the church, in violation of those same guidelines. (See Appendix VII and VIII)

5.) Material from these protected conversations was also shared with the Committee on Investigation through the testimonies of Rev. Spencer and Rev. Dodge in direct violation of Judicial Council Decision 836. (The reasons these conversations must be protected are spelled out in Appendix IX).

Limiting the Full Range of Possible Penalties

1.) The Florida Annual Conference has no means or authority to monitor or supervise any penalty which may result from judicial proceedings against Rev. Leslie that does not require a surrender of credentials, while the New England Conference does have both the ability and the authority to monitor and implement a full range of possible penalties.

2.) Any factor affecting the ability of the trial court to choose from the full range of penalties specified in 2711.3, including a perception that an annual conference does not have the means to monitor the imposition of a lesser penalty, would deprive the Respondent of a full, fair and impartial disposition of his case.

Refusal to Respond to Previous Attempts at Relief

1.) Judge Anthony Tatti, the chair of the Florida Annual Conference Committee on Investigation, stated in a memo to all parties that he believed a request to move all proceedings to the Respondent's home annual conference was not a matter for the Committee On Investigation to decide, but was a matter for the Presiding Officer to determine, and he further stated that he did not believe that conducting a COI hearing would constitute a waiver of the Respondent's right to have such a petition considered by the Presiding Officer. (See Appendix X)

2.) Bishop Devadhar of the New England Conference stated in a letter dated September 18, 2015 that he did not believe he had jurisdiction to decide upon this matter. (See Appendix XI)

3.) Bishop Carter of the Florida Conference did not respond to a letter from the Respondent sent on September 3, 2015 rescinding his agreement for the judicial processes to go forward in Florida. That letter contained a notice to Bishop Carter that a decision to go ahead with the certification of charges by the committee on investigation three weeks later could trigger the double jeopardy provisions of 2701.2.c, should an appellate body decide at some later point to uphold the jurisdictional challenge of the Respondent. (See Appendix XII)

One very significant show of bias by the presiding officer came about in relation to the exclusion of a witness which the defense wanted to call during the trial. At the committee of investigation and in an attempt to prove her claim that she was a member of the church, the complainant told the committee (COI) that she led a Bible study at the church. I knew that the complainant had not even attended a Bible study and certainly had not led one. The defense wanted to call one witness who attended the Bible study (which I had, in fact led) regularly to make the point that the complainant had not attended any of the Bible study sessions. However, as stated below, the presiding officer did not think that it was a necessary witness. The partial document below represented a section of the defense's opposition to the ruling.

Exclusion of Defense testimony

On December 21, 2015 Bishop Alfred Gwinn, Presiding Officer in the Matter of the Rev. Errol Leslie, ruled that Defense witnesses in the trial of the Rev. Errol Leslie would not be permitted to testify in the guilt/innocence phase of the trial regarding the processes that have led up to the trial. (See Appendix XIII) Specifically, he stated:
...*if (Rev. Leslie) should attempt to testify to the "validity of the charges" which relates to any procedural issues, that is not appropriate testimony for the trial court to hear. Process information is not relevant for the trial court to hear. (Emphasis added)*

Further on the Presiding Officer wrote:

This trial is not about things in the original complaint from the original Complainant. Unless the Complainant testifies to other instances besides those that are in the Bill of Specification and Charges then evidence of other alleged misconduct will be excluded from the trial court.

In excluding a witness who has direct knowledge of a false statement made in the testimony of the Complainant before the COI, a statement intended to make it appear that Rev. Leslie was an irresponsible pastor, putting the needs of the church behind his own, the Presiding Officer ruled:

Testimony as to whether the Complainant led a Bible study is not relevant to the establishment of the Bill of Specification and Charges. Therefore, Lelys Glasse may not testify as to whether the Complainant led a Bible study unless and until the study is put into issue by the Church or the Complainant.

The Defense objects to the ruling of the Presiding Officer on the following grounds:

1. His ruling prevents the Defense from impeaching testimony that was offered before the Committee on Investigation (COI) and which led to the certification of a Bill of Charges against the Respondent. Since there is no opportunity before the COI for parties to crossexamine witnesses, misstatements, untruths and half-truths remain unchallenged. Witnesses before the COI can fashion a narrative that cannot now be examined if the Church chooses not to introduce the same material before the trial court.

2. The certification of a Bill of Charges by the COI is not a thing indifferent. It has enormous prejudicial value when it comes before the trial court. If that certification occurred, in part, on the basis of false testimony, and the Defense is not permitted to demonstrate the errors in that testimony by calling relevant, reliable witnesses, justice cannot be served.

3. The Bishop's ruling severely limits the ability of the Defense to demonstrate the credibility of the Complainant. If the Defense is not permitted to bring forth witnesses who can testify to direct untruths offered before the COI, how will the trial court know whether the witness is truthful in her testimony before the trial court? If the Defense is not permitted to show that the Complainant told one story in her complaint and another before the COI, how will the trial court be able to accurately assess the reliability of the witness? While the Presiding Officer may be right when he states: Testimony as to whether the Complainant led a Bible study is not relevant to the establishment of the Bill of Specification and Charges, he also may be wrong. With all due respect to the Presiding Officer, he was not in the deliberation room of the COI and he does not have knowledge of which portions of the testimony of witnesses before that body were influential in deciding to forward a Bill of Charges and which were not. In any case, the testimony of this witness is absolutely relevant in establishing whether the Complainant testified truthfully before an official body in this judicial process and whether she can be counted upon to testify truthfully before the trial court. Without the ability to call witnesses who can impeach the testimony of the complainant before the COI, the defense is unfairly penalized in its ability to make its case.

4. It appears that the Presiding Officer intends to prevent the trial court from possessing and examining the original complaint. Judicial Council decisions 763 and 777 indicate the indispensability of such a signed complaint for the subsequent judicial processes to be valid. The original signed

written complaint is foundational in the judicial process. This complaint was forwarded to the New England Conference in support of suspending Rev. Leslie for 90 days. It was a focal point in the Supervisory sessions conducted by the Bishop the Florida Conference and his Superintendent. It was read and considered by members of the COI. To deprive the trial court of an opportunity to understand the context out of which the Bill of Charges was issued is to truncate the trial court's ability to fashion a fair and just verdict and penalty.

5. Finally, and most importantly, at no point has there been a forum in which the Respondent has been given an opportunity before an official Church body to respond to the libelous charges that have been leveled at him by the Complainant, charges that played an enormous role in destroying his reputation and led directly to the termination of his ministry in Florida. He has chosen to come to trial in the hope of having a chance to tell his story and respond to numerous lies that have been broadly dispersed by the Complainant, through her original complaint and through slanderous stories she spread among his former congregants. Now the Church proposes that its version of justice can only be accomplished if the trial court is prevented from knowing the full story. A just response by the trial court will be impossible under such circumstances.

Following on the same path, the majority of the witnesses whom we tried to introduce were rejected by the presiding officer working in tandem with the counsel for the church.

CHAPTER 9

New England Bishop Sends
Me to Be Slaughtered

So time moved along, and while I was in a property committee meeting at one of the churches I was serving in my home conference, I received a telephone call from my defense counsel stating that the trial date was set for January 16 of 2016. By this time, my defense team had just about given up on expecting any fairness in response to all the blatant demonstration of injustice which was pointed out. After further developments, I made all the plans and left my congregations in New England, where my clergy membership resided to go for a church trial in the Florida Conference to be tried by a jury of Florida clergy. As I walked into the room, I could not help but observing that Bishop Carter was making a speech as he welcomed and introduced the key persons at the trial.

At 9:05 a.m.:

BISHOP CARTER: Good morning, everyone. Good morning. Good morning. We welcome each of you to the Florida Conference and to this week. We extend our welcome and hospitality to you and are grateful for all those—come on in. We welcome you and those who are serving this week. My name is Ken Carter. I'm the resident Bishop of the Florida area and want to open us with a word of prayer and then introduce our presiding officer, so let us pray. (Prayer offered.)

BISHOP CARTER: It's an honor to introduce our presiding officer for this, Bishop Al Gwinn. (Copied and posted directly from official transcript court—Day one page 12 WASILEWSKI COURT REPORTING)

Now in the Book of Discipline, there is a clause which states that the bishop must have nothing whatsoever to do with the trial court. So here was another breach of discipline which was overlooked. Many of us who have served in the Methodist Church are aware that bishops are generally loved, respected, and revered by clergy and laity alike. If one should speculate, we could assume that Bishop Carter's illegal and unnecessary presence at the introductions was aimed more so at "gaining sympathy" and pick up sentiments for the Florida Conference with such emotion already tainting the potential jurors and working against me two days later. The irony is that as we will see later on in the appeal, the Judicial Council used the same argument to negate a ruling of law made by Bishop Devadhar. The Judicial Council merely stated that bishops are not supposed to even remotely have anything to do with a church trial. The intent of that clause in the Book of Discipline was to prevent the bishops from having any direct impact or influence over any decisions made by the trial court and the members of the Judicial Council all knew that Bishop Carter did not share any verbal opinions with the potential jury pool. However, his physical presence and welcome statement could have had more of an impact on the trial court than anything verbal which he might have said.

Interestingly, in the subsequent clergy session of the New England Annual Conference, my defense counsel asked the question as to whether or not the Florida Conference had the constitutional authority to carry through with the procedures. After the ruling by Bishop Devadhar, the ruling went to the Judicial Council for ratification. The question had nothing to do with the bishop actually impacting or influencing any actions or decisions taken by the trial court. It was a question referencing the laws or constitution of the United Methodist Church and not one referencing any direct actions of the trial court. The Judicial Council in handing down its decision was well aware of the difference but chose to ignore the truth and place sentiment over ethics and justice. They initially ruled that the bishops are not to be a part of any church trial in any way. Perhaps they were unaware that Bishop Carter had opened up the trial court in Florida.

Bishop Devadhar in his response to the question as to whether or not the Florida Conference had the constitutional authority to carry through with the procedures, and of course, after consultation with the attorney who was the chancellor for that conference danced around the subject and gave kind of a ridiculous answer. Below is a draft of the questions asked in the clergy session of the conference by Dr. Scott Campbell and also the response given by Bishop Devadhar.

STATEMENT OF FACTS

At the Clergy Session of the New England Annual Conference on Friday, June 17, 2016, a report was received concerning clergy status which listed a clergy member of the New England Annual Conference as having his conference membership terminated by trial. This clergy was tried by the Florida Annual Conference in January of 2016, where he was found guilty of three charges. The penalty imposed on him was termination of his membership in the New England Annual Conference. The clergy person was serving in a cross conference appointment at the time the complaint was brought, and he was tried under the provisions of Par. 2719.1 of the 2012 Book of Discipline ("2012 Discipline"). The New England Annual Conference clergy session had no authority to vote on the matter and merely received the report. This reply to question of law is submitted pursuant to the provisions of Par. 2609.6 of the 2012 Discipline of the United Methodist Church.

The Judicial Council has jurisdiction over this issue under Pars. 51 and 56.3 of the Constitution of The United Methodist Church and under Par. 2609 of the 2012 Discipline, interpreted by Judicial Council Decision 1244.

QUESTION OF LAW

After receiving this report in question, a clergy member requested a ruling of law from presiding Bishop Sudarshana Devadhar on five (5) questions:

1.) Is the section of Par. 2719.1 that makes an exception to the requirement that a member be subject to judicial proceedings in his or her own annual conference in conflict with Par. 33 of the Constitution of the United Methodist Church?

2.) Do not Judicial Council Decisions 1210, 1244 and 1318, among others, establish the principle that the General Conference cannot delegate powers that are constitutionally reserved to one body to another body without amending the constitution?

3.) Does the constitution authorize an annual conference to revoke the membership of a clergy member of another annual conference?

4.) If the Bishop determines that the cited section of Par. 2719.1 is in conflict with Par. 33 of the Constitution, and is thus, by definition, unconstitutional, what will be the status of Rev. Leslie pending review of this decision of law by the Judicial Council?

5.) If Rev. Leslie is determined to be a member in good standing of the New England Annual Conference while review of this decision of law is pending, is he entitled to receive an appointment in the interim?"

The clergy member asking for the Ruling of Law specifically noted that the decision to refer the matter to the Florida Annual Conference was made in compliance with the 2012 Book of Discipline, Par. 2719.1.

I indicated that I would issue my ruling within thirty (30) days as required by Par. 2609.6.

DECISION OF LAW AND ANALYSIS

I rule that Par. 2719.1 is constitutional and therefore, a clergy member tried, convicted and sentenced by trial court assembled in a different annual conference from the one in which the clergy holds his membership, can have his membership terminated in his conference of membership.

It has been argued that Par. 33 which states in pertinent part: "The annual conference is the basic body in the Church and as such shall have reserved to it the right to vote...on all matters relating to the character and conference relations of its clergy members...," means that an annual conference where a clergy is not a member, cannot vote on his conference relations. I disagree with that interpretation as it applies to the trial situation.

Par. 33 specifically refers to the annual conference's reserved right to vote on these matters, (emphasis added). In the instance of a trial and imposition of penalty, no annual conference votes. Even if the trial of the clergy at issue had taken place in New England and the same penalty had been imposed, the clergy session of annual conference still would not have had the right to vote to affirm or reject the penalty.

Par. 2711 describes the powers of the trial court. Clearly, the annual conference either as a full body or by its clergy sessions is not a part of this voting or decision making in trial matters.

Additionally, the Judicial Council has affirmed the finality of a trial court ruling in Judicial Council Decision 1201 which states: "The meaning of the Discipline is clear in Par. 2711. 'The trial court shall have full power to try the respondent.' It does so within the boundaries of the Discipline for determining guilt, and the trial court alone has the authority to reach a determination with regard to a penalty in the circumstance where it has made a finding of guilt. Only the trial court has the authority to set a penalty, and it must do so within the range of options specified by the Discipline (Par. 2711.3). No other entity outside of the operations of the trial court can usurp it, modify it, supplant it, or enter a suggestion into the decision by the trial court as the Discipline makes clear."

Par. 2719.1 does not describe an action at all similar to those actions ruled unconstitutional in Judicial Council Decisions 1210, 1244, and 1318. Rather it simply provides a venue which has been agreed to by the bishops of both conferences invoked and the respondent. That is exactly what occurred in the instant matter. There was no usurping of authority from the New England Annual Conference in violation of Par. 33.

My decision that Par. 2719.1 is constitutional makes the remaining questions moot. If, however, the Judicial Council rules Par. 2719.1 unconstitutional, then I believe that all trials ever held under this provision must be ruled invalid, and new trials must be granted to all respondents whose trial occurred in an annual conference other than the one where the respondent had his/ her membership.

DECISIONS SUMMARY

Question #1—Par. 2719.1 is not a violation of Par. 33 and is therefore constitutional.

Respectfully submitted,
Sudarshana Devadhar, Bishop
New England Annual Conference

Bishop Devadhar states in his preamble that the New England Conference "had no authority to vote...but merely received the report." It could also be argued, technically, that the penalty which the Florida trial court imposed was illegal since it does not fall within the range of the penalties suggested by the Book of Discipline. The Florida trial court ironically ended my appointment in the New England Conference, but that is not listed as one of the options for penalty in the Book of Discipline. There is an option to remove the credentials of a clergy person, but there is no option to end an appointment while the credentials of that clergyperson remains intact (as was the case in this instant). Bishop Devadhar's statement would have been in direct contradiction to what the constitution of the church explains in number 33.

As hard as Bishop Devadhar and whoever counseled him tried to dance around the truthful answer to the questions asked, Judicial Council ruling number 580 was unequivocal in its ruling on a similar case from 1987. Here is the full ruling below with the key section placed in bold print for emphasis.

DECISION NUMBER 580–April 1987

Digest of Case

In July of 1986, M.A. Kunkle, a ministerial member of the West Ohio Conference, was found guilty by a trial court of immorality under Par. 2621 of the 1984 Discipline. He appealed to the Court of Appeals of the North Central Jurisdiction. That court ruled that the procedures of the West Ohio Conference in investigating and trying the case were "so flawed that the material the trial court had before it was so tainted that it was impossible for the trial court to arrive at a fair and just decision." The case was remanded to the West Ohio Conference for a new trial, with instructions to the conference to pay specified benefits to the accused.

The accused appealed the ruling to the Judicial Council, asking that all charges be dismissed. The West Ohio Conference filed a cross-appeal which asked the Judicial Council to reverse the decision of the Court of Appeals and reinstate the verdict of the trial court.

At an open hearing before the Judicial Council on April 23, 1987, Roy Webster appeared for the accused and Eugene Frazer for the West Ohio Conference.

Evidence heard by the trial court is not within the purview of the Judicial Council, except for purposes of determining sufficiency. We may rule only on matters of law, as related to procedures of the Court of Appeals. The Judicial Council finds that the issues of law raised by the Court of Appeals in its ruling are valid, and that the court was acting within its authority to order a new trial.

The Court of Appeals was also within its authority in instructing the West Ohio Conference to pay the accused benefits, as required by Par. 2624.2(i). An Annual Conference may not escape this responsibility by arbitrarily placing a minister on involuntary leave of absence instead of calling the Committee on

Investigation into session and proceeding to trial in timely fashion if trial is warranted.

The Court of Appeals was in error on one point, although it does not affect the outcome of this particular case. Citing Par. 2626.1, the court expressed its opinion that the "process and trial should have been carried out in the Louisville Conference," where the accused was serving under special appointment by the bishop of the West Ohio Conference, instead of in the West Ohio Conference, where he is a member.

Par. 2626.1 provides that "any ministerial members residing beyond the bounds of the conference in which membership is held shall be subject to the procedures of Pars. 2620-2625 exercised by the appropriate officers of the conference in which he/ she resides." Interpreting this paragraph to include investigation and trial among those procedures places it in direct conflict with Par. 36 of the Constitution, which gives to an Annual Conference the right "to vote on all matters relating to the character and conference relations of its ministerial members." To that extent, Par. 2626.1 is unconstitutional, void, and of no effect. Though an accusation may originate in a conference where a minister resides but does not hold membership, the investigation and trial, if any, must be conducted by the Annual Conference of which the minister is a member, since that process may result in a change in ministerial relations. This does not prejudice the right of an accused to request a change of venue.

The decision of the Court of Appeals remanding the case for a new trial and ordering the payment of benefits is sustained. The opinion of the court concerning the proper venue for ministerial trials is not sustained.

The West Ohio Conference must convene the Committee on Investigation within 60 days from the date of this decision (April 24, 1987). If charges are filed by the committee, a written copy of the charges and detailed specifications must be supplied promptly to the accused. (Pars. 2622, 2623.3)

April 1987

DECISION 1331

This ruling by the Judicial Council in 1987 is the precedent that my defense counsel referenced in several of his briefs at every level and somehow and mysteriously, none of the appeal court members were able to understand that rudimentary and elementary clause in the ruling. Please note the use of the word *must* in relation to which conference the trial, if any, shall be held. In the above referenced ruling, paragraph 36 is now paragraph 33 while paragraph 2626.1 is now paragraph 2719.1

I invite you to compare the language of my defense counsel's brief (below) to the language used by the Judicial Council in the bolded paragraph above. How could the Court of Appeals for the South Eastern Jurisdiction and the Judicial Council both ignore this argument by the defense? Instead of seeing and acting on the truth that would have stared them in the face, both bodies decided to retry the case. At both levels of appeal, the issue of trial venue was totally ignored even though it was raised by my defense counsel on both occasions.

Excerpt from Judicial Council ruling #508

Par. 2626.1 provides that "any ministerial members residing beyond the bounds of the conference in which membership is held shall be subject to the procedures of Pars. 2620-2625 exercised by the appropriate officers of the conference in which he/she resides." Interpreting

194

this paragraph to include investigation and trial among those procedures places it in direct conflict with Par. 36 of the Constitution, which gives to an Annual Conference the right "to vote on all matters relating to the character and conference relations of its ministerial members." To that extent, Par. 2626.1 is unconstitutional, void, and of no effect. Though an accusation may originate in a conference where a minister resides but does not hold membership, the investigation and trial, if any, must be conducted by the Annual Conference of which the minister is a member, since that process may result in a change in ministerial relations. This does not prejudice the right of an accused to request a change of venue.

<u>Excerpt from Defense Counsel's brief</u>

Section A—2719.1 is Unconstitutional

Par 33 of the Constitution states unambiguously: The annual conference... shall have reserved to it the right to vote... on all matters relating to the character and conference relations of its clergy members. 2719.1 does not comply with this clear directive of the Constitution. The annual conference is given the exclusive right in the Constitution to adjudicate matters relating to the character and conference relations of its members. There is no provision in the Constitution for an annual conference to delegate this responsibility to any other body, nor can the General Conference ignore the clear mandate of the Constitution without amending the appropriate section. "Reserved to it" means that it is the exclusive province of the annual conference to which a clergy member belongs to

**deal with matters relating to the character and
conference relations of that member**

This argument was made both in the briefs as well as the oral
arguments presented to the Court of Appeals and to the Judicial Council.
However, in spite of the very striking similarities in the language of my
defense counsel and the language of the 1987 Judicial Council, this ruling
number 580 by the highest court of the United Methodist Church was
seemingly overruled by a subsequent meeting of that same body. The same
argument was used by several persons who wrote briefs in relation to
Bishop Devadhar's ruling of law. However, it was countered by the
referenced clause from the Book of Discipline which states that Bishops
should not have anything to do with trials. If that is truly the case, why
would Bishop Carter be asked to do the opening and welcome at the trial
when there were so many other clergy persons working right there in the
Florida Conference office who could have done the same? The truth is
that standing all by itself, there was nothing wrong with what Bishop Carter
did even if it was—as I suspect—meant to win the sentiment of those who
would eventually serve on the jury. However, Bishop Devadhar's authority
to rule on the questions asked was not anymore wrong or different from
Bishop Carter doing the opening at the trial in Florida. Again, we see an
imbalance and abuse of power where the presiding officer who presumably
knows the "ins and outs" of the Book of Discipline did not rule Bishop
Carter's presence and participation out of order.

There were a number of things relating to the trial court which would
be worth being put in perspective. Firstly, my counsel had requested that
the trial be a closed one, but Rev. Jay Therrell, the counsel for the church
determined that he wanted it to be an open trial. This essentially means
that it would be as public as any secular court trial and all the information
would be available to everyone all over the world. As such, the morning
following the verdict and sentencing, the United Methodist News had the
story on the Internet. Bishop Devadhar posted a separate story on the
website of the New England Conference. This fed into several separate
websites related to or connected with the United Methodist Church. As
such, by the end of the week, I was getting telephone calls from all over

the world about what had happened to me. The emotions ranged between anger, disappointment, surprise but for the most part, I felt support, sympathy etc. It really never had to be a public trial, and the outcome or consequence would not have been any different, but Reverend Therrell determined that to "add insult to injury," he wanted to "embarrass me and send me on my way to obscurity in the wilderness to die of hunger and thirst." Of course, once this information is on the Internet, the chances of picking up an appointment in another denomination would be "slim to none." Reverend Therrell's motive was supported by district superintendent Gary spencer who made sure that a public announcement was made to the congregation of the Palm Bay United Methodist Church where I was serving at the time of the incident.

Via one call—tell-all telephone calls—the announcement informed the congregation that the trial date had been set, that it was a trial that was open to the public, and that everyone was welcomed to attend the session. Prior to this Dr. Spencer had had a number of meetings with the congregation of the church as well as with appropriate committees and he had come under a lot of fire from the congregants who still believed in my call to ministry and who thought that the administration of the conference could have handled things much differently. Someone even used the term *overreaction* when they described the response of the annual conference. Perhaps in Dr. Spencer's mind, inviting the entire congregation to witness the trial would validate his style as they would hear from the witnesses how highly "immoral" I was and that I was essentially "the scum of the earth." However, to his disappointment but not surprising to me, no one from the congregation wasted their time to attend the trial with the exception of the one person—a retired pastor—who came at the invitation of the defense counsel to speak on my behalf and to plead my case to the jury of peers and ministerial colleagues in relation to the penalty. In fact, he was able to testify that the complainant had personally told him that her motive for reporting my behavior was to "destroy me," and seemingly, the Florida Conference was willing to help her in the process.

The fact that no one from the Palm Bay UMC showed up for the trial did not change any motive on Dr. Spencer's part so when the trial was over and the sentencing was announced, he thought it necessary to convene a meeting of the congregation through the pastor who was then serving the church. At this meeting, he would tell them all what the outcome of the trial was notwithstanding the fact that this public information was available for the whole world to see. This might have been still another effort for him to feel vindicated because even if the trial was one-sided and biased—as it turned out to be—a guilty verdict would "prove" that the church was justified in following through with the process as they did and all those who supported me would jump on the other side. I would note here that the announcement at the church regarding the meeting at which the verdict and penalty would be announced was made at midafternoon on the day of the penalty phase. However, the penalty was not officially announced until 7:00 p.m. that evening. One has to wonder if the penalty was a foregone conclusion and Dr. Spencer had access to that information. The mood of the process and trial was such that he would not have been enthusiastic about telling the congregational meeting that the penalty was minimal if this was how it turned out to be. Whereas there is no evidence that Dr. Spencer definitely knew what the outcome was going to be, I cannot help but speculate that it was that confidence that led him to have the announcement regarding the meeting made prematurely.

Of course, I was not at that meeting, but my understanding is that Dr. Spencer got "peppered" again and was under more fire for the way in which the congregation perceived the way that I was treated. So the anger at the conference from the majority of the congregation which started in August of 2014 was not quelled even up to January of 2016. Three years later and even now when I speak with persons individually, they would share that they are still angry.

It turned out that two witnesses called by the church would not have been able to attend and give live testimonies. Hence, arrangements were made to have them testify via video ahead of time.

One of the witnesses, Dr. Althea Spencer-Miller, who even though she was called as a witness for the church, was able to see through the unethical approach and vindictive intent of the counsel for the church. Therefore she tried to give a fairer picture of the situation in her deposed testimony, a testimony which would have been helpful to the defense if it were left raw and unedited. However, those "pro-defense" sections of Rev. Spencer Miller's testimony were edited out.

The second witness for the church who was asked to give a videotaped testimony was Rev. David Dodge who was in the process from the very beginning. In his testimony, Reverend Dodge indicated that he had not heard or experienced any remorse from me throughout the whole process. Having heard him say that, Dr. Campbell, my defense counsel asked him to explain an e-mail, which on day 1 he had sent to his counterpart in the New England Conference stating that *"Errol repeatedly expressed remorse over the situation."* Because Dr. Campbell made a reference to the e-mail, which would demonstrate Reverend Dodge's lack of integrity, Rev. Jay Therrell became furious and described this questioning by Dr. Campbell as a "gotcha moment." Needless to say, Reverend Therrell edited out that section of the deposed testimony as he did other sections which would have helped the defense, and he had the jury hear only the parts which were harmful to the defense but helpful to the church's arguments. Equally he omitted sections of Rev. Althea Spencer-Miller's testimony which would have helped the cause of the defense.

A few days before the trial was set to start, Dr. Campbell had actually asked Reverend Dodge for a copy of the e-mail and Reverend Dodge claimed that he was unable to find it on his hard drive. As you will see in my personal brief to the Judicial Counsel, I found it hard to believe that someone in that position would not have been careful to safely guard important documents with a pending process which would turn out to be so crucial. I mentioned in my brief that that response from Reverend Dodge was at best irresponsible and at worst unethical. Either on his own thoughts or under guidance from Reverend Therrell, he decided that he was not going to provide an e-mail which would demonstrate in his own words that I had expressed remorse from day 1. I mentioned earlier that when we had the meeting with the Just Peace representative I used the opportunity to ask the members of the Palm Bay United Methodist Church who were represented at that forum to please share my regrets and apologies with the congregation. That was, in fact, the closest I would come to having an opportunity to honestly express these sentiments to the congregation since I was instantly banned from even stepping on the church grounds after the report was made and the letter of complaint handed in. That request for forgiveness made to the congregation through the two representatives was made in the presence of Reverend Therrell, the counsel for the church, as well as Reverend Dionne Hammond, his assistant counsel. However, during his closing arguments Reverend Therrell indicated to the jury that it was only during my testimony at the trial itself that he had heard me express any remorse.

> *Respondent's counsel and Reverend Leslie himself have tried to paint the picture that all the people who have testified against him, including Ms. Hendricks and Gary Spencer and David Dodge, have either misremembered things or really, quite honestly, out-and-out lied. I find it interesting that what they are trying to say is that they all are wrong, they all have lied, they all have misremembered and that Reverend Leslie is the only one who is telling the truth. I'm pleading with you not to fall for this false narrative. The respondent and his team has tried to demonstrate that he is remorseful, and that may very well be the case. But I am here today to tell you I have been with this process for 15 months. I was asked to serve in this role by Bishop Carter in November of 2014, and yesterday and today are the first time I have ever heard one hint of remorse or regret from Reverend Leslie. As I demonstrated yesterday when I cross-examined Reverend Leslie, when the chair of the Florida Conference Committee on Investigation, a circuit judge for the state of Florida, asked Reverend Leslie, and I quote, "Do you believe the Palm Bay United Methodist Church has been harmed as a result of this incident," instead of taking responsibility for his actions and expressing remorse, Reverend Leslie said, and I quote directly from the transcript, "Judge, I believe that Palm Bay United Methodist Church, United Methodist Church has been harmed because of the actions of Dr. Spencer." He blamed Gary Spencer. (Trial day 2, page 178, Waleski Court reporting)*

He indicated something similarly the very day after the efforts to have a just resolution through Just Peace. It is contained in a letter which he sent to Bishop Devadhar the day after that meeting. In that letter, he indicated to Bishop Devadhar that throughout the entire Just Peace meeting, he did not hear me express remorse; neither was it seen in my demeanor. Was it a lapse in Reverend Therrell's memory, or was it blatant dishonesty? Once more it was very clear that Reverend Therrell was prepared to sell his soul in order to see the end of my ministry in the United Methodist Church. Thankfully, his letter was countered by a response by Dr. Campbell, my defense counsel. In his letter to Bishop Devadhar, he indicated that I was remorseful.

On the morning following the unsuccessful Just Peace efforts, I flew to Connecticut in order to meet with the joint staff parish relations committee of the two churches that I was going to serve. I remember getting on a 6:00 a.m. flight, and after picking up the rental car, I drove to the hotel, which I had reserved for my accommodation. As I pulled into the parking lot and while still sitting in my car, I received a call from my defense counsel in which he told me that Reverend Therrell had e-mailed a letter to Bishop Devadhar, requesting him not to give me an appointment. This e-mail infuriated the normally calm and soft-spoken Reverend Scott Campbell, and he responded accordingly. As you read the e-mail from Reverend Therrell, which was sent within hours after he emphatically declined to offer anything to the Just Peace Table but the surrendering of my credentials, the reader would be able to see that the person who was acting in the name of the church and in the name of God was behaving like a bloodthirsty vampire who had gotten out of control. He was hoping that Bishop Devadhar would satisfy this thirst.

VIA US & ELECTRONIC MAIL
Bishop Sudarshana Devadhar Boston Episcopal Area
Post Office Box 249
Lawrence, Massachusetts 01842-0449
Re: In the Matter of: Rev. Errol E. Leslie,
Respondent

Dear Bishop Devadhar:

Grace and peace to you in the name of our Lord and Savior, Jesus Christ! I am writing to you in my capacity as Counsel for the Church in the above referenced matter. As you know, Rev. Errol Leslie will no longer have an appointment in the Florida Annual Conference as of July 1, 2015. My understanding is that he is being considered for an appointment in the New England Conference over which you preside.

As you may know, yesterday a just resolution process was conducted in this matter, and sadly it did not come to a resolution. Accordingly, the matter has been returned to Presiding Bishop Al Gwinn for us to move toward a trial. Therefore, I am writing to request that you place Rev. Errol Leslie on suspension pending trial pursuant to paragraph 2704.2(c) of The Book of Discipline of The United Methodist Church (2012). To place Rev. Leslie on suspension pending trial under this provision requires a majority of the executive committee of the New England Conference Board of Ordained Ministry would have to concur with you.

Should you decide not to place Rev. Leslie on suspension pending trial, I am formally requesting that Rev. Leslie be placed on involuntary leave. Based on my experience of Rev. Leslie during yesterday's just resolution process, I saw very little, if any, evidence of contrition, remorse, or repentance on his part. I do not believe it is in the best interests for a local church to have Rev. Leslie as their pastoral leader in his compromised state. I also do not think Rev. Leslie and his family can find recovery and healing in the midst of serving/leading a local church—something that is challenging for clergy and family that are in a healthy spiritual, emotional, and mental state.

Thank you for considering my request. I stand ready to assist you, your Cabinet, the Executive Committee of the New England Conference Board of Ordained Ministry, or the Conference Relations Committee should you need me to do so. God bless you!

Cc: Bishop Ken Carter, Florida Episcopal Area Rev. Scott Campbell, Counsel for the Respondent 4118 Coronado Parkway • Cape Coral, FL 33904 239.542.4051 • Fax239.542.5076 www.capecoralfirst.org

Needless to say, Reverend Campbell fired back immediately as he realized that the counsel for the church was now stepping way over the line and going past his place. He sent the following letter to Bishop Devadhar in response.

Bishop Sudarshana Devadhar
Episcopal Leader of the New England Annual
Conference
June 24, 2015

Dear Bishop Devadhar,

I am both astonished and dismayed at the content of
the letter that Rev. Jay Therrel, Counsel for the Church
in the Florida Annual Conference's proceedings
against Rev. Errol Leslie, forwarded to you and to
others yesterday. His characterization of Reverend
Leslie as showing "very little, if any, evidence of
contrition, remorse or repentance" is inaccurate and
untrue. It is a subjective opinion of one who met Rev.
Leslie for the first time on Monday and has never had
so much as a single personal conversation with him. It
is further the opinion of one who from the beginning
of this process has asserted that only the surrender of
Rev. Leslie's credentials would suffice to demonstrate
his true remorse. Contrary to his description, Rev.
Leslie has expressed over and over again, even in the
face of blatantly false charges and lie after lie directed
toward him by the complainant, remarkable restraint
and a continuing willingness to accept full
responsibility for his own actions and the harm that his
actions have precipitated. He has been honest and
forthright in his conver sations with the leadership of
the Florida Annual Conference and he has fully
cooperated with every single requirement that has been
placed upon him by those leaders. He has done all that
has been asked of him with grace and dignity.

I will not attempt to discuss what transpired during
Monday's just resolution process because we agreed
that we would not share the specific content of that
meeting beyond the circle of trust. I am dismayed that

Rev. Therrell has, in my opinion, violated the explicit confidentiality agreement into which we entered at the beginning of Monday's process. It was agreed by all parties and a document was signed stating that nothing that took place in our search for a just resolution would be used in the future prosecution of the case. Less than 24 hours later, Rev. Therrell offered his own impressions of the words and demeanor of Rev. Leslie, garnered from the meeting on Monday, and sought to use what had transpired in that meeting against Rev. Leslie. His statement that his observations were based on what he saw "at yesterday's just resolution process" was, in my opinion, a violation of both the letter and the spirit of the agreement that was signed at the outset of our time together.

I am also at a loss to understand how it is within the purview of a Counsel for the Church to advise the Bishop of another annual conference regarding appointment matters. I believe that in attempting to influence the Bishop of New England in this way Rev. Therrell has exceeded his Disciplinary authority. He has no standing to make a formal request for a change in the membership status of a pastor in another annual conference. His authority extends to carrying forward the judicial process in the Florida Annual Conference related to the Reverend Errol Leslie. It does not extend to inserting himself, unbidden, into appointive matters in another annual conference. The Disciplinary paragraph he cites in his letter gives no such role to the Counsel for the Church.

Additionally, Rev. Therrell's unsolicited observations about the "spiritual, emotional and mental state" of a family he does not know were entirely inappropriate. He has not counseled these persons and he is not their pastor. He is, in fact, their adversary in this process. Likewise, his concern for the wellbeing of a local church in the New England Conference is misplaced. Other very capable persons in New England are fully prepared to carry out the oversight of ministries charged to their care.

We on the defense team vigorously protest both the content of the letter and the violations of appropriate boundaries that it represents.

In Christ, Scott Campbell
Counsel for the Respondent

Reverend Therrell was a prosecutor before he entered ministry, and one does not have to be an attorney to know that part of the strategy of prosecutors is to appeal to the emotions of the jury by making the accused look as horrible as they possibly can. There is nothing that will anger a jury like a perception that the defendant has no remorse and does not seem to care about whatever the violation was in which he/she was involved. In a secular court of law it is normal to try and portray a defendant in that way—even if unethically done; but in the church and in a church trial, one would expect honesty, integrity, and the demonstration of Christian values which Jesus taught. As Dr. Larry Lake indicates in one of his briefs to the Judicial Council, the unethical behavior of Dr. Spencer, Reverend Therrell, and Reverend reinforced by the "don't care" attitude of the presiding officer is not any different in the eyes of God than any sinful acts in which I was engaged. Below is a copy of the elusive e-mail written by Reverend Dodge which Dr.

Campbell eventually had to retrieve from the assistant to the bishop in the New England Conference. This e-mail was referenced earlier in this memoir.

Well friends, it has been a long, but fruitful day. Gary Spencer and I met with Errol Leslie for an hour and a half this afternoon. We explained to him the nature of the complaint and he shared that the complaint is accurate in regards to his involvement with the complainant.

It is Gary's and my expectation that Rev. Leslie will surrender his credentials but he asked for some time to consider his options and to determine how to handle his financial obligations. Thus, I told him we would move forward on determining a date for the supervisory response. If he does surrender credentials before the selected date we would then cancel the supervisory response.

Gary explained to Rev. Leslie that he is not to initiate any contact with church members and he is to clear out his office in a timely manner. Gary will continue to monitor that progress. We determined that neither Rev. Leslie, nor his wife, Kaye, who is the church secretary, are signers for the church's checking account He does have a pastor's discretionary fund for which only he signs. He turned over that checkbook to Gary.

Rev. Leslie was very cooperative throughout our conversation and repeatedly expressed his remorse over this situation.

I have notified our Director of Clergy Excellence who has conferred with the chair of our Board of Ordained Ministry. A conference call is scheduled for 10:00 Thursday morning to act on the request for suspension.

I also notified our communications director, Gretchen Hastings. She is expecting a call from the communications director of the New England Conference so that statements can be prepared that will be in harmony with one another.

Gary and I also met with the SPRC. They were very surprised and shocked. It is apparent that they have a lot of appreciation for both Rev. and Mrs. Leslie.

Plans are in place for Gary and I to be at the two services on Sunday to make the announcement regarding the complaint and the suspension. Gary will do the early service. He is unavailable for the 11:00 service due to a charge conference scheduled at another church that morning. So, I will make the announcement at the conclusion of that service. Gary will return to the church as soon as his charge conference is completed so that he can be present with me following the service as we seek to provide a safe place for people to deal with their emotional responses to the announcement.

Tomorrow I will construct the letters that will go to Rev. Leslie and to Ms. Hendricks and will explain the process. I will send copies to Bishop Devadhar and Rev. Robinson-Johnson. As soon as a date is established for the supervisory response 1 will notify you of that, also.

Thank you, Erica, for the sample letter to use with Rev. Leslie regarding Para. 2719.1 will correct the names and email that to Gary for Rev. Leslie's signature.

I believe that captures the activities of the day. Please let me know if there any questions or any further suggestions.

Blessings,
Rev. David A. Dodge

Nothing has been altered in this e-mail except for highlighting the section referring to my expressions of remorse, and this is just for emphasis

There were some other "secular" strategies which Reverend Therrell used to place me in a bad light. For example, in his questioning of me he wanted to know if I could explain how or why the congregation's attendance dropped from an average of 140 to 90 per Sunday. That question came out of nowhere and was not ruled irrelevant by the presiding officer even though it had nothing to do with the trial itself. Interestingly, when on the other hand my defense counsel pointed out to the jury that as many as 77 new members were added to the congregation during the six years I served there, Reverend Therrell was able to negate that by mentioning that these were just members on paper but meant nothing in reality. At that time Reverend Therrell served in Cape Coral, so I am not quite sure how he was able to determine that these numbers were on paper only except that he wanted to discredit any positive aspects of my ministry which were highlighted by Dr. Campbell. In another setting, I could have reminded him about how race affects and impacts persons who will attend or leave a church when a pastor of color is appointed to a predominantly white congregation. In a different setting I could also have told him how the ratio of the congregation changed from 70 percent White and 30 percent Black to 80 percent Black and 20 percent White within five years of my going to the church.

When Reverend David Calhoun, my district superintendent from the New England Conference, testified to my character, ministry and work in that conference in just a six-month period, Reverend Therrell once more decided to discredit the testimony and make it appear to be insignificant by suggesting to the jury that I was just being "on my best behavior" as an act of drama in response to the situation in which I found myself. Among other things, that was very painful for me to hear. I had never been one to "put on a show." I have always given sincere and enthusiastic pastoral services. It was hard because I thought about a complainant who pursued me, and I failed miserably and was not strong enough to resist. She then played the victim game successfully, and the church counsel and other leaders bought that while suggesting that I was being theatrical.

Reverend Therrell also used the opportunity to discredit any strong witnesses which my defense was able to bring forward. When the son of the complainant sat in the witness stand on my behalf, Reverend Therrell's first question to him was whether or not he had ever been to prison which in fact he had. However, he did explain that all the adults in his family had gone to prison because the complainant had told a vicious lie about her ex-husband and suggested to the police that the older kids were party to the "crime" that never happened.

It just so happened that one of our other schoolmates who lived in the Palm Bay area was also a witness on behalf of the defense. She happened to have had several conversations with the complainant who had also implicated her (the witness) as having an affair with me. Reverend Therrell's first question to her was whether or not she had threatened to strangle the complainant. Her response was that her statement then was said "tongue in cheek" because she thought that the complainant was really going overboard in trying to scandalize me in the community.

I mentioned earlier how key pieces of evidence which would have been helpful to the defense were omitted from the trial court. One such example was the original letter of complaint. At every step in the process this letter of complaint was produced and used to formulate the case against me. It was safe for the church to use this letter at all the other levels because there would not have been an opportunity to question or cross-examine the complainant about the many blatant lies which she placed in her story. On the other hand, those who believed her full story would buy the argument that she was really a victim and that she was sexually abused. It is interesting how Reverend Therrell, the counsel for the church, looked at that letter and included sexual abuse as one of the original four charges brought against me. By the time the process got to the Committee on Investigation, this charge was dropped because at least some of those members were able to look beyond the allegations and see the truth. Even though this original letter of complaint was used at every level of the process, Reverend Therrell cleverly and astutely ensured that it was not shown to the jury comprising my peers and colleagues. This is the forum at which the complainant could be questioned and cross-examined. A cross-examination based on the letter of complaint would easily have shown the gross exaggeration and lies which she told and at the very least would bring her motive into question. The original letter of complaint is referenced above.

It is important to keep in mind that in the first phase of the trial, there was a unanimous vote by the jury to convict me of the three charges which were brought against me. This was partially so because the facts were there and the evidence was clear that I had been engaged in an extramarital affair for a period of three months. In addition to that, my defense counsel and I agreed that I would admit to the charges and then wait for the penalty phase to make our case and explain the circumstances which led me to this kind of activity. However, when the penalty phase ended there were four persons who voted against ending my ministry in the United Methodist Church. One would think that if four persons who were convinced that I was guilty could decide that a lighter penalty would be more appropriate, one wonders if there would not have been three more who would move in that direction if key pieces of evidence, including the original complaint were not omitted. For example, what difference might it have made if the jury had seen the elusive e-mail which Reverend Dodge claimed he could not find and which Bishop Gwinn did not allow into the trial as evidence? What might have happened if the original letter of complaint which started the whole process was not withheld from the jury?

The very elusive e-mail referenced above was not allowed in the trial either. So while Reverend Therrell in Tandem with the presiding officer decided to hold back that key piece of evidence which stated in Reverend Dodge's own words that on day 1, I repeatedly expressed remorse, the same Reverend Therrell who helped to hide this piece of evidence told the jury of the trial court that he had not heard the words "I am sorry" or any other expression of remorse from me up until that point. Notwithstanding the acknowledgment of my own sinfulness, Reverend Therrell and his partners in dishonesty could do well with the processing of the passage from proverbs 6:16–19:

> There are six things which Jehovah hateth; Yea seven which are an abomination to Him. 'Haughty eyes; a lying tongue, and hands that shed innocent blood; A heart that deviseth wicked purposes, Feet that are swift in running to mischief, a false witness that utters lies, and he that soweth discord among brethren.

So the closing arguments end and the presiding officer wraps up the session and sends the jury off to duty to deliberate on the case. It was a very long three-plus-hour wait, and it appeared longer because every question which the jury sent back to the presiding officer suggested strongly that they were planning to nail me to the cross and nail me good. Needless to say, when we were called in for the verdict on the penalty, there was a 9–4 decision to terminate my ministry in the United Methodist Church. During the ensuing discussion, my defense counsel indicated to the presiding officer that he intended to appeal the case. Within seconds of the reading of the verdict, there was a reminder from the counsel for the church through the presiding officer to my defense counsel and my New England district superintendent that Bishop Devadhar would not be allowed to appoint me as a lay pastor or in any other pastoral capacity for the next two years. After a few exchanges, the trial came to an end, and my fate in the United Methodist Church seemed to be sealed.

CHAPTER 10

My Worst Fears Become Real

When I went to my hotel room that night following the penalty phase, I was extremely despondent. I had given all my life to serving the church. At the time it was thirty-eight years of faithful ministry. I committed an outright and blatant sin and was not afforded the opportunity of a pardon. It just so happened that Reverend Dr. David Calhoun, my New England district superintendent stayed at the same hotel as I did. We got back there about the same time, but he spent quite some time in his room before he finally came and knocked on my room door and asked me if I would like to join him for dinner at a restaurant. I found it strange that he invited me and not my wife, who was also staying there with me. Immediately I became paranoid and began to speculate that he might have been speaking with Bishop Devadhar to give him an update and that the news was not good from the New England end. As we sat down at the table, his first question to me was, "So, Errol, what are you going to do?" That question just confirmed my worst fears. There was not going to be an appointment of any kind in New England. So I saw myself, for the second time in fifteen months, packing up and leaving a parsonage where I was quite comfortable and leaving congregations that I loved and that loved me. The remainder of the conversation indicated just that, and of course, I was not able to eat. By the following morning, the information was already in the United Methodist electronic news—not surprisingly one-sided—and it felt like salt was already being rubbed into my wound. By the time I checked into a separate hotel on the evening after, I was beginning to get sympathetic texts and phone calls from my parishioners in the New England

Conference. Bishop Devadhar had done what bishops were expected to do and sent a team of "counselors" to both congregations to "break the news to them." In the process, they were asked not to make any contact at all with me claiming that any such contact could jeopardize my chances of a successful appeal. In hindsight that reminded me of Reverend Gary Spencer who had told me that I had to sign the agreement within three days to have the process take place in the Florida Conference. This was the same bishop who had set up a telephone conference among Reverend Calhoun, himself, and myself with the claim that this three-way meeting was going to be strictly pastoral, so there was no need for my defense counsel to be a part of that meeting. Had my defense counsel been a part of this meeting, I am sure that he would have challenged Bishop Devadhar's claims that there were no other pastoral options opened to me. In the circumstances, I would have been happy to serve in a "lower pastoral position," just as the bishop of the Greater New Jersey Conference was allowed to do. However, as was the case with Bishop Carter in the Florida Conference, here was Bishop Devadhar taking full advantage of my ignorance in relation to the Book of Discipline and church laws. As stated before, during the conversation, Bishop Devadhar made it very clear to me that none of the other options opened to him were going to be considered, so he was giving me thirty days to vacate the parsonage. He confirmed and supported that piece of information with a certified mail which I received during the week immediately following.

In the pursuing weeks, I received several letters of support from the parishioners in New England, and it truly felt like *déjà vu* as I had gone through this experience fifteen months before. The absurdity of the situation is such that by now, the folk in Florida thought that I was permanently placed back in ministry while I recognized that for the second time in that same period, I was going to have the experience of packing up and leaving a parsonage again. To say that this was an overwhelming thought would be an understatement. As it turned out, once more the son of the complainant flew to Connecticut in order to help me pack for the second time in a very short period, and he drove the Penske truck which I had rented back to Florida where we placed most of it in storage units. We should note that, as one of the support letters indicated, I paid my way

214

fully from Florida to the New England Conference, and after six months, I had to pay my way back to Florida even though Bishop Devadhar was aware of the pending case which he stayed away from and happily handed to the Florida Conference so that they could hang me as they actually did. While all the negative emotions continued to flow through my head, there were also some positive thoughts. The church and its team of Pharisees had made so many blunders in the process that both my defense counsel and the entire defense team was able to assure me that this was all going to be overturned. I was not personally very familiar with the process myself, but I was learning a lot and that very rapidly as the process went on. I was therefore able to see the blunders myself and so remained very hopeful that it would not be long before I was going to be reinstated. The hope became even stronger because the appeal was going to be at two levels. At the level of the South Eastern jurisdiction and then at the level of the Judicial Council. In the secular world, this would compare to a regional appeal court and then, if necessary, to the Supreme Court.

However, even with the very blatant blunders and a process which was extremely irregular, I could not help but notice that the counsel for the church, Rev. Therrell, had continued to pursue the prosecution of the case with great confidence. While I did not share that concern with my defense team, it was a little troubling, and I kept wondering if he had assurance from the top that a victory for the church in case of an appeal was guaranteed. We need to keep in mind again that the legal advisor to the council of bishops—a nationally known name—was in on the case from the pretrial period. It would be very naive to assume that he was not familiar with persons who served on the Judicial Council. It would also be naïve to believe that they were going to honor the clause from the Book of Discipline, which made it clear that this case was not to be discussed at any point or with anyone outside of the official forum where it belonged at any one point. By the same token, the chancellor for the Florida Conference served on the Southeastern Jurisdiction Committee on Appeal. The fact that he officially recused himself from serving did not mean that he might not have been in touch with other members of that committee. This was a group of human lawyers. This was really a team of professionally trained attorneys working against a pastor who was only trained in theology and who was not allowed (based on the Methodist Book of Discipline) to hire even one attorney. If one can visualize the champions of the national football league playing against a second-grade team from elementary school, then that was really the scenario. These were all legal professionals who may not necessarily have had the moral courage to be objective and practical and truthful even if that meant telling the Florida Conference that I was not given due process and even more telling them that they had no authority to carry through the process.

Even though it seemed like a slam-dunk reversal of the penalty, it was a very tense period for the next five months until the Southeastern Jurisdiction Committee on Appeal met and heard the case. Dr. Scott Campbell immediately went to work and submitted his ten-point challenge to the outcome with the most solid case relating to the lack of authority of the Florida Conference to carry through the proceeding. Here is his ten-point appeal notice below.

Notice of Appeal

In the Matter of the Rev. Errol Leslie

January 27, 2016

1.) The Respondent, the Rev. Errol Leslie, hereby appeals from the verdict of the trial court convened by the Florida Annual Conference on January 11, 2016 at Lakeland, Florida and the penalty imposed by that same trial court on January 12, 2016, to the Southeastern Jurisdiction Committee on Appeals, pursuant to paragraphs 2715 and 2716 of The Book of Discipline, on the following grounds:

2.) Under the provisions of 2719.1 of the 2012 Book of Discipline the Florida Conference did not have jurisdiction to carry forward judicial procedures involving Rev. Leslie. Rev. Leslie did not meet the requirements of 2719.1 regarding residency and appointment status as a direct result of actions taken by the Florida Annual Conference. Officials of the Florida Conference failed to provide the respondent with a copy of the complaint against him before requiring him to sign an agreement related to 2719.1 in violation of Judicial Council Decision 974. This action bound the respondent to a decision deemed irrevocable and authoritative for subsequent judicial procedures by the Florida Annual Conference without the respondent having had access to all of the information that was in the possession of the Church at the time of the signing, a violation of the fair process rights outlined in 2701.2.e).

3.) Even if the Florida Annual Conference did have jurisdiction in the matter, the Presiding Officer, Bishop Al Gwinn, applied definitions of "relevance" and "reliability" in the guilt/innocence phase of the trial in a way that was prejudicial to the defense and favored the prosecution.

4.) The exclusion of the original complaint from consideration by the trial court was an error of church law.

5.) The Presiding Officer improperly excluded relevant evidence from consideration by the trial court during the penalty phase of the trial.

6.) The Presiding Officer improperly excluded a question from the voir dire process that would have demonstrated whether members of the trial court were open to considering a full range of penalties available to the trial court under 2711.3 if the respondent were found guilty of the charges against him.

7.) The General Conferences of 2008 and 2012 (??) violated Constitutional protections guaranteed in Judicial Council Decisions 698 and 836 by allowing material from the supervisory process to go forward to the Committee on Investigation and the Counsel for the Church to be used in subsequent judicial proceedings. These legislative actions further violate the provisions of 363.1. b) that the supervisory response is not to be a part of any judicial process.

8.) To the extent that the Presiding Officer relied upon the counsel of Attorney William Waddell, legal advisor to the Counsel of Bishops, during pretrial considerations, such action is a violation of constitutionally mandated separation of powers and a conflict of interest that is prejudicial to the defense.

9.) Violations of the Respondent's fair process rights by the Florida Annual Conference, including, but not limited to an illegally imposed status of involuntary leave of absence upon the respondent by Florida officials (including one official who testified against the respondent at the trial) created an atmosphere in which the requirement of 2719.1 "that fairness will be better served" was impossible to achieve.

10.) The violation of a confidentiality agreement by the counsel for the church related to an attempt to reach just resolution constituted misconduct on the part of the Church.

Respectfully Submitted,
Scott Campbell
Counsel for Rev. Errol Leslie, Respondent

218

We will not go into all the responses from the appellant court, but it is interesting to note that just as Bishop Gwinn was able to dismiss eighteen irregularities brought up by my defense during the pretrial period, the Committee on Appeals was able to negate all the points raised after this first appeal. For now, we will just examine two of the items.

IV. Analysis

Appellant's Issue 1. The Florida Conference did not have authority to carry forward judicial procedures involving Rev. Leslie under the provisions of 2719.1 of the 2012 Book of Discipline. Rev. Leslie did not meet the requirements of 2719.1 regarding residency and appointment status as a direct result of actions taken by the Florida Annual Conference.

This is the response from the appeals court:

As for the appellant's assertion in his brief that 2719.1 is unconstitutional, we agree with the Church that this issue is waived because the appellant failed to list it in his notice of appeal. 2012 Discipline 2715.1.

It strains credulity for anyone to try and figure out how it is that the committee on appeals could determine that the defense did not list the unconstitutionality in its notice of appeal. If the Florida Conference is deemed not to have the authority or have jurisdiction, how much clearer does it need to be that it is unconstitutional? In the English language, there are synonyms such that some words are used interchangeably. As I stated in my own brief to the Judicial Council, the fact that the actual word *constitution* was not used does not mean that the message is not clear. However, the representatives of Christ's church on earth deemed that this point is moot and is therefore waived. This was easily a very strong argument which my defense counsel had been making time and time again throughout the process, so since there was no logical response to it, the committee on appeal determined that it was not legitimately before them. Oops!

Let us look at another paragraph from the Court of Appeals findings:

> Meanwhile, as a result of his meeting with Ms. Hendricks and his conversation with Rev. Dodge, Dr. Spencer contacted the appellant and directed him to report for a meeting at Dr. Spencer's Vero Beach office on July 30, 2014. The appellant was not told the purpose of the meeting. During the July 30, 2014 meeting, which Rev. Dodge also attended, the appellant was told that a signed complaint had been filed against him alleging that he had conducted an improper sexual relationship with a woman other than his wife. Dr. Spencer testified that he informed the appellant of the complainant's identity and that the appellant "confirmed" and admitted that he and Ms. Hendricks "had had a sexual relationship" during the time period Ms. Hendricks had described. *Dr. Spencer testified that the appellant did not express remorse for his actions at any point in that meeting but was "quiet and subdued."*

Please take note of what the committee claimed that Dr. Spencer testified in the last italicized sentence. Now compare this with what the same committee points out (below) about Reverend Dodge's testimony.

> *However, the email that Rev. Dodge apparently sent to Rev. Robinson-Johnson on the evening after the meeting included the following statement: "Rev. Leslie was very cooperative throughout our conversation and repeatedly expressed his remorse over this situation." Counsel for the appellant attempted to use the foregoing statement during his cross-examination of Rev. Dodge on January 5, 2016.* Counsel for the Church objected on the basis that counsel for the appellant had neither produced the July 30, 2014 email by the December 29, 2015 deadline nor made the email available to counsel for the Church, even though counsel for the appellant

had obtained the email several hours before Rev. Dodge's videotaped testimony commenced. The Presiding Officer sustained the objection and ruled that the email could not be used to impeach Rev. Dodge because the appellant had missed the deadline. Nevertheless, the appellant sought to introduce the email into evidence during the penalty phase of the trial. The Presiding Officer reaffirmed his prior ruling that the email could not be admitted because it had not been produced by the December 29, 2015 deadline.

Please note again the section in italics. It is clear that Reverend Dodge is saying one thing about my expression of remorse and Rev. Spencer is saying another. Does one of them have a bad memory or is one just blatantly lying? Let us also take note as to how Reverend Therrell, the counsel for the church and Bishop Gwinn, the presiding officer, used a so-called missed deadline to prevent the trial court from seeing the e-mail. My defense counsel, Dr. Campbell, repeatedly asked Reverend Dodge for a copy of the e-mail, but Reverend Dodge claimed that he could not find it. The request for the e-mail was made in good time, and this e-mail clearly referenced my remorse. How could the committee on appeal then make the statement below?

Additionally, even assuming the Presiding Officer erred by not allowing the appellant to use the email to impeach Rev. Dodge's testimony concerning the appellant's expression of remorse, this record does not by any means establish or suggest that this error changed the outcome of the trial court's verdict, or penalty, in this matter.

As I asked in my own brief, why was there so much effort to keep the e-mail out of the possession of the trial court if they did not think that a genuine expression of remorse could impact how the court would vote in the penalty phase? Why did the committee on appeals use the word

221

apparently in reference to the e-mail being sent by Reverend Dodge to Rev. Robinson-Johnson? The e-mail was sent on day 1. Period! Why would Reverend Therrell claim during his closing arguments that it was the first time that he had heard me express any remorse? He heard me on the very first occasion when I met him asking the two representatives from the Palm Bay UMC to apologize to the congregation on my behalf.

Very often in a secular trial court, reference is made to the demeanor of the accused which onlookers use to get a sense of his or her remorse. It is hard to understand how a panel of trained attorneys some of whom would have worked in the secular court system could not see through this very easy psychological truth.

Separate and apart from the appeal brief filed by my defense counsel, support continued to be poured out from members of the two churches that I was serving in the New England Conference at the time of the trial. The two letters below just ring with support and is representative of the sentiments expressed by the wider church community.

Dear Rev Calhoun,

I am not sure if this letter should be addressed to you or someone else but I would request that, if necessary, you would direct it to the appropriate person.

I am writing to express my concern and disappointment with the system of the United Methodist Church which resulted in the abrupt removal of The Reverend Errol Leslie from our church back in January of this year, 2016. Even though it is now four months later and another pastor has been assigned to start on July 1st, I know that I speak on behalf of the majority of the congregation in stating that he was treated very unfairly. For anyone to say that after nearly forty years of service he was 'discarded' in a callous and non-Christian way would be an understatement. These persons at the church in Vernon (and I have heard Wesley memorial in East

Hartford) are still distraught and bitter even as they try to adjust through this period of transition.

My understanding is that the bishop appointed Rev Leslie with the full knowledge of the situation which was then pending and Rev Leslie, himself, apprised the appropriate committees of that same situation when he came to meet them in the summer of 2015. As such, nobody was blindsided by the results of the trial even if they had hoped for a better ending. In addition to that, even after the full congregation/s was/ were informed of the results, there was still a strong sense of support, acceptance and forgiveness which was demonstrated by so many persons. Having met and spoken with his wife, I am satisfied that she and their two daughters have also been fully supportive of him and they have been trying to rebuild their family. Through the show of support from both the churches as well as his family, I am seeing a clear demonstration of the forgiveness which is the essence of what we preach as Christians. In that regard I would ask where, in this situation is a show of forgiveness, redemption, restoration and grace from the hierarchy of the church? What is the message that we preach at Easter? Where is the demonstration of care for himself and his family? Is this action by the church not incompatible with what we preach and proclaim? (While I do not know all the facts that led to this unfortunate end, I do think that in a case where a pastor is targeted and "falls" because of his vulnerability associated with problems in his own family situation, that is a perfect opportunity for a body of Christians to offer their love and care and support.)

On a personal note, I would like to share about the impact which Rev Leslie's ministry has had on my family in the six months that we got to know him. My husband and I were trying to find a church family where we were comfortable and after our first visit to the Vernon UMC with him as pastor and a little interaction with him, our search was over. I also know that several families who had stopped attending that church, for one reason or another, started attending again and some became very active as well.

My/Our perception is that the church has 'thrown out' a gifted pastor with a big heart for service to God and His people and this at a time when there is such a shortage of pastors. There was no attempt to have any kind of mediation. Instead, it was like a child being "kicked" out of the house by parents because he/she disobeyed their instructions. You and I both know that even in that hypothetical scenario, a parent would seek to counsel with the child and arrive at some kind of mediation.

We were told that there is an appeals process which is on the way but I should hope that regardless of how that turns out, Rev Leslie would have another opportunity to serve the church in some kind of a pastoral role. I am sure that there are still many more lives that may be touched through the ministry to which God has called him and I would urge you to help repair any damage that has been already done to him by considering my/our request to have him fully utilize his gifts and talent in ministry.

Yours Truly

AB

This second letter came from another member of the same congregation.

April 25, 2016
Rev. David Calhoun
District Superintendent

Dear Rev. Calhoun,

I write this letter in support of Reverend Errol Leslie. Rev. Leslie came to Vernon United Methodist Church in July of 2015. He immediately began his ministry by reaching out to all of our members. What a nice change for us. I was fortunate enough to accompany him on many visits to our members, and how they all loved his visits. Him getting to know us, and us him, was so moving and spiritually enriching. He made a very positive difference in my faith journey and I know this is true of many others in our congregation.

Rev. Leslie led us on a great spiritual reawakening during his very passionate sermons in the short time he was with us. We came to love and appreciate him and all his talents that he brought to us. What an absolute treasure he has been to the Vernon Methodist Church.

Rev. Leslie never claimed to be perfect, but who among us can? I have raised many questions trying to understand how he could be judged so harshly and with so little forgiveness, love and compassion. Some of my questions were:

1.) Was this affair with a minor, or someone of the same sex?
2.) Was this an ongoing issue with Rev. Leslie?

3.) Was the other person involved in the affair simple or slow and unable to know right from wrong or be easily influenced?

The southern conference knew of the affair and, if resolved, no punishment would have been done. How hypocritical is that? So you opted to punish Rev. Leslie and two churches in the New England Conference that needed him. I question the ethics of this.

What about the teachings of Jesus? Aren't you like the Pharisees? where the law is more important than people and love and forgiveness? How terrible to destroy a good man who made a mistake. I do not condone what Rev. Leslie did but I do forgive him and offer him all my support. I am praying that I can learn to forgive the Methodist Church with its law above all else.

How very sad for you people to preach the teaching of Jesus but unable to love and live as Jesus would have you do. Do you honestly believe that this is how Jesus would have handled the situation? I find it hard to believe that you are all ordained ministers. May God forgive you.

Sincerely yours,
CD

There were several other similar expressions both in writing and verbally from members of both congregations which I served in the New England Conference. However, it made no difference to the hierarchy of the church. They had the power to kick me into obscurity, and they certainly exercised that power to the maximum.

CHAPTER 11

The Blatant Disregard for Truth and Justice

This was the response of the committee on appeals in its entirety. I would ask you to judge if they were just been attorneys trying to create arguments to support their bias or Christians who were objectively looking at the truth and trying to apply ethical principles.

COMMITTEE ON APPEALS SOUTHEASTERN
JURISDICTION OF THE UNITED METHODIST CHURCH

In the Matter of the Rev. Errol Leslie, Appellant
(Original Jurisdiction: Florida Annual Conference
of the United Methodist Church)

OPINION ON APPEAL

This matter was heard on May 31, 2016. Upon consideration of the record on appeal, the briefs of the parties, oral argument, and deliberations of the Southeastern Jurisdiction Committee on Appeals ("Committee"), the Committee concludes that the weight of the evidence sustains the charges of sexual misconduct, immorality, and disobedience to the order and discipline of the United Methodist Church ("UMC") and no errors of Church law vitiate the trial court's verdict or penalty of termination of Rev. Errol Leslie's membership in the New England Annual Conference ("New England Conference").

Accordingly, the Committee affirms the verdict of the trial court and the penalty imposed.

I.   Factual and Procedural History

The appellant, Rev. Errol Leslie, was ordained in 1981 in Jamaica in the Methodist Church of the Caribbean and the Americas. In 1995, he moved to the United States and had his orders recognized by the New England Conference of the UMC. In 2008, the appellant received a cross-conference appointment to the Florida Annual Conference ("Florida Conference") of the UMC and was assigned to serve the Palm Bay UMC. The appellant, his wife, and his two children lived in the church parsonage.

In 2011, the appellant began communicating via email and/or other electronic means with Veda Hendricks, a woman with whom he had attended high school in Jamaica. Ms. Hendricks had also moved to the United States and lived in Georgia, but her mother lived in Port St. Lucie, Florida. The appellant and Ms. Hendricks communicated regularly after reconnecting. On March 4 or 5, 2014, Ms. Hendricks stopped in Palm Bay on her way to visit her mother. During that visit, the appellant and Ms. Hendricks began a sexual relationship, which continued for more than four months, during which time the couple met many times in hotels, at Ms. Hendricks's home, and at her mother's home. They also went on a cruise together. The appellant took Ms. Hendricks to events held at the Palm Bay UMC church, at which his wife was also present, including worship services. At the appellant's invitation, Ms. Hendricks preached at both services on

Mother's Day 2014, when the appellant's wife was present. The appellant did not disclose the nature of his relationship with Ms. Hendricks and often deliberately misled his wife about his whereabouts and obligations to explain his absences and keep his sexual relationship with Ms. Hendricks hidden from his wife and others.

From the outset of the extramarital affair, the appellant and Ms. Hendricks's intent was for the appellant to divorce his wife, marry Ms. Hendricks, and continue in ministry in the UMC. However, Ms. Hendricks became dissatisfied because the appellant was proceeding more slowly toward these goals than she preferred, so she informed the appellant's wife of the extra-marital affair. Additionally, on July 24, 2014, she called the office of Rev. David Dodge, Assistant to the Florida Conference Resident Bishop, to lodge a complaint against the appellant. Rev. Dodge, who was out of the office when her call came in, returned Ms. Hendricks's call the same day and advised her that if she wanted to go forward with a complaint, she must file a written and signed complaint with Dr. Gary Spencer, Superintendent of the Atlantic Central District in the Florida Conference. Dr. Spencer was responsible for supervising fifty-eight churches, including Palm Bay UMC and its pastor, the appellant. Ms. Hendricks met with Dr. Spencer on July 28, 2014, and submitted a written and signed complaint. Dr. Spencer then contacted Rev. Dodge "to indicate he had had the conversation with Ms. Hendricks, that he had indeed received a signed complaint and that the complaint specified that she and [the appellant] had had a sexual relationship outside the bounds of marriage." Later that same afternoon, Rev. Dodge emailed Florida Area Resident Bishop Kenneth H. Carter, Jr., who was then in Costa Rica, to alert him to "what was taking place." Also on that same afternoon, Rev. Dodge, aware that the appellant's clergy relationship was with the New England Conference, contacted Rev. Erica Robinson-Johnson, director of connectional ministries for the New England Conference and Assistant to New England Conference Bishop Sudarshana Devadhar. Rev. Dodge "shared with [Rev. Robinson-Johnson] that we had a signed complaint against [the appellant] that appeared to have validity, and [they] communicated together then about the process."

Meanwhile, as a result of his meeting with Ms. Hendricks and his conversation with Rev. Dodge, Dr. Spencer contacted the appellant and directed him to report for a meeting at Dr. Spencer's Vero Beach office on July 30, 2014. The appellant was not told the purpose of the meeting. During the July 30, 2014 meeting, which Rev. Dodge also attended, the appellant was told that a signed complaint had been filed against him alleging that he had conducted an improper sexual relationship with a woman other than his wife. Dr. Spencer testified that he informed the appellant of the complainant's identity and that the appellant "confirmed" and admitted that he and Ms. Hendricks "had had a sexual relationship" during the time period Ms. Hendricks had described. Dr. Spencer testified that the appellant did not express remorse for his actions at any point in that meeting but was "quiet and subdued."

Rev. Dodge testified that Dr. Spencer "took the primary lead" in the meeting on July 30, 2014, and began with prayer, before informing the appellant of the complaint. Rev. Dodge's memory of the meeting was that Dr. Spencer "talked about the content of [Ms. Hendricks's complaint], about the number of times, about meetings and hotels and cruises and those types of things." Rev. Dodge said that the appellant was "very quiet after hearing the nature of the complaint, that his speech level had dropped to a lower decibel," and that "his head pointed looking down basically from that point on." According to Rev. Dodge, the appellant admitted knowing Ms. Hendricks and having an extra-marital sexual relationship with her. Rev. Dodge stated that the appellant did not at any time verbally express regret for allowing the relationship to develop, or grief about how it would affect his family, or concern for how his local church might be affected by his behavior. Rev. Dodge stated that they discussed the processes that could occur going forward, as outlined in the UMC Book of Discipline, including the possibility of the appellant surrendering his credentials, and the appellant indicated that, "at that time that he was not—he was not prepared to make that kind of decision at that—in that moment; but that's the only thing he expressed." Rev. Dodge denied encouraging the appellant to surrender his credentials, stating "I laid that out as one option that was available to him. It was not my place to encourage him one way or the other." But Rev. Dodge acknowledged telling the appellant that if he surrendered his credentials at any point "that would end the process."

On August 1, 2014, two days after the meeting with Rev. Dodge and Dr. Spencer, the appellant, along with the Bishops of the Florida and New England Conferences, signed an agreement allowing the complaint to remain in the Florida Conference for processing. The agreement was signed pursuant to 2719 of the 2012 Book of Discipline of the UMC ("2012 Discipline), which states:

Any clergy members residing beyond the bounds of the conference in which membership is held shall be subject to the procedures of 27012718 exercised by the appropriate officers of the conference in which he or she is a member, unless the presiding bishops of the two annual conferences and the clergy member subject to the procedures agree that fairness will be better served by having the procedures carried out by the appropriate officers of the annual conference in which he or she is serving under appointment, or if retired, currently residing.

(Emphasis added.) Six days later, on August 7, 2014, a copy of Ms. Hendricks's original complaint was delivered to the appellant. On November 6, 2014, the appellant was notified that the Bishop of the Florida Conference had appointed counsel for the Church, and this notification commenced the judicial proceedings under 2701 of the 2012 Discipline. At some time thereafter, although the date is not clear from the record, retired Bishop Al Gwinn was appointed to serve as the Presiding Officer of the judicial proceeding. But, after his appointment, the Judicial Council handed down its Decision 1296 and reinstated paragraphs from the 2008 Discipline pertaining to the role of the Committee on Investigation. While the Judicial Council decision stated it was prospective only, it remained unclear how it would impact matters like this one, in which the judicial process had already commenced. The Florida Conference and counsel for the church chose to afford the appellant the benefit of decision No. 1296 and referred the complaint to a Committee on Investigation on August 5, 2015. Thereafter, the appellant twice attempted without success to rescind the 2719 agreement and asked the Committee on Investigation to dismiss all charges against him. On September 23, 2015, following a hearing, the Committee on Investigation certified a bill of charges, specifically immorality, sexual misconduct, and disobedience to the order and discipline of the UMC. 2012

Discipline 2702.1(a), (i), and (d). Additionally, the Committee on Investigation granted the request of counsel for the Church and voted unanimously to recommend to the Bishops of the New England and Florida Conferences that the appellant be suspended from all clergy responsibilities pending the outcome of the judicial process.

Following the action of the Committee on Investigation, on November 24, 2015, the Bishop of the Florida Conference confirmed that Bishop Al Gwinn would continue to serve as the Presiding Officer for the trial. On December 21, 2015, Bishop Gwinn advised the parties that any documentary evidence either party intended to introduce, other than that included in the bill of specifications and charges, should be "requested" to the Presiding Officer no later than December 29, 2015. On January 2, 2016, Bishop Gwinn ruled on a motion in limine that counsel for the Church had filed seeking to prohibit questioning and evidence about Ms. Hendricks, or any other witness, prior relationships or sexual history. In his ruling Bishop Gwinn emphasized that during the guilt-innocence phase of the trial, only evidence or testimony tending "to prove or disprove" the appellant's guilt of the charges would be deemed relevant.

On January 11, 2016, the guilt/innocence phase of the trial began in Lakeland, Florida. At the outset, the appellant admitted, through the opening statement of his counsel, that he "did have an inappropriate relationship with Ms. Veda Hendricks over a period of about four months in the spring and early summer of 2014." The appellant's counsel stated that the appellant had "made a terrible mistake which he deeply and sincerely regrets," described the appellant as "profoundly aware of the harm that his actions have caused to many people, the complainant, the church, both in the macro and the micro sense, his family and indeed himself," and stated that the appellant takes "full responsibility for his own decisions and actions." Therefore, although disputes arose during the trial as to which party instigated the affair and which party paid for the hotels and the cruise, the appellant admitted having the extramarital sexual relationship with the complainant. After hearing the proof, the trial court unanimously found the appellant guilty of the charges of immorality and sexual misconduct. By a twelve-to-one vote, the trial court also found the appellant guilty of the charge of disobedience to the order and discipline of the UMC.

The penalty phase of the trial commenced on January 12, 2016. The Church offered additional testimony from Dr. Spencer and Rev. Dodge. Dr. Spencer testified that the appellant's actions had harmed Ms. Hendricks, the appellant's family, and the parishioners of the Palm Bay UMC. Dr. Spencer explained that the appellant's family had been required to move out of the church's parsonage. As for the harm to the Palm Bay UMC congregation, Dr. Spencer testified that the appellant's actions had generated a great deal of distrust, contention, confusion, and anger within the congregation and that the situation as a whole had shifted the congregation's focus from ministry. Additionally, Dr. Spencer explained that "[f]inancially the church has been in a major decline." He explained that Palm Bay had not been able to pay "apportionments, property and casualty insurance premiums, pension premiums, [or] health insurance premiums" and that the Florida Conference had paid, meaning that "other churches" pay when Palm Bay

UMC goes into arrears. As a result Dr. Spencer stated that the appellant's actions had created a ripple effect of harm with other churches in the Florida Conference, and Dr. Spencer opined that it would be extremely difficult for Palm Bay to ever repay to the Florida Conference the debt it had incurred for back apportionments and other payments. Dr. Spencer testified that Palm Bay paid its apportionments in full in 2013 but had paid only a small portion in 2014 and none at all in 2015. Additionally, Dr. Spencer stated that Palm Bay "cannot afford a fulltime local pastor now—I mean full-time elder," that the appointed pastor's hours may have to be reduced further as well, and that it is "entirely likely" that Palm Bay may become a two-point charge. Dr. Spencer testified that the appellant's actions had also harmed the reputation of United Methodist clergy generally and that his actions had caused the local church and others, including Dr. Spencer, to focus time and attention on matters other than ministry and outreach. Dr. Spencer testified that the worship attendance had declined by ten percent as well. Based on his experience leading and supervising UMC churches, Dr. Spencer stated that surrender of credentials would be an appropriate penalty for the appellant.

Rev. Dodge testified that the last trial on allegations of sexual misconduct in the Florida Conference occurred in 2007 and that, although complaints involving sexual misconduct had been filed against other UMC clergy, the majority of those cases had been resolved by "the pastor who was involved in such surrender[ing] credentials." As to individuals harmed by the appellant's actions, Rev. Dodge identified Ms. Hendricks and also pointed to the grief and embarrassment suffered by the appellant's family, as well as the deep hurt to the "very fragile congregation" of Palm Bay UMC. Rev. Dodge also mentioned the harm done to the financial stability of Palm Bay UMC, and said that in 2013 the church paid its $10,000 apportionment in full but paid only $1,250 in 2014 and nothing in 2015. At the time of his testimony, Rev. Dodge stated that Palm Bay UMC owed the Florida Conference over $18,000 for health insurance and pension premiums, over $20,000 for property and casualty insurance premiums, and had not paid any toward those arrears since May 2014. Rev. Dodge agreed that the appellant's actions had "[a]bsolutely" affected other churches in the Florida conference and had harmed the Order of Elders as well. Rev. Dodge explained that the appellant's actions had cast a shadow on all clergy and specifically on the Order of Elders of the Florida Conference. Rev. Dodge believed the time and resources that had been required "to fully and carefully attend to this matter and all of its collateral damage" were time and resources that should have been "directed towards the making of disciples of Jesus Christ for the transformation of the world." Based on his leadership in the Florida Conference in a number of positions, including leading the center for clergy excellence and serving on GBHEM's Division of Ordained Ministry, Rev. Dodge opined that an appropriate penalty for the appellant would be not to allow him to pastor any UMC congregation or have credentials in the UMC.

The appellant testified on his own behalf and called seven other witnesses to testify on his behalf as well. The appellant's proof during the penalty phase focused on the circumstances of how the extramarital sexual relationship with Ms. Hendricks developed, on inconsistencies in Ms. Hendricks's testimony, on how Ms. Hendricks revealed the relationship to the appellant's wife, on Ms. Hendricks's character and past conduct, on the appellant's lack of any history of similar conduct and his good reputation among ministers in Jamaica, on the appellant's conduct and attitude since returning to and receiving an appointment within the New England Conference, and on the appellant's remorse for the situation. The appellant's proof focused on convincing the trial court to impose a penalty less severe than loss of recognition of the appellant's credentials and suggested several possibilities, including requiring the appellant to undergo professional counseling, and/or to participate in a structured program with the appellant's district superintendent, and/ or to participate in an accountability group, any of which would be at the appellant's expense. Additionally, during closing statements, counsel for the appellant asked the trial court to consider the options of a mandatory full clinical psychological evaluation followed by mandatory counseling with a licensed professional as specified by the psychological evaluation, mandatory spiritual direction with a certified spiritual director for not less than two years, mandatory participation in a covenant or accountability group of clergy colleagues, and/or mandatory letters of apology to the complainant, the Palm Bay UMC, and the Florida Conference.

After hearing the proof, the trial court, by a majority nine-to-four vote as to all three charges, decided that the appropriate penalty was to terminate the appellant's conference membership and revoke the recognition of the appellant's credentials for conference membership.

The appellant timely appealed the trial court's decision. Counsel for the appellant and the Church were instructed to attach as appendices to their briefs any documents made part of the record below, in addition to the transcript of the trial, that are necessary to resolve this appeal. Counsel for the appellant filed an opening brief and thirty-three appendices, and counsel for the Church filed a response brief along with five appendices. Counsel for the appellant submitted a reply brief, which, among other things, identified three issues that had been listed in the notice of appeal that the appellant had abandoned before this Committee. No issues have been raised about the record before the Committee. This Committee heard oral argument on May 31, 2016, and for the reasons explained below, upholds the trial court's verdict and penalty.

II.   Jurisdiction

The Committee has jurisdiction under 2715 and 2716 of the 2012 Discipline.

III.   Appeal Procedures

Paragraph 2715 of the 2012 Discipline provides, in pertinent part, as follows:

1.) In all cases of appeal, the appellant shall within thirty days give written notice of appeal and at the same time shall furnish to the officer receiving such notice (2716.2, 2717.1, 2718.2) and to the counsel a written statement of the grounds of the appeal, and the hearing in the appellate body shall be limited to the grounds set forth in such statement. [Footnote omitted.]

2.) The appellate body shall determine two questions only: (a) Does the weight of the evidence sustain the charge or charges? (b) Were there such errors of Church law as to vitiate the verdict and/or the penalty? These questions shall be determined by the records of the trial and the argument of counsel for the Church and for the respondent. The appellate body shall in no case hear witnesses. It may have legal counsel present, who shall not be the conference chancellor for the conference from which the appeal is taken, for the sole purpose of providing advice to the appellate body.

3.) In all cases where an appeal is made and admitted by the appellate committee, after the charges, findings, and evidence have been read and the arguments concluded, the parties shall withdraw, and the appellate committee shall consider and decide the case. It may reverse in whole or in part the findings of the committee on investigation or the trial court, or it may remand the case for a new trial to determine verdict and/or penalty. It may determine what penalty, not higher than that affixed at the hearing or trial, may be imposed. If it neither reverses in whole or in part the judgment of the trial court, nor remands the case for a new trial, nor modifies the penalty, that judgment shall stand. The appellate committee shall not reverse the judgment nor remand the case for a new hearing or trial on account of errors plainly not affecting the result. All decisions of the appellate committee shall require a majority vote. (Emphasis added.) Under the foregoing procedures, which define and circumscribe the scope of this Committee's review and authority, we are authorized to consider two questions only: "(a) Does the weight of the evidence sustain the charge or charges? (b) Were there such errors of Church law as to vitiate the verdict and/or the penalty?" In his reply brief, the appellant acknowledges that he is not contending that the evidence is insufficient to sustain any of the charges. Instead, the appellant argues that numerous errors of Church law occurred and that these errors vitiate the verdict and/or the penalty. For the reasons explained below, we uphold the trial court's verdict and penalty in all respects. Because our review is clearly limited to the issues stated in the notice of appeal and discussed in the appellant's briefs, our analysis is organized according to the statement of the issues in the notice of appeal.

IV.   Analysis

Appellant's Issue 1. The Florida Conference did not have authority to carry forward judicial procedures involving Rev. Leslie under the provisions of 2719.1 of the 2012 Book of Discipline. Rev. Leslie did not meet the requirements of 2719.1 regarding residency and appointment status as a direct result of actions taken by the Florida Annual Conference.

The appellant argues that the Florida Conference lacked authority to prosecute the complaint within its jurisdiction. According to the appellant, the requirements of 2719.1 of the 2012 Discipline were not met, and the agreement the appellant signed allowing this matter to go forward in the Florida Conference was null or void or rescinded. This Committee disagrees. Paragraph 2719.1 provides as follows:

Any clergy members residing beyond the bounds of the conference in which membership is held shall be subject to the procedures of 27012718 exercised by the appropriate officers of the conference in which he or she is a member, unless the presiding bishops of the two annual conferences and the clergy member subject to the procedures agree that fairness will be better served by having the procedures carried out by the appropriate officers of the annual conference in which he or she is serving under appointment, or if retired, currently residing.

The plain language of this paragraph lists only two criteria that must be met for it to apply. First, a clergy member subject to the judicial proceeding must be "residing beyond the bounds of the conference in which membership is held." Additionally, the presiding bishops of the two annual conferences and the clergy member subject to the procedures must agree that fairness will be better served by having the matter handled by the appropriate officers of the annual conference in which the clergy member is serving under appointment.

We agree with the Church that the judicial process began for purposes of the 2719.1 agreement when Bishop Carter notified the appellant on November 6, 2014, that he was appointing a counsel for the Church to handle the complaint. 2012 Discipline 2701 ("The judicial proceedings and the rights set forth in this paragraph commence upon referral of a matter as a judicial complaint to the counsel for the Church."); 2719.5 ("For procedural purposes, the judicial process shall be governed by the Discipline in effect on the date a complaint is forwarded to the counsel for the Church."). On that date, the appellant was living outside the bounds of the New England Conference and serving under appointment in the Florida Conference. For the reasons stated by the Presiding Officer in his January 8, 2016 ruling on the appellant's motion to dismiss (attached as appendix III to the Church's brief), we are not persuaded by the appellant's argument that Judicial Council Decision

No. 1296, which reinstated portions of the 2008 Discipline relating to the role of the Committee on Investigation, also reinstated the portion of the 2008 Discipline defining the beginning of the judicial process differently than the 2012 Discipline. Accepting the appellant's argument would be particularly inappropriate because the judicial process in this case began six months before Judicial Decision No. 1296 was rendered. The fact that the Florida Conference, out of an abundance of caution, also afforded the appellant the benefit of proceeding through a Committee on Investigation after Judicial Decision No. 1296 was rendered does not change our conclusion that the judicial process in this case began on November 6, 2014. And on that date, all the criteria for the 2719.1 agreement were met.

Also unpersuasive is the appellant's argument that the 2719.1 agreement is null and void because it was executed before the judicial process began. The 2719.1 agreement simply resolved that the judicial process would occur in the Florida Conference, not the New England Conference, if Ms. Hendricks's complaint culminated in a judicial process. No language in 2719.1 establishes a time frame for entering into such an agreement or requires that such an agreement be signed only after the judicial process had officially commenced on November 6, 2014.

As for the appellant's assertion in his brief that 2719.1 is unconstitutional, we agree with the Church that this issue is waived because the appellant failed to list it in his notice of appeal. 2012 Discipline 2715.1.

Appellant's Issues 2 and 3.

2.) Officials of the Florida Conference failed to provide the Respondent with a copy of the complaint against him at the outset of the supervisory process while at the same time requiring him to make decisions about where the complaint process would go forward.

3.) The Respondent did not have access to documents and information that were in the possession of the Church at the time he was compelled to choose the venue in which the complaint process would go forward.

While it is true that the appellant signed the 2719 agreement before receiving a paper copy of the complaint, the appellant had met with Dr. Spencer and Rev. Dodge two days before he signed the agreement. According to their testimony, the appellant was advised during the meeting of the allegations of the complaint and of the identity of the complainant. The agreement the appellant signed is straightforward and written in plain English. The appellant has failed to establish or even suggest that he was unaware of its meaning or that he was coerced into signing it. Indeed, paragraph four of the agreement establishes just the opposite, as it provides: "After consideration of the complaint and the provisions of 2719, Rev. Leslie has agreed, freely and voluntarily without coercion, that fairness will be better served by having the procedures of 27012718 carried out by the appropriate officers of the Florida Annual Conference."

We are also constrained to disagree with the appellant's assertion that the Presiding Officer erred by refusing to allow him to rescind the agreement. The

Presiding Officer correctly pointed out that the 2012 Discipline does not provide a right to rescind such an agreement and that the appellant waited for several months after he had signed the agreement, and until shortly before trial, before attempting to rescind it.

Finally, we conclude that the appellant has failed to demonstrate how any of his objections to the 2719 agreement amount to a denial of fairness or constitute an error affecting the result of either phase of his trial, in which he admitted to having an extramarital affair with the complainant.

Appellant's Issue 4. The Presiding Officer, Bishop Al Gwinn, applied definitions of "relevance" and "reliability" in the guilt/innocence phase of the trial in a way that was irreparably prejudicial to the Respondent and favored the prosecution.

We disagree with this assertion. As the appellant concedes, the 2012 Discipline does not define the word relevant but confers upon the Presiding Officer the authority to rule upon the admissibility of evidence. 2012 Discipline 2710.1, 2710.7. The Presiding Officer's definition of relevance as any evidence tending to prove or disprove the charges against the appellant was appropriately broad and neutral and neither favored nor disfavored the appellant or the prosecution. This definition properly enabled the Presiding Officer to exercise the discretion the 2012 Discipline afforded him. Furthermore, although we conclude the Presiding Officer properly defined relevance, we alternatively conclude that even if the definitions were erroneous, the appellant has failed to demonstrate that the error affected the result of his trial. Again, as previously stated, the appellant admitted to having an extramarital affair with the complainant.

Appellant's Issue 5. The exclusion of the original complaint from consideration by the trial court was an error of church law.

The appellant's argument on this point is not persuasive. The appellant fails to point to any provision of the 2012 Discipline requiring the Presiding Officer to admit the original complaint into evidence for the trial court to consider. Rather, the trial court's role is to determine whether clear and convincing evidence has been introduced during the trial to establish the appellant's guilt of the charges and specifications that have actually been brought. The trial court fulfilled this obligation. Additionally, as the Church points out, the original complaint contains allegations not relevant to the charges and specifications, and these allegations, if presented, actually could have biased the trial court against the appellant. Where, as here, the complainant appeared at the trial and was available for cross-examination, the Presiding Officer did not err in excluding the original complaint from evidence. The appellant seems not to recognize that the Presiding Officer did not foreclose use of the original complaint. To the contrary, the Presiding Officer appropriately ruled that the appellant could use statements in the original complaint for impeachment purposes to challenge the credibility of any witness that provided testimony inconsistent with the complaint during trial. The appellant has failed to establish a denial of fair procedures or that any alleged error in excluding the original complaint affected the result of this trial, in which the appellant admitted having an extramarital affair with the complainant.

Appellant's Issue 6. The Presiding Officer erred in a llowing the Church's Motion in Limine to influence the cross examination of witnesses for the prosecution.

In his reply brief the appellant expressly abandoned this issue for consideration on appeal. Appellant's Issue 7. The Presiding Officer erred in excluding relevant and reliable evidence from consideration by the trial court during the penalty phase of the trial.

As the Church notes, it appears this issue relates to the Presiding Officer's exclusion of a July 30, 2014 email Rev. Dodge sent to Rev. Robinson-Johnson of the New England Conference. The following facts are necessary to place this issue in context.

On December 21, 2015, the Presiding Officer advised the parties that any documentary evidence either party intended to introduce, other than that included in the bill of specifications and charges, should be presented to the Presiding Officer no later than December 29, 2015, twelve days before the start of trial. On that same date, December 21, 2015, counsel for the appellant sent an email to Rev. Dodge requesting a copy of a July 30, 2014 email Rev. Dodge sent to Rev. Robinson-Johnson of the New England Conference. Counsel for the appellant described the email as relating "to the alleged confession [of the appellant] earlier that day." Counsel for the appellant copied all parties on his email to Rev. Dodge requesting a copy of the July 30, 2014 email, including counsel for the Church and the Presiding Officer. Rev. Dodge replied that he would be out of the office until January 4 and would be "glad to forward" the requested correspondence at that time. Rev. Dodge sent another email on January 4, 2016, explaining that he had just returned to the office and apologizing because he apparently had not kept a copy of the July 30, 2014 email. He said he would continue searching his files and would forward it immediately should he locate it. Later that same day, January 4, 2016, counsel for the appellant asked Rev. Dodge for permission to contact Rev. Robinson-Johnson and inquire whether she could provide him with a copy of Rev. Dodge's July 30, 2014 email to her. Rev. Dodge responded, "Yes, that would be fine."

Counsel for the appellant contacted Rev. Robinson-Johnson and obtained the July 30, 2014 email from Rev. Dodge before Rev. Dodge's videotaped testimony on January 5, 2016. Rev. Dodge stated during his testimony that the appellant had not expressed remorse during the July 30, 2014 meeting. However, the email that Rev. Dodge apparently sent to Rev. Robinson-Johnson on the evening after the meeting included the following statement: "Rev. Leslie was very cooperative throughout our conversation and repeatedly expressed his remorse over this situation." Counsel for the appellant attempted to use the foregoing statement during his cross-examination of Rev. Dodge on January 5,

2016. Counsel for the Church objected on the basis that counsel for the appellant had neither produced the July 30, 2014 email by the December 29, 2015 deadline nor made the email available to counsel for the Church, even though counsel for the appellant had obtained the email several hours before Rev. Dodge's videotaped testimony commenced. The Presiding Officer sustained the objection and ruled that the email could not be used to impeach Rev. Dodge because the appellant had missed the deadline. Nevertheless, the appellant sought to introduce the email into evidence during the penalty phase of the trial. The Presiding Officer reaffirmed his prior ruling that the email could not be admitted because it had not been produced by the December 29, 2015 deadline.

The appellant argues that the Presiding Officer erred because disclosure deadlines are not mandatory.

This may be true, but the Presiding Officer has the authority under 2710.1 to set such deadlines. The Presiding Officer did not err by establishing the deadline or by refusing to allow the appellant to utilize evidence neither disclosed to counsel for the Church nor provided to the Presiding Officer by the deadline. Additionally, even assuming the Presiding Officer erred by not allowing the appellant to use the email to impeach Rev. Dodge's testimony concerning the appellant's expression of remorse, this record does not by any means establish or suggest that this error changed the outcome of the trial court's verdict, or penalty, in this matter. The appellant does not contest the facts of the case. He testified at trial about the meeting in question. Accordingly, the appellant is not entitled to relief on this ground.

Appellant's Issue 8. The Presiding Officer erred by excluding a question from the voir dire process that would have shown whether members of the trial court were open to considering the full range of penalties available to the trial court under 2711.3 if the Respondent were found guilty of the charges against him.

In his reply brief, the appellant has expressly abandoned this issue for consideration on appeal. Appellant's Issue 9. The General Conference violated Constitutional protections guaranteed in Judicial Council Decisions 698 and 836 by removing the protection of confidentiality from the supervisory response and thereby allowing material from the supervisory process to go forward to the Committee on Investigation and to the Counsel for the Church to be used in subsequent judicial proceedings. These legislative actions violate the separation of powers and deprive the Respondent of fair process rights.

This Committee concludes that this issue is without merit for the reasons explained in the referral and ruling of the Committee on Investigation, which is attached as Appendix IV to the Church's brief. In particular, the Judicial Decisions on which the appellant relies involved earlier versions of the Discipline that differ fundamentally from the 2012 Discipline, which applied in this matter. Appellant's Issue 10. To the extent that the Presiding Officer relied upon the counsel of Attorney William Waddell, legal advisor to the Council of Bishops, during the judicial process, such action is a violation of constitutionally mandated separation of powers and a conflict of interest that was prejudicial to the Respondent.

The Committee concludes that this issue is without merit and that the Presiding Officer acted consistently with 2708.1 of the 2012 Discipline. As the Church points out, legal counsel to the Council of Bishops is not the Florida Conference chancellor. The fact that counsel sometimes provides advice to bishops does not hinder his ability to provide neutral advice to a Presiding Officer under very different circumstances. The Committee also rejects the appellant's argument that the Presiding Officer may not consult with legal counsel during pretrial phone conferences. As the Presiding Officer stated when ruling on this issue, the pretrial process is designed to address issues that will arise during the trial, and consultation with counsel on these matters will aid the Presiding Officer in properly ruling on trial issues.

Nevertheless, even assuming the Presiding Officer's consultation with legal counsel during pretrial conferences was held to be error, it was not an error that affected the outcome of this proceeding, in which the appellant admitted to a months' long extramarital affair. The trial court did not know about or consider this issue, and it therefore made no difference in their deliberations.

For the same reasons, the Committee denies the request of appellant renewed April 13, 2016, to require the Presiding Officer to make a detailed disclosure of his communications with Mr. Waddell. Regardless of any advice received by the Presiding Officer, he remains responsible for the rulings he made. This Committee reviews only his rulings, not the source of his information.

Appellant's Issue 11. Violations of the Respondent's fair process rights by the Florida Annual Conference, including but not limited to, an illegally imposed status of involuntary leave of absence upon the Respondent by Florida officials (including one official who testified against the Respondent at the trial) created a biased and prejudicial atmosphere in which the judicial process occurred.

The Committee concludes that this assertion does not entitle the appellant to relief. Long before this trial occurred, the Florida Conference admitted it made an error by placing the appellant on involuntary leave of absence and rectified this mistake by returning the appellant to active ministry status and compensating him with back pay, benefits, housing, and interest. The error in placing the appellant on involuntary leave of absence in no way affected the outcome of the trial in which the appellant admitted to having an extramarital affair with the complainant.

Appellant's Issue 12. The creation by the Florida Annual Conference of an illegal verbatim of a supervisory session that was subsequently shared with the Counsel for the Church and the Presiding Officer was a violation of the rights of the Respondent and created a presumption of guilt that was prejudicial to the Respondent.

The Church admits that it erred by making a partial verbatim account of a discussion between the appellant, appellant's counsel, the Atlantic Central District Superintendent, and others. The Church asserts, however, that this error in no way affected the trial court's verdict because the Church never submitted the partial verbatim account to the trial court or to the Committee on Investigation. Thus, the partial verbatim account could not possibly have influenced the trial court or created a presumption of guilt. Again, the appellant repeatedly admitted and never denied engaging in the extramarital affair with the complainant.

Appellant's Issue 13. The failure of the Counsel for the Church to contact or interview the Respondent during his investigation of the complaint was indicative of a presumption of the Respondent's guilt on the part of the Church.

In his reply brief, the appellant has expressly abandoned this issue for consideration on appeal. Appellant's Issue 14. The request by Counsel for the Church to the Committee on Investigation that it recommend suspension of the Respondent from his ministry in The New England Annual Conference during the balance of the judicial process represented prosecutorial overreach and was indicative of the prejudicial and biased atmosphere created by the Church throughout the supervisory and judicial process.

This assertion also is without merit. Paragraph 2704.2c of the 2008 Discipline (which applied to proceedings before the Committee on Investigation) permits Church Counsel to ask the Committee on

251

Investigation to recommend the appellant's suspension. The Committee unanimously granted the request and recommended to the Bishops of the Florida and New England Conferences that the appellant be suspended from all clergy activities pending the outcome of the judicial process. Church counsel's decision to pursue an option available under the 2008 Discipline is not indicative of a prejudicial and biased atmosphere. Rather, it is a decision to utilize processes clearly permissible under the 2008 Discipline. Additionally, although the request was not erroneous, even if it were, the error in no way affected the outcome of the appellant's trial in which he admitted having an extramarital affair with the complainant.

Finally, although appellant in his initial and reply brief may be deemed to have raised some other issues, the Committee considers them waived because they were not raised in the original notice of appeal. 2012 Discipline 2715.1.

V.   Decision

The facts substantiating the charges in this case have never been disputed. The appellant contests only the severity of the penalty imposed. However, the penalty is within the range authorized by 2711.3 for such offenses. There has been no mixing or matching of penalties as prohibited by Judicial Council decisions 240 and 1270. The trial court, though not unanimous, imposed the penalty after careful consideration of all facts and evidence. While errors were made, the members of this Committee cannot say that the admitted or alleged errors are of such a nature as to vitiate the verdict or penalty imposed.

For all the foregoing reasons, the Committee concludes that the weight of the evidence sustains the charges of sexual misconduct, immorality, and disobedience to the order and discipline of the UMC, and that no errors of Church law vitiate the trial court's verdict or penalty of termination of the appellant's conference membership and revocation of the recognition of appellant's credentials for conference membership. Accordingly, the Committee affirms the verdict of the trial court and the penalty imposed.

From this committee's response, one can see that the members essentially retried the case in absentia rather than looking at the many indications of injustice and unfairness as well as a failure to demonstrate fundamental Christian ethics by leaders of the Florida Conference as well as by the presiding officer. Of course, there were also several technical flaws which the church tried to cover up and which flaws my defense counsel had brought to their attention. My counsel made every effort to point out the deliberate and unethical acts on the part of the church as well as all the professionally trained attorneys who made up the committee on appeal and who merely looked for loopholes in trying to rationalize on behalf of the church. This was like a judge trying a case with his friend or relative as the complainant and who overlooks the truth in order to declare the otherwise innocent accused defendant guilty. Here is one of the many quotes from the committee's response which proves the point.

Appellant's Issue 10. To the extent that the Presiding Officer relied upon the counsel of Attorney William Waddell, legal advisor to the Council of Bishops, during the judicial process, such action is a violation of constitutionally mandated separation of powers and a conflict of interest that was prejudicial to the Respondent.

The Committee concludes that this issue is without merit and that the Presiding Officer acted consistently with 2708.1 of the 2012 Discipline. As the Church points out, legal counsel to the Council of Bishops is not the Florida Conference chancellor. The fact that counsel sometimes provides advice to bishops does not hinder his ability to provide neutral advice to a Presiding Officer under very different circumstances. The Committee also rejects the appellant's argument that the Presiding Officer may not consult with legal counsel during pretrial phone conferences. As the Presiding Officer stated when ruling on this issue, the pretrial process is designed to address issues that will arise during the trial, and consultation with counsel on these matters will aid the Presiding Officer in properly ruling on trial issues.

Nevertheless, even assuming the Presiding Officer's consultation with legal counsel during pretrial conferences was held to be error, it was not an error that affected the outcome of this proceeding, in which the appellant admitted to a months' long extramarital affair. The trial court did not know about or consider this issue, and it therefore made no difference in their deliberations.

For the same reasons, the Committee denies the request of appellant renewed April 13, 2016, to require the Presiding Officer to make a detailed disclosure of his communications with Mr. Waddell. Regardless of any advice received by the Presiding Officer, he remains responsible for the rulings he made. This Committee reviews only his rulings, not the source of his information.

Finally, although appellant in his initial and reply brief may be deemed to have raised some other issues, the Committee considers them waived because they were not raised in the original notice of appeal. 2012 Discipline 2715.1.

CHAPTER 12

A Call For Justice

That final paragraph in the decision of the committee on appeal speaks volumes both in terms of how it is worded and also in terms of the message it sends. I have addressed this in my own brief which I felt compelled to file even if that was a little unusual.

> Finally, although appellant in his initial and reply brief may be deemed to have raised some other issues, the Committee considers them waived because they were not raised in the original notice of appeal. 2012 Discipline 2715.1.

My defense counsel was as thorough and meticulous as could be in relation to the arguments which he was putting forward in support of a reversal of the penalty imposed. There was not one issue which he raised which was not in the original notice of appeal. Both the Committee on Appeals as well as the Judicial Council merely found a reason for not addressing any issue which stared them right in the face as another blunder by the church.

Anyone who reads my defense counsel's case for an appeal and then reads the response of the committee with a level of objectivity would be able to see the blatant bias on the part of committee on appeals. In a very rare move, I felt compelled to file my own brief to the Judicial Council as printed below. This document below is the actual brief which I submitted to the Judicial Council for its consideration. They were my own thoughts as I reflected on and analyzed everything.

Brief Submitted Regarding Docket No. 2016-7 By the Rev. Errol Leslie

Introduction

On June 3, 2016 the Committee on Appeals of the Southeastern Jurisdiction issued a decision upholding the findings of a trial court convened by the Florida Annual Conference that on January 12, 2016 had removed the membership of the Appellant from the New England Annual Conference of the United Methodist Church.

The Appellant would like to start off by making the observation that the Committee on Appeals largely relitigated the case, finding the Appellant guilty and then affirming the penalty. The first half of the opinion under the caption "factual and procedural history" is replete with information regarding testimony and a very large portion of what is regarded as 'factual' is not only false but was not even raised as testimony during the actual trial. The inclusion of disputed testimony as "Factual History" portrays the Appellant in the worst possible light and made it difficult for the Committee to look dispassionately at the legal issues that were actually being appealed. In the church counsel's oral argument he did not deal with the legal issues raised in the appeal; instead he focused on questions of guilt and innocence or about how angry the conference was or about what he deemed to be the Appellant's strategy. He did not address the violations of fair process issues by the Church.

Rebuttal to Assertions by the Committee on Appeals

The factual and procedural history as portrayed by the Committee seems to be an extension of the prosecution's arguments. Not only is that "factual history" filled with exaggerations and untruths carried over from the Committee on Investigation and the trial, but some additional statements have been included which were not even mentioned at the trial. The opinion of the Committee on Appeals does not reflect the appearance of balance. The purpose of the appeal is to show or contest the procedural issues and it is very clear from the Appellant's briefs that there were multiple violations of fair process which would easily have vitiated the penalty.

As an example of the inaccuracies contained in the "Factual and Procedural History" of the Committee on Appeals, the document refers to the Appellant taking Mrs. Hendricks to several Church events including Church services. The Appellant never took Mrs. Hendricks to any event at the Church. Not even one. For those VERY FEW times that she went on the Church campus, she would always drive herself there—and with the exception of the first time, it was always without the prior knowledge of the Appellant. To suggest that the Appellant would take her there is not only a ploy intended for effect, but it is also trying to 'tie' Mrs. Hendricks to the congregation as if she was actually a part of the Church family. The Counsel for the Church continuously made that implication during the earlier part of the process and even included a charge of sexual abuse in his initial charges, claiming that Mrs. Hendricks was a member of the Appellant's congregation.

Another example of an exaggeration of the facts in order to portray the Appellant in a bad light is the claim made by the Committee that the Appellant was planning to marry the complainant and continue his ministry at PBUMC. In his testimony, the Appellant clearly stated that his plan was to communicate his personal emotional struggles with the District Superintendent and was waiting for the right opportunity to do so in a timely manner. However, Mrs. Hendricks went ahead and communicated with the DS before the Appellant had an opportunity to do so.

A third example is that the testimony of the Appellant's wife, Kaye Leslie, shows that the telephone call which the complainant made to her was not to tell her about the affair but instead, it was to encourage Mrs. Leslie to divorce her husband (the Appellant) so that they could then get married. She even told the Appellant's wife during one of the telephone calls that her daughters 'were old enough to handle a divorce.' The problem here is that the statement of factual history is basically drawn from the prosecution's version of history and largely ignores conflicting testimony from the defense.

It is this kind of perception which led to a penalty which was imposed by the trial court because it was led to believe that the Appellant had absolutely no place in ministry, was definitely not remorseful and would only continue to be a danger to parishioners and to any congregation which he served. The fact that there was no previous history to support such an assertion and the fact that his current District Superintendent testified on his behalf showing and expressing appreciation for his ministry in Connecticut was not persuasive with the trial court, largely because of the image of the Appellant that was communicated by the Church.

It is worthy of note that throughout the written opinion there is a consistent reference to the fact that the Appellant admitted to the charges. The implication is that the violations of fair process by the Church are irrelevant. Instead the committee implies that based on the admission alone, the penalty should be affirmed. The Appellant contends that there are two separate phases of the trial and while an admission of an affair may have justified the verdict, there is every reason to believe that a fair process would have changed the outcome of the penalty. It is important that the Judicial Council keep that in mind as they examine all the facts related to the multiple violations of fair process and the ongoing pattern of bias and prejudice against the Appellant. The Appellant would therefore ask the Judicial Council to ignore the summarized statement of "Factual and Procedural History" as presented by the Committee since it is inaccurate. Instead, the Appellant would request that the Judicial Council read the actual transcripts which portray the real story.

As mentioned before, at the appeals level, the focus needed to be on whether the Church had observed its own laws. While the Appellant raised many challenges to the legality of the Church's behavior, both in briefs and oral argument, the Counsel for the Church failed to engage any of these issues substantively. Instead he largely focused his arguments on the character and the strategy of the Appellant, and insisted repeatedly that the actions of Florida officials could not be challenged because these persons were above reproach. The facts, however, are otherwise.

One example of unethical behavior is the decision of District Superintendent Spencer to pressure the Appellant (citing a false deadline) to sign a document about where subsequent judicial processes would take place while the Appellant was under duress and without counsel. Additionally, the Superintendent refused to give the Appellant a copy of what he had signed, which meant that the Appellant did not even have a chance to review it. (The Appellant was also compelled to sign this statement before he had been allowed to see the written complaint against him.) The Presiding Officer falsely states that attempts to rescind this document were not made for more than a year. In reality, the first attempts were made in February of 2015, before the Appellant had even been provided with a copy of the bill of charges. There was a pattern of behavior by the leadership of the Florida conference which was unfair. This action by the District Superintendent was one such act.

The Appellant also has several concerns about how the process on July 30th, 2014 played out in the office of Dr. Spencer. Once more, the Committee on Appeals is eager to accept the prosecution's version of what transpired, opining that a statement from Rev's Spencer and Dodge that they shared the contents of the complaint with the Appellant was true. In fact, they withheld 90% of what was in the complaint and refused to let the Appellant have a copy. The Committee also chooses to believe the testimony of the Florida officials that they shared the name of the complainant with the Appellant at that meeting, even though the Appellant testified otherwise and his spouse testified that the Appellant called her immediately after the meeting to ask if she had filed the complaint against him, the point being that the complainant was never identified by name. The bias of the Committee on Appeals was clearly and consistently to accept the testimony of Church witnesses at face value and to ignore the testimony of Defense witnesses, unless, of course, that testimony corroborated the Church's narrative.

The simple truth is that if the mandate of JC 974 had been followed and all materials had been shared with the Appellant at the outset, there would be no dispute about what was shared during the July 30 meeting. The Church dropped the ball on this one, but the Appellant is the one who pays the price when the Committee on Appeals chooses to adopt the prosecution's version of what transpired.

The Committee also reported that Rev Dodge did not encourage the Appellant to surrender his credentials. However, the Appellant testified that both men as well as Bishop Carter at the supervisory session asked him to surrender his credentials. Rev Spencer made that request at every opportunity.

The fact is, from the outset of the process, the only alternative acceptable to the Florida Conference was the surrender of credentials on the part of the Appellant. This was stated repeatedly by Superintendent Spencer, the Counsel for the Church, Bishop Carter and the Chancellor for the Florida Conference. It was the non-negotiable position of the Church blocking just resolution. The Counsel for the Appellant reported in a March 2015 letter to the Presiding Officer on the first conversation he had with the Counsel for the Church the previous month in which he quotes the Counsel as saying: "This is Florida. He has two choices. Either he voluntarily surrenders his credentials or they will be taken away from him." The illegally imposed involuntary leave of absence was also an indication that there was a very biased and highly charged prejudiced atmosphere which prevailed among the leadership in the Florida Conference. The end goal was to give the ultimate punishment to the Appellant—to do whatever it took to ensure that he was not in good standing with the Church.

The Committee's token reference to the signing of the "2719 Agreement" is also a matter of serious concern. In spite of the very obvious indication that this was a coerced signature as pointed out by the Counsel for the Appellant, the Committee states that it is written in plain English and cited paragraph number four of the document as justification of their position. Once more, the Appellant explained how the District Superintendent had given him a false deadline for a time when the agreement had to be signed. No such deadline exists in the Book of Discipline but the Superintendent abused his power by playing on the Appellant's ignorance and lack of knowledge in Church law by coercing him with this false deadline. The Superintendent did not dispute giving this false deadline but the Committee claims the Appellant signed the document without coercion.

In relation to the committee's claim that the document signed was written in plain English so it did not need to be explained to the appellant, is irrational. There is a reason that attorneys will seek to interpret documents that are written in plain English to their clients. There is a reason why many persons will have their attorneys examine documents that are written in plain English before they sign it. There is a reason why most persons would have attorneys draft a document before it is signed and issued. The fact that a document is written in plain English does not mean that the contents is clear or easily understood. There is a reason why members tend to nominate or elect attorneys to serve on many Committees in the United Methodist Church that deal with judicial matters. It is simply that attorneys are supposedly better able to interpret laws which ARE ALL written in plain English. There is a reason why bishops within the United Methodist Church will pass on documents that are written in plain English to conference chancellors in the respective conferences. There is a reason that every business that requires a signature on a document will ensure that the person who signs receive a copy of the document and there is a reason why in all instances, time is given to a 'would be' client to read and consider his/ her options before a contract is signed. Very often, business documents and contracts would be referred to attorneys even if they are written in plain English. For the Committee on Appeals to arbitrarily dismiss this obvious but deliberate tactic by the Church is unbelievable.

While the Committee has concluded that "the Appellant has failed to demonstrate how any of his objections to 2719 agreement amount to a denial of fairness or constitute an error affecting either phase of the trial," it did not make any reference to the Appellant's stating very early in the process in a letter to the Presiding Officer dated March 30, 2015 that because of so many violations of fairness up to that point, he did not believe that he could receive a fair trial in Florida.

It cannot be overemphasized that the Appellant was not allowed to carefully review the agreement nor was he given time to consider it. As such the Committee's point that the Appellant did not express at any time that he did not understand it, does not make any sense. He did not have the time to process the information in order to see whether or not he understood it, including sentence number four! He was given a document and asked to sign it after five minutes and this after he was intentionally misled into believing that there was an urgent time constraint. In addition, his request for a copy of the document so that he could review it was denied.

The Appellant urges the Judicial Council to look objectively at the circumstances in order to determine if justice and fairness have been executed in the circumstances. In the secular world, attorneys may look for legal technicalities but in the world of the Church, we are urged to look at a strong display of Christian Ethics, justice and fairness.

According to the Committee, Dr. Spencer testified that the Appellant did not express any remorse for his actions at any point during the meeting but was "quiet and subdued." Rev Dodge testified that "the Appellant did not at any time verbally express regret for allowing the relationship to develop or grief which he caused to his family…"

(This testimony came after his September 23, 2015 testimony before the Committee on Investigation that he "honestly could not remember" whether the Appellant showed remorse. It also came after his July 30, 2014 email to colleagues in New England in which he stated that the Appellant "was very cooperative and repeatedly expressed remorse for his actions.")

It is ironic that both men testified along those lines; the Appellant testified very clearly in plain English that he not only expressed regret and showed remorse, but that in doing so, he actually reached over to both men individually and hugged them one at a time as he expressed his apologies. However, for reasons known only to itself, the Committee has chosen to totally leave the Appellant's portion of the testimony out of its "narrative" while later on supporting and defending the ruling of the Presiding Officer not to allow the email which was composed by Rev Dodge himself and which email would show the exact opposite of what both men testified to be used at the trial. The Church through the Counsel for the Church blocked this email from going before the trial court and the Presiding Officer supported his effort. In his closing argument to the trial court, the Counsel for the Church claimed that the only time that he had heard any expression of remorse from the Appellant was earlier that day through the Appellant's own testimony. Here were three persons from the Church claiming that the Appellant was not remorseful but they blocked their own email which contradicted that assertion from going before the trial court. Is this the best the Church can do in the pursuit of truth?

The Appellant pointed out in great detail the efforts which he made to obtain the copy of the email from Rev Dodge in a timely manner but the Assistant to the Bishop, 'misplaced' such an important document in such an important matter. The Committee on Appeals did not see a problem with all of that. In fact, it stated that even if the email was viewed by the trial court, it would not have vitiated the penalty. If the viewing of the email by the trial court would not have vitiated the penalty, why would all three men insist that Rev Leslie did not express any regrets but blocked that email showing otherwise from going before the trial court?

Later in its report, the Committee stated that the forced signing of the 2719 agreement was of little significance since there is nothing in the Book of Discipline setting any time frame for when it should be signed. There is, however, in 363.1.b) an explicit statement that the supervisory response is "not to be a part of any judicial process." The Committee read The Discipline selectively, choosing to lift up those portions which supported its preferred narrative and ignoring those that did not.

The Committee has been clear with its details about what the witnesses for the Church testified but was very vague and passive when it came to reporting on any testimony of the witnesses for the Appellant. For example, what little evidence the defense was able to use showed very clearly that Mrs. Hendricks was the aggressor and the instigator in the relationship, yet the Committee (even with that evidence) states "disputes arose during the trial as to which parties instigated the affair and which party paid for hotels and cruise."

There was no reference in the Committee's report to the Appellant's testimony or the opening statement of the Appellant's counsel regarding the fact that the Appellant was going through a VERY ROUGH TIME in his marriage at the time when the complainant came into his life and started to pressure him to leave his wife and marry her. This was a fact which the Church and its Counsel have downplayed because this may have caused the trial court to be a little more sympathetic to the Appellant and may have given a lesser penalty. The Committee that is supposed to be unbiased did not seem to give equal weight to each side of the testimony that was given at the trial. The Committee merely stated consistently throughout its statement that the Appellant confessed to being guilty so the violations of his fair process rights did not matter.

Another example of this is that the Committee again gave details of Dr. Spencer's testimony regarding the harm that the Appellant's actions caused his family, the Church and to Mrs. Hendricks including the fact that his family had to move out of the house. This detail was again exaggerated and for effect. A second example is the reference to Rev Dodge's testimony regarding the grief and hurt and embarrassment suffered by the Appellant's family as well as to the "very fragile congregation at Palm Bay UMC." All this detail from the testimony from the Church's witnesses amounts to a retrying of the case and serves the purpose of portraying the Appellant as a horrible person who does not deserve to be in ministry. Interestingly, the Committee did not make any references to the fact that the Appellant's wife testified on the Appellant's behalf which itself was a show of support or that the complainant's son testified against his mother but in support of the Appellant because he knew her history.

There is no detail given in the committee's report on the testimony of the Rev Denzel Southwood Smith who testified that the complainant told him that she filed the complaint because her motive was to destroy the Appellant. There was no reference in the committee's report to the testimony of the District Superintendent of the Connecticut/Western Massachusetts district who testified that the Appellant had been doing a good job in his new appointment and was already creating a positive atmosphere after only six months in the appointment. There was no detail given in the committee's report on the testimony of the Rev Althea Spencer Miller who testified that the complainant was inconsistent and untrue in the stories which she (the complainant) was telling. Is there any reason why details are given in reference to the testimony given by the witnesses for the Church but the only reference to the testimony given by the witnesses for the Appellant is that "the Appellant testified on his own behalf and called seven other witnesses to testify on his behalf as well?" **The account of the Church's witnesses is accounted for in six or seven pages while the account of the defense's witnesses is summarized in two sentences.**

There is a reference in the reported opinion to Rev Dodge testifying that in previous situations which were similar in the conference, in the majority of cases, the pastor would surrender his/ her credentials. However, the Committee did not mention anything from the opening statement of the Appellant's Counsel that the Appellant did not surrender his credentials because of the many lies which were mentioned in the complaint.

The Appellant had stated to the bishop of the Florida conference and to every other officer of the Florida conference who had asked him to surrender his credentials that he would not do so because of the many lies which were in the complaint. In his mind, to surrender his credentials based on so many false allegations would be tantamount to his admitting to all of these other allegations.

In fact, it is pretty offensive that the Committee could even detail Rev Dodges' testimony regarding his opinion that "the time and resources that had been required 'to fully and carefully attend to this matter and all of its collateral damage' were time and resources that should have been 'directed towards the making of disciples of Jesus Christ for the transformation of the world'." His statement is in keeping with a similar statement which Bishop Carter had made to the Appellant during the supervisory hearing when he told the Appellant that he (Bishop Carter) does not want to be spending money on a trial which could be better spent on feeding persons who are poor. While the Appellant remains enthusiastic about making disciples for Jesus Christ and was, in fact, a pioneer in establishing food pantries and other feeding programs in the Churches (including Palm Bay UMC) he has served, statements like these suggest that it is wrong for him to exercise his constitutionalright to go to a trial especially in a case where a complaint has been filed against him with so many outrageous allegations. It further suggests that a pastor who has given almost forty years of his life serving the Church is of little or no worth so that spending time and resources on a case involving him is poor stewardship. The implication is that he should just be discarded—kind of ironic when Jesus Christ whose disciples we want to make with the resources and time, welcomed and sought to restore everyone who was lost or went astray. This line of thinking again shows very clearly the bias, anger, vindictiveness and harsh feelings towards the Appellant which could not have led to a fair and impartial trial. It is little wonder that the Church through its counsel as well as the Presiding Officer blocked every effort of the Appellant to produce evidence or witnesses which would show that some witnesses for the Church could have been impeached for not telling the truth.

The Appellant also finds it interesting that Rev Dodge talks about "fully and carefully attending to the matter." This was another statement intended for effect. With all the errors resulting in multiple violations of the Appellant's rights, including a claim that he could not find an important email, it is ironic that Rev Dodge could be talking about "carefully attending to the matter."

Finally in this section, even though the Appellant was clear in his attempt to show how many times the effort was made to have the proceedings go back to New England, the Committee seemed to have ignored all the documentation confirming that and has gone along with the Church and the Presiding Officer's assertion stating that the Appellant waited until almost before the trial to rescind the agreement. In this documentation, there was a timeline of letters and requests submitted to appropriate persons involved in the process.

The Committee also stated that it was not persuaded by the Appellant's argument that the decision JC 1296 reinstated all matters relating to the Committee on Investigation. The contention of the Appellant is that there is only one way to interpret "All." As far as the Committee is concerned, the fact that the Counsel for the Church was able to suppress one of his original documents and the fact that the chair for the COI used the term "a new process" seem to be of little significance. The Appellant would invite the Committee or the Church to indicate or itemize which matters relating to the Committee on Investigation should be returned to the 2012 Discipline. The ruling by the JC clearly says "all" but somehow the Church and the Committee seem to be able to handpick which matters are referred to in the "all." The directive did not say 'some matters"; it clearly says "all matters"

On page 3 of the Committee's opinion, it is stated that Judicial Council ruling JC 1296 was prospective "but it remained unclear how it would impact matters 'like this one'." It is hard to see what is unclear about a decision being prospective. It simply means that it relates to any matter going forward. A judicial process had started but since this new ruling was prospective, any judicial process moving forward should have been sent to the New England Conference. The process had to be started over if the matter was going through the Committee on Investigation. The Counsel for the Church needs to state clearly why he insisted that Florida would "hold on" to the case. The insistence on "holding on" to the case is another sign of the highly charged prejudicial atmosphere which prevailed. The Counsel himself stated that Rev Leslie wanted to go to

New England in order to receive a lesser penalty. This would again indicate that he along with the other leaders in the Florida conference had only one result in mind and they were going to obtain that result regardless of what it would take to get it.

The Committee on Appeals was very careful in its language when it stated that the Bishop of the Florida Conference confirmed that Bishop Alfred Gwinn would **"continue"** to serve as Presiding Officer for the trial. The Counsel for the Appellant submitted two documents in which language such as **"reappointed"** was used. In his email to the Counsel for the Church, Bishop Gwinn mentioned that he had not heard anything from Bishop Carter so he could not have acted on communication from the Counsel for the Church. Judge Tatti mentioned in one of his documents that **"a new process"** had started. In fact, the Counsel for the Church also mentioned this to the Committee on Investigation. The quote below is from the COI transcript on page # 190.

That and the fact that under the old system, when I had prepared charges and we were going to trial, unbeknownst to any of us, the Judicial Council decided in April to then bring the Committee on Investigation back. We had to wait until June for the Annual Conference to meet to elect you all. You all had to have time to elect a chair. It just began a whole new process for us too.

The cumulative effect is obvious here, but the Committee on Appeals chose to disregard all arguments that did not support its preferred narrative.

The Exclusion of The Issue of the Constitutionality of 2719.1

The Appellant strongly contests the ruling of the Committee that the matter relating to 2719.1 being unconstitutional is waived because it was not mentioned in the notice of appeal. As the Appellant argued in the response brief, the notice of appeal is intended to state what the basis/es of the appeal would be and not meant to argue the case. The case was well and appropriately made in the notice of appeal that one of the grounds on which the appeal was being made is that the Florida conference did not have the authority to proceed with the trial. The exact language used in the notice of appeal was:

"The Florida Conference did not have authority to carry forward judicial procedures involving Rev. Leslie under the provisions of 2719.1 of the 2012 Book of Discipline"

The fact that the word "constitution" or "unconstitutional" was not used in the sentence does not mean that the issue is waived or moot. The argument of the Appellant is that the Florida conference did not have the authority to carry out judicial proceedings because 2719.1 is, for all intents and purposes rendered null and void. In the mind of the Appellant that paragraph in the Book of Discipline is what is actually moot or nonexistent. Florida would only have authority to carry out judicial proceedings if the Appellant was a member of that conference.

As an example or illustration, If an attorney in representing a client, establishes the "irretrievable breakdown of a marriage" as grounds for divorce that attorney will not have to argue the ways in which the breakdown is irretrievable or even give the details of that breakdown until he/ she goes to court. Nothing needs to be said prematurely about what issues have taken place in the home which would constitute an irretrievable breakdown. That attorney needs only to establish what the GROUND/S is/are.

In this instant case, the Appellant made it very clear that the Florida conference did not have the authority to carry out the judicial proceedings and that was clear enough for the case to have been made. As such the Appellant contests that ruling by the Committee and asks that the matter be allowed to stay on the table for further discussion and debate.

The Issue of Relevance

The Committee indicated that the Presiding Officer did not err in his narrow definitions of relevance. The initial brief of the Appellant makes mention of the fact that the complainant was given a free reign to tell multiple untruths in a way that severely tarnished the reputation of the Appellant but the Appellant was not given an opportunity to prove that these were untruths because the Church and the Presiding Officer blocked every request which was made to show evidence or bring witnesses which would prove that the complainant was lying. Everyone knows that one factor which may influence a jury or trial court as they consider the penalty for an accused person is their perception of that person.

As such, someone who is convicted of a crime but is perceived as being truly repentant or remorseful may receive a lesser penalty than someone who is convicted of the same crime but who is perceived to be a villain. Both the Church and the complainant portrayed the Appellant as being a villain and he was never given an opportunity to bring witnesses or evidence to show that this was not the case. Even without him having that opportunity, there were still four persons who voted against the penalty to end his clergy membership in the New England Conference. Unlike the Committee on Appeals, the Appellant is convinced that in spite of the admission of the Appellant, there would have been enough votes not to terminate his membership if the Appellant had been given a fair opportunity to show the trial court that he was not the villain which the Church and the complainant intentionally portrayed him to be.

There has not been any consistency in how the Presiding Officer applied the use of "discretion" or when he followed the Discipline. The Committee on Appeals has been just as inconsistent. For example, the Presiding Officer did not allow the original complaint or testimony from defense witnesses which would show that the complainant was lying throughout her testimony because he did not think that it proved the guilt or innocence of the Appellant. However, he allowed both the complainant as well as the Church to introduce testimony regarding the effectiveness of the Appellant's ministry at the Palm Bay United Methodist Church. Both Rev Spencer and Rev Dodge, under questioning from the Counsel for the Church, went to great lengths to depict the Appellant as an ineffective pastor and tried to show that the Church had "fallen apart" under his ministry. This reference dealt with a time prior to the filing of the complaint. Apart from the fact that that testimony was false, nothing in that part of the testimony was relevant to the case and it certainly did not help to prove the guilt or innocence of the Appellant. It just showed up once more the bias in favor of the Church and the Presiding Officer's effort to block any testimony or witness from the Appellant which could impeach the Church's star witness.

Original Complaint

The Committee mentions also on page 9 that the Appellant fails to point out any Disciplinary provisions requiring the Presiding Officer to admit the original complaint into evidence. In fact that is not the case. In the Appellant's initial brief, it was pointed out that the Discipline makes it clear that the respondent has a right to possess all the documents which have been used against him. He went on further to say that having or possessing the documents is of no consequence if he is not able to use it in his defense. In addition, the Book of Discipline cannot and does not spell out every detail as to how the Presiding Officer ought to make his judgments. It is interesting to observe how often both the Committee and the Presiding Officer make reference to what the Book of Discipline does not say—as the case may be—when it comes to defending the Church. However, when the Church has ignored the Book of Discipline multiple times, the same persons excuse, defend and rationalize on behalf of the Church and deem the issue as being of little or no significance. There is a point when the Presiding Officer is expected to not only use his/ her discretion but also to be fair and balanced when doing so.

The Committee also claims that the Presiding Officer did not err by not allowing the original complaint to be seen by the trial court. In fact the Committee went along with the Church's claim that if the trial court had seen the complaint it would have biased them more against the Appellant. As it turned out, the Church did not worry about the Committee on Investigation being biased against the Appellant so that body was allowed to see the complaint. The Church did not worry about the Board of Ordained ministry in two separate annual conferences being biased against the Appellant when the complaint was shown to those two bodies. The Church did not worry about Counsel for the Church being biased against the Appellant when he was given the complaint. It is extremely disingenuous to suggest that this was the stated reason why they did not want the complaint to be seen by the trial court. On the contrary, the Church went out of its way to exaggerate stories about the Appellant and tried to portray him in a very negative light to the trial court and that was in order to establish as much bias against the Appellant as they could muster.

In fact, the Counsel for the Church opined that the reason the Appellant wanted to use the complaint in his defense is that it would have shown up the complainant in a negative light. If in fact, the using of the complaint may have shown up the complainant in a negative light, the Appellant cannot and should not be held responsible for that; neither should he be punished. Obviously, if the trial court perceived her in a negative light, it would have created sympathy and understanding for the Appellant and as such, could have resulted in a lesser penalty. The sole reason the Church did not want the trial court to see the original complaint was that it would have portrayed the complainant as a dangerously unstable person and would potentially have created sympathy for the Appellant. All other explanations are smoke and mirrors. Once again, however, the Presiding Officer blocked evidence which would have shown that the complainant was not speaking the truth. The Counsel for the Appellant was not permitted to cross examine the complainant on the contents of the complaint.

Interestingly, the Committee on Investigation was allowed to read the complaint because the Church knew that cross examination is not permitted in that forum. The Counsel for the Church claimed that he only wanted the relevant charges to go before the trial court. If so, he could have let the same "relevant" charges with the accompanying evidence go before the Committee on Investigation. This is but one more example of the double standard that was used throughout this process.

More on the David Dodge Email

The Appellant gave day by day detailed descriptions of his effort to obtain the copy of the email from Rev Dodge. It seems more than a little strange that a document as important as that one which was sent right at the beginning of the process was not secured by someone in such a high office. Rev Johnson Robinson was able to locate her copy of the email because she considered it an important document to secure. Rev Dodge's claim that he could not locate the email is at best, irresponsible and at worst, unethical. In spite of this detailed description of the painful effort to get a copy of the email, somehow the Committee did not recognize the significance of this issue. It is important that this was another piece of evidence which would have helped to show the trial court that the Appellant was not the villain that the Church and the complainant were portraying him to be. The trial court could definitely have been less severe in its penalty if they were made to see this true side of the Appellant.

The Appellant is offended by the language used by the Committee in its reference to the transmission of the above referenced email to Rev Robinson Johnson. The Committee used the word "apparently." The Appellant would like to request that the communication be called for what it is. The email was not 'apparently' sent. It was definitely sent. Copies of the entire email chain have been provided to the Committee. The use of the word "apparently" disparages the integrity of the Counsel for the Appellant and once again reveals the pro-Church bias of the Committee on Appeals. The Committee appears to be picking up on the demeaning remarks of the Counsel and Co-counsel for the Church in a sidebar conversation on the second day of the trial [See pp. 59–68 of the trial transcript, Day Two] in which they imply that the Dodge email was a fabrication of the Defense. Such insinuations are beneath the dignity of the Counsels, and certainly way out of bounds for an official Church body like the Committee on Appeals.

Relating to the Legal Advisor to The Council of Bishops

The Committee does not see a problem with the Presiding Officer seeking counsel from Attorney Bill Waddell who is the legal advisor to the council of Bishops. Consider the following example. Recently, the Bishop of the New England Conference was asked to make a ruling of law on an issue relating to this case. It is conceivable that the Bishop would have quite appropriately turned to the legal advisor to the Council of Bishops for advice in the matter. Can one seriously argue that there would not now be a conflict of interest and a 'separation of powers issue'? More to the point, it is Attorney Waddell who has been training bishops in the conduct of trials as a part of his responsibility for the Council of Bishops. For him to then participate in pre-trial decisions about the admissibility of evidence blurs the line separating the episcopal and the judicial roles. Some of the pretrial motions which were decided upon that blocked the evidence and witnesses which the Appellant wanted to bring in were made by the Presiding Officer, presumably on the advice of attorney Waddell. Despite the opinion of the Committee on Appeals, this is improper, represents a conflict of interest and blurs the separation of powers long held to be an essential tenet of our United Methodist polity.

Similarly when the Committee states that "the fact that counsel sometimes provides advice to bishops does not hinder his ability to provide neutral advice to a Presiding Officer" is like saying the mayor of a city, acting in an official capacity, can provide advice to the chief of police of that same city regarding charges brought up against a member of that mayor's own family. Conference chancellors are human beings and it is for this reason that the Book of Discipline does not allow them to become the Counsel for the Church in any matter or case. It is the same rationale which determined that members of the Committee on Appeals who are from an appellant's annual conference must recuse themselves from considering that case. It is the same rationale which would make it impossible for the spouse of a pastor in a local Church to serve on the staff parish relations committee. It is another case where common sense alone would dictate that human beings even with the best intentions can allow their emotions and bias to get in the way of objectivity and fairness.

In addition to this, the Committee is also saying that the trial court did not know about this issue so it would not have vitiated the penalty. The Appellant's contention is that nothing regarding the procedure was allowed to go before the trial court but as the Appellant opined in its earlier brief, the trial court may well have been more understanding of the injustice meted out to the Appellant if it had been given either directly or indirectly the information regarding the unfair process that led up to the trial.

On page twelve the Committee states that it reviews only the rulings of the Presiding Officer and not the source of his rulings. This does not stand up to the test of rationality. This is like saying that it would not have mattered if the chancellor for the Florida Conference or the Bishop himself had advised the Presiding Officer. It would not matter to the Committee because the Committee only checks the rulings of the Presiding Officer and not the source of his rulings. The Appellant refers the Judicial Council to a question which was asked in the Appellant's brief as follows: If that is the case, would the Committee have given the same response if the Presiding Officer had sought his legal guidance from the attorney for "Associates in Advocacy," a pro-defense organization in the Church? The reality is that bias is subtle and almost impossible to detect after the fact. Sometimes those who harbor a bias don't even know it themselves. It is not unlike racism in that regard. Therefore, every effort must be made to eliminate all potential sources of bias from the process. It is disappointing that the distinguished members of the Committee on Appeals failed to understand this important principle.

The Illegal Leave of Absence

The Committee completely missed the point of the Appellant's concern in issue number 11. The fact that the conference compensated the Appellant for his financial loss as a result of placing him in an illegal status of involuntary leave does not make what they did right. In the secular world, there have been several persons who have spent years in prison and who were subsequently released because DNA or other evidence proved that the person was wrongly convicted. Some of these persons were compensated financially but that compensation did not replace the humiliation they experienced; neither can it replace the many years of freedom in their lives which disappeared as a result of the imprisonment. In such cases, the compensation is merely a token gesture and acknowledgment that the state or the court did wrong. Even more, that release would have shown that there was a level of enthusiasm and zeal to convict the person charged to the point where very little, if any effort was made to balance the evidence presented. In this instant case, the Appellant's contention is that the illegally imposed status of involuntary leave is a reflection of the highly charged prejudicial and biased atmosphere that prevailed in any discussions relating to the case. It was so bad that the leadership of the Florida Conference felt free to impose such a penalty without going through the proper process.

As stated, reimbursing the Appellant for what would have been rightfully his anyway, does not nullify the prejudice and the bias which prevailed; as such it does not excuse the leadership either. One will have to conclude that this illegally imposed status was done knowingly because it would be hard to believe that at that level of leadership in the Church, there would not have been one person who would have recognized that the illegally imposed status was wrong. That is a clear indication that there was bias and as such, the Appellant could not have been expected to receive a fair trial. The imposition of that status was just their way of ensuring that the Appellant was punished to the maximum.

In spite of this very clear demonstration of an annual conference acting autonomously and disregarding the Disciplinarily mandated approach to dealing with cases, the Committee has chosen to excuse and rationalize on behalf of the Conference its inexcusable behavior. The trial court was not given the opportunity to examine these violations of process and the Presiding Officer blocked this information from going to the trial court. This also reaffirms the very heavily biased and prejudicial atmosphere which prevailed over the proceedings. The court was never allowed to see and examine for itself the witnesses or evidence which would have demonstrated this bias and prejudice.

The Illegal Verbatim

The Committee seeks to protect the Church once more in its reference to the illegal verbatim relative to the discussion between the Appellant, Appellant's counsel and the Atlantic Central District Superintendent. The Committee claims that "the Church asserts that this error in no way affected the trial court's verdict because the Church never submitted the partial verbatim account to the trial court or to the committee on investigation."

It is true that the Church did not submit this document to trial court but it was submitted to the Counsel for the Church so already a heavy bias and prejudice was developed. This was important because it demonstrated a pattern of fair process violations by the Florida Conference, a topic that the Presiding Officer would not allow to be considered by the trial court. The Appellant made many requests for the process errors to be looked at by the Presiding Officer and the trial court but he declined all such requests.

This, in fact, had the same result and effect as did the denial of the request of the Appellant that the original complaint be allowed as part of the trial proceedings.

COI Request for Suspension

The Committee on Appeals also failed to understand the concern regarding the request for suspension made by the Florida Committee on Investigation upon the recommendation of the Counsel for the Church. The Book of Discipline may have a paragraph that allows for this but the usage of any of these options is a matter of discretion. This request to place the Appellant on suspension was made twice and followed upon the original suspension at the very beginning of the process. An illegally imposed involuntary leave of absence was also placed upon the Appellant. When one looks at the big picture, it is not difficult to see that all of this is reflecting an insatiable desire to punish the Appellant to the maximum without even wanting to go through the proper process as dictated by the Book of Discipline. This speaks to a highly charged atmosphere of bias and prejudice which did not allow for the Appellant to have been given a fair trial.

Conclusion

If the actions of the Florida Annual Conference go unchallenged or if there is not careful scrutiny of the process which was followed, then the Church will be sending a message to other annual conferences and other bishops that they do not have to be guided by the Book of Discipline or previous decisions of the Judicial Council. Instead, these parties can take matters into their own hands and operate as if they are independent entities. While the Counsel for the Church claims that the Appellant has not taken responsibility for his actions, the Counsel and also the Committee on Appeals need to know that the Church also needs to take responsibility for a continued and consistent tendency to be unfair, biased and prejudiced. To make excuses for and to defend the leaders of the Florida Annual Conference is to invite them and others to repeat their unacceptable behavior in future situations. I respectfully request that the Judicial Council send a strong message to all annual conferences and committees on appeal that fair process still matters and that Disciplinary mandates and Judicial Council precedents cannot be ignored with impunity. That message will best be sent by setting aside the verdict and the penalty imposed by the Florida Conference upon the Appellant. Respectfully Submitted, The Rev. Errol Leslie Appellant

CHAPTER 13

The Strongly Made Case in the Pursuit of Justice

As indicated, it was unusual, if not unprecedented, for an appellant to file a brief on his own behalf. However, the evidence of injustice on the part of the Florida Conference was so blatant; I could not sit still and only have other persons speak on my behalf when the pain was getting stronger as I processed all that was happening. In this next section, I have chosen to reference some of the other briefs which were submitted to the Judicial Council. Some of the points made may appear to be a little vague if the reader does not either have prior knowledge of or background information on the subject.

One of the most compelling briefs responding to the Committee on Appeals was from Rev. Dr. Larry Lake. For me to have tried to summarize his argument would be to do it some injustice. Hence, I have it below in its entirety. Dr. Larry Lake also makes reference to some of the many holes in the response of the Committee on Appeals as stated in his full brief below. Dr. Lake served at one point as my assistant defense counsel.

THE JUDICIAL COUNCIL OF THE UNITED METHODIST CHURCH DOCKET ITEM NUMBERS 1016-7 & 1016-8

IN RE: Reverend Errol Leslie v. Florida Annual Conference
(Appeal from the Decision of the Southeastern Jurisdiction Committee on Appeals)
And
IN RE: A Review of a Bishop's Decision of Law in the New England Annual Conference Concerning Questions Related to the Trial Decision in Florida Annual Conference v. Reverend Errol Leslie
REPLY BRIEF OF AMICUS CURIAE

SUBMITTED BY
The Reverend Dr. Larry B. Lake

INTRODUCTION

The Counsel for the Church is learned and articulate. Perhaps the type of reasoning expressed in the brief he submitted to the Judicial Council served him well in his previous career as a prosecutor. His fundamental point, made multiple times, was that the Respondent-Appellant confessed and that his admission of guilt is the central focus. But in The United Methodist Church we are required to focus on more than guilt alone. According to the Discipline, the supervisory, administrative and judicial processes of the Church are purposeful, holistic, and focused on healing, reconciliation, restoration, and a just resolution. See 362-364 and 2701-2707. Sometimes these high standards cannot be met fully, and there are times that conference relations and credentials are involuntarily changed. But under our order and

286

discipline this is only allowed if and when conference officials apply the fair process procedures specified in the Discipline, in a manner that is consistent with the decisions of the Judicial Council and the Constitution. The officials of the Florida Annual Conference did not meet this standard in their application of supervisory and judicial procedures against the Respondent-Appellant in this case. And their actions must be rendered null, void and of no legal effect.

II

AUTHORITY FOR SUBMISSION OF BRIEF

This amicus curiae reply brief is submitted pursuant to the Rules of Practice and Procedure promulgated by the Judicial Council, especially Rule V.I. The jurisdiction and powers of the Judicial Council are provided pursuant to 2609 of the Discipline and also 51 & 55-58 of the Constitution. See also Judicial Council Decision No. 1244.

III

ANALYSIS AND RATIONALE

It is not necessary to reply to each of the arguments put forward in the brief submitted by the Counsel for the Church in this case. The following points are stated here to supplement the more detailed arguments presented in my previously submitted amicus curiae brief on Docket Item Nos. 1016-7 & 1016-8:

1.) Officials of the Florida Annual Conference did not have disciplinary or constitutional authority to apply judicial procedures against the Respondent-Appellant in this case. The Counsel for the Church argued in his 1016-7 and 1016-8 briefs that 2719.1

is constitutional and that there is no Judicial Council authority on this matter. He is in error. Judicial Council Decision No. 580 makes the unconstitutionality of 2719.1 all but settled law in the Church, a point of law the Counsel for the Church failed to address in either of his briefs. The General Conference action contained in 2719.1 is unconstitutional because it is an unlawful delegation of constitutional powers and directly conflicts with 20 and 33 of the Constitution.

2.) Even if 2719.1 was constitutional, officials of the Florida Annual Conference did not follow the plain language of its provisions, because it was not possible to rely on those provisions in applying judicial procedures against the Respondent-Appellant in this case. At the time charges and specifications were referred to the Committee on Investigation, the Respondent Appellant did not live within the boundaries of the Florida Annual Conference and was serving an appointment in the New England Annual Conference.

3.) Decision No. 1296 makes the "but for" opinion of the Presiding Officer ascribing the beginning of the judicial process to some prior time irrelevant, moot and without merit. Church officials are not free to make up critical aspects of fair process procedures, especially when they are in conflict with the explicit provisions of the Discipline, merely based on their preferences or to effect some prejudged outcome to their liking.

4.) Both the presiding bishop of the New England Annual Conference and the Counsel for the Church insinuate that declaring 2719.1 unconstitutional would have dire consequences, reversing "multiple verdicts... around the globe" litigated over a long time span. These arguments are without merit. The judicial procedures for appeal provide ample safeguards related to timely notice. Neither a jurisdictional committee on appeals nor the Judicial Council have the jurisdiction and powers to review verdicts and penalties without the proper notice and other appellate procedures being followed in conformity with the Discipline and the Constitution. Any such case could be dispensed in a few sentences. The rendering of 2719.1 unconstitutional would create no known consequences involving prior trials and any unknown consequences would be dealt with procedurally and in favor of the Church.

5.) The Counsel for the Church's arguments in his brief generally relied upon the flawed, erroneous and unfair rulings of the Presiding Officer. For example, the Counsel for the Church on page 4 of his brief related to Docket Item No.10167 "commends the entire ruling to the Judicial Council because it is excellent and thorough in its logic and decisions…" He provides the ruling in its entirety in Appendix II of his brief regarding Docket Item No. 1016-7. The Counsel for the Church also states on page 4 of his brief related to Docket Item No.10167 that he "has been involved in all levels of the discussions surrounding submitting the instant matter to the Florida Committee on Investigations."

6.) The Presiding Officer at the trial provided his ruling denying the Respondent-Appellant's motion to dismiss on January 8, 2016. His rationale states, on page 7, "I denied the motion on this issue based on the lack of any specific authority for the argument and because of the prejudice due to the timing of the issue being raised so long after the judicial process had begun." The Counsel for the Church repeats and relies on this rationale in his brief related to Docket Item No. 1016-7. When he made that ruling on January 8, 2016 the Presiding Officer was well aware that this assertion is based on a false premise, and the Counsel for the Church also knew it was false when he relied upon it in making his arguments. Here is what actually happened:

⊕ After the delivery of the November 20, 2014 letter from the resident bishop of the Florida Conference—a communication that conference officials have admitted violated the fair process rights of the Respondent-Appellant— Reverend Leslie was reeling from the impact of having to move his family on short notice. This letter and its violations of fair process was well-known to both the Presiding Officer and the Counsel for the Church when the Presiding Officer's ruling was handed down on January 8, 2016.

⊕ Shortly, after naming his counsel, the Reverend W. Scott Campbell, the bishop of the New England Annual Conference was approached, in February 2015, about bringing the case back to New England in the interest of fair process. That request was denied.

⊕ The Counsel for the Respondent wrote to the Presiding Officer in March 2015 raising the issue that the Respondent Appellant could not receive a fair trial in Florida, due to the numerous and irreparable violations of fair process, and requested a change of venue.

- The Presiding Officer is well aware that procedures were suspended to pursue a just resolution a process he acknowledged in writing in April of 2015.

- The Presiding Officer was made aware that the just resolution conference took place on June 22, 2015 and that it was not successful.

- While the detailed discussions of the just resolution conference are confidential in nature, it should be noted for this purpose that there were extensive discussions raised by the Respondent-Appellant regarding the invalidity, for multiple reasons, of the 2719.1 Agreement. There also were detailed discussion about Judicial Council No. 1296, which was handed down on April 18, 2016.

- The Presiding Officer was made aware that the Respondent-Appellant took an appointment in the New England Annual Conference beginning July 1, 2015.

- On July 23, 2015, the Counsel for the Church communicated to the Presiding Officer and others that he had decided to refer his charges and specifications to the newly formed Committee on Investigation and that the Committee had recently chosen their chair.

- The Presiding Officer wrote to the Counsel for the Church in response and expressed his support for this decision.

- The Presiding Officer was made aware that in early August 2015 charges and specifications were referred to the Committee on Investigation and that the Respondent-Appellant had thirty days to provide a response.

- In his response, the Respondent-Appellant raised multiple issues related to the so called "2719 Agreement" and these were discussed in the first preliminary organizational meeting between the parties and the chair of the Committee on Investigation on September 1, 2015

- The chair of the Committee on Investigation ruled that a formal ruling would be deferred for action by the Presiding Officer without prejudice.

- Prior to the Committee on Investigation's meeting extensive documentation was provided to the chair of the Committee on Investigation documenting the invalidity of the so called "2719 Agreement" and documenting that the Florida Annual Conference did not have authority to apply judicial procedures against the Respondent-Appellant.

- At the hearing of the Committee on Investigation September 23, 2015, there was extensive information provided about the Florida Conference's lack of authority to apply judicial procedures against the Respondent-Appellant.

- The Discipline provides for a thirty day period after a decision by a Committee on Investigation before further procedures are applied

- Throughout his written rulings the Presiding Officer has shown direct knowledge of what transpired before the Committee on Investigation.

⊕ The Presiding Officer was not reappointed, as he indicated in writing was required, until November 2, 2015.

⊕ On November 19, 2015, the Respondent Appellant's counsel wrote to the Presiding Officer and raised the issue that the Florida Annual Conference did not have authority to apply judicial procedures against the Respondent-Appellant. Another formal motion was put forward, timely, based on the Presiding Officer's instructions, on December 29, 2015.

7.) The Respondent-Appellant did not raise the legal issues related to the so called "2719 Agreement" until late in the process. It is disingenuous and a denial of fair process for the Presiding Officer to use timeliness as a basis for his denial, especially when he knows his premise is factually false. The Respondent-Appellant raised the legal issues related to the so called "2719 Agreement" timely and at every step in the process. Moreover, it is disingenuous for the Counsel for the Church now to continue to rely on this known falsehood.

8.) On page 3 of his brief the Counsel for the Church quotes directly from the disputed "2719 Agreement." He states: "After consideration of the complaint and provisions of 2719, Reverend Leslie has agreed, freely and voluntarily without coercion, that fairness will be better served by having the procedures of 2701 through 2718 carried out by the appropriate officials of the Florida Annual Conference" (emphasis added by the Counsel for the Church).

9.) The plain language quoted by the Counsel for the Church indicates that the Respondent Appellant had considered the complaint. The Counsel for the Church knows and has acknowledged in writing in his briefs that the Respondent-Appellant did not have possession of the written complaint and had not even seen it when he signed the so called "2719 Agreement." The specified factual basis of the alleged agreement of the Respondent-Appellant is clearly false. In fact, the Respondent-Appellant had not considered nor seen the written complaint. He was unaware of the scurrilous and numerous lies it contained. It strains credulity to assert that these actions by Florida Conference officials were not purposeful. Forcing the Respondent-Appellant to sign an agreement based on the consideration of the complaint when the Respondent-Appellant had not been given a copy of the complaint is a form of coercion and certainly violates the fair process procedures required by the Discipline and Judicial Council Decision No. 830.

10.) In his ruling handed down on January 8, 2016 part of the Presiding Officer's rationale dealt not only with the timing of the Respondent Appellant's motion to dismiss, but also a theory on when the judicial process began. The Presiding Officer states "but for the decision of the Judicial Council in Decision 1296, a decision that was issued after the complaint had been referred to the Counsel for the Church, the complaint against Reverend Leslie would have proceeded under the judicial process as defined in the 2012 Book of Discipline, pursuant to 2704.2."

11.) Judicial Council Decision No. 1296 was handed down on April 18, 2015. It strains credulity and is improper for the Presiding Officer to be making rulings based on propositions that are premised on "but for the decision." By this time the process was well established. Decision No. 1296 was a requirement. The Counsel for the Church decided to submit his referral to the Committee on Investigation. The Committee on Investigation had acted and the process had moved forward. Decisions of law and legislation cannot be retroactive; hence, in its Decision No. 1296 the Judicial Council, rightly, said that its decision was prospective. This does not mean that officials of the Florida Annual Conference had the option to ignore it. Even the Counsel for the Church and the Presiding Officer acknowledged this in July 2015. It is irrelevant what might have happened "but for" Decision No. 1296. This line of reasoning is an obfuscation and based on a knowingly false premise related to how late a motion was first put forward in the process (see points Nos. 6 and 7 above).

12.) The Counsel for the Church interpretation of Judicial Council Decision No. 1094 is a misreading of that decision. He directly quotes from that decision "the error of Church law occurred due to the failure to deliver the five letters to Dr. Kendall with the letter of complaint was harmless in light of subsequent events" (emphasis added by the Counsel for the Church). The subsequent events in that case had to do with the execution of a "Statement of Resolution" and that document was an integral basis of the Judicial Council's decision.

13.) Judicial Council Decision No. 1094 is actually supportive of the Respondent-Appellant's claim that the officials of the Florida Annual Conference violation of fair process is an "error of church law." The Judicial Council pointed out that the five letters supporting the letter of complaint was in Dr. Kendall's hand and reviewed by him prior to execution of the statement of resolution. In this case, Florida Conference Officials are basing their entire case on a so called "2719 Agreement" executed prior to the Respondent-Appellant reviewing the written complaint.

14.) The Presiding Officer opined in his January 8, 2016 ruling that the Discipline does not provide for the recension of a so called "2719 Agreement." This rationale is based on flawed logic and erroneous. On January 8, 2016, the Presiding Officer made a substantive ruling on fairness based on what is not in the Discipline. Justice would have been better served if he had based his ruling on what actually is in the Discipline and faced the clear, numerous, substantial, and irreparable violations of fair process explicitly provided for in Church law.

15.) The Presiding Officer's definition of relevance and his application of it is prejudicial and problematic to fair process. For example, the Presiding Officer erred and violated the Respondent-Appellant's fair process rights when he excluded from evidence a written communication from the bishop's assistant that was written to New England Annual Conference officials on the same date of the first supervisory session. That communication indicates that the Respondent-Appellant was remorseful. Later, before the Committee on Investigation, the bishop's assistant testified that he could not remember whether or not the Respondent-Appellant was remorseful. At trial, he testified that the Respondent-Appellant showed no remorse.

The Counsel for the Church argues that even if this is an error it "does not rise to the level of an error that would change the outcome of the trial." This is not for the Counsel for the Church to decide. It is for the trial court to decide, and they were deprived of the evidence.

16.) There is little question that remorse could have had an effect on the penalty assigned by the trial court. But this error was repeated during the penalty phase when the Presiding Officer denied the Respondent-Appellant's motion to allow the trial court to have the written evidence. The Presiding Officer ruled that it was not relevant but it would have been if it had been seen earlier in the process. It was the fault of the bishop's assistant that it took extra time to produce the document stating contemporaneously that the respondent showed remorse. So, the trial court heard testimony from the bishop's assistance that the respondent had no remorse, when the Presiding Officer knew that the testimony was impeachable. This is a fundamental violation of the Respondent-Appellant's fair process rights.

17.) The Counsel for the Church is in error when he asserts that the Respondent-Appellant waived his right to make constitutional arguments in his notice to the Southeastern Jurisdiction Committee on Appeals. In the first issue raised on appeal, the Respondent-Appellant stated "the Florida Conference did not have authority to carry forward judicial procedures involving Reverend Leslie under the provisions

of 2719.1 of the 2012 Book of Discipline." The Committee on Appeals quoted this very sentence in their written opinion on page 7. Once this issue was identified in the Notice of Appeal, the Respondent-Appellant was free to develop all disciplinary and constitutional arguments related to the issue pursuant to the Notice of Appeal.

18.) A Notice of Appeal does not require developing arguments. It would not further the cause of justice and would not be in keeping with the Church's fair process requirements to affirm this argument from the Counsel for the Church and the opinion of the Southeastern Jurisdiction Committee on Appeals.

19.) The Discipline provides in 2708 that "the presiding officer may have legal counsel" during the trial. But this provision also included explicit qualifications. Legal counsel for the presiding office "shall not be the conference chancellor" and legal counsel is "for the sole purpose of advice to the presiding officer during the trial" (emphasis added). These limitations preserve important constitutional principles.

20.) The Constitution provides for the right of "trial by committee," and this means a committee of peers (20 and 33 of the Constitution). Even the terminology in the Discipline is used to convey this fundamental principle. There is no "jury" and a "judge" per se. In the civil courts, the judge is often referred to as the "court." In our polity, the committee of peers is the "trial court." There is a "presiding officer," but his or her role is more limited under the Discipline than that typically afforded to a secular judge. These differences preserve another fundamental principle of the Constitution; i.e., the importance of the separation of powers.

21.) It is under the authority of the annual conference, not the bishop, our Constitution provides for trial by a committee of peers who also are conference members. In our polity, trial of a conference member by episcopacy is not permitted. In this case, the Presiding Officer over stepped his constitutional authority by keeping evidence from the trial court and providing rulings outside of the hearing of the trial court. This usurps the trial court of its constitutional role and authority. Disallowing a conference chancellor from serving as counsel for the presiding officer also reinforces the separation of powers. In this case, the Presiding Officer used the chancellor of the Council of Bishops as legal counsel and that advice was not for the sole purpose of advising to the Presiding Officer during the trial.

22.) In some instances, fair process requires that officials not only recognize the letter of the law but also apply those principles fairly by extension and analogy, especially when fundamental constitutional principles are in play. It would make little sense for the Discipline to prohibit, as it does explicitly in 2708, the use of the conference chancellor for legal counsel to a presiding officer only to allow the chancellor for the Council of Bishops to fulfill that role and to have the separation of powers undermined by another means.

23.) Free floating advice from the chancellor for the Council of Bishops, the arguing of objections and motions out of the hearing of the trial court (except for those matters explicitly provide for to be ruled upon in pretrial motions by the Discipline) and requiring a respondent to conduct extensive pretrial and sidebar litigation undermines the preeminent place that the trial court occupies in our jurisprudence and undermines the constitutional principles of trial by committee and the separation of powers which are enshrined in the constitution.

24.) The Counsel for the Church focuses in his Docket Item No. 1016-7 brief on diminishing the consequence of only one error of church law. But the consequences of the multiple, substantive and irreparable violations of fair process in this case are cumulative. Florida Conference officials did not provide the Respondent-Appellant with a copy of the written complaint in a timely fashion and made an unlawfully verbatim of a supervisory session. The Respondent-Appellant was placed on involuntary leave of absence without notice or exercising his rights to be heard. Florida Conference officials did not afford the Respondent-Appellant his constitutional right to the presumption of innocence. These are not matters that can be diminished, for they are at the very heart of our rights as clergy to constitutionally guaranteed fair process.

IV

CONCLUSIONS, REMEDIES AND
REQUESTED RULINGS

The violations of fair process in this case have been at all levels of the proceedings, and those violations have been numerous, substantial and irreparable. There has been a cumulative effect to all of the instances where officials of the Florida Annual Conference failed to afford the Respondent-Appellant his constitutionally protected fair process rights. Therefore, the following suggested conclusions, remedies and rulings are requested of the Judicial Council:

1.) Either under its review powers of a bishop's ruling of law or under its powers to hear appeals, the Judicial Council should render 2719.1 of the Discipline unconstitutional and, therefore, null, void and without legal effect.

2.) The procedures applied against the Respondent Appellant by Florida Annual Conference officials, including the trial verdict and penalty, should be rendered null, void and of no legal affect.

3.) The original complaint should be remanded to the New England Annual Conference to begin all disciplinary complaint procedures, including a supervisory response, de novo. Instructions should be provided with the remand for all fair process procedures to be followed carefully and diligently.

4.) The remand instructions also should emphasize the Respondent-Appellant's rights against double jeopardy.

5.) The Judicial Council should rule that use of the chancellor of the Council of Bishops in advising a presiding officer in a trial is a violation of the separation of powers.

6.) Further, the Judicial Council should rule that the constitutional principal of trial by committee does not allow extensive litigation of issues outside of the hearing and presence of the trial court and stress the essential and preeminent role of the trial court under the Constitution.

CERTIFICATION AND SIGNATURE

In compliance with the promulgated Rules of Practice
and Procedure of the Judicial Council of The United
Methodist Church, I, Larry B. Lake, hereby, do certify
this 2nd day of September 2016 that I submitted the
Reply Brief of Amicus Curiae related to Docket Item
Nos. 1016-7 & 1016-8 which bears my name on the
title page of this document.

Larry B. Lake

_____

Electronic Signature of Larry B. Lake

The third brief from my defense counsel to the Judicial Council spells out some additional errors of the committee on appeals.

A Brief to the Judicial Council
Addressing Docket No. 2016-7
Concerning the Matter of The Rev. Errol Leslie

Submitted by The Rev. Scott Campbell

Introduction

On January 11, 2016, the Rev. Errol Leslie was found guilty of sexual misconduct, immorality and disobedience to the order and discipline of the United Methodist Church under the provisions of 2702.1 of the 2012 Book of Discipline by a trial court convened by the Florida Annual Conference. On January 12 the court imposed a penalty which revoked Rev. Leslie's membership in the New England Annual Conference, although it did not revoke his orders, which were through the Methodist Church in the Caribbean and the Americas. On February 4, 2016 Rev. Leslie's counsel, Rev. Scott Campbell, a retired elder in the New England Annual Conference, submitted a notice of appeal to the Presiding Officer of the trial, Bishop Alfred Gwinn, and the Resident Bishop of the Florida Annual Conference, Bishop Ken Carter. Bishop Gwinn subsequently forwarded the notice of appeal to the chair of the Committee on Appeals of the Southeastern Jurisdiction, the Honorable Constance Clark.

On May 31, 2016, meeting in Atlanta, GA, the Committee on Appeals heard oral arguments from counsels for both the Church and the Appellant and on June 3, 2016 issued an opinion upholding both the verdict and the penalty of the trial court.

Basis of this Appeal

The Appellant contends that the Committee on Appeals ignored significant constitutional issues, disregarded direct requirements of The Discipline, and failed to understand and/or apply precedential rulings of the Judicial Council. Further, the Committee was profoundly influenced and prejudiced by the question of whether the evidence presented at the trial was sufficient to support the verdict and/or the penalty, a question that was never raised or appealed in the brief or in the arguments of the Appellant. In fact, the Appellant's counsel explicitly waived this basis of appeal, a fact acknowledged by the Committee on page 7 of its opinion. The Appellant claimed, rather, that there were errors of church law sufficient to vitiate the verdict and/or the penalty. This acknowledgment did not prevent the Committee, however, from repeatedly dismissing procedural matters raised by the Appellant by claiming that admissions made by the Appellant at trial sustained a guilty verdict. On at least seven occasions in the body of the Committee's opinion it bolstered its ruling by claiming that the Appellant admitted during the trial to having an extramarital affair. This was not the basis of the appeal and should never have been considered in the Committee's rationale, let alone repeatedly cited as justification for its rulings.

Specifically, this brief will focus upon the following violations of fair process:

1.) The clear mandates of Judicial Council Decision 974 were ignored by the Florida Conference and the Committee on Appeals, which substituted its own definition of fairness in place of that defined by the Judicial Council.

2.) The process surrounding the signing of the socalled "2719 Agreement" was coercive, failed to comply with JC 974 and violated the letter and the spirit of 363.1.b) of The Discipline.

3.) The actions of the General Conferences of 2000, 2004 and 2008 in removing confidentiality from the supervisory process were unconstitutional and directly violated precedents clearly spelled out in JC 698 and JC 836. Further, the Committee on Appeals failed to provide even a single citation in its decision that would demonstrate how alleged differences between the judicial system in effect in 1998 and that in effect in 2016 would render the constitutional protections provided for in JC 836 irrelevant and unnecessary in the present.

4.) The Committee on Appeals invented a rationale for the exclusion from evidence of a letter at trial that directly impeached testimony of a key witness for the Church, claiming that it was excluded on the basis of a missed deadline for submission, a rationale never raised by the Presiding Officer in his rulings.

5.) The Committee on Appeals failed to understand the significant prejudicial influence created by the participation of the Legal Advisor to the Council of Bishops in the pretrial process in direct violation of 2708.1 of The Discipline. It failed to address either the separation of powers or the conflict of interest issues that this inappropriate involvement raises.

6.) The hyper-focus of the Committee on Appeals on the admissions by the Appellant of involvement in an extramarital affair prevented it from fairly addressing numerous fair process violations by the Church.

Issues Related to JC 974

Judicial Council Decision 974 states unambiguously:

The respondent has a right not only to examine but to possess the written complaint and any supporting material accompanying it at the initiation of the supervisory process. A respondent cannot make an adequate response to a complaint without being privy to the complaint in its totality. Fairness alone dictates access to such written complaints and their supporting documents. Full disclosure of all information concerning a complaint must occur for the respondent to make an adequate response. (emphasis added)

In the present instant a signed, written complaint was in the hands of the Florida Conference on July 28, 2014. It was not shared with the Appellant until August 7, 2014. In the meanwhile, District Superintendent Gary Spencer and Assistant to the Bishop David Dodge conducted an in-depth interview with the Appellant from which they extracted information that they later would use to testify against him at trial. Rev. Leslie was without counsel at that meeting. Further, the Appellant was coerced into prematurely signing a document on

August 1 agreeing that the judicial process would take place in Florida, again without benefit of counsel. This document would later be used by officials to deny the Appellant's constitutional right to undergo judicial processes in his own annual conference.

The Committee on Appeals argued that a claim by Superintendent Spencer and Assistant Dodge that the Appellant was advised during the meeting of the allegations of the complaint and the identity of the complainant was a sufficient substitute for the requirements of JC 974. It ignored the fact that testimony at the trial by the defense strenuously disputed this claim and that neither of the Florida officials ever claimed to have given the Appellant a full accounting of the allegations contained in the complaint. In fact, both testified that they only informed Rev. Leslie that the complaint alleged an affair with the Complainant. Neither testified that they informed Rev. Leslie that the signed, written complaint also alleged that he had engaged in numerous sexual affairs with parishioners or that he had sexually abused his own daughters. If this material had been disclosed to the Appellant at the outset of the complaint process, as is required by JC 974, he certainly would have approached his conversations with conference officials from an entirely differently perspective. This is what JC 974 means when it says: Full disclosure of all information concerning a complaint must occur for the respondent to make an adequate response.

The Florida Conference took these spurious allegations seriously enough to launch their own investigation (under the auspices of Rev. Dionne Hammond) of the charges contained in the original complaint. The entire complaint was also shared with the Bishop of the New England Annual Conference, without the Appellant having seen it or even being fully advised of its contents, as the Florida Conference attempted to secure the agreement of the New England Conference to suspend Rev. Leslie from active ministry. The Committee on Appeals failed to see how one party having exclusive access to all the information, and using that information to move the process forward in the way it desired during a crucial decision-making period, was unfair. By the time the Appellant received a copy of the complaint he had already:

1.) participated in a meeting without being accompanied by an advocate during which statements he was alleged to have made would later be used against him at trial,

2.) been coerced into signing a binding, irrevocable agreement about where judicial proceedings would go forward, and

3.) been suspended from active ministry.

All this took place without the Appellant knowing what the Church had it its possession. The train was already hurtling down the track to convict Errol Leslie and expel him from ministry and the complete disregard for the provisions of JC 974 was instrumental in achieving that goal. The Committee on Appeals did not have the authority to substitute its own opinions about acceptable alternatives for the clear, unambiguous requirements spelled out by the Judicial Council in JC 974.

Issues Related to the "2719 Agreement"

It is undisputed in the transcripts of the hearing before the Committee on Investigation and the transcripts of the trial itself that Rev. Gary Spencer informed the Appellant on July 31, 2014 that if he did not sign a document indicating where he wanted judicial proceedings to go forward by noon the next day that he would lose the possibility of having the process occur in Florida. There are so many things wrong with this approach that it is difficult to know where to begin. The following list of objections will have to suffice:

1.) 2719.1 is a paragraph that deals with judicial processes. It has nothing to do with the supervisory response. At the time the Appellant was compelled to sign the document in question there was no judicial process, only allegations by a complainant and a fledgling supervisory process. 363.1.b) makes it clear that the supervisory response is not to be "part of any legal process." It would be more than three months before it was determined that the supervisory process had failed to produce a just resolution and the matter would be referred to a counsel for the church, thus triggering judicial proceedings under the terms of the 2012 Book of Discipline.

2.) The Appellant had asked on July 30 to have a copy of the complaint against him. That request was denied by Rev's Spencer and Dodge, so at the time he signed the document on August 1, he still had not seen the complaint against him, nor did he have any knowledge of the majority of its contents. The Committee on Appeals highlights sentence four of the document as evidence that the process under which it was signed was above reproach. Sentence four reads: *After consideration of the complaint and the provisions of 2719, Rev. Leslie has agreed, freely and voluntarily without coercion, that fairness will be better served by having the procedures of 2701-2718 carried out by the appropriate officers of the Florida Annual Conference.* How, one wonders, was the Appellant able to consider a complaint he had never seen and which was being intentionally withheld from him? No Book of Discipline was provided to the Appellant to review prior to the signing. How was he supposed to understand the provisions of 2719 in relation to the judicial process outlined in 2701–2718? How was his signing free and voluntary if he were told that if he didn't sign it by noon on August 1 (more than three months before there was a judicial process) that he would lose any privileges that 2719 might afford him? The document was signed on the Church's timetable, not the Appellant's. He was not informed that it would be binding and irrevocable. He was not given sufficient time to process the implications of signing this document, nor was he advised to consult with counsel before doing so. The time to sign a binding agreement about where judicial proceedings would take place would have been after it had been determined that such proceedings would even occur and after the Appellant had had sufficient time to reflect on such an important question and to secure the advice of counsel. Superintendent Spencer also denied Rev. Leslie's request on August 1 to be given a copy of the "2719 Agreement." His Counsel never saw the document until it arrived with the charging documents of the Counsel for the Church on February 17, 2015, a further serious violation of JC 974.

3.) The plain language of 2719.1 requires an agreement among the appropriate bishops and the member that fairness will be better served by having a process go forward in a particular venue. No such conversation ever took place among the parties. No consideration of the various options was ever discussed among the three. In fact, to this day no such conversation has ever taken place. Instead, a District Superintendent, who was not a party to the agreement, compelled a signature from the Appellant by resorting to threats of removing options. The signature obtained in this flawed process was subsequently used to deny the Appellant's request to be tried in New England.

4.) The Presiding Officer at the trial ruled that JC 974 was irrelevant to the signing of the "2719 Agreement." He could not see a connection between the requirement of the Judicial Council that a respondent have access to all materials in the possession of the Church at the outset of the complaint process because "fairness alone" dictates such, and the signing of a document that required the respondent to affirm that he had considered a complaint he had never seen under threat of losing the privilege of having a choice about the venue for a potential trial, if such ever came to be. The Presiding Officer made this ruling in response to the Appellant's request to set aside the "2719 Agreement" and exercise his constitutional right to be tried in his own annual conference. The Committee on Appeals was likewise oblivious to the coercive elements in this process. One can only hope that the Judicial Council, long a defender of fair process, will see the connections these parties could not.

The Unconstitutionality of Removing Confidentiality from the Supervisory Process

The most egregious dereliction of its responsibilities by the Committee on Appeals came in its two sentence dismissal of the very carefully developed constitutional arguments raised by the Appellant in relation to the removal of confidentiality from the supervisory process by the actions of successive General Conferences from 2000-2008. The Appellant respectfully requests members of the Judicial Council to carefully review at this time the arguments raised on pp.12-16 of his brief to the Committee on Appeals. In summary, he argues that JC 698 held that passing information from the supervisory process to the judicial process without allowing a respondent to have the fair process protections of verbatims and legal counsel during supervision was unconstitutional. When a new judicial process came into being in the 1996 Book of

Discipline it, likewise, did not provide for verbatims or legal counsel during supervision. When the Minnesota Annual Conference questioned this lack of protection in a request for a Declaratory Decision, the Judicial Council issued Decision 836 which held that such protections were unnecessary under the new system because there was an impenetrable wall in the new system between the supervisory and the judicial processes. If the supervisory process failed to yield a just resolution, nothing was to go forward but the "bare complaint." The General Conferences of 2000, 2004 and 2008 then proceeded, step by step, to remove this barrier, first permitting supervisory material to be shared with the Committee on Investigation, then with the Counsel for the Church, and finally removing the provision that the supervisory process was to be confidential from 363.1.b).

The Counsel for the Church argued that the judicial systems of 1996 and 2012 were completely different from one another and that JC 698 and JC 836 were thus no longer relevant. The Committee on

Appeals bought his argument. Neither the Counsel nor the Committee was able, however, to offer a single citation to demonstrate how such alleged differences in processes now provide the protections for a respondent during the supervisory process that previous Judicial Councils deemed essential. When the respondent is denied the opportunity to have an accurate record of what transpired in supervisory sessions or to be represented by legal counsel during those sessions, he or she is completely vulnerable to misremembering or, worse, misrepresentation of what was said if that material is allowed to go forward. JC 698 recognized and named this danger and called this vulnerability unconstitutional. JC 836 also understood what was at stake and was at pains to assure the Church that the problem was solved by fixing a wall between the supervisory and the judicial processes. The above cited General Conferences then proceeded to take the wall apart, brick by brick, and never made provision for the fair process concerns named in JC 698 and acknowledged in JC 836 to be addressed. The burden is on the Committee on Appeals to show how the allegedly different system provides for those fair process rights that previous Judicial Councils determined not only to be essential, but to be constitutionally mandated. Their one-sentence dismissal of this critical issue does not fulfill their obligation.

This is not an incidental issue. Information from supervisory sessions was used in framing the Bill of Charges issued against the Appellant and disputed testimony regarding what transpired in supervisory sessions was offered by both sides at trial. The clear intention of the present judicial system, as interpreted by JC 836, was that none of this material should have been before the trial court. The purpose of the supervisory response, according to 363.1.b) is to attain a just resolution among all parties. Such a resolution cannot be easily achieved when material from the supervisory process is being extracted and preserved for later use at trial. The Judicial Council itself recently acknowledged this problem in JC 1318 when it ruled unconstitutional a legislative attempt before the General Conference to introduce penalties (which belong to the judicial sphere) into the just resolution process. The Decision states in relevant part: *A Just Resolution is an alternative way of handling chargeable offenses... The three amended paragraphs, 363.1, 2701.5 and 2706.5c3, as acted upon by the Judicial Administration Legislative Committee are unconstitutional.*

Mischaracterization by Appeals Committee of Exclusion of Dodge Testimony

The Committee on Appeals mischaracterized the reason that an email from Assistant to the Bishop, David Dodge, was excluded from evidence. It states in its ruling on page 11: *The Presiding Officer reaffirmed his prior ruling that the email could not be admitted because it had not been produced by the December 29, 2015 deadline.* This statement is in error and it is significant for reasons that will follow.

First, there was never any mention in any of the original correspondence among the parties that took place on January 5, 2016 of the email being excluded because the December 29 deadline had been missed, nor did that factor enter into any of the official objections of the Church nor the original ruling of the Presiding Officer on this matter. The issue was always that the Church had not had the item in question before it was introduced in the out of-court commissioned testimony of Rev. Dodge. There was no ruling that a deadline had been missed and therefore the document was excluded.

Because there was no such ruling, the Defense attempted once more to introduce the email during the penalty phase of the trial in order to bolster the testimony of the Respondent that he had repeatedly expressed remorse for his actions. By this point the Church had had the document in its possession for a week and had had ample time to examine it. The Church once more objected, citing doubts about the authenticity of the email, and claiming that it was a backdoor way to impeach the testimony of Rev. Dodge. Still there was no claim made that the December 29 deadline had been missed. The Presiding Officer did once more sustain the objections of the Church to the introduction of this document, but not on the basis of the deadline having been missed. He did mention in passing that if the document had been submitted with the original documents he probably would have allowed it, but that had to do with the question of the Church having ample time to review it, and did not reference a missed deadline. Here is exactly what the Presiding Officer said in excluding the document for a second time:

You know, in my opinion, had you had this document in the series of documents that you gave us under standard time, I would have probably admitted this into evidence, but the reason I chose not to do that was the way it was presented at the time of testimony without the Church counsel having any opportunity to see the document or know about it. I do not believe this document is relevant to the penalty phase. So I'm not—I'm ruling that this document cannot be used in the penalty phase. [Emphasis added.]

The email was excluded because the Presiding Officer could not see its relevance, plain and simple. At no point in the entire process was a missed December 29 deadline referenced by anyone other than the Committee on Appeals. Because the Committee on Appeals believed the Presiding Officer's ruling to be based on a missed deadline it never dealt with the actual reason for his exclusion of the material, namely his belief that it was irrelevant in the penalty phase.

This question is important because it allowed an impression of an unrepentant, unremorseful respondent to linger with the trial court. While we cannot know with certainty the extent to which this false impression influenced the trial court, we do know that it was very important to the Committee on Investigation, taking up two pages of transcript. The Appellant believes the Presiding Officer erred when he determined that a document bolstering his testimony that he was extremely repentant from the outset of the complaint process was irrelevant. He also believes that the rationale offered by the Committee on Appeals was erroneous.

The fact is that the Defense made extensive efforts to obtain the document in question in a timely and appropriate fashion and was prevented from doing so by a chief witness for the Church. Further, there is no requirement in The Discipline that materials be shared in advance with the other party, only that they be made available to the other party. There was never a question of the document being withheld from the other party. It was a document from the Church's own witness and was shared with the Counsel for the Church within hours of being received, unlike the Church's determination to withhold the original complaint from the Appellant for nine crucial days. Even if the

Presiding Officer was correct in excluding the document from the pretrial cross-examination of Rev. Dodge, the Appellant believes he was in error in excluding the material from consideration by the trial court in the penalty phase.

Issues Relating to the Involvement of the Legal Advisor to the Council of Bishops

For a number of years Attorney William Waddell has been training bishops about how to conduct trials. He legitimately undertakes this task in his role as legal advisor to the Council of Bishops. However, in addition to that training role, Attorney Waddell has, in a number of instances, served as a legal advisor to presiding officers during the pretrial phase and throughout the trials themselves. When Attorney Waddell was present for a pretrial conference phone call in the present matter, the Counsel for the Respondent objected to his presence, citing 2708.1 which states: The presiding officer may have legal counsel...for the sole purpose of advice to the presiding officer during the trial. The Presiding Officer overruled the objection of the Defense, stating that he considered the pretrial phase to be a part of the trial.

It is not clear the extent to which Attorney Waddell continued to advise the Presiding Officer in the present matter. A request from the Defense to the Presiding Officer to disclose this information went unanswered, as did two subsequent requests to the Committee on Appeals to solicit this information. The very fact that these requests were ignored gives the appearance that there was something to hide. The Appellant spelled out his objections to Attorney Waddell's involvement in detail on pp. 27-29 of his brief to the Committee on Appeals and will not reiterate those objections here. In summary, there are issues of both the separation of powers and conflict of interest raised by the legal advisor to the Council of Bishops advising presiding officers during the pretrial phase and trials themselves. While the Appellant has no questions about the integrity of Attorney Waddell, the conflict of roles is problematic. The Council of Bishops is not a neutral body. Bishops are consecrated to care for the spiritual and temporal affairs of the Church. Bishops appoint Counsels for the Church.

Once again, the Committee on Appeals was insensitive at best to issues that the Judicial Council has long held as central to our judicial polity, in particular the issue of the separation of powers. JC Decisions 799 and 1156 provide further interpretation of this issue. The Committee refused to hold the church accountable for this blurring of the lines by once again referring to the Appellant's admitted guilt.

Nevertheless, even assuming the Presiding Officer's consultation with legal counsel during pretrial conferences was held to be in error, it was not an error that affected the outcome of this proceeding, in which the appellant admitted to a months' long extramarital affair.

The Misguided Focus of the Committee on Appeals

On at least seven occasions in its opinion the Committee on Appeals references admissions by the Appellant that he was involved in an extramarital affair, usually in order to excuse the Church for violating the Appellant's fair process rights. The argument goes something like this. "Yes, the Church might have been in error here, but the error didn't affect the outcome because the Appellant admitted he had an affair." The fact is, the Appellant had no other defense strategy left to him because of the Church's violation of his fair process rights. The admission of testimony regarding the supervisory process left him in an untenable position. Without an accurate record of what was actually said during supervision and without counsel to advise him, he didn't have a chance when it came to countering the testimony of his District Superintendent and the Assistant to the Bishop, persons whom the Counsel for the Church refers to as "great statesmen of the Church." Without having been privy to all that the Church knew from the outset of the process, he was unprepared to make an adequate response to the complaint or to make an informed choice about the venue for his trial. When he honestly admitted having made a terrible mistake for a short period in his life, the Committee on Appeals took that as license to ignore Disciplinary requirements and Judicial Council precedents which applied to this case, stating, in effect, that these violations were irrelevant because Rev. Leslie admitted his guilt. Once again, the Appellant never claimed that there was not sufficient evidence to sustain the verdict and/or the penalty in his appeal. He claimed that the Church made errors of Church law sufficient to vitiate the verdict and/or penalty. That means that the focus of the Committee on Appeals needed to be on the Church and its behavior, not on the first question with which it was so preoccupied. Unfortunately, a serious consideration of the violations of fair process rights at every level of the Church is almost entirely absent from their document. Their dismissal of the constitutional arguments around the removal of confidentiality from the supervisory process with a single sentence is just one example of the almost total failure of this Committee to do its job responsibly.

The Appellant has raised a number of other issues in his brief to the Committee on Appeals that he hopes will be duly considered by the Judicial Council, but for reasons of focus and brevity, he chooses to lift up for special consideration only the above issues in this document.

Conclusion

Rev. Errol Leslie's fair process rights were repeatedly violated by the Church.

- He was not provided with a copy of the complaint against him in a timely fashion in violation of JC 974.
- He was coerced into prematurely signing a document that deprived him of his constitutional right to be tried in his own annual conference by his own peers and was then denied possession of the document he was compelled to sign.
- He was deprived of rights identified by the Judicial Council in decisions 698 and 836 as being constitutional by the actions of three successive General Conferences to remove the boundaries between the supervisory and judicial processes.
- He was prevented from introducing exculpatory and relevant evidence in the penalty phase of the trial by an erroneous ruling by the Presiding Officer. The Committee on Appeals then misattributed the motivation for this ruling and did not deal with the question of the relevance of the document in question.
- The involvement of the legal advisor to the Council of Bishops in advising the Presiding Office during the trial process was a violation of the separation of powers and a conflict of interest.

- The Committee on Appeals did not properly address the issues that were appealed, focusing undue attention on the question of whether the evidence sustained the verdict and/or penalty.

Remedy Sought

The Appellant requests that the verdict and penalty imposed by the trial court of the Florida Annual Conference be set aside and Rev. Leslie be returned to full membership in the New England Annual Conference.

Respectfully Submitted, Scott Campbell
Counsel for the Appellant
August 20, 2016
Certification of Service
Docket 2016-7

There were other pastors who became aware of the case, observed the flaws referenced multiple times above, and chose to submit their own briefs. One such was in this fourth brief from a full elder associated with the New York Conference. This one primarily referenced the decision of law handed down by Bishop Devadhar regarding whether or not a conference has the authority to terminate the conference membership of an elder in another conference.

DOCKET NO. 1016-8

BRIEF OF AMICUS CURIAE REV. PAUL A. FLECK IN OPPOSITION TO THE BISHOP'S DECISION OF LAW IN THE NEW ENGLAND ANNUAL CONFERENCE CONCERNING WHETHER 2719.1 UNCONSTITUTIONALLY CONFLICTS WITH 33 OF THE CONSTITUTION

OF THE UNITED METHODIST CHURCH
("THE CONSTITUTION"), WHETHER
GENERAL CONFERENCE CAN DELEGATE
POWERS CONSTITUTIONALLY RESERVED
TO AN ANNUAL CONFERENCE, AND
WHETHER THE CONSTITUTION ALLOWS AN
ANNUAL CONFERENCE TO REVOKE THE
MEMBERSHIP OF A CLERGY MEMBER OF
ANOTHER ANNUAL CONFERENCE

I.

RECOMMENDED ACTION BY THE JUDICIAL COUNCIL

This amicus curiae recommends that the ruling of Bishop Devadhar be reversed in its entirety. Rev. Errol Leslie should likewise be reinstated as a Member in Full Connection of the New England Annual Conference.

II.

FACTUAL BACKGROUND / STATEMENT OF FACTS

This amicus takes issue with Bishop Devadhar's mixed statement of fact and law when he states "[t]he New England Annual Conference clergy session had no authority to vote on the matter and merely received the report." The question of the Annual Conference's authority is, of course, what is directly at issue in this case. The New England Annual Conference had every right to determine the conference relations of one of its clergy members in full connection, and that clergy member had every right to seek recourse via a jury trial in the Annual Conference where he had his membership.

Bishop Devadhar's factual background also neglects to mention whether fair process was followed in Rev. Leslie's case. In fact, fair process was denied Rev. Leslie when he initially agreed to undergo the complaint process in Florida only three days after learning of a complaint against him. He had not seen the complaint. He was not represented by counsel. He then attempted to exercise his constitutional right to be tried in his own annual conference, but Bishops Devadhar and Carter refused to allow him to do so. His request was made prior to any charges being presented.

III.

JURISDICTION

The Judicial Council has jurisdiction of this case under pars. 51 and 56.3 of The Constitution and par. 2609.6 of the Discipline.

IV.

ARGUMENT AND AUTHORITIES

A. Clergy Members Are Guaranteed a Right to Trial by Jury in the Conference in Which They Have Their Membership by The Constitution, Pars. 20 & 33

Fair process under both the Constitution and other provisions of the Discipline demands the right to trial by one's peers. That is why, in the trial of a bishop, for example, the jury pool consists of clergy in full connection from within that bishop's jurisdiction named by the College of Bishops. 2712, Discipline. Correspondingly, in writing the provision concerning the "Trial of a Clergy Member of an Annual Conference, Local Pastor, Clergy on Honorable or Administrative Location, or Diaconal Minister" [underline/ emphasis added] pursuant to par. 2713 of the Discipline, the General Conference must have likewise contemplated a pool of persons consisting of clergy in full connection from the clergy member's own annual conference. 2713.3, Discipline. Why would we have a system where bishops are guaranteed a trial by their peers within their jurisdiction but clergy are not within their annual conference?

B.   A Jury Trial Determination Constitutes a Vote of the Annual Conference Pursuant to Par. 33 The jury trial determination is what should properly constitute the vote of the annual conference pursuant to paragraph 33 of the Constitution. Trial court juries of an annual conference vote both upon matters of whether to convict (9 votes per 2711.2 of the Discipline) and upon the penalty (7 votes per 2711.2 of the Discipline). The trial court can vote to "terminate the conference membership, and revoke the credentials of conference membership, commissioning, ordination, or consecration of the respondent..." However, that is subject to the constitutional requirement that the annual conference "shall have reserved to it the right to vote... on all matters relating to the character and conference relations of its clergy members..." 33, Constitution, Discipline.

C. Separation of Powers Prevents a Bishop from Ceding the Rights of an Annual Conference to Determine the Character and Conference Relations of One of Its Members

A bishop is not a member of the annual conference by virtue of his or her role and should not be allowed to cede rights specifically reserved to the annual conference by transferring venue of a matter to another conference pursuant to par. 2719.1. See, e.g., Judicial Council Decisions 22, 925, 1023. Paragraph 33 of the Constitution specifically reserves to the annual conference the question of the conference relations of its members, not the presiding Bishop. Our polity's delicate balance would be undone if a bishop were allowed to abdicate the role reserved to the annual conference of determining the character of its clergy members through jury trial. Such a result is not contemplated in our polity.

D. This Is Not a Question Venue for the Trial, It Is a Question of Personal Jurisdiction of the Trial Court

The Bishop has confused venue for the trial with whether the trial court in Florida properly had jurisdiction over Rev. Errol Leslie and his status in the first instance. Paragraph 2719.1 is a venue provision established for convenience. See also 2708.4 (Governing a request for change of venue immediately prior to trial). But, as the Judicial Council has always recognized in its own rubrics for decisions, you first must determine jurisdiction of the court before proceeding any further. There has to be jurisdiction of the subject matter, i.e., the issue in dispute (for example, this Judicial Council has subject matter jurisdiction of this particular matter by virtue of 51, 56.3, and 2609.6 of the Discipline).

There also has to be jurisdiction over the person, or personal jurisdiction. In this instance, the matter of personal jurisdiction is governed by the member's home conference. Paragraph 33 of the Constitution is the only provision in the Discipline that speaks to this. There are no Judicial Council decisions that speak to this either, to this amicus' knowledge.

E. Even If Par. 2719.1 Is Found Constitutional, There Has Been No Finding That "Fairness Will Be Better Served" by Having the Complaint and Trial Process Take Place in the Florida Conference

Constitutional fair process demands that the requisites of Paragraph 2719.1 be so much more than mere agreement of the parties. There must be a finding by the parties (the bishop of the clergy member's home conference, the bishop of conference where the clergy serves/resides, and the clergy member) that "fairness will be better served" by having the complaint and trial process take place in the conference where the clergy member serves/ resides as opposed to the conference where membership is held. The record here indicates that no such finding was made by the parties to the agreement. Quite to the contrary, the record demonstrates fundamentally unfair process.

V.

CONCLUSION AND PRAYER

Therefore, circumstances considered, this amicus curiae respectfully requests that the Judicial Council reverse Bishop Devadhar's ruling, and that Rev. Errol Leslie be reinstated as a Member in Full Connection of the New England Annual Conference.

Rev. Paul A. Fleck
Full Member Elder, New York Annual Conf

Between my personal brief and the additional three briefs stated above in their entirety, there were some strong and compelling arguments which would cause a normal and objective court of appeal or Judicial Council to reverse the actions of the Florida Conference. However, that was not to be. It seemed that at every level, the original trial court; the committee on appeals as well as the Judicial Council, the case was just relitigated rather than acknowledging the level of ethics—or lack thereof—as demonstrated by the Florida Conference. The partial brief below submitted by Rev. Jay Therrell is a case in point where the higher courts were asked to rule based on guilt or innocence and not based on the Methodist laws and its constitution.

CHAPTER 14

A Rebuttal of the Same Old...Same Old

Throughout this sharing, I have mentioned several times that the representatives of the church used my confession to sin as leverage to ignore the blatant and deliberate unethical practices of the church and even after appeal, to uphold the penalty at both levels. The issue of fairness which the Book of Discipline emphasized did not come into play. I would hope that anyone reading this narrative and who is looking at this with an objective eye would be able to recognize that the church continued to replay my confession over and over. In this chapter, I am going to include excerpts from the actual rebuttal which the counsel for the church, Rev. Jay Therrell submitted both to the Committee on appeal as well as to the Judicial Council. There was very little change in the arguments presented because, really and truly, they had no defense of the unfair process. As I reference the redundant snippets below, I will include my own commentary on each section as they appear so as to point out the flaws which both appellant courts would have seen but chose to ignore.

THE FLORIDA ANNUAL CONFERENCE OF
THE UNITED METHODIST CHURCH

BRIEF ON BEHALF OF THE CHURCH IN THE
MATTER OF REV. ERROL LESLIE V. FLORIDA
ANNUAL CONFFERENCE

(Appeal from the decision of the Southeastern
Jurisdictional Committee on Appeals)

Docket No. 1016-7

The Counsel for the Church for the Florida Annual Conference of The United Methodist Church brings this brief in opposition to the Brief of the Appellant in the Matter of the Rev. Errol E. Leslie v. Florida Annual Conference.

Introduction & Matters Related to Questions/ Standards

This is not an appeal where the Respondent has denied his wrongdoings. To the contrary, Rev. Leslie has admitted to his gross misconduct: immorality, sexual misconduct, and disobedience to the Order and Discipline of The United Methodist Church. (See p. 232-3 of Trial Transcript Day One) The Respondent had a months-long affair with the Complainant with the end goal of divorcing his wife and marrying the Complainant.

To this first point, as my defense counsel pointed out, the issue of my confession or my guilt was not one which was up for debate. This was already dealt with in the trial phase of the process. This case is now at the stage of the appeal and it was never raised by my defense counsel or by anyone else on the defense team. As such, there is no reason to try to prove guilt or innocence:

1.) Because the Church is submitting a brief without knowing what points the Appellant will continue to raise with the Judicial Council, the Counsel for the Church is going to include arguments for all of the original points of appeal raised by the

Appellant before the Southeastern Jurisdictional Committee on Appeals ("SEJCOA").

My thought is that the real reason why he was raising these points again was that he had no other point to try and manufacture. He really did not have a solid response to the flaws raised by the defense.

2.) The Church presented overwhelming physical evidence proving the Respondent's sexual misconduct, immorality, and dis-obedience to the Order and Discipline of The United Methodist Church. Moreover, the Respondent admitted his guilt of all the charges on day one of the trial (see pages 232-3 of the trial transcript, Day One).

I thought that he already stated this in his first point. For some unknown reason, he got comfort and satisfaction out of repetition.

3.) Any procedural errors have been rectified and cured without prejudice to the Respondent and without effect on the trial's outcome. The arguments below will bear this out.

The fact that "any procedural errors have been rectified and cured" is an admission to the procedural errors which the defense talked about. Since they were so many—and that was what the appeal was all about—how could he determine that it would not have had an effect on the outcome of the penalty? The other real question was, were these procedural errors really "errors," in which case they demonstrate ignorance and incompetence, or were they intentional in which case they demonstrate dishonesty?

Second, the Respondent argues that because a judicial process was not started at the time the document was signed, the agreement is rendered null and void. The

Church agrees with the fact that a judicial process had not commenced on the date the 2719 agreement was put in place, but this does not render it null and void. The two have nothing to do with each other. The agreement simply determined that if and when a judicial process commenced that it would happen in the Florida Conference and not the New England Conference. The plain language of 2719.1 does not say when the agreement must be made. It does not speak to time frames or deadlines. It does not state the conditions under which such an agreement must be made. All of the arguments of the Respondent along this line are simply the Respondent's opinion. The Appellant's Brief to the SEJCOA does not point to any paragraph in the Discipline or Judicial Council decision requiring otherwise. As the Respondent points out, fairness is subjective and in the eye of the beholder.

The counsel is here stating his opinion and stretching his interpretation of the law but then he is reprimanding the defense for stating what he determines is "an opinion." He did not respond to the charge that the district superintendent falsely and knowingly placed an artificial deadline for the agreement to be signed thereby taking full advantage of the respondent's ignorance. Additionally, it must be pointed out that both the counsel for the church as well as the committee on appeals continuously rebuffed points made by the defense by stating that there is no clause in the Book of Discipline which mandates a particular action. At the same time when there are such disciplinary clauses which are referenced, the response is that it would not have changed the outcome of the verdict or penalty. It is clear that there was no sense of objectivity. Instead, inconsistent reasoning prevailed in order to sustain the implicit bias.

The argument that Rev. Leslie was asked to sign the document before he knew the contents of the complaint is untrue. Reverend Leslie was very much aware, by that time, of the fact that a complaint had been made against him regarding sexual misconduct.

Once more, the counsel is choosing to make statements which he knew were untruths. I knew that a complaint had been filed against me alleging sexual misconduct, but I did not know of the other twenty-six allegations—many of which are inflammatory and portrays me in a far worse light than I would have expected. My response to the complaint would have been much different had I known all the contents. In fact, I chose to include the original complaint in the handwriting of the complainant, not because I am proud of the contents, but in order to make the point that the church acted cruelly in withholding it from me initially while I am making seemingly irrevocable decisions and also withheld it from the trial court as they were considering the penalty.

The Appellant's SEJCOA Brief argues

Perhaps it was assumed by officials of the Florida Conference that it was only a matter of time until judicial proceedings would occur and they wanted to get a head start on that process. If so, such an assumption would be indicative that they presumed the appellant to be guilty of the allegations contained in the complaint, a direct violation of 363.1.b which specifies that complaints are to be treated only as allegations during the supervisory process.

Throughout the Appellant's SEJCOA Brief, the Respondent's Counsel seems to assert the power of clairvoyance by knowing what thoughts and emotions the officials of the Florida Conference had, the members of various Judicial Councils had, and the delegations of multiple General Conferences. Just because the Respondent believes something to be the case does not make it so. The Church was simply trying to cover all contingencies and possibilities. It should not be penalized for performing due diligence.

The counsel is suggesting that forcing a respondent to sign a document prematurely is now synonymous with "performing due diligence"? This is not demonstrating the power of clairvoyance, this is basic common sense. It is not just a matter of believing an opinion that is formed out of a vacuum to be true; there is a continuous pattern by the church to demonstrate their bias and prejudice throughout the process.

> Furthermore, when Rev. Leslie agreed to have a judicial process go forward in Florida, he signed a document which contained the following paragraph four which reads in its entirety, "After consideration of the complaint and the provisions of 2719, Rev. Leslie has agreed, freely and voluntarily without coercion, that fairness will be better served by having the procedures of 2701— 2718 carried out by the appropriate officers of the Florida Annual Conference." [Emphasis added.] If Rev. Leslie did not believe this to be the case, he did not have to sign the document. This is a revisionist attempt at forum shopping that has gone on throughout this entire process. Once Rev. Leslie determined that if he could get the instant matter handled in the New England Conference that there was a greater probability of having a minor penalty imposed on him, he has done everything he could to get this issue removed from Florida.

This is the same counsel who just criticized the defense for claiming the power of clairvoyance but now he has the power to know of "Rev Leslie's revisionist attempt." *Once Rev. Leslie determined that if he could get the instant matter handled in the New England Conference that there was a greater probability of having a minor penalty imposed on him, he has done everything he could to get this issue removed from Florida.* This statement confirmed the point that Florida had only one penalty in mind so that going through the motions of the trial was routine. The counsel makes it clear that Reverend Leslie did everything in his power to have the proceedings removed from Florida because he thought that there was a greater probability of having a minor penalty imposed on him. The suggestion here is that the Florida Conference fought to hold on to the case because their bias led them to the conclusion that they were going to get the maximum penalty out of the trial court. In actuality, I was merely seeking justice and fairness. The point is further confirmed by this other statement immediately below.

> There are two criteria required to invoke 2719. Both were met. It should be well noted that first, 2719, on its plain language, does not provide a mechanism by which an agreement can be rescinded. To allow such a rescission would encourage forum shopping for the annual conference that would be most favorable to the respondent.
>
> The many references to Judicial Council decision 974 are a complete overreach and there is nothing in that decision that relates to agreements under 2719. Much ink is spilled on this argument, but it is all opinion.

How can it be an overreach when the Judicial Council decision makes it clear that this has to do with fairness? The actual wording from the Judicial Council is that "fairness…*dictates.*"

> There is no paragraph of the Discipline or a Judicial Council decision directly on point. The Council can only make its decisions based on the plain language of the Discipline or decisions rendered by its predecessors. To do otherwise would turn the Council into a legislative body with powers that the Discipline does not give to it. The Respondent's attempt to argue

that he was stopped at every point along this journey from raising this issue only shows that the Respondent was trying to raise the issue inappropriately. It is appropriate for the Committee on Appeals and Judicial Council to consider this issue. It was not appropriate for the Committee on Investigation to consider it because the Discipline did not empower them to do so. The presiding officer of the COI preserved the issue rightly for appeal and the Judicial Council is now rightly empowered to rule.

Somehow I am not able to understand the point which the counsel for the church is trying to make in his paragraph immediately above. It seems that the Committee on Appeal and the Judicial Council were both able to understand it. The attempts to get the case moved from the Florida Conference to the New England Conference started very early in the process.

Point of Appeal #2:

The Respondent argues that the Florida Conference did not provide the Respondent with a copy of the complaint against him at the outset of the supervisory process while at the same time requiring him to make decisions about where the complaint process would go forward.

First, as noted above, the two matters are not related. The 2719 agreement has nothing to do with the time frame of the original complaint being given to the Respondent. There is nothing in the plain language of 2719 regarding the original complaint. This is an overreach.

Here again is another case in point that whatever the counsel is not able to respond to adequately, he dismisses it by saying that it is an overreach. The Judicial Council ruling 974 determined that the complaint is supposed to be given to the respondent. That is just the policy of the United Methodist Church. However, as usual, the counsel is trying to dance around the established fact and policy.

> Second, the Florida Conference has already acknowledged that it failed to give the Respondent a copy of the original complaint on the day the Respondent met with his district superintendent. The original complaint, however, was forwarded to the Respondent nine days later. The Florida Conference argues that this error was cured by giving Rev. Leslie a copy of the complaint and also argues that it does not rise to the standard of vitiating the verdict of the trial court as required by the Discipline.
>
> The Judicial Council felt similarly when it rendered its decision 1094 on April 28, 2008, which has similar circumstances to the instant matter: a clergyperson accused of sexual misconduct who was not given a copy of five letters of complaint at the very beginning of his disciplinary process. The decision held
>
> *Dr. Kendall should have been provided with the five letters when he was provided with a copy of the May 16, 2005 letter of complaint as a matter of fair process. The failure to do so was an error of church law. The letters were supplied to Dr. Kendall on June 12, 2005, prior to his execution of the Statement of Resolution. Providing letters at that time remedied the failure to do so previously. Dr. Kendall had the opportunity to review the letters at that time and he voluntarily entered into the Statement of Resolution with knowledge of the contents of the letters. The error of church law that occurred due to the failure to deliver the five letters to Dr. Kendall with the letter of complaint was harmless in light of subsequent events. Dr. Kendall was not prejudiced in any way by this error and, under the circumstances,*

the error is not sufficient to vitiate the verdict or the penalty.
(Emphasis added)

The major difference in this case is that Dr. Kendall had an opportunity to review the five letters before he voluntarily entered into an agreement. That is a huge difference. I did not have the opportunity to review any documents before I was forced to sign the agreement.

> This instant process took 14 months to get to a trial. Nine days constitutes a very minor error on behalf of The Rev. Dr. Spencer and The Rev. Dodge and it was harmless in light of subsequent events. The Respondent was not prejudiced in any way by this error. The trial court's decision was not influenced at all by the delay in giving Rev. Leslie a copy of the complaint.
>
> Lastly, the Respondent testified to his guilt to the charges brought against him, similarly in fashion to Dr. Kendall agreeing to his conduct and entering into a Statement of Resolution. JC 1094 is entirely on point.

Here again, a testimony of admission is supposed to overshadow everything that the church did wrong?

Point of Appeal #3:

> The Respondent argues that he did not have access to documents and information that were in the possession of the Church at the time he was compelled to choose the venue in which the complaint process would go forward.
>
> The 2719.1 Agreement relates to which annual conference will carry out procedures. There is no requirement in the judicial process that would require the respondent to see the written complaint before

agreeing to the annual conference where it will be processed. The Presiding Officer has not discovered any Judicial Council decision that would impose that condition on such an agreement and would invite the Counsel for the Respondent to point out that decision should it exist.

The Judicial Council has ruled that the complaint must be given before the respondent can make any adequate response. That is written in plain English, and it is hard to see how the counsel as well as the presiding officer could continue to pretend that they were unable to understand this very clear policy of the church.

The ruling in Decision 974 does not appear to apply to the process envisioned in 2719.1. Even if the Judicial Council should decide later to impose a condition that the Respondent see the complaint before agreeing to the annual conference where it is to be processed, the Council would surely take into consideration that Reverend Leslie waited over a year after signing the Agreement to attempt to rescind it. (Emphasis added) Further, his current motion was submitted only a short time before the trial is scheduled to begin.

I deny the motion on this issue based on the lack of any specific authority for the argument and because of the prejudice due to the timing of the issue being raised so long after the judicial process had begun. This issue is noted so that the Jurisdictional Committee on Appeals and the Judicial Council may review the issue if there is any appeal.

The Church agrees with Bishop Gwinn that there is no specific authority for the Respondent's argument. The Church also agrees with Bishop Gwinn that the Respondent taking over a year to decide to argue about this matter and attempt to rescind the 2719 agreement demonstrates this is a "hail Mary" pass and an attempt at forum shopping for a lighter penalty.

This is just blatantly disingenuous on the part of both the presiding officer and the counsel for the church. In the previous briefs from the defense, the time table for requesting a change of venue to the New England Conference was already established. It started within a very short time after the matter was given to the counsel for the church.

Lastly, the Respondent in his SEJCOA Brief essentially intimates that there was an ulterior motivation on behalf of the Rev. David Dodge and the Rev. Dr. Gary Spencer in keeping a copy of the original complaint from the Respondent. The brief says, "Perhaps officials of the Florida Conference were afraid that if the Appellant saw the numerous inflammatory and false allegations contained in the original complaint it might have made it more difficult to persuade him to surender his orders." This is, again, offensive. The Respondent and his counsel are attempting clairvoyance again and subtly accusing senior leaders of the Florida Conference of intentionally being biased against Rev. Leslie. This line of argument is unhelpful to the Respondent and it is doing harm to the reputations of two senior leaders who are not on trial and who have long, exemplary records of ministry. Moreover, the Church reminds the Council that the Counsel for the Respondent, in his opening statement, affirmed the Respondent's guilt of the charges brought against the Respondent by the Committee on Investigation. Further, the Respondent testified to his guilt of the charges brought against him. (See the transcript of the opening day of the trial p. 64–5 and p. 232-3.)

Here is another case where the counsel for the church is pretending to be offended and putting up Dr. Spencer and Reverend Dodge on a pedestal and being beyond reproach. His ongoing reference to "senior leaders" and "statesmen" are plainly for effect. The dishonesty has already been pointed out in previous pages of this narrative. It was frustrating to read or listen to this continuous rhetoric when the actions of both men showed otherwise.

Point of Appeal #5:

The Respondent argues that the exclusion of the original complaint from consideration by the trial court was an error of church law. In making this assertion, the Appellant's SEJCOA Brief fails to cite one paragraph from the Discipline requiring the original complaint be considered by the trial court.

Really? The United Methodist Church is also governed and guided by a constitution as well as Judicial Council rulings. For him to suggest that the Book of Discipline does not mandate that the complaint should be considered by the trial court is not only non-sensical, but it is totally irrational. The defense referenced Judicial Council ruling number 974 over and over. Now the counsel is asking for confirmation from the Book of Discipline.

Moreover, the Respondent develops a strange argument that the original complaint should have been introduced to the trial court so the Respondent would have the chance to clear his name of certain allegations made in the document but not acted upon by the Counsel for the Church. Why would the Respondent need to rebut an allegation that was never made by the Church? The Counsel for the Church investigated the allegations contained in the original complaint. Some of those allegations were brought forward to the Committee on Investigation.

Actually, all the allegations were brought to the Committee on Investigation because they saw the original complaint in its entirety. As my defense counsel pointed out, the committee's knowledge of the allegations from the complaint, helped to formulate the charges which would have gone forth to the trial court. The counsel also knew that there was no opportunity for cross-examination of the complainant at the level of the committee on investigation. On the other hand, plain and simple, the complaint did not go to the trial court because there would have been the opportunity for cross-examination.

Moreover, one could argue, these additional allegations might bias the trial court against the Respondent.

The defense virtually begged for the complaint to be given to the trial court, and now the counsel is saying that that would have prejudiced the court against the respondent? It is ironic since the counsel tried to paint a picture of the respondent which certainly tainted the impression which the court had of the respondent. As such, there was no real concern for protecting me against any bias.

Throughout the entire judicial process the Respondent sought to discredit the Complainant. That is his right. The Respondent wanted the original complaint included in the trial court to try and paint the Complainant in a negative fashion. Yet, the Complainant was not on trial; the Respondent was. Further, the Respondent admitted conduct to the trial court which proved the allegations (See pages 232–3 of the Trial Day One Transcript).

The counsel makes reference to my confession again. The fact that the complainant was not on trial does not mean that there should not have been an opportunity to question her credibility. A trial court can find a defendant guilty and still be lenient in the penalty depending on factors other than guilt or admission.

Point of Appeal #11:

The Respondent argues that the Respondent's fair process rights were violated because Rev. Leslie was placed on Involuntary Leave of Absence by the Florida Conference and that it created a biased atmosphere for the judicial process.

The Church has admitted that it made a mistake by placing Rev. Leslie on involuntary leave of absence. This mistake was cured. Reverend Leslie was returned to active ministry status and given back pay, benefits, housing, etc. with interest. This error in no way affected the outcome of the trial.

Additionally, a mistake related to procedures concerning involuntary leave of absence has nothing to do with the trial court's decision as to whether there was clear and convincing evidence to sustain the charges brought against Rev. Leslie by the COI. The Appellant's SEJCOA Brief tries to argue that this is not true, but is very unconvincing. One of the arguments put forth by the Respondent is that calling Rev. David Dodge and Rev. Dr. Gary Spencer as witnesses to testify to the fact that Rev. Leslie had confessed to the specified charges somehow requires the trial court to consider the Florida Conference's error regarding Rev. Leslie and involuntary leave of absence. Yet, the Respondent does not demonstrate how this negatively affected the outcome of the trial.

Compensation for the church error does not rectify the lack of fairness. All along, my defense counsel argued that the so-called error and rush to place me in a status of involuntary leave was indicative of the mindset of the church hierarchy. One does not need to be a brain surgeon nor a rocket scientist to figure that one out. There was an implicit bias and prejudice throughout the entire process and that bias drove the many irrational arguments which the counsel for the church, the presiding officer as well as the committee on appeals put forward in response to the concerns of the defense.

THEREFORE, because the Appellant fails to demonstrate that the weight of the evidence did not sustain the charges and also fails to show any error of Church law rose to the level of "plainly" affecting the result of the trial, the Counsel for the Church requests that the Appellant's Brief be DENIED, and the verdict and penalty imposed by the trial court be AFFIRMED.

Date: August 26, 2016 Respectfully Submitted,

Rev. James J. Therrell, Jr.
Elder in Full Connection
Counsel for the Church of The Florida Annual
Conference of The United Methodist Church

Reverend Therrell continuing his established bias, which blinded him from any logic or rational thinking, also chimed in on why he thought that Bishop Devadhar was correct to rule that it was okay for the Florida Conference to carry through with the proceedings even though my clergy membership was with the New England Conference. Here is his reasoning below.

It is a well settled principle of American criminal law that a trial is held in the location where the crime occurred. It is right and appropriate to hold trials in the jurisdiction where the crime occurred because it is the people of the jurisdiction that were harmed in addition to the victim. (More often than not, the victim of a crime also lives in the jurisdiction where the crime occurred.) Paragraph 2719.1, without conflicting with 33, allows this to take place within The United Methodist Church.

Since I am not an attorney, I cannot speak to what happens in criminal cases. However, this is not a criminal case. It was a case within the United Methodist Church, and this body has its own policies which guides its operations. It is hard to understand how the counsel for the church could have come up with that kind of reasoning but even harder to understand how the Judicial Council did not point out the obvious irrationality in comparing apples and oranges.

Reverend Leslie had a months-long affair with the Complainant with the intention of marrying her after divorcing his wife. The evidence presented at the trial proved this point and the Appellant did not appeal the weight of the evidence. The ramifications of his actions victimized the Complainant, who lives within the bounds of the Florida Conference and who, at times, attended his church. Moreover, Rev. Leslie's actions have directly hurt the churches of the Florida Conference who have had to cover tens of thousands of dollars in costs for the litigation of this church trial, unpaid apportionments, and unpaid property and casualty insurance premiums. It is only right and fair that this trial take place in the Conference where Rev. Leslie's actions hurt others. Paragraph 2719.1 allows this to take place without ever conflicting with 33.

The counsel for the church points out that the appellant did not appeal the weight of the evidence, yet he spends so much time and in so many instances explaining that I confessed to wrongdoing so that negates all the errors and dishonest process which the church used. Now he is claiming that because the church chose to spend tens of thousands of dollars on the process, that fact makes it right for the process to be held in Florida. Once more, this is very irrational thinking, and the sad thing is that he knew that it was irrational thinking but still decided to throw it out to see if the Judicial Council would catch it, and apparently it did. The counsel is also referencing the narrative portrayed by the complainant that she was a member of my church. It continues to be painful that he never seemed to even question the truthfulness of the complainant in spite of him having examined the contents of the complaint.

> It is important for the Judicial Council to know why this Decision of Law was requested from Bishop Devadhar. In the original Notice of Appeal timely filed, the constitutionality of 2719.1 was never raised. Later, when the Appellant's Brief was filed, there were arguments included about the instant paragraph's constitutionality. The Church appropriately argued that pursuant to 2715.1 and 2715.4 that because that argument was not included in the grounds for the appeal, it was barred from consideration. The Southeastern Jurisdiction Committee on Appeals concurred and barred the question. Reverend Campbell's request for a Decision of Law from Bishop Devadhar is a back-door attempt to get it in.

Earlier on in this narrative, I pointed out how the committee on appeals upheld the claim by Reverend Therrell that the question for authority of the Florida Conference to carry through the proceedings was a moot point and waived. I also stated that because they could not find a rational argument to counter that very important point which my defense counsel was making from the beginning of the process that it was their way of getting out of having to embarrass the Florida Conference and let them know that they really did not have the authority. For Reverend

Therrell to use the power of clairvoyance which was gifted exclusively to him and determine why the issue was raised at the New England Conference is not relevant to the matter. What is relevant is the fact that the Florida Conference had no authority to carry through with the proceedings as Judicial Council ruling number 580 so clearly determined.

> Lastly, Bishop Devadhar is correct in noting that should the Judicial Council reverse Bishop Devadhar's decision that multiple verdicts from 24 years of previous trials around the globe will have to be reversed. This would trigger the double jeopardy provisions found in 2701.2.d. Accordingly, those clergy could not be retried. Presumably those persons would have to be restored to active ministry even though they have committed chargeable offenses deemed egregious enough to end their careers and potentially be paid back pay. This is unjust to the **victims** of Rev. Leslie and the others who have had their orders terminated. The Counsel for the Church is aware that Rev. Scott Campbell has argued that there are not many cases of this type. First, Rev. Campbell has absolutely no way of knowing this and has offered no proof. **Second, even one case where a pastor who has hurt others is allowed to return to ministry is a grave injustice.**

I ask us to note that in the sentence above Reverend Therrell makes reference to "the victims (plural) of Reverend Leslie." This is very significant as it proves the point that the bias which the church had may very well have been rooted in the original complaint which was provided to the church and which as readers, you have seen. This complaint had all those crazy allegations and portrayed me as a predator. It clearly resonated with the church since Bishop Carter had actually referenced this during the supervisory session when he said to me "I am only interested in justice for all these women" (plural). Now here is Reverend Therrell's real thinking coming out without him even realizing it. His words were, "This is unjust to the victims of Reverend Leslie." Reverend Therrell had also interviewed at least one young lady who was my daughter's age. This he did because the complainant just arbitrarily gave him a list of names that came to her head and he acted upon it. Bishop Carter and Reverend Therrell clearly bought the tales told by the complainant in her complaint but withheld the said complaint from the trial court under the guise of just bringing the "provable" charges. When they get called out for dishonesty and unfairness, they plead "statesmen who have served the church for several years." I may not be considered a statesman, and I do not care to be so considered by human beings since it was God who called me into ministry. However, I will state that at the time when the charges were brought, I had served the church faithfully for thirty-eight years. In a few months, I would be celebrating the fortieth anniversary of my ordination and the forty-fourth of my ministry. No one can take that away from me. The hierarchy of the church can take away my appointment within the United Methodist Church, but they cannot take away my call by and ordination from God. In their effort they may even kick me out of the clergy of the United Methodist Church, but they cannot kick me out of heaven or out of the kingdom of God. That is why God chose to rescue me because He called me and ordained me.

Conclusion

Paragraph 2719.1 is constitutional. It is not in conflict with 33 because it has nothing to do with changing how Annual Conferences (or their clergy sessions) vote on matters of ordination, character, and the like. The Counsel for the Church respectfully asks the Judicial Council to affirm Bishop Devadhar's Decision of Law and not allow a miscarriage of justice to occur restoring Rev. Leslie to ministry and potentially others as well.

Rev. James J. Therrell, Jr. Elder in Full Connection

So after four strong briefs submitted to the Judicial Council, the ruling came in favor of the church. The entire ruling is below. It does not take into consideration any of the fair process rights established by the defense. The worst offense is that it totally ignored the law (JC ruling number 580) already established by a precedent body in 1987. This ruling was addressed by two of the briefs and also in the oral arguments for the defense. I ask you to note though that rather than trying to counter the argument, the Judicial Council totally and comprehensively ignored the argument and made no reference to it in its response because it could not. It is apparent that this was one time when they could not dance around it, so they chose the next best option that suited them—ignore it. How disconcerting it was for the defense? The two bodies which are supposed to be objective and point out acts of unfairness and injustice especially where it is blatant, are themselves, flawed with injustice!

By ignoring it, the Judicial Council has set a very bad precedent for other cases that may come up. It does not seem that there is a place for the church to follow its own laws. Anyone serving in high places can break the law as they see fit and get away with it because the Judicial Council now seem to be making its decisions based on class and status as opposed to truth and honesty. Interestingly, in the opening paragraph the council makes mention that "the Southeastern Jurisdiction Committee on Appeals [hereinafter Committee] affirmed the conviction and penalty assessed against a clergy member of the Florida Annual Conference." In so doing and straight out of the gates, the council is not acknowledging that I was a member of the New England Conference and not the Florida Conference. I have to wonder whether or not this was another convenient error. The council also vaguely mentions that I received the complaint in August 2014 but made no reference to the actual timing of the receipt of that complaint as it relates to decisions which I was forced to make. The council in handing down its decision also references Judicial Council rulings number 240 and 1270, which were *not* brought to their attention by anyone but totally ignores Judicial Council ruling number 580, which was brought to their attention in four separate briefs. Here is the full decision of the Judicial Council below.

October 28 2016
In Re: Rev. Errol Leslie v. Florida Annual Conference

Digest of Case

The Appellant admitted that the evidence sustained the charges of immorality, sexual misconduct, and disobedience to the order and discipline of the United Methodist Church. The enumerations of error asserted by the Appellant are not such as to vitiate the verdict and penalty. The decision of the Committee on Appeals of the Southeastern Jurisdiction is affirmed.

SUBJECT TO FURTHER CORRECTION AND REVISION.

Statement of Facts

In May of 2016, the Southeastern Jurisdiction Committee on Appeals [hereinafter Committee] affirmed the conviction and penalty assessed against a clergy member of the Florida Annual Conference. The Committee concluded that (i) the weight of the evidence sustained the charges of sexual misconduct, immorality, and disobedience to the order and discipline of the United Methodist Church and (ii) that no errors of Church law vitiate the trial court's verdict and penalty of the termination of his membership in the New England Annual Conference.

The Appellant, Errol Leslie, was ordained in the Methodist Church of the Caribbean and the Americas in 1981. He moved to the United States in 1995 and had his orders recognized by the New England Annual Conference of the United Methodist Church. In 2008, he received a cross-conference appointment in the Florida Annual Conference to serve Palm Bay United Methodist Church.

In 2011, the Appellant began communicating via email and/or other electronic means with a woman [hereinafter Complainant] with whom he had attended high school in Jamaica. The Appellant and the Complainant communicated regularly after reconnecting. In March of 2014 she visited him in Palm Bay and they undertook a sexual relationship.

From the outset, the Appellant's intention was to divorce his wife and marry the Complainant. However, when the Complainant became convinced that he was proceeding too slowly toward those goals, she informed his wife and the assistant to the Resident Bishop of her affair with the Appellant. The Appellant was contacted by his District Superintendent and informed of the allegations being made against him. In August of 2014, the clergy member received a copy of the complaint and was notified that the Bishop of the Florida Annual Conference had appointed counsel for the church and that judicial proceedings had commenced under 2701 of The Book of Discipline 2012 [hereinafter The Discipline]. The case proceeded to trial, verdict, penalty and this appeal.

An Oral Hearing was conducted in Lisle, Illinois on October 25th. Rev. Scott Campbell appeared on behalf of the Appellant. Rev. Jay Therrell appeared on behalf of the Church.

Jurisdiction

The Judicial Council has jurisdiction under 2715 and 2716.

Analysis and Rationale

We have reviewed the bill of specifications and charges, the testimony of the witnesses in the trial

350

court, the Appellant's brief, and the applicable provisions of The Discipline. We agree with the Committee's conclusion that the evidence sustained the charges of immorality, sexual misconduct and disobedience to the order and discipline of the United Methodist Church and that the enumerations of error asserted by the Appellant are not such as to vitiate the verdict and penalty.

Since the Committee amply described the issues and controlling law, we hereby adopt the Committee's Analysis of the Appellant's fourteen enumerations of error together with its Decision:

The facts substantiating the charges in this case have never been disputed. The appellant contests only the severity of the penalty imposed. However, the penalty is within the range authorized by 2711.3 for such offenses. There has been no mixing or matching of penalties as prohibited by Judicial Council decisions 240 and 1270. The trial court, though not unanimous, imposed the penalty after careful consideration of all facts and evidence. While errors were made, the members of this Committee cannot say that the admitted or alleged errors are of such a nature as to vitiate the verdict or penalty imposed.

For all the foregoing reasons, the Committee concludes that the weight of the evidence sustains the charges of sexual misconduct, immorality, and disobedience to the order and discipline of the UMC, and that no errors of Church law vitiate the trial court's verdict or penalty of termination of the appellant's conference membership and revocation of the recognition of appellant's credentials for conference membership. Accordingly, the Committee affirms the verdict of the trial court and the penalty imposed.

Decision

The Appellant admitted that the evidence
sustained the charges of immorality, sexual misconduct
and disobedience the order and discipline of the
United Methodist Church. The enumerations of error
asserted by the Appellant are not such as to vitiate the
verdict and penalty. The decision of the Committee on
Appeals of the Southeastern Jurisdiction is affirmed.

Deanell Reece Tacha was not present.

First lay alternate Warren Plowden participated in
this decision.

That ruling was the proverbial final nail in my coffin. It was a strong
affirmation of the Florida Conference and the Committee on Appeals of
the South Eastern Jurisdiction. However, let us take note of the concurring
opinion from Beth Capen who was absent. Beth is also an attorney by
profession and served on the Judicial Council. She was absent from that
particular gathering but would have received the relevant information. This
last section in bold italics speaks for itself and clearly suggests that she
recognized that fairness was not in play throughout the process.

Concurrence

*I generally concur with my colleagues and also
strongly believe that the time is ripe for a long
overdue close examination and critical
constitutional analysis of fair process rights as
currently expressed in the Discipline (2012 and
2016) and clarified and controlled by Judicial
Council Decisions (see, e.g., 698, 836, 1296, 1318).
Furthermore, given that the 2016 General
Conference passed legislation which would
permit a direct appeal to the Judicial Council
during Administrative and Judicial proceedings, it*

would presumably behoove us to engage in this constitutional inquiry as soon as possible particularly as to whether and what extent the intended purpose of the supervisory response (for a just resolution) has been undermined by conflicting Disciplinary provisions and misapplication thereof, and the extent to which it has become a mechanism that serves to further deprive individuals of their fair process rights.

Respectfully Submitted,

Beth Capen

CHAPTER 15

The Elusive Dodge Emails

The "elusive" e-mail that Reverend Dodge sent to his counterpart in the New England Conference evoked quite a bit of controversy. For his part, the counsel for the church was extremely dramatic and theatrical in expressing his disappointment in the defense counsel for bringing it up during the videotaped testimony. In this instance, Reverend Dodge was caught with his hand in the cookie jar, and the best response that the counsel for the church could come up with was to put the blame on my defense counsel by pretending to be angry. It was no "gotcha moment" as Reverend Therrell suggested. From all appearances, he may have been the one who advised Reverend Dodge to "steal the cookie" in the first place. A gullible presiding officer fell for the theatrics even though he would have been able to see through the contradictory pieces of information that Reverend Dodge gave between his videotaped testimony and the e-mail that he sent to the New England Conference from day one of the very first meeting between Reverend Spencer, himself, and me.

As my defense counsel pointed out, the fact of the matter is that during Reverend Dodge's testimony to the committee on investigation, he hedged his words when he was pressed by one of the committee members about whether or not I had shown remorse. On page 148 of the COI transcript, he says, "You know, I don't really recall one way or the other." By the time he got to the trial, he declared with no uncertainty that there was no remorse expressed. His story changed from time to time, and this may very well have been a direct result of the coaching that he would have gotten from the counsel for the church who seemed to have forgotten that he was not in his former role of being a prosecutor in the secular court but was now in a church trial—a trial in the church of Jesus Christ!

Reverend Therrell's reference to surprise witnesses in television shows and movies is on point. Very often, this is what happens in the regular court system when a witness lies and is caught lying with the evidence of lying staring them in the face. This was no drama on the part of my defense counsel. The only drama centered around Reverend Therrell's pretense to be angry and suggesting that in the regular court of law, he would have been requesting sanctions be imposed against the Counsel for the Respondent and request a referral to the "Bar" for his conduct. Reverend Therrell even stated, "If the secular world can handle things in this manner, surely the Church should be better." That was such an ironic statement given the fact that there were so many indications of unethical behavior and violations of fair process on his part. Here is the e-mail exchange below. The first one is from my defense counsel.

> Bishop Al Gwinn, Presiding Officer
> On Tue, Jan 5, 2016 at 5:54 pm,
> <Campbellwscott@aol.com> wrote:
>
> Dear Bishop Gwinn,
>
> There was a dispute this afternoon during the commissioned out-of-court testimony about the Defense's use of a letter written by David Dodge to officials of the New England Conference on July 30, 2014. Rev. Therrell believed its use to be a violation of the requirement to share documentation with the other side. I'm sure that he will be in touch with you about his concerns. I'll let him speak for himself. I did want you, however, to have some background on how the letter came into our possession and how we understood it.
>
> I wrote to Rev. Dodge on December 21, asking for the letter. He replied to me that he was out of his office

and would not return until January 4, and that he would be happy to forward the letter at that time. Yesterday, January 4, Rev. Dodge wrote to me telling me he could not find a copy of the letter. I asked his permission to approach Rev. Robinson Johnson, the Assistant to the Bishop in New England, to see if she had a copy that could be shared with the Defense. Rev. Dodge agreed and I contacted Rev. Robinson Johnson by email yesterday. When I had not heard from her by 9:00 this morning, I contacted her by phone. I opened an email from her at 10:30 this morning which contained a copy of the letter.

As I read through the letter, it was clear that it pertained to the process, and would not be something that the Defense would or could introduce as evidence. I did, however, hold on to the letter in case testimony should be introduced by the Church which the letter might impeach. You will recall that in my letter to you of 12/29 I stated the following:

The Defense also has in its possession several receipts and bank statements that may or may not be relevant, depending on the testimony of the Church's witnesses. We will not be introducing them as exhibits in our own case, and, thus, are not submitting them at this time, but would like to reserve the right to introduce them should they become necessary to impeach the testimony of one of the Church's witnesses during cross-examination.

The Church made no objection to this statement, nor did you as the Presiding Officer address the matter.

We believed this letter to fall into the same category as those receipts and bank statements. It was not an appropriate document for the Defense to introduce. It would not be our exhibit and it related to process.

An occasion arose during the direct examination of the Church today when the witness stated three times that Rev. Leslie had shown no remorse for his actions at his July 30 meeting with Rev. Dodge and Dr. Spencer. A statement in the letter he sent that same afternoon appeared to directly contradict that statement, so I quoted from the letter and asked the witness to explain.

When I asked a follow-up question based on the same letter, the Counsel for the Church strenuously objected and accused me of bad faith in not sharing the document with him prior to the examination of the witness.

If I have violated a rule, I sincerely apologize to Rev. Therrell and to you. I had no idea that the letter would turn out to be relevant, but when it appeared that the witness was telling one story to colleagues in New England and another to the trial court, it seemed important to point out. I recalled your guidance in a December 6 email: *If, at any time, either counsel should feel that testimony being given is not accurate then it is relevant and appropriate for that counsel to establish such by questions and witnesses.*

Grace and Peace,
Scott Campbell
Counsel for Rev. Leslie

From: bishopgwinn@gmail.com
To: Campbellwscott@aol.com
CC: jtherrell@capecoralfirst.org, dhammond. fumc@ gmaii.com, llake@bay-view.org, reveel@ cfl.rr.com
Sent: 1/5/2016 10:22:45 p.m. Eastern Standard Time
Subj: Re: David Dodge July 30 Letter

Reverend Campbell,

Thank you for your response to the matter of the unexpected letter that was used in the commissioned testimony of Reverend Dodge today. The spirit you have in offering up your view of how and what happened today is a spirit that makes this a church trial and not a civil trial. I commend you for practicing what you expressed a concern for in an earlier email.

I have not yet heard from the Counsel for the Church regarding this issue so I will speak only tentatively about how we might agree on moving forward now that this has happened. Had we been in a court session, after Reverend Dodge had answered in a way that you describe the transcript will read and you were aware of a letter that you believed would impeach the testimony then you would have ask the Presiding Officer if you could approach the bench. The Presiding Officer would have granted your request and invited the Counsel for the Church to join us. You would have then revealed the document that you had and ask for permission to use the document for impeachment. You would have explained why you had the document and had not yet made it known to the Presiding Officer and the Counsel for the Church for possible use. We would have listened to a response from the Counsel for the Church. The Presiding Officer would have then made a ruling. I will not state a ruling because this is only a hypothetical situation but

I will say that reliable documents would be relevant regarding impeachment.

Here is the possible way (remember we have not heard from the Counsel for the Church) we will deal with this matter. Since this is a shortcoming of a commissioned testimony in that the Presiding Officer is not present to make a ruling, the questioning and testimony dealing with this subject will be deleted from the video and the unknown and unexpected letter will also be deleted.

I am confident that we all want fairness at every point so either counsel may have potential documents that may be needed for impeachment or the introduction of a conversation that opens up a previously closed area of the trial. Then these documents can be approved for such use only.

I am asking each counsel to respond to this possible way of moving forward and/or suggest another way of handling this matter.

Al Gwinn
Bishop, Retired

From: jtherrell@capecoralfirst.org \
To: bishopgwinn@gmail.com
Sent: 1/5/2016 9:40:56 P.M. Eastern Standard Time
Subj: David Dodge's Commissioned Testimony

Dear Bishop Gwinn:

This afternoon we videotaped the commissioned testimony of the Rev. David Dodge, assistant to Bishop Carter. The court reporter just forwarded me the transcript and I have sent it to all parties. The reporting firm has requested that we have our edits as soon as possible—tomorrow afternoon if possible— so the video can be appropriately edited and DVDs/video files produced. I will forward you my objections later tonight.

This afternoon during the Counsel for the Respondent's cross examination of Rev. Dodge an issue arose that is on the record for you to review. I am writing to you because the Church, including both the counsel and the assistant counsel, are gravely concerned about the conduct of the Counsel for the Respondent. Reverend Campbell attempted to impeach Rev. Dodge's testimony through the use of an email he claimed to have received from Bishop Devadhar's assistant. The Church was at no time provided a copy of this letter. For that matter, Rev. Dodge was not shown a copy of the letter during the testimony. He was asked about a document that he was not able to see and that the Church could not examine. For as much as the Respondent complains about not seeing Ms. Hendricks' written complaint at his first meeting with District SuperintendentSpencer so Rev. Leslie could accurately respond to it, one would think the Respondent would ensure this didn't happen as it did today.

This conduct is, in the opinion of the Church, inexcusable. We are expected to share all of our evidence with one another. The Church has given every piece of evidence it has to the Respondent. We have even given the Respondent copies of potential pieces of evidence that we will not be using—to make sure we go above and beyond the call of duty. Moreover, because all of the Church's witnesses have testified before the Committee on Investigation, the Respondent knows in advance to what they will testify and the general line of questioning the Church will conduct. There are absolutely no surprises on the side of the Church.

In his email earlier tonight, Rev. Campbell told you that he received a copy of the alleged email at 10:30am today. The testimony occurred at 3:00pm this afternoon. On the record, Rev. Campbell said the email "just arrived just before this meeting." (See page 25 of the transcript.) Which is the true statement? The Church contends this was done in bad faith in an attempt for a "gotcha" moment to discredit a senior statesman not only of the Florida Conference but the Southeast Jurisdiction, and indeed the denomination. Additionally, in an email to you at 7:24 a.m., Rev. Campbell stated, "I appreciate your sensitivity on this matter and your willingness to make room for it in your very busy schedule today. It is difficult to respond to your question without providing the Counsel for the Church with information that will make it more difficult for us to establish an important point this afternoon, since he will have the first opportunity to examine Rev. Dodge" (emphasis added). At the time, I wondered what the Respondent's Counsel meant when he wrote that. The Church contends that Rev. Campbell knew full well what he was planning to do all along.

On court television shows and movies it makes great drama and plot intrigue to have surprise witnesses and surprise evidence. The reality is in real courts of law this never happens. I distinctly remember in my evidence class at the University of Florida College of Law that my evidence professor told us that we should disregard every court drama that we had ever seen because there should never be a surprise in a trial. In secular criminal proceedings this is required by law. If we were in a secular court, I would be requesting sanctions be imposed against the Counsel for the Respondent and request a referral to the Bai' for his conduct. If the secular world can handle things in this manner, surely the Church should be better. This is not Rev. Campbell's first time dealing with a church trial. This should not be a surprise to him.

Moreover, the Church's counsel and assistant counsel are offended that the Respondent's Counsel seems to place the blame on not sharing the alleged email on you and me. In his email earlier tonight Rev. Campbell said, "The Church made no objection to this statement, nor did you as the Presiding Officer address the matter." Quite honestly, there have been so many emails from the Respondent's Counsel over the course of the last 15 months with so many requests, charges, complaints, motions, responses to motions, etc. that it is often hard to follow everything that he says. I don't think that the responsibility for this should be placed on you or me. The requirement to share evidence does not go away.

The vast majority of the Respondent's witnesses have not appeared before the Committee on Investigation. We do not know to what they will testify or what evidence they may offer. It would be horrible if this should happen again next week before the trial court.

The Church moves that everything related to the "gotcha" email (which still as of this writing has not been provided to us, even though, on the record, Rev. Campbell said that it would be) be stricken from the record, removed from the video, and that Counsel for the Respondent be admonished not to engage in such conduct again.

Sincerely,
Jay Therrell and Dionne Hammond
Counsel and Assistant Counsel for the
Church

Trust in the Lord with all your heart; don't rely on your own intelligence. Know him in all your paths, and he will keep your ways straight." (Proverbs 3:5–6)

From: bishopgwinn@gmail.com
To: jtherrell@capecoralfirst.org
CC: dhammond.fumc@gmail.com,
Campbellwscott@aol.com, llake@bay-view. org,
reveel@cfl.rr.com, wdean@flumc.org
Sent: 1/5/2016 10:38:41 P.M. Eastern Standard Time
Subj: Re: David Dodge's Commissioned
Testimony

Reverend Therrell,

I have just noticed your email since I have been working on the email I just sent. Your frustration is understandable and I trust that a lesson has been learned and we will not face such an issue again.

I refer all to my recent email and for a continuation of this conversation.

Please note again the rage and rant in the tone of Reverend Therrell's letter to the presiding officer, Bishop Gwinn. I invite you to examine Dr. Campbell's account of how the entire communication regarding the e-mails unfolded. This account is followed by copies of the original e-mails in their entirety that include dates and parties who received copies of the respective e-mails. Dr Campbell starts off his account to the Committee on Appeals by referring to the evening of the videotaped out of commission testimony.

The reference to "That same evening" was in relation to the evening when the out-of-court commissioned testimony was given.

That same evening the Counsel for the Church filed an objection with the Presiding Officer to any reference to the Dodge letter being included in the video of Rev. Dodge's testimony and the next day, January 6, the Presiding Officer upheld his objection and the section was excised.

The Appellant believes that the ruling of the Presiding Officer to exclude the testimony of Rev. Dodge relating to this letter was an error of Church law for the following reasons:

1.) The letter was relevant. This written contemporaneous statement made by Rev. Dodge to colleagues in New England (sent on July 30, 2014, the same day of the first supervisory session directly contradicted his out-of-court commissioned testimony.

2.) The letter was reliable. When Rev. Dodge was unable to produce the letter himself, he gave permission to the Defense to approach the Rev. Erica Robison-Johnson, Assistant to the Bishop in the New England Conference, to request a copy of the letter. Rev. Dodge did not dispute the accuracy of the letter in his commissioned testimony, nor did he claim there was any problem with its authenticity. A copy of the letter was emailed to the Counsel for the Church on the evening of January 5, exactly as it had been received from Rev. Robinson-Johnson.

The relevant portion of this letter states: *Rev. Leslie was very cooperative throughout our conversation and repeatedly expressed his remorse for the situation.* The Counsel for the Church raised questions about the authenticity of this letter in a side bar conversation on January 12, 2016, implying that the Defense may have introduced a false or doctored document. The Counsel for the Appellant respectfully reminds the Committee that this was a church trial. We do not do such things.

3.) The Defense followed fair and reasonable procedures in attempting to acquire this letter, keeping all parties apprised of the process.

On December 21, 2015 the Presiding Officer sent the following notice to all parties:

Should you intend to introduce any documentary evidence other than that included in the Bill of Specifications and Charges that proposed evidence should be requested to the Presiding Officer not later than December 29, 2015.

Seeking to comply with the Presiding Officer's directive, that same day, December 21, the Counsel for the Respondent sent the following request to Rev. Dodge:

Grace and Peace to you in this holy season. Would you please forward to me a copy of the email that you sent to the Rev. Erica RobinsonJohnson on July 30, 2014. This email relates to the alleged confession of Rev. Leslie earlier that day.

This request was copied to all parties, including the Counsel for the Church and the Presiding Officer. They were made aware of the existence of the letter and that the Defense believed it to be in the possession of the Church's own witness.

Rev. Dodge replied on December 21:

You probably received my "out of office" message indicating that I am away from the office until January 4. I will be glad to forward that correspondence to you at that time.

On January 4, 2016 Rev. Dodge sent the following email to the Defense:

Today is my first day back in the office since receiving this request from you. I have searched my email files and do not locate an email sent on July 30, 2014 to Rev. Erica Robison-Johnson that relates to the topic you identified. Since the meeting with Rev. Leslie occurred on July 30 at the superintendent's office in Vero Beach, Florida (about 3 hours from Lakeland), I suspect that such communication regarding that meeting would have occurred on July 31, 2014. However, as I searched my email files for that date, I still do not locate such an email. Somehow, I must have missed keeping a copy of it. I will continue to check the files and, if I find it, I will immediately forward it to you.

Counsel for the Respondent replied that same day:

Thanks for looking. I believe that Erica may have a copy. Would you authorize her to share it with us?

Rev. Dodge answered in an email that was copied to both the Counsel for the Church and the Presiding Officer:

Yes, that would be fine.

If the Counsel for the Church had doubts about the authenticity of the letter, he had had it in his possession for a week by that point and could have raised any question he had with Rev. Dodge, who was both a witness for the Church and the author of the letter.

The Appellant is curious about the awkward English phrasing in this email: i.e. I have searched... and do not find (as opposed to cannot find or have not found) and again: as I searched...I still do not locate such an email (as opposed to could not locate).

Rev. Robinson-Johnson forwarded the letter at 9:30 AM on January 5 (the next day) and the Counsel for the Defense opened the email approximately one hour later. (See Appendix XXXIII)

The video examination of Rev. Dodge was scheduled for 3:00 that same afternoon.

4.) The Defense did not intend to introduce this letter as documentary evidence since it related to process and the Presiding Officer had specifically excluded anything related to process from the trial. It was reserved to be used only in the event that it was necessary for impeachment. It did not become necessary until the apparent contradiction between Rev. Dodge's testimony and the letter emerged. It had not been immediately forwarded to the Church that morning because the Defense did not intend to introduce the letter as a part of its own case and because of the last-minute nature of the acquisition of the document. The Counsel for the Defense was heavily involved in preparing his cross examination and direct examination of Rev. Dodge scheduled for later that same afternoon.

5.) There is no Disciplinary requirement that all materials used at trial be shared in advance with the other party. 2701 states only:

The respondent and the Church shall have access to all records relied upon in the determination of the outcome of the committee on investigation, trial court, or appeal committee or body.

There was never any question of access being withheld from the Church. The document was forwarded to the Counsel for the Church on the evening of January 5, 2016. The Church had been made aware of the existence of a letter in the possession of its own witness and had ample lead time to do its own investigation into the contents of that letter. The Church was copied on the request to Rev. Robinson-Johnson for the letter and chose not to follow up on the matter itself.

The Defense should not have been penalized in the presentation of its case because the Church had not done due diligence in the preparation of its witness, who himself had given permission the previous day (in an email that was also copied to the Church) for the Defense to acquire the letter. The Defense sought once more to introduce the letter in question prior to the penalty phase of the trial on January 12, 2015 to be used to support the testimony of the Respondent that he had indeed expressed remorse during the first supervisory session. The Church had now had the letter in its possession for an entire week and had had ample opportunity to prepare a response and to validate its authenticity. Still, the Presiding Officer excluded the letter from being introduced, leaving the trial court with only the uncorroborated assertion of the Respondent that he had repeatedly expressed his remorse during the July 30, 2014 meeting, a claim that could not be substantiated by any written record of that meeting and that had been disputed by the testimony of Rev. Dodge.

A copy of the letter would have been passed across the table, or submitted to the Presiding Officer, had we not been in the unique position of securing out-or-court commissioned testimony via video conference across a distance of some 1500 miles. The parties were also without the services of the Presiding Officer. This is a prime example of the way in which a respondent is denied fair process by the erosion of the separation between the supervisory process and the judicial process that was assured in JC 836. It is instructive to note that Rev. Dodge testified before the committee on investigation on September 23, 2015 that he could not actually recall whether the respondent expressed remorse in the July 30 meeting (COI transcript, p. 148, lines 7–8), but three and a half months later he was able to categorically deny three times that there was any expression of remorse (Commissioned testimony, p. 10, ln. 20 through p. 11, ln 5). Without fair process safeguards in the supervisory process (or a wall between the processes) a respondent is inevitably at risk of faulty memories or possible bias on the part of those testifying about what transpired during a supervisory session

This was the original e-mail thread below:

From: Campbellwscott@aol.com [mailto:
Campbellwscott@aol.com]
Sent: Monday, December 21, 2015 12:59 pm To:
David Dodge <ddodge@flumc.org>
Cc: bishopgwinn@gmail.com; Jay Therrell
<jtherrell@capecoralfirst.org>; dhammond. fumc@
gmail.com; Lake Larry <llake@bay-view. org>;
reveel@cfl.rr.com
Subject: Request for Evidence

Dear Rev. Dodge,

Grace and Peace to you in this holy season. Would you
please forward to me a copy of the email that you sent
to the Rev. Erica Robinson-Johnson on July 30, 2014.
This email relates to the alleged confession of Rev.
Leslie earlier that day.

Thank you for your cooperation. Christmas
Blessings,

Scott Campbell Counsel for Rev. Leslie.

Rev. Dodge replied on December 21:

You probably received my "out of office" message
indicating that I am away from the office until January
4. I will be glad to forward that correspondence to you
at that time.

From: Campbellwscott@aol.com [mailto:
Campbellwscott@aol.com]
Sent: Monday, January 04, 2016 1:23 PM
To: David Dodge <ddodge@flumc.org>

Subject: Re: Request for Evidence

In a message dated January 4, 2016, 1:02:51 p.m., Eastern Standard Time, ddodge@flumc.org writes,

Dear Rev. Campbell,

Today is my first day back in the office since receiving this request from you. I have searched my email files and do not locate an email sent on July 30, 2014 to Rev. Erica Robison-Johnson that relates to the topic you identified. Since the meeting with Rev. Leslie occurred on July 30 at the superintendent's office in Vero Beach, Florida (about 3 hours from Lakeland), I suspect that such communication regarding that meeting would have occurred on July 31, 2014. However, as I searched my email files for that date, I still do not locate such an email. Somehow, I must have missed keeping a copy of it. I will continue to check the files and, if I find it, I will immediately forward it to you.

My apologies for this situation.

Blessings,
Rev. David A. Dodge

Assistant to Bishop Kenneth H. Carter Jr. 450 Martin
Luther King, Jr. Avenue Lakeland, FL 33815
863-688-5563 x152
From: Campbellwscott@aol.com [mailto:
Campbellwscott@aol.com]
Sent: Monday, January 04, 2016 1:23 PM
To: David Dodge <ddodge@flumc.org>
Subject: Re: Request for Evidence

Dear Rev. Dodge,

Thanks for looking. I believe that Erica may have a
copy. Would you authorize her to share it with us?
Blessings,

Scott Campbell Counsel for Rev. Leslie

Yes, that would be fine.

Rev. David A. Dodge
Assistant to Bishop Kenneth H. Carter Jr.
450 Martin Luther King, Jr.
Avenue Lakeland, FL 33815
863-688-5563 x152

CHAPTER 16

Full Appellant's Brief to the Committee on Appeals

In the Matter of the Rev. Errol Leslie Submitted to the Appeals Committee of the Southeastern Jurisdiction

Introduction

On January 11, 2016, the Rev. Errol Leslie was found guilty of sexual misconduct, immorality and disobedience to the order and discipline of the United Methodist Church under the provisions of 2702.1 of the *2012 Book of Discipline* by a trial court convened by the Florida Annual Conference. On January 12 the court imposed a penalty which revoked Rev. Leslie's membership in the New England Annual Conference. On February 4, 2016 Rev. Leslie's counsel, Rev. Scott Campbell, a retired elder in the New England Annual Conference, submitted a notice of appeal to the Presiding Officer of the trial, Bishop Alfred Gwinn, and the Resident Bishop of the Florida Annual Conference, Bishop Ken Carter.

Bishop Gwinn subsequently forwarded the notice of appeal to the chair of the Committee on Appeals of the Southeastern Jurisdiction, the Honorable Constance Clark.

In the following brief the Appellant will show that the findings against Rev. Leslie should be reversed in their entirety because of numerous errors of Church law and multiple violations of Rev. Leslie's fair process rights. The challenges of the Appellant fall into three broad categories:

- The lack of authority of the Florida Annual Conference to try the case
- The violation of the Appellant's Fair Process rights prior to the trial
- Errors of Church law related to rulings of the Presiding Officer before and during the trial This brief will address each of these areas in turn.

Part I—Lack of Authority of the Florida Conference
The Context

Rev. Errol Leslie was a member of the New England Conference who served a cross conference appointment in the Florida Conference from 2008 until 2014 as the pastor of the Palm Bay United Methodist Church. On July 29, 2014 Rev. Leslie was summoned to a meeting the following day at the office of his District Superintendent, the Rev. Gary Spencer. When Rev. Leslie asked what the meeting was about, Rev. Spencer refused to tell him. The next day Rev. Leslie met with Rev. Spencer and the Assistant to the Bishop of the Florida Conference, the Rev. David Dodge, where he was informed that a signed written complaint had been received alleging that he had been involved in a sexual relationship with a woman who was not his wife. He was not provided with a copy of the signed written letter of complaint, contrary to the clear directive of church law (see Judicial Council Decision 974), nor was he informed of the contents of that letter. Neither was the complainant identified to him by name.

Rev's Spencer and Dodge informed Rev. Leslie that he was being placed on suspension and asked him whether he wished to surrender his orders at that time. He declined to do so. The next day, July 31, 2014 Rev. Leslie was contacted by Rev. Spencer and informed that he had to choose where the complaint process against him would go forward, either in Florida or in New England. Rev. Spencer requested that the choice be made that day and a document to that effect be signed. When

Rev. Leslie informed Rev. Spencer that he could not meet with him on that day he was told that the document had to be signed by noon on Friday, August 1, or the case would automatically revert to the New England

Annual Conference.[1] The two arranged to meet on that Friday morning, whereupon Rev. Leslie, without benefit of counsel, and without informed consent, was presented with a one-page document entitled "Paragraph 2719 Agreement." In a meeting that lasted approximately five minutes Rev. Leslie signed the document.

Grounds

The Florida Annual Conference had no authority to conduct judicial proceedings in the case of Rev. Leslie. This assertion rests upon three claims. First, 2719.1 is unconstitutional.[2] Second, even if it were constitutional, the circumstances under which the so called "Paragraph 2719 Agreement" was signed rendered it null and void. Third, under the rules of the *2008 Book of Discipline* the Appellant did not qualify for the exemption provided in 2719.1.

Section A—2719.1 is Unconstitutional

33 of the Constitution states unambiguously: *The annual conference… shall have reserved to it the right to vote…on all matters relating to the character and conference relations of its clergy members.*

2719.1 does not comply with this clear directive of the Constitution. The annual conference is given the exclusive right in the Constitution to adjudicate matters relating to the character and conference relations of its members. There is no provision in the Constitution for an annual conference to delegate this responsibility to any other body, nor can the General Conference ignore the clear mandate of the Constitution without amending the appropriate section. "Reserved to it" means that it is the exclusive province of the annual conference to which a clergy member

---

1   COI transcript, p.121. Lines 1–17, Wasilewski Court reporting.

2   All Disciplinary passages are cited from the 2012 Book of Discipline unless otherwise noted.

belongs to deal with matters relating to the character and conference relations of that member.[3]

The 1992 General Conference made a decision that an exception could be made, under limited circumstances, to the constitutional mandate that judicial procedures must be exercised by the appropriate officials of the conference in which the clergyperson is a member. Prior to 1992 members of one annual conference living and serving in another annual conference were required to face judicial procedures in their own annual conference, regardless of where the alleged offense took place. The intention of the 1992 General Conference may well have been to facilitate fairness, but it failed to take the appropriate corresponding step of amending the Constitution in order to bring it into compliance with this legislation. No General Conference since has addressed this matter.

16.7 of the Constitution gives the General Conference the right to provide a judicial system and a method of judicial procedure for the Church, but it adds this important caveat: *except as herein otherwise prescribed.* In other words, judicial procedures must comply with all other relevant portions of the Constitution. The General Conference cannot enact legislation that is not in compliance with requirements of the Constitution. (See JC 1210 for one recent example of this principle.) The Constitution goes to great lengths to prevent the General Conference from interfering with the legal rights of clergy members, even to the point of including the protection of the right of clergy to a trial among the Restrictive Rules. (See 20). Not the General Conference, nor the bishops of the respective conferences in the present instant, nor the clergy member himself have the authority to undo the assignment of matters of character and conference relations to a member's own annual conference.

2719.1 is unconstitutional.

---

3   It is instructive to note that the Florida Annual Conference acknowledges this Constitutional mandate in a March 12, 2015 letter from the bishop's office to the Appellant. Rev. David Dodge, writing on behalf of Bishop Carter, states to the Appellant: "The process of placing you on leave of absence was to be the responsibility of the New England Conference rather than the Florida Conference."

Section B—Even if 2719.1 were constitutional, the circumstances under which the "Paragraph 2719 Agreement" was signed made it null and void

2719.1 deals exclusively with judicial procedures. It reads:

> *Any clergy members residing beyond the bounds of the conference in which membership is held shall be subject to* **the procedures of 2701–2718** *exercised by the appropriate officers in which he or she is a member, unless the presiding bishops of the two annual conferences and the clergy member subject to the procedures agree that fairness will be better served by having the procedures carried out by the appropriate officers of the annual conference in which he or she is serving under appointment, or if retired, currently residing. (emphasis added)*

It is important to note that *2701–2718* deal exclusively with judicial procedures. There is no reference to the supervisory process in these paragraphs. This is important because when the Appellant was compelled to sign the so called "Paragraph 2719 Agreement" on August 1, 2014, there **was no judicial proceeding taking place.** Judicial proceedings would not commence for at least another three months while the *Disciplinarily* mandated 90-day supervisory response was taking place (see 363.1.c). The "Paragraph 2719 Agreement" was not required for a supervisory response to a complaint to occur.

2719.1 does not deal with the supervisory process. (*It is instructive to note that The Discipline provides no guidance whatsoever regarding the form that the agreement referenced in 2719.1 must take. No document is required. No written contract is specified. The Presiding Officer presumes too much in his ruling in response to the Appellant's Motion to refer the Matter to the New England Conference when he states:* **"The Book of Discipline does not provide a right to rescind such an agreement."** *In fact, The Book of Discipline does not provide even a right to create such a document. No guidance is given about when or if such a document should be used, what its authority is in relation to subsequent proceedings, or whether it is to be considered binding or irrevocable. The Presiding Officer chose to support arbitrary* *assumptions advanced by the Florida Conference that have no Disciplinary basis. He denied the request of the Appellant to withdraw from the "Paragraph 2719 Agreement" based on a lack of cited authority, but honored the contention of the Florida Conference that their document was binding and irrevocable, requiring no citation of authority for this assertion. Further, Counsel for the Church insists (without Disciplinary authority) that it takes the agreement of all three parties to the agreement to rescind it. The Appellant wonders whether the Church would have argued the same point had Bishop Carter decided at some point along the way to refer the matter back to New England. The Church made up its rules as it went along and the Presiding Officer supported these arbitrary formulations.)*

There is a difference of opinion in the present instant between the Church and the Appellant about when the relevant judicial process commenced. If one believes it began under the terms of the *2012 Book of Discipline*, the judicial process began in November of 2014 when the matter was referred to a counsel for the church.[4] If one believes that the choice the Florida Conference made following Judicial Council Decision 1296 to return to the procedures of the *2008 Book of Discipline* meant that judicial proceedings commenced with the referral of the matter by the Counsel for the Church to a committee on investigation, that event did not occur until August of 2015.[5] In either case, the Appellant was compelled to sign a document relating to where judicial proceedings would occur long before any determination was even made that such proceedings would take place or were warranted. (See COI transcript, p. 121 lines 1–5) The decision was required before he had seen the complaint against him or knew its contents, before he knew what the charges against him would be and before he had an opportunity by exposure to the supervisory process to assess for himself whether "fairness (would) be better served" by choosing to proceed judicially in Florida. He was prematurely forced to make a

---

4   Bishop Carter notified the Appellant in a letter dated November 6, 2014 that he intended to refer the matter to a counsel for the church. That action, once taken, under 2701 of the 2012 Book of Discipline, would constitute the commencement of judicial proceedings.

5   The Counsel for the Church submitted a formal complaint to the Committee on Investigation on August 5, 2015. That action, under the provisions of 2701 of the 2008 Book of Discipline, would constitute the commencement of judicial proceedings.

judicial decision at the outset of the supervisory process, without benefit of counsel and without adequate time being given for careful consideration of all relevant factors and contingencies.[6]

Perhaps it was assumed by officials of the Florida conference that it was only a matter of time until judicial proceedings would occur and they wanted to get a head start on that process. If so, such an assumption would be indicative that they presumed the Appellant to be guilty of the allegations contained in the complaint, a direct violation of 363.1.b which specifies that complaints are to be treated only as allegations during the supervisory process.[7] The nature of the supervisory response, according to this same paragraph:

is pastoral and administrative and shall be directed toward a just resolution among all parties. It is not to be a part of any judicial process.

The only *Disciplinary* requirement placed on the Florida Annual Conference on August 1, 2014 was to make a good faith effort to resolve the complaint and find healing for all parties. Officials irreparably compromised their ability to carry out this responsibility by jumping the gun and prematurely injecting elements of the judicial process into the supervisory response.

The circumstances under which the 2719 document was signed are also important. The Committee will note that there are a number of Disciplinary paragraphs cited in the document. 2701–2718 are referenced as well as 363.d and 2704.2.c. The Appellant was given an artificial deadline by the District Superintendent, no interpretation of the cited paragraphs

---

6   If the Appellant had known, for instance, that the Florida Conference intended to attempt to place him on Involuntary Leave of Absence while the Counsel for the Church prepared a case against him, his decision to proceed in Florida might well have been different.

7   The presumption of innocence is also lifted up as essential in the judicial process in 2701 when it states: "The presumption of innocence shall be maintained until the conclusion of the trial process. The assumption is that a respondent is presumed innocent during the supervisory phase as well because it is not possible to maintain something that is not already in place."

was provided for the Appellant, and no Book of Discipline was reviewed with the Appellant by the Superintendent. When Rev. Leslie asked for a copy of the document for his own records Rev. Spencer denied his request. Rev. Leslie did not receive a copy of the 2719 document until it arrived more than six months later on February 18, 2015 as a part of the formal judicial complaint against him forwarded by the Counsel for the Church. Yet, the Church has insisted that the Appellant's signature on a document he was not permitted to possess was irrevocable and binding throughout the entire subsequent judicial process.

The Appellant believes Judicial Council Decision 974 is directly relevant to the issue at hand. JC 974 places a strong burden on the Church to make certain that basic fairness is maintained throughout the complaint process. In particular, it cites the need for the Respondent to have access to and possession of the original complaint and copies of all supporting material from the very outset of the process.

A respondent cannot make an adequate response to a complaint without being privy to the complaint in its totality. Fairness alone dictates access to such written complaints and their supporting documents. Full disclosure of all information concerning a complaint must occur for the respondent to make an adequate response.

JC 974 is all about fairness. Insisting that a clergy member sign a document three months prior to the initiation of a judicial process without the benefit of counsel and without providing ample time for careful consideration of the implications of signing such a document, and then insisting that this signed document allows no possibility of reconsideration is even more egregious than withholding the original complaint (which the Church also did for eight days, including the period when the signing of the 2719 document took place). The Appellant believes the actions herein described deprived the Appellant of rights guaranteed to him by the Constitution and were simply and undeniably unfair.

The Florida Conference had multiple opportunities to return the process to its rightful place in New England, but rebuffed every request by the Appellant to do so. The counsel for the Appellant approached Bishop Devadhar of the New England Conference in February of 2015 (less than one month after becoming Rev. Leslie's counsel) to request that the

"Paragraph 2719 Agreement" be set aside and the judicial process be returned to New England. Bishop Devadhar reported that after consulting with Bishop Carter, the two contended that it was too late to grant the request.

On March 30, 2015 the Appellant submitted to the Presiding Officer a request for a change of venue based upon his claims of the violation of fair process in the Florida Conference. This motion was never ruled upon because the parties agreed shortly thereafter to enter into a mediated attempt at a just resolution under the auspices of Just Peace. By the time the efforts at just resolution failed (June 22, 2015), the Florida Conference was considering whether to apply the provisions of Judicial Council Decision 1296, issued April 17, 2015, and submit the entire matter to a committee on investigation.[8] On July 23, 2015 the counsel for the church announced his intention to refer the matter to the committee on investigation and on August 5, 2015 he submitted a new formal complaint to the chair of the committee.

Under this new process, the Appellant notified the chair of the Committee on Investigation on September 1, 2015 of his intent to introduce a motion to set aside the "Paragraph 2719 Agreement." (See transcript of COI conference call, p. 20) Judge Anthony Tatti, chair of the committee, did not believe he had jurisdiction in the matter. His response is summarized in these words from a memo by Judge Tatti of the conversation in question:

> *Counsel for the Respondent advised that he intended to file a motion seeking to set aside the "Paragraph 2719 Agreement," executed by the Respondent, whereby the Bishop of the New England Conference, the Bishop of the Florida Conference, and the Respondent agreed that the procedures of 2701– 2718 in regard to the instant complaint would be carried out by the appropriate officers of The Florida Annual Conference. The Chair opined that the Respondent's proposed motion was jurisdictional in nature and any ruling on such a motion would*

---

8   JC 1296 held that portions of the 2012 Discipline relating to the elimination of the Committee on Investigation were unconstitutional.

be beyond the province of the Chair or the Committee on Investigation and **properly addressed by the Presiding Officer of a Church Trial.** *The Chair further expressed the opinion that no waiver of the Respondent's ability to challenge the agreement would result from the Respondent's appearance and participation in the Hearing of the Committee on Investigation of the Florida Annual Conference.* (emphasis added)

The Appellant subsequently notified the bishops of both annual conferences in a letter dated September 3, 2015, that he was rescinding his consent to the "Paragraph 2719 Agreement. "Bishop Devadhar responded in a letter dated September 18, 2015 that he did not believe he had jurisdiction in the matter. Bishop Carter did not respond to the letter.

A document entitled "Motion to Dismiss the Complaint" was filed by the Appellant on December 29, 2015 in compliance with filing requirements provided by the Presiding Officer, Bishop Al Gwinn. He denied the motion, stating in part:

> *I deny the motion on this issue based on the lack of any specific authority for the argument and* **because of the prejudice due to the timing of the issue being raised so long after the judicial process had begun.** *This issue is noted so that the Jurisdictional Committee on Appeals and the Judicial Council may review the issue if there is any appeal.* (emphasis added)

With all due respect to the assertion of the Presiding Officer, this issue was presented at every appropriate point along the way. Bishop Gwinn also denied the request to refer the matter back to New England, in part, because he determined that JC 974 was not relevant to the issue at hand. He wrote:

> *The 2719.1 Agreement relates to which annual conference will carry out procedures. There is no requirement in the judicial process that would require the complainant (sic) (to see the written complaint before agreeing to the annual conference where it will be processed.[9] The Presiding Officer has not discovered any Judicial Council decision that would impose that condition on such an agreement and would invite the Counsel for the Respondent to point out that decision should it exist. The ruling in Decision 974 does not appear to apply to the process envisioned in 2719.1.*

In fact, just the opposite is true. It is precisely the kind of difficulty which arose in this situation that JC 974 sought to eliminate. JC 974 holds that a respondent cannot make informed decisions or mount an adequate defense without access to all of the material that is in the possession of the Church.

Furthermore, the exception in 2719.1 itself is made to promote fairness. The Appellant vigorously disagrees with the ruling of the

Presiding Officer that fairness is ***better served*** by allowing the Church to withhold information from the respondent while at the same time compelling him to make a critical, irrevocable decision about his future three months before *The Discipline* requires him to do so. Even retail outlets allow 30 days to change one's mind after a purchase. In this case, the Church would not even issue the Appellant a receipt until six months later.

---

9   It is presumed that the Presiding Officer meant to refer to the respondent here rather than the complainant. No argument was advanced for the complainant to see her own complaint.

Section C—Under the rules of the *2008 Book of Discipline* the Appellant did not qualify for the exemption provided in 2719.1

Judicial proceedings in the instant matter began under the provisions of the *2012 Book of Discipline*. Midway through the process, on April 17, 2015, the Judicial Council issued Decision 1296 which stated:

> *The action of the 2012 General Conference to delete the role of the Committee on Investigation for clergy members of an annual conference is unconstitutional. The portions of The Discipline that relate to the role of the Committee on Investigation for clergy members of the annual conference that existed in the 2008 are restored. This decision is prospective and takes effect on April 18, 2015.*

In a letter dated July 23, 2015 the Counsel for the Church wrote:

> *The purpose of this email is to let you know that after seeking advice from several people, I've decided to submit my charges against Rev. Leslie to the Florida Conference Committee on Investigation. Annual Conference elected a new committee last month, and the committee has just elected their chair: Judge Anthony Tatti.*[10]

On August 5, 2015 the Counsel for the Church submitted a formal judicial complaint to the Committee on Investigation, thereby triggering the commencement of judicial proceedings under ¶2701 of the *2008 Book of Discipline*.

2719.1 requires that a clergy member, in order to qualify for an exemption to the requirement that a member undergo judicial proceedings

---

10 The Counsel for the Respondent supported and encouraged this decision, believing that this process would provide an ideal opportunity to return the whole matter to New England. (See point three on the page 9 of this brief.)

in that member's own conference, must be residing and serving in another annual conference. By August 5, the Appellant was neither living nor serving under appointment in the Florida Annual Conference. He was back in his own annual conference serving a two-point charge in central Connecticut. He no longer met the test established in 2719.1 for an exemption. It is important to note that the reason the Appellant was no longer under appointment in Florida was that in a letter dated March 12, 2015, Rev. David Dodge informed the Appellant that his appointment in the Florida Annual Conference would be terminated effective June 30, 2015. The termination of the appointment was initiated by Florida, not by the Appellant.

The Counsel for the Church has argued, and the Presiding Officer has ruled that the choice of the Florida Annual Conference to refer the matter to a committee on investigation did not constitute a new judicial process. Counsel argued that JC 1296 refers only to the portions of the *2008 Discipline* that relate to the role of the committee on investigation and that the *2012 Discipline* guides all other aspects of the judicial process. The Appellant would make three points in this regard.

First, the matter at hand *does* relate directly to the role of the committee on investigation. In receiving a formal complaint from the counsel for the church, the committee initiates judicial proceedings. The committee is referenced directly in the preamble to 2701 in the *2008 Discipline*, which states:

> *The judicial proceedings and the rights set forth in this paragraph commence upon referral of a matter as a judicial complaint from the counsel for the Church to the committee on investigation.*

The role of the committee on investigation is essential in defining a fair judicial process. JC 1296 notes:

> *...the change in the discipline that occurred at the 2012 General Conference raises serious questions about both fair process and balance between the episcopal and other clergy processes. As*

Judicial Council Decision 1226 notes, "fair process procedures, trials and appeals are integral parts of the privilege of our clergy of right to trial by a committee and of appeal."

Decision 1296 removes the authority of the bishop to initiate judicial proceedings unilaterally. It delays that process until a complaint is submitted to the committee on investigation. The election by the Florida Conference to proceed under the provisions of the *2008 Discipline* made the previous process null and void.[11]

Indeed, the Counsel for the Church took advantage of the new process to suppress an illegal verbatim made by the Florida Conference of a supervisory session (see 363.1.b) that had been included with his first submission of documents to the Presiding Officer on February 18, 2015. The Church cannot have it both ways. It cannot pick and choose which portions of the previous process it deems useful and which it does not. Florida made a choice to begin judicial proceedings anew when it chose to refer a judicial complaint to the committee on investigation.

Second, the only significant differences between the *2008 Discipline* and the *2012 Discipline* regarding judicial proceedings have to do with the role of the committee on investigation. It is not as if there are distinct guidelines in the *2012 Discipline* (apart from the role of the committee on investigation) that now govern judicial proceedings in some hybrid fashion.

---

11 The Presiding Officer stated in an e-mail to the Counsel for the Church dated November 9, 2015 that he had not received confirmation of his role in the new process. His email reads: "I have delayed answering your email due to the fact that I have not received any word from Bishop Carter concerning a trial. I have checked my e-mails, and there was a period when I was away from e-mail, but have been unable to find any such notice. I am confident this matter will be corrected soon. However, I believe it would be inappropriate for me to discuss any process until we have documentation of my role." Bishop Ken Carter issued the following statement on November 24, 2015: "To clear up any confusion that I have appointed Bishop Al Gwinn as the presiding officer in this matter, I have reappointed Bishop Gwinn *following the referral of the bill of charges and specifications by the committee on investigation*" (emphasis added). It is clear that a new judicial process had begun, replacing the previous process.

Third, because the Florida Conference was ready to begin the judicial process anew, this would have been an ideal time for the Florida Conference to refer the matter back to the place where the Appellant had membership and was living and serving at the time.

The counsel for the Respondent suggested this course of action to the Counsel for the Church in an email dated July 25, 2015.

He wrote:

> *(A)re you interested in having a conversation about the possibility of moving the whole process to New England at this point? A part of the problem earlier was the we had already moved so far down the road. If we are backing up, is there any wisdom in transferring the case here?*

There was no obstacle placed by the Appellant to returning the process to New England. To do so would have cleared up many thorny problems, but, for reasons of its own, Florida elected not to avail itself of this possibility, choosing instead to insist that a deeply flawed document, signed prematurely and under duress, continue to determine all subsequent proceedings.

Part II—Fair Process Violations
The Context

2719.1, the paragraph under which the supervisory process and the judicial process were conducted in Florida, offers one justification for making an exception to the Constitutional requirement that a member go through judicial processes in that member's own annual conference. It is in order *that fairness will be better served.* There is no other rationale offered for the exception. It does not lift up justice for the complainant or protection of the annual conference. The location of the alleged offense is not deemed relevant. The only reason that an exception can be made is if the two bishops *and the member* determine that fairness will be better served by judicial proceedings going forward in the host conference.

Admittedly, fairness is, to some degree, in the eye of the beholder. What seems fair to the Church may well be experienced as unfair by a respondent and vice versa. And it is also true that even the best efforts to assure fairness to all parties are sometimes inadequate. Yet, when there is a pattern of behavior over many months in which the laws of the Church that safeguard fair process are repeatedly violated, it becomes necessary for an impartial third party to determine whether the interests of fairness were indeed better served by those entrusted with the responsibility to assure fair process, or whether the actions of those parties have so compromised the process that it cannot be redeemed and must be set aside.

Judicial Council decision 1189 is direct and to the point about where the responsibility for assuring fairness rests:

> *Officers of the church who are involved in the administration of disciplinary process with respect to the conduct of clergy that can result in an adverse effect on the conference relations of a clergy member must strictly comply with disciplinary provisions. Said officers are guardians of a sacred trust to follow faithfully and adhere to disciplinary process. Important rights are in play and the clergy person, as well as those who have grievance against them, must be treated with the utmost fairness. The bishop, the cabinet, the Board of Ordained Ministry, and the clergy session*

of the Annual Conference all have the responsibility of ensuring that disciplinary procedures and processes are faithfully followed.

That same decision goes on to say:

Deviations from the careful processes set forth in the Discipline, even when undertaken in good faith or for the sake of efficiency, fall below acceptable standards of fair process.

The Appellant will show that his fair process rights were repeatedly violated by the Florida Annual Conference and that the cumulative effect of these violations made it impossible for him to receive a fair trial in that annual conference.

Section A—*Matters Related to the Original Complaint*

Judicial Council Decision 974 states unambiguously:

*The respondent has a right not only to examine but **to possess** the written complaint and any supporting material accompanying it **at the initiation of the supervisory process**. A respondent cannot make an adequate response to a complaint without being privy to the complaint **in its totality**. Fairness alone dictates access to such written complaints and their supporting documents. Full disclosure of all information concerning a complaint must occur for the respondent to make an adequate response.* (emphasis added)

In the present instant the Appellant was not provided with a copy of the complaint against him at the initiation of the supervisory process. The Appellant's request to have a copy of the complaint was delayed by the District Superintendent for nine days. Even though he was summoned to a meeting with the Superintendent and the Assistant to the Bishop on July 29, 2014, and even though the Superintendent had the complaint in his possession, the Appellant was not provided with a copy of the complaint until August 7, and then it was only released after the Appellant wrote to the bishop's assistant citing JC 974.

(Lines 13–25 on page 144 of the transcript of the hearing before the committee on investigation confirm that the complaint was in the physical possession of the Superintendent at the site of the July 30 meeting.) The Church has argued that this difference was inconsequential and of no effect. Counsel for the Church cites JC 1094 as precedent, which he claims involved similar circumstances. In that case Dr. Wesley Kendall had not been provided five letters of complaint at the outset of the complaint process, as required by JC 974. The Judicial Council found this violation inconsequential in light of the *very different circumstances* which ensued in Dr. Kendall's case. Decision 1094 reads, in part:

> *The May 16, 2005 letter of complaint filed by the district superintendent referenced five letters which served as the bases for the complaint. Dr. Kendall was entitled to receive these five letters at the same time he received the letter of complaint. In Decision 974 the Judicial Council declared that "[a]t the initiation of the supervisory process the respondent has a right not only to examine but to possess the written complaint and any supporting material accompanying it." Dr. Kendall should have been provided with the five letters when he was provided with a copy of the May 16, 2005 letter of complaint as a matter of fair process. The failure to do so was an error of church law. The letters were supplied to Dr. Kendall on June 12, 2005, prior to his execution of the Statement of Resolution. Providing the letters at that time remedied the failure to do so previously. **Dr. Kendall had the opportunity to review the letters at that time and he voluntarily entered into the Statement of Resolution with knowledge of the contents of the letters.**[12] The error of church law that occurred due to the failure to deliver the five letters to Dr. Kendall with the letter of*

---

12 The Counsel for the Church deliberately omitted this sentence printed in bold from his citation of this passage to the Presiding Officer, indicating that he fully understood this important difference between the two cases.

complaint was harmless in light of subsequent events. Dr. Kendall was not prejudiced in any way by this error and, under the circumstances, the error is not sufficient to vitiate the verdict or the penalty.

The case cited by the Church differs materially from the instant case in at least two important respects. First, a Statement of Resolution was reached in the Kendall case subsequent to his receipt of all documents, rendering the mistake of the Church harmless. No such resolution was reached in the instant case. Indeed, the Church insisted that a document signed by the Appellant during this interim period, without him ever having seen the complaint against him, was irrevocable and binding. The harm here is enormous. Second, the Church used information from the supervisory session with Rev's Spencer and Dodge on July 30, 2014, eight days before the Appellant had been permitted to see the complaint or any of the supporting material, to prosecute its case. Both Rev. Spencer and Rev. Dodge testified about the contents of that first supervisory session before the Committee on Investigation and before the trial court and the Counsel for the Church referenced this session in his charging documents. Unlike in the case of Dr. Kendall, the omission of information the Church had in its possession at the time, information that it was **mandated** to share with the Appellant, was extremely harmful to him. He was unable to mount an adequate defense without knowing the plethora of patently false allegations to which the Church was privy and he was not. (*The influence on the Church of numerous lies contained in the original complaint cannot be overstated. It would be another two months before the Rev. Dionne Hammond completed her report to the conference indicating that she had found no basis for the allegations contained in the complaint that the Appellant had been sexually involved with numerous women in his current local church and in previous appointments in New England. These allegations colored much of the supervisory process, even as late as October 23, at the very end of the supervisory period, when Rev. Spencer was still quizzing the Appellant about his alleged involvement with other women.*)

The final sentence in the citation quoted above from JC 1094 is: *Dr. Kendall was not prejudiced in any way by this error and, under the circumstances, the error is not sufficient to vitiate the verdict or the penalty.* The implication here is that had the circumstances been different, this error would have been sufficient to vitiate the verdict or the penalty.

Had a just resolution not been reached *after* the materials had been shared with Dr. Kendall, the weight of the error would have been much greater. If actual harm had occurred this error in Church law would have and should have been taken very seriously.

The Appellant is at a loss to understand the motivation of the Church in keeping the information contained in the original complaint from him until after he signed the so-called "Paragraph 2719 Agreement." Both Dr. Spencer and Rev. Dodge testified before the trial court that they did not share the libelous allegations contained in the original complaint with the Appellant during the July 30 supervisory session. Perhaps officials of the Florida Conference were afraid that if the Appellant saw the numerous inflammatory and false allegations contained in the original complaint it might have made it more difficult to persuade him to surrender his orders. That certainly was the case once the Appellant became aware of the contents of the complaint. Though he was asked on many occasions throughout the supervisory process if he would willingly turn in his credentials, he stated each time that he could not do so on the basis of false allegations.

Section B—Legislation passed by the General Conferences of 2000, 2004 and 2008 violated Constitutional fair process protections guaranteed in Judicial Council decisions 698 and 836 by removing confidentiality from the supervisory response.

Paragraph 363.1.b in the *2012 Book of Discipline* provides that the supervisory response of the bishop is to be:

> *pastoral and administrative in nature and shall be directed toward a just resolution among all parties. It is not part of any judicial process* **At all supervisory meetings no verbatim record shall be made and no legal counsel shall be present.** *The person against whom the*

complaint was made may choose another person to accompany him or her with the right to voice (emphasis added)

Judicial Council Decision 698, issued in October of 1993, found that the provisions barring a verbatim and legal counsel from the supervisory process were unconstitutional under the previous judicial system. It held that because there was no clear line of separation between the supervisory process and the judicial process in that system, material from the supervisory process was being relied upon to determine the outcome of the judicial process. The decision held that respondents could not be denied an accurate record of those proceedings, nor could they be denied legal counsel, if the supervisory process was indeed being comingled with the judicial process.

Such a prohibition, according to JC 698, is unconstitutional. Referring to the prohibition against legal counsel JC 698 states, in part:

> *To deny the respondent to select his/her advocate, albeit an attorney, would be to infringe upon his/her right to choose the advocate. This prohibition is in contradiction of the ensurance of fair process (due process) which is accorded in Par. 2622, under the provisions of Par. 18 of the Constitution. The respondent should have the opportunity to have legal counsel present at every level of the administrative or judicial process pursuant to Par. 2622.3.*

In 1996 a new judicial system was introduced which made a sharp distinction between the supervisory process and the judicial process. The basic elements of that system remain intact today. A request from the Minnesota Annual Conference in 1998 for a declaratory decision from the Judicial Council raised a constitutional question about whether the continued inclusion of the provisions barring verbatims and legal representation during the supervisory process (currently contained in 363.1.b) were legal. Were not these prohibitions still unconstitutional as JC 698 had held? The Judicial Council did not agree. In Decision 836 it held that barring these fair process protections during the supervisory process was not an impediment to fair process under the new system because there was an impenetrable wall in the new system between the supervisory and the judicial processes. Referring to the Minnesota brief, JC 836 reads, in part:

> *It is argued that the new supervisory process, which has no fair process safeguards, is contradictory to Decision 698. Such is not the case. Decision 698 was rendered under the procedures of the 1992 Discipline wherein everything in the supervisory process upward made its way to the Committee on Investigation.* **The fair process protections were needed because each body involved was using the information of the person or body below. The new procedures require a fresh start if the supervisory response fails to produce resolution or reconciliation.**
>
> **Nothing but the bare complaint is referred. Neither the Committee on Investigation if the complaint is a chargeable offense, nor the Board of Ordained Ministry, if the complaint is to be handled administratively, <u>has any documentation from the supervisory response.</u>** *In secular terms, these bodies to whom the referral is made hear the case "de novo," i.e. from the beginning. The current supervisory process as defined in the 1996 Discipline does not deny the respondent the rights of fair process or the constitutional right of trial. (emphasis added).*

The fair process safeguards identified in JC 836 lasted only two years before they were effectively obliterated by the General Conference of 2000, when it included language in the *2000 Discipline* that was explicitly contradictory to JC 836. Judge Anthony Tatti, in forwarding a bill of charges from the committee on investigation, included an excellent summary of the erosion of the constitutional safeguards guaranteed by JC 836 by three successive General Conferences. The following summary is drawn from his document:

a.) 358 (*Complaint Procedures*) of the 1996 Book of Discipline, *provided in 358.1.d.1 as follows:*

If the bishop determines that the complaint is based on allegations of one or more offenses listed in 2624.1, the bishop may refer the complaint to the counsel for the Church who shall be appointed by the bishop. The counsel for the Church shall be an elder in full connection and shall have the right to choose one assistant counsel without voice who may be an attorney. **The counsel for the church shall sign the complaint as a judicial complaint, forward it to the committee on investigation and represent the Church in any proceedings of the committee on investigation.** (*emphasis added*)

b.) The 2000 Book of Discipline *renumbered 358 of* The 1996 Discipline *to 359 and amended the 1996 provision in the new 359.1.d.1 as follows:*

If the bishop determines that the complaint is based on allegations of one or more offenses listed in 2702.1, the bishop may refer the complaint to the counsel for the Church, who shall be appointed by the bishop. The counsel for the Church shall be a clergyperson in full connection and shall have the right to choose one assistant counsel without voice who may be an attorney. The counsel for the Church shall draft and sign a judicial complaint, **attaching as exhibits all relevant written materials, including but not limited to information from the supervisory process and a suggested list of witnesses as deemed appropriate,** *forward the judicial complaint to the committee on investigation and represent the church in the judicial process. (emphasis added)* c.) *2626 (Committee on Investigation) on the 1996 Book of Discipline, provided in 2626.6e as follows:*

The committee on investigation may call such persons as it deems necessary to establish whether or not there are reasonable grounds for formulating a charge or charges. The chairperson shall have the power, whenever it is appropriate in the committee's own discretion, to appoint a member(s) of the committee to interview any witness(es), provided that all parties may be present (without voice) and that three days' notice of the time and place of such interview shall have been given to all parties. The person(s) so appointed shall create a verbatim record of the interview and certify the record by signature for transmittal to the chairperson.

d.) The 2000 Book of Discipline *renumbered 2626 of the 1996 Discipline to 2706 and amended the 1996 provision in the new 2706.4c as follows:*

*The committee on investigation may call and question such persons or request such written information **including but not limited to materials from the supervisory process**, as it deems necessary to establish whether or not there are reasonable grounds for formulating a charge or charges. The committee may receive the counsels suggested lists of persons to be questioned, sources of written material or questions. There shall be no right of cross-examination by either the respondent or the person(s) bringing the original complaint. (emphasis added)*

e.) *2704. (Referral of Original Complaint to Counsel for the Church, Who Shall Prepare Judicial Complaint and Supporting Material for Consideration by Committee on Investigation) of* The 2004 Book of Discipline, *provided in 2704.2a as follows:*

If the bishop determines that the complaint is based on allegations of one or more offenses listed in 2702.1, the bishop shall refer the complaint to the counsel for the Church, who shall be appointed by the bishop. The counsel for the Church shall be clergyperson in full connection and shall have the right to choose one assistant counsel without voice who may be an attorney. The counsel for the Church shall draft and sign a judicial complaint, attaching as exhibits all relevant written materials, **including but not limited to information from the supervisory process,** *and suggested list of witnesses as deemed appropriate, forward the judicial complaint to the committee on investigation and represent the Church in the judicial process. (emphasis added)*

f.) *(Committee on Investigation-Procedures) of* The 2004 Book of Discipline, provided in 2706.4c *as follows:*

The committee on investigation may call and question such persons or request such written information **including but not limited to materials from the supervisory process** *as it deems necessary to establish whether or not there are reasonable grounds for formulating a charge or charges. (emphasis added)*

g.) 2704. *(Referral of original Complaint to Counsel for the Church, Who Shall Prepare Judicial Complaint and Supporting material for Consideration by Committee on Investigation) of* The 2008 Book *of Discipline, provides in 2694.2.a as follows:*

If the bishop determines that the complaint is based on allegations of one or more offenses listed in 2702.1, the bishop shall refer the complaint to the counsel for the Church, who shall be appointed by the bishop. The counsel for the Church shall be a clergyperson in full connection and shall have the right to choose one assistant counsel without voice who may be an attorney. The counsel for the Church shall draft and sign a judicial complaint, attaching as exhibits all relevant written materials, **including but limited to information from the supervisory process** *and a suggested list of witnesses as deemed appropriate, forward the judicial complaint to the committee on investigation and represent the Church in the judicial process. (emphasis added)*

h.) *Committee on Investigation-Procedures of* The 2008 Book of Discipline, *provides in* 2706.4c *as follows:*

The committee on investigation may call and question such persons or request such written information, **including but not limited to materials from the supervisory process,** *as it deems necessary to establish whether or not there are reasonable grounds for formulating a charge or charges. (emphasis added)*

i.) The 2000 Book of Discipline *clearly amended and altered the parallel provisions of the* 1996 Book of Discipline *to: (1) require Counsel for The Church to include information from the supervisory process as attachments to a judicial complaint; and (2) provide for the Committee on Investigation to request and consider materials from the supervisory process.*

Between 1996 and 2004, The Book of Discipline provided, in the "Supervisory Response" paragraphs, that "the supervisory response should be carried out by the bishop and district superintendent in a **confidential** *and timely manner..." (emphasis added)*

The 2008 Book of Discipline *amended the "Supervisory Response" paragraphs to read that "the supervisory response should be carried out by the bishop and district superintendent in a timely manner"* **deleting the word "confidential"** *from the sentence appearing in the 1996, 2000 and 2004 Disciplines.*

The amendment of The Book of Discipline in 2000 *requiring The Church's Counsel to attach information from the supervisory process to a judicial complaint and specifically authorizing the Committee on Investigation to request and consider materials from the supervisory process,* **clearly and unequivocally superseded that portion of JC 836 which suggested that committee on Investigation is not permitted to have or rely upon information obtained during the supervisory process.** (emphasis added)

Judge Tatti provides an excellent summary of what transpired between 2000 and 2008 at the various General Conferences, but **he reaches the wrong conclusion**. The actions of these General Conferences did not supersede JC 836. Rather, they placed the Church back in the untenable constitutional position that was addressed in JC 698. Basic fair process provisions for the respondent of legal representation and an accurate record are still prohibited during the supervisory response, while the Church is free to incorporate material from that process into the prosecution of the case during the judicial phase.

Therefore, the actions of the collective General Conferences to raze the wall between the supervisory and judicial processes does not supersede JC 836 as the judge claims. Rather, **these accretions are unconstitutional**. As chair of the committee on investigation Judge Tatti may not have had the authority to find *Disciplinary* paragraphs unconstitutional, but the Committee on Appeals is empowered to make such a determination. It is charged with identifying errors of Church law in ¶2715.7.b. Only the Judicial Council can ultimately decide if a particular piece of legislation is unconstitutional, but there is nothing in *The Discipline* that prevents The Committee on Appeals from making a provisional finding that particular passages of *The Discipline* that have been relied upon during judicial proceedings are in conflict with the Constitution or that they are not in compliance with previous Judicial Council decisions. Such is clearly the case in the present instant.

Furthermore, in the case at hand, the deprivation of counsel and accurate record keeping was especially harmful to the Appellant. He was summoned to a meeting with his district superintendent on July 30, 2014 without being informed of the nature of that meeting, even though he had asked about the purpose of the meeting. Because he did not know the subject matter of the meeting he could not know that he was entitled to be accompanied by an advocate as is clearly specified in 363.1.b. He was not informed that anything he said in this ostensibly pastoral and administrative session would make its way up the line into any subsequent judicial process that might ensue. The content of the conversations that took place was disputed at trial and there was no means to ascertain what was actually said.[13] Either the supervisory process needs to be openly acknowledged as a part of the judicial process and the full fair process safeguards required by the Constitution need to be available to the respondent, or the supervisory response needs to be separate and distinct from the judicial process as required in JC 836 and specified in 363.1.b so that the pastoral work of reconciliation can proceed unencumbered by looming threats and gathering clouds.

Section C—Information from the supervisory process was passed to the Counsel for the Church and the Presiding Officer in the form of an illegal verbatim transcript of a supervisory session.

---

13   Rev. Dodge, for instance, wrote in a letter to officials in the New England Annual Conference that the Appellant was "very cooperative throughout our conversation and repeatedly expressed his remorse for the situation." Rev. Dodge then testified before the trial court that the appellant expressed no remorse whatsoever during the session in question. There is no record available to establish which version is accurate, but it is clear that Rev. Dodge's testimony at the trial was prejudicial to the Appellant.

363.1.b clearly prohibits any verbatim record of supervisory sessions being kept. Nevertheless, the Administrative Assistant to Rev. Gary Spencer, Mrs. Linda Graham, prepared a partial verbatim of a supervisory session with the Appellant that took place on October 23, 2014. This material was later incorporated by the Counsel for the Church into his initial Judicial Complaint and forwarded to the Presiding Officer. While the document in question, after the strong protests of the Appellant, was eventually suppressed from the second complaint that went forward (after the judicial process was begun anew before committee on investigation), its inclusion in materials that were used to prepare the case against the Appellant and its likely use in persuading the Board of

Ordained Ministry of the Florida Conference to place the Appellant in the status of Involuntary Leave of Absence constitute a violation of the Appellant's fair process rights.[14] The Appellant reminds the Committee of the strong statement by the Judicial Council in Decision 1189:

> Deviations from the careful processes set forth in the Discipline, even when undertaken in good faith or for the sake of efficiency, fall below acceptable standards of fair process.

Section D—The Florida Conference illegally placed the Appellant in the status of Involuntary Leave of Absence

Bishop Carter informed the Appellant in a letter dated November 20, 2014 that he had been placed on Involuntary Leave of Absence by the Board of Ordained Ministry of the Florida Annual Conference.[15]

---

14 It is impossible for the Appellant to know what was shared with the Board of Ordained Ministry because he was not permitted to be present for the session at which material was presented to the Board, in direct violation of JC 1189. Whatever communication there was between Bishop Carter and the Board was entirely ex parte.

15 This same letter gave the Appellant ten days to find new living quarters, pack up his belongings, and move everything he owned, this after six years in the parsonage. While the deadline for moving was later extended, the original expectation

The same letter erroneously informed the Appellant that any counsel he retained must be from the New England Annual Conference, effectively depriving him of the assistance of the elder who had been advising him from mid-August onward, the Rev. Sydney Sadio, a retired member of the New Jersey Annual Conference. It was several months before the Appellant was able to secure his present counsel, who is a member of the New England Conference.

(The 2012 Discipline requires that counsels for administrative matters be from the member's own annual conference. There is no such restriction for judicial matters. (See 362.2.c and 2701.2.c). This counsel, in a letter dated February 23, 2015 informed the Bishop of the Florida Annual Conference that *The Discipline* had not been followed in depriving the Appellant of his salary, benefits and housing. That letter stated, in part:

- Paragraph 355.1 specifies that the bishop and superintendent must give to the clergy member and the Board of Ordained Ministry a written statement of the specific reasons involuntary leave is being requested. No such document was ever provided to Rev. Leslie. Judicial Council decision 1189 underscores this point: *The bishop and the district superintendent are required to give specific reasons for the request in writing to the member and the Board of Ordained Ministry.*

- Paragraph 355.2 requires that the Board of Ordained Ministry hold a hearing that follows the fair process guidelines of *The Discipline* (2701). No such hearing ever took place. Judicial Council decision 1189 makes it clear that the bishop cannot approach the Board of Ordained Ministry to request involuntary leave without the presence of the member: *Fair process requires that the member is entitled to hear all information considered by the Board. Fair process requires the bishop's point of view to be received in the presence of the member...and not in the absence of the member or in an ex parte manner.* Rev. Leslie was not provided with a chance to be heard before any final action was taken

---

communicated by the Florida Conference is indicative of the inhumane way in which the Appellant was treated throughout the process.

(2701.2 a), was not given notice of such a meeting (2701.2 b), and was not represented by an advocate before the Board (2701.2 c). The *Judicial and Administrative Procedures Handbook* of the General Council on Finance and Administration sheds further light on the procedures that must be followed by the Board, none of which were observed in the present case.

- The fact that 355.4 was cited in justifying the action taken by the Board does not excuse the conference from its responsibility to strictly adhere to the fair process provisions called for in 355. Again, JC 1189 speaks to this point: *355.4 is not a stand alone provision, but must be read and applied in its entirely. Even when pursued as an interim action between sessions of the Annual Conference, all provisions of 355 are applicable and must be observed.*

The Assistant to the Bishop of the Florida Annual Conference, Rev. David Dodge, admitted in a March 12, 2015 letter to the Appellant that the conference had made an error, but still refused to acknowledge the multiple violations of fair process that were involved, admitting only that it was the New England Board of Ordained Ministry that should have made a decision about conference relations. The Appellant was reinstated to active ministry and financial restitution was made for the months that he had been suspended without pay and benefits, but by this point it was more than clear to the Appellant that the interests of fairness were not being better served in Florida. *(This point was driven home in June of 2015 when, the day after a failed attempt at just resolution, the Counsel for the Church sent a letter to the Bishop of the New England Conference requesting that the Appellant be suspended for the balance of the judicial process, stating: **Based on my experience of Rev. Leslie during yesterday's just resolution process, I saw very little, if any, evidence of contrition, remorse or repentance on his part.** Not only was this description entirely at odds with the perceptions of others in the process, it was sent after the counsel had signed a confidentiality agreement with all parties to the just resolution process which stated: What is shared in the context of this facilitated conversation may not be used against the parties in any other church judicial or administrative proceeding (including but not limited to a potential church trial) or civil action. When the New England Bishop did not grant the Counsel's request, he did* *not give up. He later prevailed upon the Committee on Investigation to make the same request to New England, a request that was also denied. Nothing in The Discipline empowers a counsel for the church to make recommendations to another annual conference regarding a respondent's appointment status.)* The same March 12, 2015 letter from Rev. Dodge informed the Appellant that his appointment in the Florida Conference would be terminated after June 30, 2015. While it is certainly the right of an annual conference to take such action, it is worth noting that this decision was made before any hearing or trial had ever taken place, certainly calling into question whether the presumption of innocence called for in 2701 was ever in play in the instant matter.

It may be argued that because the Florida Conference took steps to indemnify the Appellant financially for the harm it had done to him by failing to follow the mandates of *The Discipline*, that there was no lasting damage to him. Such a perspective would fail to take into account the serious mental, emotional, and spiritual damage that is caused to a member and his family when they are forced from their home and livelihood as a result of violations by conference officials of the clear procedures mandated in *The Discipline*. Much was made at the trial about how the actions of the Appellant had let down the Church. Over and over again the prosecution declared that the Appellant had harmed his church, his colleagues and his conference. Not one word was permitted to be spoken at the trial about how the Church had harmed the Appellant. When the Church fails to live up to the highest standards of fairness in the way it prosecutes offenses, the message that is sent to the world is that the Church cannot be trusted, and the harm that emanates from that message is incalculable.

It may also be argued that, while regrettable, the error regarding a matter of conference relations was unrelated to the judicial process. That is precisely what the Presiding Officer ruled when he wrote:

> *Reverend Leslie's status as a clergy person during the pendency of the complaint does not affect his guilt or innocence under the*

*Bill of Charges and Specifications. Therefore, the motion to
dismiss on this argument is denied.*

What the Presiding Officer fails to acknowledge is the tremendous
interrelatedness of all of the pieces. Two of the same officers who placed
the Appellant in an illegal status that violated every semblance of fair
process, who withheld the original complaint from him in the initial
supervisory meeting, who produced an illegal *verbatim* of a supervisory
session, and who compelled him to sign the "Paragraph 2719 Agreement"
prematurely and without due process, **testified against him at the trial!**
The counsel for the church made two separate efforts during the judicial
process to place the Appellant on suspension. We are not dealing with
separate and distinct processes staffed by different individuals. As far as
the Appellant knows, the District Superintendent who testified against him
at trial may have even submitted nominations for those to be included in
the trial court pool before which body he would then testify. The Appellant
was certainly not informed that Dr. Spencer had recused himself from that
responsibility. Taken all together, the fair process rights of the Appellant
were trampled underfoot by the Florida Conference, and to assume that
the judicial process born out of this web of indifference to fair process
would now be unaffected is too much to ask. There is a reason that *The
Discipline* does not provide only for a fair trial, but for a **fair process** as
well, a fair process that encompasses the entire complaint procedure. In
the words of JC 1296: **(F)air process procedures**, *trials and appeals are
integral parts of the privilege of our clergy of right to trial by a committee and of appeal.*
(emphasis added)

Part III—Legal Errors by the Presiding Officer

The Grounds

The Appellant believes that certain rulings of the Presiding Officer
involved errors of Church law. These errors fall into three categories. First,
the Appellant believes that the Presiding Officer's definition of
"relevance" as being limited only to what tends to prove or disprove a bill

of charges and specifications forwarded by the committee on investigation is too narrow and is prejudicial to the defense. Second, certain rulings on the admissibility of evidence were in error. Third, the use by the Presiding Officer of the legal advisor for the Council of Bishops violated the separation of powers mandated in the judicial process and violated the provisions of 2708.1. This brief will deal with these issues in three sections.

Section A—The Presiding Officer defined "relevance" too narrowly and in a way that was prejudicial to the defense.

2708.3 gives the Presiding Officer the authority to rule on matters of procedure prior to the commencement of a trial. It reads:

> *All appeals of any procedural or substantive matters that have occurred prior to referral of the charges to trial must be appealed to the presiding officer of the trial court before the convening of the trial. Otherwise, the right to appeal on such matters is forfeited. All objections to and motions regarding the regularity of the proceedings and the form and substance of charges and specifications must be made before the convening of the trial court. The presiding officer may determine all such preliminary objections and motions; in furtherance of truth and justice may permit amendments to the specifications or charges not changing the general nature of the same; and may dismiss all or any part of the bill of charges upon a finding by the presiding officer (1) that all or such part is without legal or factual basis or (2) that, even assuming the specifications to be true, they do not constitute a basis for a chargeable offense.*

Judicial Council Decision 1230 declares:

> *It is a long-standing policy in The United Methodist Church to handle any administrative or judicial process within guidelines of fair process. **Fair process can never be presumed, but it must be clearly demonstrated at <u>all times</u>**. The*

concept of fair process is one that has been engrafted upon the
constitutional standards of our Church. (emphasis added)

The Presiding Officer, failed to consider the entire complaint process in his rulings. He chose instead to tie his definition of relevance only to the way in which the Church chose to frame its case against the Appellant. Only evidence that tended to prove or disprove the case as the Church presented it would be permitted to be examined at trial. The Presiding Officer stated:

> *I continue to believe that relevant evidence in the guilt or innocence*
> *phase of the Trial is evidence that tends to prove or disprove the*
> *Bill of Charges and Specifications.*

Such a definition precluded the consideration by the trial court of major misconduct by the Church. In the same ruling the Presiding Officer declared:

> *Process issues do not relate to whether the Respondent is innocent*
> *or guilty of the charges so they are not relevant.*

The problem with this perspective is that there is now no body within the annual conference that holds conference officials accountable to adhere to the highest standards of fairness in the complaint process. *(There has been a fondness among counsels for the church and presiding officers in recent years for declaring "The Church is not on trial" as they have sought to justify the narrow scope of the definition of relevance they employ. The Appellant believes this to be misguided dicta. The Discipline mandates fair process throughout the complaint procedures and in every trial the Church's compliance with this mandate must be open to examination by the trial court. There is nothing in The Discipline that prevents the trial court from considering whether fair process has been followed by the Church in complaint procedures. In the administrative process the Administrative Review Committee is charged with examining the entire preliminary process. 636 reads, in part:*

The entire administrative process leading to the action for
change in conference relationship shall be reviewed by the

administrative review committee, and it shall report its findings to the clergy session of members in full connection with the annual conference prior to any action of the annual conference. *("This safeguard does not exist for the judicial process. There is no body specifically charged with reviewing the fidelity of the Church to the requirements of The Discipline, although JC 1273 does state: Questions as to fair process, judicial process, and administrative process ought to be dealt with through the appropriate manner and bodies set forth in the Discipline. (emphasis added) Only the Presiding Officer is charged with reviewing challenges to fair process in ruling on pretrial motions by the Defense. If the Presiding Officer employs a standard of relevance restricted by the blinders of believing that all that is relevant in the judicial process is whether the bill of charges and specifications is true, there is no mechanism in United Methodist polity at the annual conference level to hold the Church accountable to Disciplinary mandates. The only relief for a respondent is the costly and time-consuming route of appeal. Further, burdensome and damaging penalties imposed by the trial court continue throughout the appeal process. This untenable situation could be remedied by employing a definition of relevance that permits the trial court to examine the entire narrative that unfolded from the time a written signed complaint was received, and not simply what the Church ended up with without regard to how it got there.")* They are free to take a haphazard approach to fair process, knowing that the slate will be wiped clean prior to trial because violations of fair process do not tend to prove or disprove whatever charges they draw up. They are even free to introduce evidence at trial that was garnered through the violation of Church law and the Defense is not permitted to even point that out to the trial court.

In the present instant, the Presiding Officer excluded process questions raised by the Defense from consideration by the trial court and himself refrained from ruling on the merits of those claims. Every challenge was weighed by the standard of whether it proved or disproved the Church's Bill of Charges. The Presiding Officer ruled, in effect, that the failure of the Church to share the signed written complaint with the Respondent at the initiation of the supervisory response, as is mandated by JC 974, was irrelevant, even though he permitted testimony to be offered to the trial court about the contents of a supervisory session that took place before the Respondent had seen the complaint. He permitted the Church to testify about the process under which the "Paragraph 2719

Agreement" was signed, but would not permit the Defense to dispute the validity of that document or to allow the trial court to know that the Respondent had rescinded his consent to the agreement. *(The Presiding Officer ruled on January 5, 2016 in response to a question from the Counsel for the Respondent: The validity of the Paragraph 2719.1 Agreement made between Bishop Carter, Bishop Devadhar and Reverend Leslie is not a matter for the Trial Court. The trust (sic) of your request seems to be a procedural issue. The Guilty or Innocent phase of the trial is about what happened and not why it happened. However, you may make a proffer of that evidence outside the presence of the Trial Court.)* The trial court was not permitted to know that the Florida Conference had trampled on the fair process rights of the Respondent when it ignored The Discipline in placing him on Involuntary Leave of Absence, but two of the officials responsible for that travesty of justice were permitted to testify against the Respondent at trial. The Defense was barred from sharing anything having to do with this issue. The Presiding Officer ruled:

> *Reverend Leslie's status as a clergy person during the pendency of the complaint does not affect his guilt or innocence under the Bill of Charges and Specifications. Therefore, the motion to dismiss on this argument is denied.*

He ruled that the original, signed complaint, that had been shared with the Committee on Investigation by the Church, could not be seen by the trial court, stating:

> *Although both the original signed grievance and a judicial complaint are both called a "complaint" in the Book of Discipline, they are different. Both are indispensable for the judicial process, but I do not believe both are indispensable for the Trial itself. The fact that the original grievance/complaint was reviewed by the Committee on Investigation or was used to address Reverend Leslie's status in the New England Annual Conference is not relevant, in my opinion.*

The Presiding Officer ruled that the violation of ¶363.1.b by the Church when it made a verbatim of a supervisory session and subsequently shared that document with the Counsel for the Church to assist him in preparing his case did not matter. He wrote:

> *The Presiding Officer does not view an "illegal verbatim" becoming the basis for dismissal of the Bill of Charges and Specifications certified by the Committee on Investigation and denies the motion on this basis.*

The only evidence permitted to come before the trial court under the narrow construction of the Presiding Officer was material that related to the way the Church wanted to frame the narrative. It did not matter that evidence used at trial was obtained through violations of fair process, nor was it deemed relevant that the Church had violated the only requirement that 2719.1 placed upon it—namely to serve the interests of fairness throughout the judicial process. Misconduct by the Respondent was fair game. Misconduct by the Church was buried under a series of pro-prosecution rulings by the Presiding Officer.

It is true that The Discipline authorizes the Presiding Officer to rule upon the relevance of evidence during a trial. It is also true that The Discipline does not define what it means by the word relevant. What is beyond dispute, however, is that The Discipline is unapologetically focused on fairness. The same can be said of an overwhelming majority of Judicial Council cases. Fair process means that there is equal treatment under the law of the Church. The Church, no matter how just its cause, must operate within the same constraints in the judicial process as the respondent. The way in which terms are defined and applied cannot unduly privilege one side or the other. In the present instant the definition of relevance favored the prosecution and put the defense at a disadvantage. To the degree that this is so, it is a violation of the fair process requirements of The Discipline.

The Appellant also believes that employing different definitions of relevance in the guilt/innocence phase of the trial and the penalty phase of the trial is problematic. In ruling on the Church's Motion in Limine, the Presiding Officer wrote:

> *The issue of "what transpired" is relevant as it relates to the truth of the Bill of Charges and Specifications. "[W]hy it happened" is not relevant in the guilt or innocence phase of the trial. "[C]ontributing factors to the offense" are not relevant unless there is a defense that is expressly provided for in The Book of Discipline or Judicial Council decisions.*

He went on in that same ruling to state:

> *In the penalty phase of the trial any "contributing factors," subject to their reliability, are likely relevant to the appropriate penalty.*

Requiring citations from *The Discipline* or Judicial Council decisions masks the reality that the Presiding Officer's definition of relevance is his own personal formulation and not a definition grounded in the law of the Church. Simple fairness and common sense ought to be all that is required to adjust such an opinion.

The Appellant respectfully requests that members of the Appeals Committee read at this time Appendix XXVII, *A Proffer Offered in the Matter of the Rev. Errol Leslie*. This document was read into the record of the trial court and offers further discussion of the ramifications of defining relevance too narrowly and excluding process matters from consideration by the trial court.

Section B—Errors of law relating to the admissibility of various pieces of evidence

The exclusion of a letter from Rev. David Dodge to colleagues in the New England Conference was an error of law. The letter was both relevant and reliable, the only tests for evidence provided by *The Discipline* according to 2710.7 and 2710.9. The letter had a complicated history which is outlined in the following letter that the Counsel for the Respondent sent to the Presiding Officer on January 5, 2016, the same day that Rev. Dodge was examined by both counsels in commissioned out-of-court testimony:

Dear Bishop Gwinn,

There was a dispute this afternoon during the commissioned out-of-court testimony about the Defense's use of a letter written by David Dodge to officials of the New England Conference on July 30, 2014. Rev. Therrell believed its use to be a violation of the requirement to share documentation with the other side. I'm sure that he will be in touch with you about his concerns. I'll let him speak for himself. I did want you, however, to have some background on how the letter came into our possession and how we understood it.

I wrote to Rev. Dodge on December 21, asking for the letter. He replied to me that he was out of his office and would not return until January 4, and that he would be happy to forward the letter at that time. Yesterday, January 4, Rev. Dodge wrote to me telling me he could not find a copy of the letter. I asked his permission to approach Rev. Robinson-Johnson, the Assistant to the Bishop in New England, to see if she had a copy that could be shared with the Defense. Rev.

Dodge agreed and I contacted Rev. Robinson Johnson by email yesterday. When I had not heard from her by 9:00 this morning, I contacted her by phone. I opened an email from her at 10:30 this morning which contained a copy of the letter.

As I read through the letter, it was clear that it pertained to the process, and would not be something that the Defense would or could introduce as evidence. I did, however, hold on to the letter in case testimony should be introduced by the Church which the letter might impeach. You will recall that in my letter to you of 12/29 I stated the following:

"The Defense also has in its possession several receipts and bank statements that may or may not be relevant, depending on the testimony of the Church's witnesses. We will not be introducing them as exhibits in our own case, and, thus, are not submitting them at this time, but would like to reserve the right to introduce them should they become necessary to impeach the testimony of one of the Church's witnesses during cross-examination."

The Church made no objection to this statement, nor did you as the Presiding Officer address the matter.

We believed this letter to fall into the same category as those receipts and bank statements. It was not an appropriate document for the Defense to introduce. It would not be our exhibit and it related to process.

An occasion arose during the direct examination of the Church today when the witness stated three times that Rev. Leslie had shown no remorse for his actions at his July 30 meeting with Rev. Dodge and Dr. Spencer. A statement in the letter he sent that same afternoon appeared to directly contradict that statement, so I quoted from the letter and asked the witness to explain. (The relevant portion of this letter states: **Rev. Leslie was very cooperative throughout our conversation and repeatedly expressed his remorse for the situation.**)

When I asked a follow-up question based on the same letter, the Counsel for the Church strenuously objected and accused me of bad faith in not sharing the document with him prior to the examination of the witness.

If I have violated a rule, I sincerely apologize to Rev. Therrell and to you. I had no idea that the letter would turn out to be relevant, but when it appeared that the witness was telling one story to colleagues in New England and another to the trial court, it seemed important to point out. I recalled your guidance in a December 6 email: "If, at any time, either counsel should feel that testimony being given is not accurate then it is relevant and *appropriate for that counsel to establish such by questions and witnesses."*

That same evening the Counsel for the Church filed an objection with the Presiding Officer to any reference to the Dodge letter being included in the video of Rev. Dodge's testimony and the next day, January 6, the Presiding Officer upheld his objection and the section was excised.

The Appellant believes that the ruling of the Presiding Officer to exclude the testimony of Rev. Dodge relating to this letter was an error of Church law for the following reasons:

1.) The letter was relevant. This written contemporaneous statement made by Rev. Dodge to colleagues in New England (sent on July 30, 2014, the same day of the first supervisory session) directly contradicted his out-of-court commissioned testimony.

2.) The letter was reliable. When Rev. Dodge was unable to produce the letter himself, he gave permission to the Defense to approach the Rev. Erica Robison-Johnson, Assistant to the Bishop in the New England Conference, to request a copy of the letter. Rev. Dodge did not dispute the accuracy of the letter in his commissioned testimony, nor did he claim there was any problem with its authenticity. A copy of the letter was emailed to the Counsel for the Church on the evening of January 5, exactly as it had been received from Rev. Robinson-Johnson.[16]

---

16 The Counsel for the Church raised questions about the authenticity of this letter in a side bar conversation on January 12, 2016, implying that the Defense may have introduced a false or doctored document. The Counsel for the Appellant respectfully reminds the Committee that this was a church trial. We do not do such things. If the Counsel for the Church had doubts about the authenticity of the letter, he had had it in his possession for a week by that point and could have raised any question he had with Rev. Dodge, who was both a witness for the Church and the author of the letter.

3.) The Defense followed fair and reasonable procedures in attempting to acquire this letter, keeping all parties apprised of the process. On December 21, 2015 the Presiding Officer sent the following notice to all parties:

Should you intend to introduce any documentary evidence other than that included in the Bill of Specifications and Charges that proposed evidence should be requested to the Presiding Officer not later than December 29, 2015.

Seeking to comply with the Presiding Officer's directive, that same day, December 21, the Counsel for the Respondent sent the following request to Rev. Dodge:

Grace and Peace to you in this holy season. Would you please forward to me a copy of the email that you sent to the Rev. Erica Robinson-Johnson on July 30, 2014. This email relates to the alleged confession of Rev. Leslie earlier that day.

This request was copied to all parties, including the Counsel for the Church and the Presiding Officer. They were made aware of the existence of the letter and that the Defense believed it to be in the possession of the Church's own witness. Rev. Dodge replied on December 21:

You probably received my "out of office" message indicating that I am away from the office until January 4. I will be glad to forward that correspondence to you at that time.

On January 4, 2016 Rev. Dodge sent the following email to the Defense:

Today is my first day back in the office since receiving this request from you. I have searched my email files and do not locate an email sent on July 30, 2014 to Rev. Erica Robison-Johnson that relates to the topic you identified. Since the meeting with Rev. Leslie occurred on July 30 at the superintendent's office in Vero Beach, Florida (about 3 hours from Lakeland), I suspect that such communication regarding that meeting would have occurred on July 31, 2014. However, as I searched my email files for that date, I still do not locate such an email. Somehow I must have missed keeping a copy of it. I will continue to check the files and, if I find it, I will immediately forward it to you. (The Appellant is curious about the awkward English phrasing in this email: i.e. *I have searched…and do not find (as opposed to cannot find or have not found)* and again: *as I searched…I **still do not locate** such an email (as opposed to could not locate).*

Counsel for the Respondent replied that same day:

Thanks for looking. I believe that Erica may have a copy. Would you authorize her to share it with us?

Rev. Dodge answered in an email that was copied to both the Counsel for the Church and the Presiding Officer:

Yes, that would be fine.

Rev. Robinson-Johnson forwarded the letter at 9:30 AM on January 5 (the next day) and the Counsel for the Defense opened the email approximately one hour later. The video examination of Rev. Dodge was scheduled for 3:00 that same afternoon.

1.) The Defense did not intend to introduce this letter as documentary evidence since it related to process and the Presiding Officer had specifically excluded anything related to process from the trial. It was reserved to be used only in the event that it was necessary for impeachment. It did not become necessary until the apparent contradiction between Rev. Dodge's testimony and the letter emerged. It had not been immediately forwarded to the Church that morning because the Defense did not intend to introduce the letter as a part of its own case and because of the last-minute nature of the acquisition of the document. The Counsel for the Defense was heavily involved in preparing his cross examination and direct examination of Rev. Dodge scheduled for later that same afternoon.

2.) There is no Disciplinary requirement that all materials used at trial be shared in advance with the other party. ¶2701 states only:

> *The respondent and the Church shall have access to all records relied upon in the determination of the outcome of the committee on investigation, trial court, or appeal committee or body.*

There was never any question of access being withheld from the Church.

(A copy of the letter would have been passed across the table, or submitted to the Presiding Officer, had we not been in the unique position of securing out-or-court commissioned testimony via video conference across a distance of some 1500 miles. The parties were also without the services of the Presiding Officer.) The document was forwarded to the Counsel for the Church on the evening of January 5, 2016. The Church had been made aware of the existence of a letter in the possession of its own witness and had ample lead time to do its own investigation into the contents of that letter. The Church was copied on the request to Rev. Robinson-Johnson for the letter and chose not to follow up on the matter itself. The Defense should not have been penalized in the presentation of its case because the Church had not done due diligence in the preparation of its witness, who himself had given permission the previous day (in an email that was also copied to the Church) for the Defense to acquire the letter.

The Defense sought once more to introduce the letter in question prior to the penalty phase of the trial on January 12, 2015 to be used to support the testimony of the Respondent that he had indeed expressed remorse during the first supervisory session. The Church had now had the letter in its possession for an entire week and had had ample opportunity to prepare a response and to validate its authenticity. Still, the Presiding Officer excluded the letter from being introduced, leaving the trial court with only the uncorroborated assertion of the Respondent that he had repeatedly expressed his remorse during the July 30, 2014 meeting, a claim that could not be substantiated by any written record of that meeting and that had been disputed by the testimony of Rev. Dodge.[17] **The exclusion of the original complaint from consideration by the trial court was an error of Church law.**

The Presiding Officer ruled on January 8, 2016 that the original signed complaint was not relevant to the concerns of the trial court. He allowed that he was open to being approached by counsels if certain limited conditions developed during the trial in which the complaint might become relevant, particularly, he noted, for reasons of impeachment. He stated:

I can see that there may be circumstances in which the original grievance/complaint could be relevant based upon circumstances, which may include issues of impeachment due to inconsistent statements or matters of credibility.

---

17   This is a prime example of the way in which a respondent is denied fair process by the erosion of the separation between the supervisory process and the judicial process that was assured in JC 836. It is instructive to note that Rev. Dodge testified before the committee on investigation on September 23, 2015 that he could not actually recall whether the respondent expressed remorse in the July 30 meeting (COI transcript, p. 148, lines 7–8), but three-and-a-half months later, he was able to categorically deny three times that there was any expression of remorse (Commissioned testimony, p. 10, ln. 20 through p. 11, ln 5). Without fair process safeguards in the supervisory process (or a wall between the processes), a respondent is inevitably at risk of faulty memories or possible bias on the part of those testifying about what transpired during a supervisory session.

The Appellant contends that the trial court needed to have before it the entire complaint history in order to understand the state of mind of the Appellant during the supervisory process, a topic that was introduced at trial by the Church. This is especially relevant in the penalty phase of the trial. It would have been entirely reasonable for a trial court deliberating over a penalty to wonder why the accused had not simply surrendered his orders if he had admitted to having a sexual affair with the complainant. The Defense was prohibited from showing the trial court that the main reason the Appellant chose to go forward to trial was that he had been accused in the original complaint of numerous affairs and egregious sexual misconduct by the complainant, including the abuse of his own daughters. He was unwilling to surrender his orders on the basis of these scurrilous and libelous allegations. He wanted a forum in which to clear his name of the numerous untruths contained in that document. It was not until February 18, 2015 that the Appellant had any inkling of what would be contained in the charges that would be filed against him. He believed up until that time that the full scope of the original complaint would be used by the Church. Had it been shared with the trial court, and the court been permitted to see for itself the outrageous accusations of that original complaint, such knowledge could have cast an entirely different light on the actions of the Respondent, showing him in a far more sympathetic light than the Church desired for him to be seen.

The original signed written complaint is indispensable in the complaint process according to JC 777. It triggers the supervisory response and it shapes all attempts to reach just resolution. In the instant case it was used to justify the suspension of the Appellant during the supervisory process and it was forwarded to the committee on investigation for that body's consideration as it formulated a bill of charges and specifications. Because the Complainant had broadly disseminated the same accusations in the Appellant's former church and community, it provided the background against which the Appellant sought to clear his name. This complaint was used at every step of the supervisory and judicial process by the Church until it came to the trial, the one place where the Appellant had an opportunity to set the record straight, and then, because it was an embarrassment to the star witness for the Church, the trial court was barred from knowing about it. The document was referred to multiple times in the testimony of both Dr. Spencer and Rev. Dodge, but the trial court was not permitted to know what that document contained because of the narrow construction of relevance employed by the Presiding Officer. While it may not have been deemed relevant to the Church's case under the narrow construction of relevance employed by the Presiding Officer, it was most certainly relevant to the Respondent's case.

C—The use of the legal advisor to the Council of Bishops by the Presiding Officer was an error of Church law.

The Presiding Officer involved Attorney William Waddell, legal advisor to the Council of Bishops, in the initial organizing conference call of all parties in the matter of Rev. Errol Leslie. Attorney Waddell often advises Presiding Officers at trials.[18] While the Counsel for the Appellant has the greatest personal respect for Mr. Waddell and considers him a friend, there is a serious issue around the separation of powers at stake when the legal advisor to the Council of Bishops provides handson legal advice throughout the pretrial phase to Presiding Officers who are expected to remain as neutral as possible in judicial proceedings. Bishops represent the interests of the Church in judicial proceedings. They are not neutral parties.

The Appellant raised his concerns about Attorney Waddell's involvement in the instant matter in a pretrial motion:

1.) *Attorney William Waddell is the legal advisor to the United Methodist Council of Bishops. Attorney Waddell was present by telephone for the first pretrial conference called by the presiding officer over the objection of the Defense. Mr. Waddell has possibly played a consulting role with the Presiding Officer before and after that time. If this is the case, such is a violation of 2708.1 which clearly states that the Presiding Officer may have counsel "for the*

---

18 The Appellant is aware the Mr. Waddell was counsel to the Presiding Officers in the trials of Rev. Amy DeLong and Rev. Frank Schaefer, to name two.

__sole purpose__ of advice to the presiding officer __during the trial.__" (Emphasis added) The Defense objects to the interpretation of the Presiding Officer during that conference that he considered the pretrial process to be a part of the trial. (The Appellant does not have a transcript of this call, but it should be noted that the Presiding Officer does not dispute the Appellant's claim that Mr. Waddell was involved or that he considered the pre-trial phase to be a part of the trial in his ruling on this matter.) "During the trial" is an unambiguous phrase referring to a particular announced time and location. The trial has not yet been convened.

2.) *Further, 2708.1 bars the conference chancellor from fulfilling the role of counsel to the Presiding Officer during the trial in deference to the separation of powers identified in item 5 of the __Fair Process Issues__ stated above. The same concern applies to the legal advisor for the Council of Bishops. While it may be appropriate for an advisor to the Council of Bishops to give general advice to bishops about approaches to trials in the abstract, it is a violation of the Constitutionally mandated separation of powers for a person serving as legal advisor to the Council of Bishops to be giving active advice to a presiding officer in a specific case. This would include advice about the general approach to take to a specific case, suggested possible rulings in the pretrial phase, and giving advice to the presiding officer during a trial. It was the Bishop of the Florida Conference, himself a member of the Council of Bishops, who forwarded the complaint against the Respondent to a counsel for the church. To have an attorney who represents that Council giving advice to the Presiding Officer during judicial proceedings is a clear conflict of interest and a violation of the separation of powers.*

3.) *If the presiding officer has used the services of Attorney Waddell beyond his listening to the first pretrial conference call, the Respondent respectfully requests, for appellate purposes, a complete record of such interactions, including a full and detailed disclosure of the ways in which those services were used, including but not limited to the number of telephone conversations or electronic communications between the two, any role played by Attorney Waddell in framing the presiding officer's general approach to the trial, and any role played by Mr. Waddell in shaping responses to questions and/or challenges by the Respondent.*

In response to the motion, the Presiding Officer ruled:

The Presiding Officer does not view Mr. Waddell's advice to me regarding any pretrial matters which I may ask of him as being precluded by 2708.1. The pretrial process is designed to address issues that the Presiding Officer will face during the trial. Any pretrial consultation with Mr. Waddell is intended to help the Presiding Officer be fair and objective in the handling of those anticipated issues. Mr. Waddell is not serving the function of a conference chancellor.

Further, he is not acting as the legal advisor to the Council of Bishops when he advises me as my counsel for a particular judicial process to which I have been appointed to be the Presiding Officer. The motion based upon these arguments is denied.

The Presiding Officer did not provide the requested record of interactions with Attorney Waddell. The Appellant's particular concern as it relates to the instant matter is twofold. First, the direct link between the Council of Bishops and the judicial process presents a separation of powers problem, an issue that has most recently been directly addressed in JC 1296.

(JC 1296 held that the elimination of the committee on investigation by the 2012 General Conference was unconstitutional because, in part:... the change in the Discipline that occurred at the 2012 General Conference raises serious questions about both fair process and balance between the episcopal and other clergy processes.) Second, the violation of 2708.1, which intentionally limits the role of legal counsel for the Presiding Officer to the trial itself, expands the influence of the legal advisor to the Council of Bishops beyond the trial, where the Counsel

for the Respondent has a direct on-the-record opportunity to participate in conversations leading to rulings, to the entire off-the-record process of the Presiding Officer formulating rulings in response to Defense motions. The legal advisor to the Council of Bishops ought not to have hidden influence in the judicial process. The Appellant believes this situation to be a direct violation of 2708.1.

Summary

- The Florida Annual Conference had no authority to host judicial proceedings against the Appellant. 2719.1 is unconstitutional, the process under which the so called "Paragraph 2719 Agreement" was signed was a violation of the Appellant's fair process rights, and under the terms of the 2008 Discipline the Appellant did not meet the tests of appointment and residency at the time judicial proceedings began which are necessary to qualify for the exception provided in 2719.1.
- The fair process rights of the Appellant were violated at multiple points throughout the supervisory and judicial processes. He did not receive a copy of the complaint against him at the outset of the complaint process. The elimination of confidentiality during the supervisory process by the General Conferences of 2000–2008 was unconstitutional. An illegal verbatim of a supervisory session was made and shared with the Counsel for the Church to assist him in the preparation of his case against the Appellant. The Florida Annual Conference illegally placed the Appellant in the status of Involuntary Leave of Absence.
- There were serious errors of Church law in the rulings of the Presiding Officer. The Presiding Officer employed a definition of "relevance" that was prejudicial to the Defense. The ruling to exclude a letter from David Dodge from consideration by the trial court that was both relevant and reliable (by any definition) was an error of Church law. The exclusion of the original signed written complaint from consideration by the trial court was an error of Church law. The use of the legal advisor to the Council

of Bishops by the Presiding Officer throughout the pretrial process was an error of Church law.

Taken all together, the violations of Church law and the indifference to the fair process rights of the Appellant that characterized both the supervisory and judicial processes in the instant matter made it impossible for the Appellant to receive a just verdict and penalty.

Relief Requested

The Judicial Council has long maintained that fair process and strict adherence to The Discipline are indispensable in matters that affect the conference relations of clergy members. In reversing the action of an annual conference to place a clergy person on Involuntary Leave of Absence, JC 1189 stated: Deviations from the careful processes set forth in the Discipline, even when undertaken in good faith or for the sake of efficiency, fall below acceptable standards of fair process. In JC 1230 the Judicial Counsel reversed the actions of the South Central Jurisdictional Committee on Episcopacy that placed a bishop in the status of Involuntary Retirement (d)ue to the numerous errors in violation of the principles of fair process and the inability to articulate what constitutes "best interests of the bishop and/or the Church"... In JC 1270 the Judicial Council upheld the decision of the Northeast Jurisdictional Committee on Appeals to overturn a penalty imposed by a trial court removing the credentials of a clergy person because the penalty did not comply with the law of the Church.

In the present instant the numerous violations of fair process and Church law cited in the foregoing pages leave the Committee on Appeals with only one fair option. The Appellant respectfully requests that the

Southeastern Jurisdictional Committee on Appeals declare the verdict and the penalty imposed on the Appellant by the Florida Annual Conference to be declared null and void and of no effect and, further, that it direct the New England Conference to immediately return the Appellant to active membership in that conference. The Appellant further requests that the Florida Annual Conference be directed to reimburse the Appellant for all lost salary and benefits incurred since the discontinuation of his membership in the New England Annual Conference.

Respectfully Submitted this day of April, 2016,
Rev. Scott Campbell
Counsel for the Appellant

CHAPTER 17

Additional Documents and Exhibits

In this section of the narrative, I have chosen to include some miscellaneous documents that would be helpful in providing additional information on how this story unfolded and the many missteps within the Florida Conference. The documents are not necessarily in any special sequential or chronological order.

David Dodge's Letter RE Jury Selection
Exhibit A

Right at the very outset, Reverend David Dodge sent the following e-mail below to the (then) cabinet. The content of the e-mail suggested that he really did not even know the process involved. As such, my defense counsel, Dr. Campbell, had to "straighten him out" on this as indicated in his response e-mail to Reverend Dodge. Between Reverend Dodge's own ignorance and the pressure, he was under from Dr. Spencer, combined with the enthusiasm and anxiety to get rid of me, he was once again operating in a way that was totally outside of the book of discipline. This disobedience to the order and discipline of the United Methodist Church is also what drove the same bishop and cabinet to place me on involuntary leave because, for them, it was the easiest and fastest way to punish me to the maximum.

From: David Dodge ddodge@flumc.org
To: Appointive Cabinet appcab@flumc.org
Sent: Mon, Mar 30, 2015 11:26 am
Subject: Errol Leslie Trial

Dear Friends,

On behalf of Bishop Carter, and pursuant to ^[2713 of the Book of Discipline, I am asking that each of you send to Rev. Annette Pendergrass, Dean of the Cabinet, the names and addresses (including email) of seven full clergy members of the Florida Conference (deacons and/or elders) in your district who may be appointed as members of the trial court pool for the trial of Rev. Errol Leslie. The date and the place of the trial will be determined in the next few days by Bishop Al Gwinn, the presiding officer.

Upon the receipt of those names from you, Bishop Carter will determine who he is appointing to the trial court pool and Rev. Pendergrass will write to the individuals to indicate their appointment.

Please carefully consider the following Disciplinary requirements when you send Rev. Pendergrass the names of clergy:

"Special consideration should be given so that the pool includes persons representative of racial, ethnic, and gender diversity."*, [2709.2

"No person shall serve as a member of the trial court who was a member of the cabinet, board of ordained ministry, or committee on investigation who considered the case in the process of coming before the trial court." ^ [2709.3

"The trial court for a clergy member shall...

[consist of] clergy in full connection." ^[2713.3
Please forward these names to Rev. Pendergrass no later than Monday, April 6. Please let me know if you have any questions on this matter.

Blessings,
Rev. David A. Dodge

With his eagle eye, Reverend Campbell caught the problem and then responded as indicated below.

Dear Rev. Dodge,

Please review once more Paragraph 2713.3.a) There is no role whatsoever for Bishop Carter to choose which nominees are to constitute the trial court pool. In fact, if he were to do so, this would be grounds for excluding the entire pool. Bishop Carter is not an impartial party in this process. The Discipline is clear that all appointments to the pool are to come from the Superintendents, not the bishop. I would appreciate it if you would communicate this clarification to the Superintendents at your earliest convenience.

Sincerely,
Scott Campbell
Counsel for Rev. Leslie

Motion in Limine and Scott's Response Exhibit B

One of the issues that the defense tried to introduce during the trial was the credibility and motive of the complainant. This is a normal practice in a regular court of law. However, in this instance, we were unsuccessful as the counsel for the church did not want to have anything introduced that could cause me to face any penalties even remotely less than not being able to pastor again. Bishop Gwinn who was the appointed presiding officer was a mere figurehead who allowed Reverend Therrell to "run the show" as he pleased. Hence, Reverend Therrell introduced this motion in Limine below. However, as always, the presiding officer thought that he had to grant the request of this counsel for the church. The fact is that this trial was not so much about fairness as it was about protecting and satisfying the appetite of the Florida Conference.

The Florida Annual Conference of the United Methodist Church Motion in Limine Regarding Complainant's Past History And Relationships

In the Matter of Rev. Errol E. Leslie, Respondent

The Counsel for the Church files and serves this Motion in Limine requesting the Presiding Officer enter an order preventing and prohibiting the Respondent's counsel from questioning the Complainant, or any other witness, or to introduce evidence, whether solicited or not, about the Complainant's prior relationships or sexual history. In support of this motion, the Church states the following:

1.) The Committee on Investigation of the Florida Annual Conference certified a bill of charges and specifications against the Respondent on September 25, 2015. This bill of charges and specifications charges the Respondent, the Rev. Errol E. Leslie, with three charges: immorality, sexual misconduct, and disobedience to the

Order and Discipline of The United Methodist Church.

2.) The aforementioned charges are based on conduct between the Complainant, Ms. Veda Hendricks, and the Respondent. No other chargeable conduct was alleged by the Counsel for the Church nor sustained by the Committee on Investigation.

3.) During the preparation phase prior to the Committee on Investigation hearing, the Respondent submitted proposed questions for the

Complainant and other witnesses about the Complainant's prior relationships (sexual and otherwise) as well as her relationship history with other people.

4.) The Complainant is not on trial; the Respondent is. It is irrelevant and there is no probative value to questioning the Complainant, Respondent, or any other witnesses about Complainant's prior relationships and sexual history. The only facts at issue are the guilt or innocence of the Respondent based upon his conduct with the Complainant. To allow any testimony or evidence of the Complainant's sexual history and prior relationships would place her on trial and she has not been charged with anything before this trial court. Any such testimony or evidence would be purely to harass and embarrass the Complainant and would be overly prejudicial and irrelevant.

WHEREFORE, the Counsel for the Church, respectfully requests the Presiding Officer to instruct the Respondent's counsel not to question the Complainant, Respondent, nor any other witness, nor to introduce evidence, about the Complainant's prior relationships or sexual history, and not to make any reference to the fact that this motion has been filed, granted, or denied.

Elder in Full Connection
Counsel for the Church of The Florida Annual
Conference of The United Methodist Church

My defense counsel, Reverend Dr. Scott Campbell, responded with the following statement below.

A Response to the Church's Motion in Limine Exhibit C

The Defense does not dispute points 1–3 in the Church's Motion in Limine. It does, however, contend that the conclusions drawn in point 4 are misguided and prejudicial to the Respondent's ability to receive a fair trial. The Defense objects to the motion on the following grounds:

1.) The Defense agrees that the Complainant is not on trial. She will not face any penalty in this process, no matter the outcome. Her calling to ministry is not under threat. The trial court will not pronounce any judgment on her, nor will the Defense.

2.) The Complainant's behavior, however, is open to examination, particularly as it affects any penalty that might be imposed on the Respondent.

3.) During the guilt/innocence phase of a church trial the common standard used to weigh the relevance of testimony is whether that testimony makes it more or less likely that the charges and specifications are true. During the penalty phase of a trial, a version of that same principle must apply. The penalty phase is not concerned with the mere facts of the case. In the penalty phase there is an opportunity for the Respondent to explore factors which contributed to the commission of the offense, including the role played by the Complainant in shaping whatever took place. In this case, there are conflicting versions of what transpired and why it happened. The principle that must be applied in weighing the relevance of testimony is whether that testimony makes it more or less likely that the Respondent's version of the story is true. If this standard is to be applied, the Complainant's past history is directly relevant to being able to determine which version of the contributing factors to the offense the trial court should believe. In order to carry out its role responsibly in fixing a penalty, the trial court must know not only the bare facts of the case, but as much as it can know about the story behind those facts.

4.) The Church's motion raises the issue of the Complainant's history being embarrassing to her. The Defense respectfully reminds the Church that the Complainant has already made the claim that she engaged in a sexual relationship with a married man in the instant case. Further, when the Defense broached the question with the Church of whether it was open to having a closed trial out of concern for the privacy of all parties, the Counsel for the Church issued the following response in an email dated March 25, 2015:

I have spoken with Ms. Hendricks and she would prefer for the trial to remain open as is the presumption. Accordingly, we'll be opposing any motion to close it.

5.) Further, while her history might be embarrassing for the Complainant, that temporary embarrassment does not compare with the very real and possibly permanent penalty being faced by the Respondent. The Respondent, out of basic fairness, must be allowed during the penalty phase of the trial to cite all contributing factors to the events that transpired.

6.) The Defense can only conclude that the Church does not want the trial court to know that the Complainant has a long history of entering into relationships with married men (and married pastors in particular) because it knows that if the trial court is aware of this fact that it will be less likely to see the Respondent as the sexual predator he has been made out to be in the original complaint and in the testimony of the Complainant before the Committee on

Investigation. It will make it more difficult for the Church to achieve the surrender of orders that it has sought from the very beginning of the supervisory process.

7.) It will be the contention of the Defense during the penalty phase of the trial, should there be one, that the Complainant initiated contact with the Respondent and aggressively pursued a relationship with him, trying to induce him to leave his wife and marry her. This will not be offered as justification for the behavior of the Respondent, but it will set the context in which he made certain decisions. Establishing the fact that this has been a repeated pattern in the Complainant's life will contribute to the likelihood that the claim of the Respondent is true. The probative value of allowing statements that the Complainant has made concerning her past, both orally and in writing, to a witness in this case is clear. The probative value of the direct knowledge of a member of her family concerning her past is likewise indisputable. The Church will be free to cross-examine witnesses who so testify to establish the veracity of their testimony.

8.) Finally, the Defense believes the trial court is perfectly capable of weighing all relevant factors in fixing an appropriate penalty. It does not need to be shielded from considering the whole story. Trials are about considering the whole truth, not only the parts that are convenient to the narrative the prosecution would like to promulgate.

The Defense respectfully requests that the Presiding officer deny in its entirety the Church's Motion in Limine.

Respectfully submitted,
Scott
Scott Campbell
Counsel for the Respondent

Meanwhile, the complainant had sent these texts below to my pastoral colleague whom I had invited to help me through the moral dilemma that I faced during the early period of my emotional struggles. It is a document that the defense thought would have been helpful in establishing motive, intent, and credibility on the part of the complainant. As indicated earlier, it was not allowed to be used during the trial.

Complainant's Texts to Church's Witness Exhibit D

<Messages (1) Veda>

Just wanted to say thanks again for your time and Prayers.

I feel guilty I did not pray with you but I had so much going on in my head and God knows my heart I can't hide my true feelings from God. It is so easy to use words in Prayer to sound so Spiritual and Holy.

God has to give me the strength to try to love myself. I hate all I have done to displease Him and disobey

His Word.

Thanks again for your time and concern.

God knows the future and I just have to trust Him.

<Messages (1) Veda>

I needed to tell you this and I did not but it is important that I tell you this

I have allowed fourteen men to sexually abuse me and I am torn to pieces by my experiences.

Errol knows I shared this with him so he could be using this against me also... name at this time in my mess.

Letter RE Appointing Bishop Gwinn
Exhibit E

Bishop Carter and the rest of the leadership in the Florida Conference did everything they could to hold on to the procedure so the bishop sent this short letter below as another attempt to negate the fact that I was very much settled, living, and working in the New England Conference at the time this letter was sent.

Subject: For Clarification

Dear Friends,

To clear up any confusion that I have appointed Bishop Al Gwinn as the presiding officer in this matter, I have reappointed Bishop Gwinn following the referral of the bill of charges and specifications by the committee on investigation.

The Peace of the Lord,
+Ken Carter
Resident Bishop, Florida Conference
The United Methodist Church

Notes Taken by a Member of the Palm Bay United Methodist Church Who Accompanied Me to Another Meeting with District Superintendent, Dr. Gary Spencer

Exhibit F

Before the start of the judicial process and even before the effort to arrive at a just resolution through Just Peace, I was summoned to a third meeting with Reverend Gary Spencer while he again lied to me—this time in relation to what the meeting was about.

It turned out that he had been informed by the complainant that I had "started a church," which was meeting at BCASCA, and he wanted to let me know that as a Methodist minister, I was not allowed to do that. BCASCA is acronym for Brevard Caribbeann American Sports and Cultural Association. It is a club comprising a group of residents mostly from the Caribbean but is also opened to Americans.

I had asked a male parishioner to drive me to the meeting, and he not only obliged but also sat in on the meeting. He supplied the notes below as his summarized recollection of the meeting. He was angry at the condescending treatment that I received from Dr. Spencer and indicated that to him right to his face.

Meeting with District Superindent

Date: 04/24/2015

Today Pastor Errol Leslie and I travelled together to meet with Dr. Gary Spencer. The day before Dr. Leslie called to ask me to accompany him to see the DS. This is not an unusual request, since I have often accompanied the Pastor on many occasions before. Furthermore, I had heard that he was being reinstated and granted back his credential to resume his pastoral duties and I wanted to discuss the matter with him. It was my opportunity.

I picked up Errol at about 9:00 am and we headed to Vero Beach, where the DS's office is located. On our way, I enquired what this meeting is about. Errol informed me that he was not quite sure, but based on conversation with the DS, he believes the meeting is to discuss his (Leslie's) role in the Church, moving forward. We even discussed the usefulness of such a meeting, if only to avert any potential misunderstanding in the future.

We arrived, and were greeted cordially. I had brought my iPad with me, so I enquired of the DS whether I could record the proceedings. He emphatically told me: NO!

We entered a room adjacent to the main office (presumably the DS private office). As would be expected, the meeting started with a short prayer by the DS. He proceeded to inform Errol that he (EL) is assigned to his District and as such, under his control and supervision. Any religious activity by Errol must first have to be vetted by him. He then proceeded to inform Errol that he (EL) was illegally conducting church services at the BCASCA club. Errol reminded him that was not what he understood the meeting would be about the DS. continued to press on the BCASCA issue and at this time, Leslie invoked the fifth. The meeting almost ended there, and, for all intent and purpose, it was. I even stopped taking notes, sensing that the BCASCA issue would be the center of the remaining discourse.

Two things became evident to me: 1) The meeting was called to assert the dominion rights of the DS over Pastor Leslie, and 2) To declare a "gotyou-moment" as evidenced by his relentless focus on the BCASCA issue.

I felt outraged. I had expected that the DS would say: Leslie, we have had our differences; but it's incumbent on us to put that aside and work together for the next couple of months to rebuild the PBUMC. Our congregants expect that of us, and we cannot let them down. Rather, what I gathered from the tone of the DS, Pastor Leslie is prohibited from even praying with anybody in Palm Bay without the approbation of the DS. And that's it!!

Listening to such unchristian garbage, led me to suggest that he should go back and read 1 Corinthians 13. Dare me to imply that the DS was not acting in a Christian-like manner. I had completely forgotten that I was in the presence of a man of God. But, to me, his tone was not of a good Christian Solder make.

The matter of Pastor Leslie's imperative to pray with whom he wishes in the community; to hold bible classes; or even to visit the sick, seem at variance with the presumed job description of the DS, who insists that any religious activity perform by Pastor Leslie must first be approved by him. Not even in an emergency situation, cases when the Pastor may be called to administer to the sick and dying. At this point a heated discussion ensued over what Pastor Leslie can and cannot do. Pastor Leslie argued that his calling and training to the church ministry entitle him to interact morally and spiritually with people without undue interference from anyone. The DS agreed in principle, but insisted that as his supervisor, it is his duty to oversee what he, Leslie, does.

One obvious thing was settled: Pastor Leslie cannot go out and form a church, at least not under the banner of the Methodist Church. But, as far as this layperson is concerned, I was so disappointed, I was so torn. I even found myself addressing the DS, telling him that he is responsible for the turmoil that exists in our church today.

Somebody ought to inform the DS that his master-slave approach to solving problems is an outdated paradigm that has no place in a modern society, and certainly not in a Christian church. I am fairly new to the Methodist Church. 1 have only been a member for six years, thanks to Pastor Leslie. I fail to comprehend, how the Church could have survived with such hegemonic behavior, as displayed by the DS.

It might be presumptuous of me, but I strongly feel that the DS should at least be reprimanded over the way he handled the whole Pastor Leslie's saga. Over six months ago he informed us of the suspension of Pastor Leslie because some sexual misconduct, whatever that is. At the time, he assured us that a thorough investigation would ensue. We are still awaiting the outcome of his investigation. In the meantime, Pastor Leslie, not only had to endure the indignity of suspension, he was subsequently fired from his pastoral job. Think of the embarrassment, humiliation and the financial plight this DS put this family through, only to have his decisions over turned.

What is even sadder, he suffers no remorse, shows no regret, and offers no apology. Rather, he is still trying to find some dirt to fan at Pastor Leslie, as evidenced by the line of questioning about BCASCA.

In fact, his method of investigation centers on finding anyone who could corroborate his own belief rather than seeking the facts.

Church's Objections to Financial Projections Done by Expert Exhibit G

An official from the New England United Methodist Foundation prepared the financial projections that would have shown the trial court what I would stand to lose if I lost my credentials. Rev. Jay Therrell, counsel for the church, fought against having this document admitted to the trial court using the arguments contained in the letter to the presiding officer as shown below. Let us keep in mind that this is the same pastor who had responded with the words "I don't care" when my assistant defense counsel had asked him if he had any concerns about my family including two teenagers and an older senior losing a substantial part of the family income.

The line in his argument, which really demonstrates how he was grasping for straws, is the one where he indicated that "Reverend Leslie could get a better paying job" if he was no longer working for the church. At this time, I was age sixty-two years old and had sent so many applications out for jobs without success. I would have made close to one hundred job applications to a variety of organizations. I may have had a response from two or three of them, but there was no fruit borne from even the very few that responded. While companies will advertise that they are equal opportunity employers, the chances of one employing a sixty-two-year-old would normally be slim to none. However, Reverend Therrell, being the kind and generous pastor, determined that, in my interest, I may indeed end up with a higher-paying job than what the church was able to pay me. How did the presiding officer rule on the omission of this personal financial projection from the court? He upheld it, and so the trial court did not have that document that may have caused some of them to show some collegial pastoral care and offer a lighter penalty. This was Reverend Therrell's letter to the presiding officer below.

From: Jay Therrell [jtherrell@capecoralfirst.org]
Sent: Friday, January 08, 2016 1:26 pm
To: Al Gwinn1; Campbellwscott@aol.com
RE: Testimony of Mrs. Kaye Leslie and two other matters

Bishop Gwinn,

The Church doesn't have any objection to Mrs. Leslie not testifying in the guilty/not guilty phase of the trial.

Concerning the document from Dr. Metzer, the church does have objections. First, I would argue the document isn't relevant. If someone is found guilty, they don't get to influence the penalty by documenting how hard one might be. If someone is guilty of a chargeable offense (or three), then by the Discipline, they've opened themselves up to whatever penalty the trial court feels is appropriate. Moreover, Dr. Metzler's work has to be based on a set of assumptions—that are very speculative. The Church is assuming this document is being prepared to show the economic impact on Rev. Leslie should his orders be terminated. The reality, however, is that Rev. Leslie could potentially earn a job making a substantially higher income. If you see what I mean—it's not knowable what Rev. Leslie might choose to do—and therefore the document seems not to be probative at all. For that reason, I'm not sure how to even effectively cross-examine such a witness or deal with such a document. Anyone could come up with such a document and have it contain all sorts of scenarios that are all unknowable.

Should you rule the document in evidence, the Church would like to request the ability to call a witness to rebut it. At this late date, I have no idea who it would be, however.

Grace and peace,
Jay

Rev. Jay Therrell, Senior Pastor Cape Coral First United Methodist Church

Trust in the Lord with all your heart; don't rely on your own intelligence. Know him in all your paths, and he will keep your ways straight. (Proverbs 3:5–6)

442

Earlier in this story, I indicated that I had applied for several jobs, and only two or three times that I even got an acknowledgment. This made Reverend Therell's statement about me making more money very impractical. I have included the general template that I had used for most of my applications. For this particular one, which I include, I assumed that my experience as a pastor plus my natural affinity to helping the needy would have made me more than qualified for the position, but that turned out not to be the case. Once more, I did not even receive an acknowledgement.

One of Several Regular Job Applications That I Made Exhibit H

February 9, 2015
The Manager
Human Resource Department
Food for the Poor

Dear Sir/Madam,

I am writing to apply for the position of "Fulfillment and Review Writer" as advertised on your website.

I trust that I will be considered for this position especially that I have given several years of volunteer service in this field. I have also worked with fundraising teams in trying to secure funding for this very important specialized ministry.

My years of pastoral experience working in a mainline denomination with many opportunities to be engaged in pastoral counseling and guidance would make me a suitable candidate for this position. In my pastoral experience, I have been involved in working on both large and small projects especially in the area of building and construction. When I served in Jamaica (my home country), I was general secretary for the denomination's property committee and this necessitated my having to communicate and negotiate with several overseas groups in order to get the necessary funding and personnel for accepting and completing projects for the church and building of homes at both the local and national level. This position also included writing reports for the appropriate groups involved in the projects. As superintendent for several large circuits of churches, I also had to write reports relating to the growth of the circuit on a regular basis.

My pastoral experience has also given me an opportunity to counsel persons who come from a wide variety of cultural experiences and socioeconomic background. Equally I have counseled with persons with various ethnicities and from all social classes of life. I have worked for years with the homeless and underprivileged and I am very gifted in connecting with persons who feel that they cannot fit into the average social class because of their economic situation. This experience would certainly make me an asset to your organization especially that I could also use my familiarity and prior association with poor living conditions in making it an enriching experience for all persons who would be involved.

If I am offered the position, I assure you that I would be totally committed to doing everything in my power to ensure the continued success of the organization and would do all I can to enhance the quality of life for those who would be beneficiaries. I certainly look forward to being invited for an interview soon.

Please feel free to email me at reveel@cfl. rr.com or telephone me at (321) 615-4978.

Yours respectfully,
Errol E. Leslie

Proffer Offered by Defense
Exhibit I

**A Proffer Offered in the Matter of the Rev. Errol Leslie
January 11, 2016**

The contention of this proffer is that the Respondent, the Rev. Errol Leslie, has been deprived of a full and fair defense by the pre-trial rulings of the Presiding Officer, Bishop Alfred Gwinn, relating to 2710.7 in The Book of Discipline the United Methodist Church (2012 Edition), which states: The presiding officer shall determine all questions of relevancy and competence of testimony. In the matter before the court the Defense contends that relevance and reliability have been too narrowly construed by the Presiding Officer and have been inconsistently applied in a way that benefits the Prosecution.

The Presiding Officer has repeatedly defined relevance in terms of whether a piece of evidence makes it more or less likely that the bill of charges and specifications is true. He attempts to define a priori what can only be determined contextually. Such a definition is inherently biased toward the prosecution because it puts the defense in the position of proving a negative—of proving that something did not happen. Given this definition of relevance, there would be no distinction at the guilt/innocence phase of the trial between self-defense and murder. All that matters is whether the trigger was pulled.

Convict first and then determine the penalty. Only the bare facts can be considered and the why and how are deemed irrelevant. This is not the way people live their lives or the way meaning is created in the human community, but it is the way this court experience is structured.

The Defense contends that the full story is as relevant in the guilt/innocence phase of the trial as it is in the penalty phase. The trial court has a right to know if the Complainant launched her complaint by telling terrible lies about the Respondent and spreading those lies at his local church. It is an important part of what happened in this case and it calls into question the narrative that the Complainant is trying to shape before the trial court. The trial court needs to know if the Church has treated the Respondent disrespectfully and unfairly throughout the supervisory process because it calls into question the assessments that conference officials make about the Respondent's demeanor and remorsefulness. The filters applied to the concept of relevance in the present instant make reliability much harder to ascertain because they give the trial court only snippets and glimpses of what transpired and shield the Complainant from accountability for egregious behavior. They make it nearly impossible to demonstrate that the Complainant began her interaction with the Church by lying about the Respondent and continued to testify untruthfully during the hearing before the Committee on Investigation, as she sought to shape a narrative that the Respondent was the initiator and the aggressor in the relationship that developed. They bring us to the absurd position where the Complainant is the chief witness for the Church, but she is protected from being questioned about what she originally complained about and that document itself is not permitted to come before the trial court. The standard for relevance employed by the Presiding Officer is irredeemably biased towards the Prosecution.

Specifically, the Defense contends that the Presiding Officer's ruling that the exclusion of the original written signed complaint from the consideration of the trial court is prejudicial to the Defense, and that the Presiding Officer's determination that matters of process are not relevant to the trial is an impossible standard, inconsistently applied in a way that benefits the Prosecution.

Prejudicial Effects of the Original Complaint

In his ruling on the inadmissibility of the written signed complaint the Presiding Officer stated:

Although both the original signed grievance and a judicial complaint are both called a "complaint" in the Book of Discipline, they are different. Both are indispensable for the judicial process, but I do not believe both are indispensable for the Trial itself. I continue to believe that relevant evidence in the guilt or innocence phase of the Trial is evidence that tends to prove or disprove the Bill of Charges and Specifications. However, I can see that there may be circumstances in which the original grievance/complaint could be relevant based upon circumstances, which may include issues of impeachment due to inconsistent statements or matters of credibility. The fact that the original grievance/complaint was reviewed by the Committee on Investigation or was used to address Reverend Leslie's status in the New England Annual Conference is not relevant, in my opinion.

This ruling makes the relevance of the original written signed complaint contingent on whether it would be useful in impeaching a witness rather than recognizing the pervasive and significant destructive influence the complaint has had on the entire process.

The Defense contends that the original written signed complaint is foundational to the ability of the

447

trial court to render a fair verdict because of the enormous prejudicial influence that it has exerted throughout the supervisory, administrative and judicial processes leading up to the present moment. It has been a hidden toxic presence that has infected every step of the process and now is excluded from consideration in the culminating event. The Church has used the document all along the way when it has been helpful to its claims, and now it is excluded as an irrelevant distraction at the end of the process.

Testimony that would have been provided by witnesses for the Defense would have shown that the original written signed complaint was largely false, concocted by the Complainant with the express purpose of destroying the Respondent's ministry. The Church has vigorously fought the disclosure of the lies and scurrilous accusations contained in the written signed complaint because it knows that if the trial court were aware of them it would immediately have serious questions about the credibility and integrity of the Church's chief witness.

Specifically, excluded testimony would show that:

- The accusations contained in the original complaint shaped the initial response of the Church to the Respondent. Arrangements to suspend him from his ministry were underway before any church official even spoke with him. He was presumed guilty from the outset, even though 363.1 specifically admonishes church officials that a complaint should be treated as an allegation or allegations during the supervisory process and 2701 states that The presumption of innocence shall be maintained until the end of the trial process. Rev. Leslie was told by Superintendent Spencer at the first meeting on July 30, 2014 to turn over the checkbook he had for the pastor's discretionary fund and to vacate his office at the church. A preacher was lined up for the following Sunday at the Palm Bay UMC and a meeting with the PPRC already set up. These latter two steps were taken not only before any action to suspend the Respondent had taken place in either the New England or the Florida Conferences, but before the Superintendent had even spoken with the Respondent about the complaint.

• On July 28, two days before officials in the Florida Conference met with the Respondent, the Assistant to the Bishop of the Florida Conference summarized the contents of the original complaint to Erica Robinson Johnson, Assistant to the Bishop in the New England Conference, potentially influencing a decision to seek the Respondent's suspension by the New England Conference.

• The supervisory process itself was sabotaged by the other allegations. When the Respondent met with Bishop Carter on September 12 the Respondent was accompanied by the Rev. Dr. Sydney Sadio who would have confirmed for the trial court through his testimony the following contemporaneous notes on that meeting from the Respondent:

After I asked for an opportunity to make a statement, I started to present my case. Within the first minute of my presentation, the bishop asked me to stop talking and indicated that he was not interested in details. He refused to look at any documentary evidence which I had to prove that the complaint was full of blatant lies and he just kept insisting that he wanted justice for her and all the other women whom I had abused.

Based on the original complaint, the Rev. Dionne Hammond was assigned the task of investigating the allegations of inappropriate behavior by the

Respondent contained in the original complaint. She reported on September 28 that there was no evidence of other inappropriate relationships. Still, even with this report in hand, Bishop Carter directed Superintendent Spencer to ask the following question of the Respondent in an October 23, 2014 meeting:

Ms. Hendricks has also alleged that you have had intimate sexual relationships with persons other than your wife during your present marriage. Is this allegation true? If so, please provide details regarding those relationships, including any information you can give concerning the names, addresses, and telephone numbers of any persons with whom you have had a sexual relationship.

The prejudicial influence of the false allegations contained in the original complaint effectively deprived the Respondent of any meaningful possibility of realizing a just resolution in his case. Although not included in the final bill of charges certified by the Committee on Investigation, the suspicion of officials that there was a degree of truth contained in the original complaint beyond the allegations of an affair with the Complainant made it impossible for the Respondent to receive fair treatment at multiple points during the process.

• Finally, the original signed complaint was presented to the Committee on Investigation and was read by each member of the committee, but no opportunity was given to the defense to respond to any of the unfounded allegations it contained. It is impossible to say what influence the allegations contained in that document might have had in the decision of that committee to certify a bill of charges.

Reverend Campbell's Response to Church's Argument on His Original Motion to Dismiss Exhibit J

Following the motion of the defense to the presiding officer to dismiss the case, the church filed its objections, which, of course, was not surprising. It was more of the "same old…same old" effort where the church tried to create a genuine rationale for all its mistakes and unethical practices. It was not difficult to counter these arguments.

Response of the Defense to the Church's Response
To the Motion to Dismiss
January 3, 2016
Preamble

A theme running throughout the Church's response seems to be that the Florida Conference is the only place where justice can be achieved in the instant matter. Despite the unambiguous requirement of The Discipline that judicial matters be adjudicated in a member's own annual conference (with one very limited and highly conditioned exception) the Church again and again equates the Respondent's efforts to exercise this fundamental principle of our polity as a travesty of justice and equates it with "jury shopping." Needless to say, the Respondent does not agree that Florida is the only place where justice can be accomplished. In fact, officials of the Florida Conference, from the very beginning of this process have had the single-minded focus that the surrender of the Respondent's orders is the only result that will satisfy their definition of justice, a focus that has skewed the supervisory response and inhibited every subsequent attempt to reach a just resolution of the case.

Issues Not Addressed in the Church's Response

1.) The Constitutional imperative that judicial matters be addressed in a member's own conference.

2.) The March 12, 2015 communication from the Florida Conference that it was discontinuing the appointment of Rev. Leslie, effective June 30, 2015.

3.) The fact that allegations by the Complainant relating to behavior alleged to have occurred in New England were withheld from the Respondent as he was making a choice about where judicial proceedings should proceed.

The Response

The Defense will comment briefly on points made by the Church with which it disagrees. The original motion best articulates its overall position.

Church Pt 1—The Defense does not argue that the prosecution began anew. It argues that the judicial process and its attendant rights for the Respondent began with the referral of a complaint to the COI. Further, the Florida Conference lost its standing to adjudicate the complaint for multiple reasons—the termination of the Respondent's appointment, the failure to disclose the full nature of the complaint prior to the signing of the agreement, the imposition of a false timeline on the Respondent, the withdrawal of the Respondent's agreement that the process go forward in Florida, and the referral of the matter to the COI at a time when the Respondent did not qualify for the exception made in ¶ 2719.1.

Church Pt 2—The Counsel for the Respondent did and does still believe this to be the best course of action, in part because, as the cited email indicates, it would provide a seamless opportunity for Florida to return the instant matter to the New England Conference, where it belonged. For its own unexplained reasons, Florida chose not to honor the mandates of The Discipline at that point.

Church Pt 3—¶ 2701 in the 2008 Discipline deals directly with the role of the COI. It identifies the moment the COI receives a formal complaint from the Counsel for the Church as the moment the judicial process begins. The Church correctly points out that this is the moment certain rights of the Respondent come into play, including the right for the judicial process to go forward in his own conference. The Church presumes too much when it claims that it can distinguish which portions of paragraphs referring to the COI deal with its "role" and which do not.

Church Pt 4—The Respondent does not argue that a new process began. It argues that a new judicial process began and that the previous judicial process was null and void. That is why it was necessary for Bishop Carter to reconfirm his intent that Bishop Gwinn would serve as the presiding officer. It was not necessary to reappoint a new counsel for the church because such an appointment is not a part of the judicial process, which does not begin until a complaint is forwarded to the COI. Further, if the Florida Conference had simply returned the matter to New England, as The Discipline specifies, to do so would not have constituted "a miscarriage of justice." It would have been in keeping with Disciplinary provisions.

Church Pt 5—The Defense disputes the assertion that it takes the agreement of all three parties to dissolve an agreement. That certainly was not the assumption of the Florida Conference when it decided to revoke the appointment status of the Respondent, nor does this line of reasoning apply in most other agreements. Counsel for the Church needs to show precedent in The Discipline or in Judicial Council decisions to support such a contention.

Arguments Related to the Respondent Not
Receiving the Complaint in a Timely Manner

Church Pt 1—The Church misunderstands the basic distinction between the present case and the Kendall case. In the Kendall case there was no harm rendered by the late delivery of supporting documents. In the present instant there was enormous harm done. The Respondent was pressured into signing an agreement two days after being notified of a complaint against him, without ever having seen that complaint, and the Church now insists that the document that was signed is binding in the present. It is astonishing that such a difference goes unnoted by the Church!

Church Pt 2—First of all the Respondent makes no assertion in its motion that Dr. Spencer gave an "ultimatum." This is an invention of the Counsel for the Church. The word "ultimatum" was used by the chair of the COI in examining Rev. Spencer, but does not appear in the motion of the Defense. The exact words of Rev. Spencer before the COI in response to the question by the chair "Was he given any sort of ultimatum?" were: "We did say we needed it done by the next day, by 12:00, because at some point we had to make a decision—he had to make a decision— for the process to continue." The Church prioritized its process anxieties (which were based on an erroneous interpretation of ¶ 2719.1) over the clear right of the Respondent to see the complaint against him before signing any such document.

Fair Process Issues

Church Pt 2—It is more than interesting to the Respondent that whenever the Church refers to the decision of the Florida Conference to reverse its action of placing the Respondent on Involuntary Leave of Absence, it neglects to mention that this decision was only made after the Respondent's counsel sent a letter to Bishop Carter detailing multiple violations of The Discipline committed by the Florida Conference in the process leading to the imposition of that status. The motive for the reversal is then reduced to the "discovery" that Florida could not place an elder from another conference on involuntary leave. No citation for the authority for that "discovery" has ever been given. The reason this whole incident is important is that it provides concrete evidence that fairness was not being better served in Florida and directly contributes to the subsequent withdrawal of agreement by the Respondent for judicial procedures to go forward in that conference. It is also noteworthy that Florida in this instance recognizes the primacy of an annual conference dealing with its own member and then rigidly seeks to deny that right subsequently.

Church Pt 3—The importance of the illegal verbatim is once again that it demonstrates how Florida's disregard for fair process undermined the Respondent's confidence that fairness could be better served in that conference, leading to the withdrawal of his consent for judicial processes to go forward in that conference.

Church Pt 4—The primary point that both the Church and the chair of the COI miss in their arguments is that JC 698 ruled the previous judicial process unconstitutional because it failed to provide basic fair process protections to a Respondent. JC 836 responds to a question about whether the new system corrects those mistakes and it opines that it does because of the wall that is built between the supervisory process and the COI. Subsequently the General Conference has chipped away at that wall by removing the word "confidential" from the description of the supervisory process and allowing material from the supervisory process to be shared with the counsel for the church and the COI, but the current Discipline does not specify what kind of information can be shared. The Administrative and Judicial Procedures Handbook of GCF&A does talk about the kind of information that is appropriate to share from the supervisory process, but, of course, that document is not official. Thus, we are left with a vacuum. It is the contention of the Defense that in this vacuum, we must be guided by the principles of fair process, by the clear spirit of ¶363.1 as it describes the nature and purpose of the supervisory process, and by the concerns addressed in JC 698 and 836. The offensive characterization of both the Chair of the COI and the Counsel for the Church of these arguments as being "patently false and misleading" demonstrates their failure to appreciate the principles at stake.

Church Pt 5—The appendix that addresses this point cites the appropriate Disciplinary paragraph and quotes from the Disciplinarily mandated guidelines of GCF&A. (See Appendix VI of the original Defense motion.)

Arguments Relating to the Full Range of Penalties

As an example of what the Defense has in mind, from time to time trial courts will create penalties that involve assignments to a board of ordained ministry to implement a process of supervision and support. Such a creative penalty would be difficult to implement under the current circumstances.

Argument Related to Failure of Previous
Attempts at Relief

The Defense is not trying to argue that any of the named officials should have taken jurisdiction, only that it had previously exhausted all possible avenues to seek relief. In addition to the attempts named in the Defense motion, the counsel for the Respondent approached the bishops of both conferences in February of 2015 to request that the entire process be remanded to New England, a request that was denied. This attempt was prior to the submission of the first judicial complaint by the Counsel for the Church. It was also prior to the revocation of the Respondent's appointment in Florida and before the subsequent referral of a complaint to the COI. All this is to say that the raising of a concern about the process going forward in Florida was not a last minute interjection by the Defense.

Arguments Related to the Attorney for the
Council of Bishops

The Defense has two concerns about this topic. First is a concern that The Discipline be followed. Second is a concern related to a conflict of interest in that the legal advisor to the Council of Bishops has a role in shaping the outcome of case. While the Defense recognizes that the presiding officer is a bishop as well and a member of the Council of Bishops, the presiding officer must make every attempt to be impartial in adjudicating the case. It is the position of the Defense that the presence of an advisor with a direct connection and accountability to the Council of Bishops as an intimate consultant on every decision makes that impartiality more difficult to achieve.

Arguments Related to the Exclusion of Testimony

Church Pt 1—It is apparent in the response of the Church that it considers Fair Process to be a distraction to the purpose it is attempting to achieve.

Church Pt 2—The original intent of the Church is not relevant to the current intent of the Defense.

Church Pt 4—The COI did not provide an opportunity for the Respondent to respond to the charges leveled at him in the original complaint. All questions that dealt with that complaint were ruled out by the chair, and there was no opportunity to cross examine the Complainant.

The Defense requests that its original Motion to Dismiss be granted.

Respectfully Submitted,
Scott
Scott Campbell,
Counsel for The Respondent

459

Letter Rescinding 2719 Agreement
Exhibit K

As indicated earlier, because I was now living in and serving in my home conference and also because there was every indication that the Florida Conference was making every effort to help the complainant destroy my life, on the advice of my defense counsel, I sent the following letter to Bishops Devadhar and Carter. Bishop Carter, in his usual style, totally ignored the letter while Bishop Devadhar took the escape route and replied as printed below. It was hard to understand why Bishop Devadhar kept passing the buck and making excuses when he knew that he could have intercepted the plans of the Florida Conference.

September 3, 2015
Bishop Sudarshana Devadhar
Resident Bishop
New England Annual Conference

Bishop Kenneth Carter
Resident Bishop
Florida Annual Conference

Dear Bishops Devadhar and Carter,

Grace and Peace to you both.

I am writing to you to rescind my agreement that the present judicial process in which I am involved will take place in Florida.

The 2012 Book of Discipline states:

Any clergy members residing beyond the bounds of the conference in which membership is held shall be subject to the procedures of HU2701-2718 exercised by the appropriate officers of the conference in which he or she is a member, unless the presiding bishops of the two annual conferences and the clergy member subject to the procedures agree that fairness will be better served by having the procedures carried out by the appropriate officers of the annual conference in which he or she is serving under appointment, or if retired, currently residing. H2719.1 [Emphasis added]

On August 1, 2014 I signed a document under the above provisions choosing for the complaint process directed towards me to go forward in Florida. Since that time, much has changed. These changes are enumerated in the attached formal notice. Of special concern, however, are the following violations of fair process already acknowledged by the Florida Conference.

- The document in question was signed two days after I was informed that I was being placed on suspension in a supervisory meeting with Superintendent Gary Spencer. During that meeting I was refused the right to see the complaint against me, and I was not informed of my right to be accompanied by an elder of my choice. When I signed the document on August 1,I still had not seen the complaint, nor did I have it in my possession, both clear violations of JC 1189.
- On October 23, 2014, Superintendent Spencer and Rev. David Dodge made an illegal verbatim of a supervisory session and subsequently shared that document with the Counsel for the Church. (See 1)363.l.b))
- On November 5, 2014 I was informed by Bishop Carter that he was requesting that I be placed on Involuntary Leave of Absence. This recommendation was approved by the Board of

461

Ordained Ministry of the Florida Annual
Conference without any of the fair process
requirements of The Discipline being observed.
On March 12, 2015 the Conference admitted its
errors and reimbursed me for back pay and
benefits and continued under appointment until
June 30, 2015.

Not yet admitted by the Conference, but presently
being contested before the Committee on
Investigation of the Florida Conference, is my claim
that an unknown official or officials of the Florida
Conference illegally shared information from my
supervisory file with the Counsel for the Church, a
direct violation of the Supervisory File Guidelines for
Clergy, published by the General Council on Finance
and Administration and mandated by 11416.7 of The
2012 Discipline.

On March 12, 2015 I was informed in a letter from
Rev. David Dodge that my appointment status in the
Florida Conference would be terminated as of June 30,
2015. This was done at the initiation of the Florida
Conference and not at my request.

For all of these reasons it is apparent to me that it
is no longer the case "that fairness will be better
served" by continuing the current judicial procedures
in the Florida Conference. I hereby withdraw my
agreement to the process going forward in Florida and
exercise my right to adjudicating the complaint against
me in the New England Conference, where I am a
member and am currently serving. Since the
Committee on Investigation has not yet held a hearing,
this would be a propitious moment to initiate such a
change. Justice and accountability will more effectively
be served where there is a direct link between the

judicial processes which occur and the conference in which my membership resides and my current appointment is held.

Lastly, there is some urgency associated with this matter. The Florida Committee on Investigation is scheduled to hold a hearing on my case on September 23, 2015. Should a Bill of Charges be certified by that body and should my allegations of violations of fair process later be upheld on appeal to the Presiding Officer or an appellate body, the provisions of double jeopardy (1)2701.2.c)) will be in effect and no further process will be permitted in either conference. I respectfully request that the two of you direct the continuation of the process to occur in the New England Annual Conference as the fairest alternative at your earliest convenience.

Please do not hesitate to contact my advocate, the Rev. Scott Campbell, if you have further questions about this matter.

Grace and Peace,
The Rev. Errol Leslie

September 18, 2015
978-682-7555 x250 FAX: 978-682-9555
e-mail: bishopsoffice@neumc.org
Sudarshana Devadhar Bishop
New England Conference
Rev. Scott Campbell
Counsel for Respondent 36 May Street
Cambridge, MA 02138
Re: Rev. Errol Leslie Dear Rev. Campbell:

Greetings in the precious name of our Lord and Savior Jesus Christ.

I have received and reviewed the documents you sent by e-mail on September 3, 2015. As resident bishop of the New England Annual Conference. 1 no longer have jurisdiction over this matter. Your concerns should be directed to the Committee on Investigation of the Florida Annual Conference.

Please share this information with Rev.

Leslie.

Please remain assured that I continue to keep you. Rev. Leslie and all concerned parties in my thoughts and prayers.

In Christ's love.

Sudarshana Devadhar SD:wh
cc: Bishop Kenneth Carter

CHAPTER 18

VENGEANCE IS MINE; I WILL REPAY SAITH THE LORD

By now, I hope that you are seeing the very clear case of collusion and conspiracy which was intended to get me out of the clergy membership of the United Methodist Church. This was done at any cost including dishonesty and unethical behavior. I shared earlier how brutally dishonest Rev Jay Therrell was as he pursued me relentlessly and mercilessly. I also observed how Bishop Carter rewarded him for his part in the effort by appointing him as a district superintendent in the conference. I remember how Rev Therrell had started using the email address for the district before he even officially started in that capacity of district superintendent. However, this effort by Bishop Carter to reward Rev Therrell in that way actually backfired. Almost as soon as he got unto the cabinet, Rev Therrell as well as Rev Dionne Hammond who was the assistant counsel for the church and who received the same reward by being made a district superintendent became part of a movement which sought to split the United Methodist Church and in so doing, created a schism within the cabinet. From that point on, Rev Therrell's aggression and arrogance which was on full display during the period of my church trial shifted and Bishop Carter became the target of this anger and aggression.

The infighting within the hierarchy of the Florida conference is now beginning to look like both Bishop Carter and Rev Therrell are getting a taste of their own medicine. We sometimes refer to this as karma. In my mind, I honestly saw it coming but did not know that it would come so clearly and with such force. Bishop (Carter) and Rev Therrell had previously teamed up to make my life miserable but...........I have come to realize that my God DOES NOT SLEEP and is always watching out for His sheep – especially those who have gone astray.

There were at least two separate occasions in the history of Israel when the enemy nation who sought to fight against God's people, turned against each other and started killing each other. These stories are recorded in 2 Chronicles 20:22&23

22 As they began to sing and praise, the Lord set ambushes against the men of Ammon and Moab and Mount Seir who were invading Judah, and they were defeated. 23 The Ammonites and Moabites rose up against the men from Mount Seir to destroy and annihilate them. After they finished slaughtering the men from Seir, they helped to destroy one another.

The second such passage is recorded in 1 Samuel 14:20-23.

20 Then Saul and all his men assembled and went to the battle. They found the Philistines in total confusion, striking each other with their swords. 21 Those Hebrews who had previously been with the Philistines and had gone up with them to their camp went over to the Israelites who were with Saul and Jonathan. 22 When all the Israelites who had hidden in the hill country of Ephraim heard that the Philistines were on the run, they joined the battle in hot pursuit. 23 So on that day the Lord saved Israel, and the battle moved on beyond Beth Aven.

I wondered if this was the experience which Bishop Carter, Rev Therrell and the entire cabinet may have experienced. Please observe the following excerpts from communication between these two men who just a year or so before had teamed up against one who was genuinely called by God for ministry. Now they are both verbally abusing each other – and doing so publicly.

Excerpt number one from Rev Therrell. This is from a letter which he sent to Bishop Carter.

............*The leadership of this annual conference has done everything it could to harass me and try to keep me from fulfilling my duties as a hired employee of the Wesleyan Covenant Association Florida Regional Chapter These efforts began on May 21,2020, when I was approached by your office to enter a brokered covenant using a hired consultant to ensure that I would be silenced and prevented from speaking to colleagues and churches. This was done before I had even been approached about serving as president of the Florida Wesleyan Covenant Association. This unprecedented step has never been taken before with a departing district superintendent in the Florida Conference. Nor has it been done since. I am the only one. This is surely not a coincidence. When I declined to enter into such an agreement, the determination with which you have had to harass and silence me has only grown.*

............On September 1st, 2020,1 was sent a letter signed by you and every member of your appointed cabinet You all accused me of' bearing false witness,'* "maligning appointments, *' and disparaging the camps of the Florida Conference. One can only assume that you believe that once someone becomes an ordained elder in the Florida Conference, they give up Their right to express an opinion or a critique or perhaps it's only an opinion with which you do not agree.

In the months to follow you continued to attempt to ascertain the names of the churches, clergy, and laity with whom 1 have spoken. One begins to wonder exactly why you desire to know this information so badly. Your assistant, Alex Shanks, called me in March of this year. Once again, he requested that I inform him of every church and clergyperson where I have shared a presentation. I declined that request. He pressed again and I informed him that my WCA-Fl Council would never authorize me to disclose that Information.

Churches and clergy are extremely fearful of allowing the Florida Conference Cabinet to know they are traditionalists for fear of retaliation.

Then on June 8, 1 received a letter (from the executive committee of the Board of Ordained Ministry. In that letter the executive committee accused me of violating my status of personal leave with bogus arguments that are so beyond the pale as to be laughable.

I found it interesting that I received the letter from the executive committee precisely three hours before I was scheduled to meet with you and your assistant io discuss the present impasse and see if a way could be worked out to move forward. You sat across a table from me in your office, allegedly in good faith, and yet you never had the courtesy to even mention the letter. Your failure to mention something I'm quite sure you must have known about is terribly disappointing.

I'm aware that the Discipline separates the episcopal office and the Board of Ordained Ministry, but basic human decency and certainly Christian love would argue for your speaking with me about it. While I cannot prove inappropriate collusion between the bishop's office and the Board of Ordained Ministry, it seems oddly coincidental that the letter would arrive on that day and at that time. It also seems beyond coincidence that the way I could rectify my alleged "violations* would be to disclose the names of the clergy, churc*hes, and laity with whom I have met - the very thing your office has consistently demanded from me.

Then in an obvious reference to the case he prosecuted against me, he griped about how much effort he had put into the case and did not think that he received enough recognition or appreciation.

.........When l was commissioned and later ordained almost 20 years ago. it meant that the Florida Conference believed that God had called me to be set apart and serve as a spiritual leader; to shepherd and order the life of a local church. I was humbled and grateful. Over the years, as both a layperson and a clergyperson, I have given my life to this Conference. I have sacrificed with my prayers, presence, service, gifts, and witness. I have offered countless hours to serve on district annual conference, and Jurisdictional committees. I have served as a counsel for the

church and having to argue a case successfully all the way to the Judicial Council. I would conservatively estimate I gave 700-800 hours in that over two-year matter all without compensation. I never asked for it nor would I want it. It was not enjoyable; in fact, it was one of the worst assignments I have ever had to carry out. Yet, I did so willingly. I have served honorably as a district superintendent with great joy - again, a humbling privilege.

The way I am thanked is to hold me to standards and provisions not required by the Discipline. I am harassed. My family is harmed. Misleading letters are written about me and sent to the global president of the WCA . Attempt after attempt is made to silence me so that the Florida effort to contend for God's Word and the 2,000 year orthodox doctrine of Christianity is stopped.

What has been meant for evil, God has redeemed for good. I will always stand for the Word of God and contend for my faith. I believe that these actions against me, though intended to subvert our cause and intimidate traditionalists, will be used by God to awaken those who are unaware of the current ethos of the Florida Conference and many in The United Methodist Church. The relentless efforts against me will strengthen the resolve of those who are standing up for the faith entrusted to us. This is certainly true for me. I pray that we can quickly move toward an amicable separation and end the fighting.

I sincerely wish you the best. As I have said, my heart is at peace a deep. abiding peace I recognize your sacred worth and love you. I pray that you will experience the fullness of Jesus and His saving love and grace that is available to everyone, but that also calls us to a sanctified life of holiness

God bless you

The following are excerpts from a document sent to Rev Jay Therrell from the board of ordained ministry of the Florida United Methodist Church Conference.

REQUIREMENTS

Given these premises. the Executive Committee of the Board of Ordained Ministry acknowledges your past failures to comply with these premises and therefore requires of you the following:

1.) *Provide a full and complete list of all ministerial activities performed while on leave, such as funerals, weddings, baptisms, preaching, and worship leadership. This list shall include the dates and locations for all past and henceforth meetings with United Methodist clergy and laity in your leadership role with WCA-EL As stated above, these meetings are considered ministerial activities and shall include gatherings virtual and in person, on both church owned and non-church owned properties.*

2.) *Provide proof of permission received by the district superintendent of the community for all past and henceforth meetings with United Methodist clergy and laity HI your leadership role with WCA-FL*

3.) *To ensures that you are fulfilling the expectations named in Premise 1. all gatherings with United Methodist clergy and laity in your leadership role with WCA-fl. shall be video-recorded in total and made available for review by the supervising district superintendent and the Board of Ordained Ministry*

These requirements are to be fulfilled by July 8,2021. Let us know if you have questions about any of these premises or requirements. Your cooperation is expected and appreciated.

Sincerely.

Subsequent to the sharing of the correspondence above, a situation arose where Rev Therrell's newly formed group held a meeting at one of the traditional United Methodist Churches. Apparently, they had permission from the pastor of that local church. The district superintendent got wind of the meeting and determined that he needed to attend this meeting which was being held at one of the churches in his district. As such, both himself and his wife showed up at the church for the meeting but they were both harassed and eventually turned away. Bishop Carter chose to issue a statement in relation to this and published it on the church's website.

Statement by Bishop Carter

Ken Carter

March 9 at 7:48 AM ·

Yesterday one of our members, the wife of a district superintendent and her husband, the superintendent, were refused entrance into one of our United Methodist churches. I both publicly grieve the wrongness of this action and affirm the goodness and courage of Wayne N Ramona Wiatt.

I turn now to the spirit of 1 Peter 3. 15, and I appeal to us to take the high road and "give an account for the hope that is in us".

I have consistently and persistently stated who we are, as United Methodist disciples of Jesus Christ. This is a never-ending task, as there is misinformation out there, and we are mischaracterized.

So, I simply remind you of these resources, which are available to you in a variety of formats. I ask that you use them, share them and improve upon them. Some is my own work, and some is collaboration with others.

We are a people under the cross of Jesus Christ, and the warmth of the Holy Spirit calls us into connection with each other.

My appeal again: Take the high road. Give an account for the hope that is in you.

We are scriptural, grace-filled and missional people who want a church for all, no exceptions. And we do not want to stand at the door and turn anyone away.

Why? Because, Jesus did not turn us away.

Amen?

Here is the newspaper article which described this impasse in greater detail from the United Methodist News

Meeting at church shut down
Meeting at church shut to district leader, wife By Sam Hodges
March 11, 2022 | UM News

A Florida Conference district superintendent and his wife were denied entry to a meeting the Wesleyan Covenant Association Florida Chapter was having at a church in the superintendent's district.

The WCA of Florida says the meeting was only open for those wanting to leave The United Methodist Church and that the superintendent was sent to intimidate those attending.

The superintendent says he went at Florida Conference Bishop Ken Carter's request, not to disrupt but to be a resource for those with questions about the disaffiliation process.

The superintendent's wife and the leader of the Wesleyan Covenant Association's Florida chapter have both posted Facebook videos about the March 8 episode at Waukeenah United Methodist Church.

Conflict in The United Methodist Church took an unusual and highly public form on March 8, when a Florida Conference district superintendent was denied entry to one of the churches he oversees.

The Rev. Wayne Wiatt, superintendent of the conference's North West District, and his wife Ramona were told to leave Waukeenah United Methodist Church in Monticello, Florida, where the Wesleyan Covenant Association Florida Chapter was holding a meeting for local churches wanting to depart The United Methodist Church.

Ramona Wiatt posted to Facebook what has become a widely viewed video of herself and her husband standing outside the church after they had been told to leave.

"This is a first for me," Ramona Wiatt says as the video begins. "I'm at Waukeenah United Methodist Church, and I've been thrown out of the church." Her video pans to show a sheriff's deputy by the church's entrance.

"There's even an officer at the door who is keeping the peace, he says," Ramona Wiatt notes in her narration.

Jay Therrell, president of the Wesleyan Covenant Association Florida Chapter, responded with his own, longer Facebook video. He said the chapter rented the church building for the meeting, that the meeting was meant only for those wanting to exit The United Methodist Church and that Waukeenah United Methodist made the decision to have an officer present for security.

Therrell asserts in the video that Wayne Wiatt was sent by Florida Conference Bishop Kenneth Carter to intimidate meeting participants, and that Ramona Wiatt's taking of video contributed to that.

"Make no mistake. This was a power move," Therrell says.

Wayne Wiatt confirmed in a phone interview that he went to the meeting at Carter's request, accompanied by his wife and district lay leader Randy Clay. But Wiatt insisted his purpose was to be available to answer questions about the disaffiliation process.

He said he left when Therrell told him he was not welcome.

"I did not want to cause a scene," he said. "I did question Jay on 'why,' and then I just accepted his authority for his meeting, though I felt as a district superintendent I should have some authority there (Waukeenah United Methodist) just because it's a United Methodist church still, and a United Methodist property."

Carter declined to answer questions from UM News, but pointed to his own Facebook post about the Wiatts being kept out of the meeting at Waukeenah United Methodist.

"I both publicly grieve the wrongness of this action and affirm the goodness and courage of Wayne and Ramona Wiatt," he said in the post.

That decision prompted the Global Methodist Church to move up its formal launch to May 1, and the WCA, including the Florida chapter, is busy sharing how local United Methodist churches can explore options for leaving the denomination with their properties.

Therrell used social media to announce a series of March meetings by the WCA's Florida chapter. The March 8 afternoon meeting at Waukeenah United Methodist was the first.

"These are not public meetings," Therrell says in his video. "We've made them known publicly, but that doesn't make them public. They are strategy meetings. And, yes, legal meetings."

Therrell says in the video that Carter planned to send teams to the meetings. In an email response to questions from UM News, Therrell said the attorney for the WCA's Florida chapter informed Carter ahead of the meetings that neither Carter nor anyone representing him would be welcome — and also warned Carter against having anyone try to take video of the proceedings.

The policy extended to the Wiatts, Therrell said.

"Neither Wayne nor Ramona will be departing the UMC for the GMC," he said, a fact the couple confirmed. "Accordingly, clearly this meeting was not for them."

Therrell himself once served as a district superintendent under Carter, and while doing so made news by joining two other conference leaders in filing articles of incorporation for a new traditionalist Methodist denomination in Florida. He went on leave and eventually gave up his United Methodist clergy credentials, claiming he had been harassed by conference leaders for his work organizing traditionalist churches. He now works full time as president of the WCA Florida Chapter.

The Wiatts said they have known Therrell for years and have always considered him a friend.

Wayne Wiatt said he has attended other meetings for churches trying to determine whether they will remain in The United Methodist Church, including one in January where Therrell made a presentation. Wiatt described that meeting in Alachua, Florida, as amicable, and he insisted he has not sought to prevent churches from leaving.

"I've already done two disaffiliations in my district," he said.

Wiatt — who serves as pastor of Trinity United Methodist Church in

Tallahassee, along with overseeing the North West District — said he and other district superintendents heard from the bishop's office about the WCA Florida Chapter meetings and were asked to attend if they could.

He said there was no request to gather information about who attended or what was said.

"Absolutely not — just to go and be a presence, see if anybody had any questions," Wiatt said. "I had the checklist for disaffiliation with me, so I could have that available."

Wiatt said he never got word that he would be unwelcome at the meeting at Waukeenah United Methodist.

"The last thing I expected was to be turned away at the door," he said. "I was really surprised when Jay approached me and said, 'You're not allowed to stay.' I said, 'I'm the district superintendent and this is one of my churches.' He said, 'This is a private meeting. I have a letter from our lawyer.'"

Therrell confirmed that he had been at church forums with Wiatt where disaffiliation options were discussed but said this was a WCA meeting organized solely to help those committed to leaving The United Methodist Church.

Wiatt's presence alone was a problem, according to Therrell.

"Anytime a district superintendent, bishop or conference official is in a room, the power dynamics change," Therrell told UM News. "Every DS knows that."

Ramona Wiatt said she too heard from Therrell directly that she was not welcome at the meeting, since she was married to Wayne Wiatt. She said she used her phone to document a situation she found "physically intimidating," especially when the sheriff's deputy walked over.

Ramona Wiatt said Therrell warned her that recording someone without permission is against the law in Florida. She said she deleted the video she'd taken inside.

Therrell offered this account:

"Ms. Wiatt clearly started videoing the participants inside, panning across the room before I reminded Ms. Wiatt (that) in Florida it is a felony to record people without

their consent. I observed the deputy approach both of us inside the church, and he acted appropriately at all times."

Stan Monroe, lay leader of Waukeenah United Methodist, backed up Therrell's account and confirmed that he and the church board chose to hire the sheriff's deputy, anticipating that there might be an attempt to disrupt the meeting.

Therrell noted that Ramona Wiatt continued to take video outside of people coming and going, a move he described as further intimidation.

Ramona Wiatt disputed Therrell, saying, "I never panned the room with my phone." She said that while outside she took and posted video of herself and her husband, as well as the sheriff's deputy, by then standing in front of the church.

The posted video includes, in the background, a few people waiting to enter the church, though mostly their backs are on view.

As for why she posted the video, Ramona Wiatt said wanted to share the dismay that she — daughter of a United Methodist minister, and the wife of one — felt at being turned away from a United Methodist church. She said emphatically that she was never encouraged to report any images or names to the bishop's office, and would never have done so.

"I don't spy," she said. "I don't play games. I'm just a very normal preacher's wife."

While declining to answer UM News' questions about the incident, Carter issued a pastoral letter on March 10 that said, in part, "I do not condone the turning away of persons at the door of a church. I do not condone falsehoods being shared about The United Methodist Church."

The bishop said in the letter that the Florida Conference will soon have district meetings, hosted by superintendents, for sharing the vision of the continuing United Methodist Church, and that those meetings will be "open to all."

So in a significant turn of events, both Bishop Carter and Rev Therrell gave each other a taste of the same bitter medicine that they had teamed up to give to me just a few years before that.

CHAPTER 19

Do Not Conform to This World
But Be Ye Transformed

Here again was the concluding statement from the Judicial Council after the appeal was made:

> For all the foregoing reasons, the Committee concludes that the weight of the evidence sustains the charges of sexual misconduct, immorality, and disobedience to the order and discipline of the UMC, and that no errors of Church law vitiate the trial court's verdict or penalty of termination of the appellant's conference membership and revocation of the recognition of appellant's credentials for conference membership. Accordingly, the Committee affirms the verdict of the trial court and the penalty imposed.

That is really a powerful conclusion because it is loaded with power. So this is the lesson which we can all learn about how Jesus expects the leaders in the church to operate.

1.) The district superintendent and the assistant to the bishop can hold back a complaint that is loaded with lies for nine days and have me make important life changing decisions about my own fate without seeing that complaint, but the Judicial Council sees nothing wrong with that.

477

2.) The district superintendent can falsely tell me that I have to sign an agreement by a false deadline which he created and set without me seeing the complaint, but the Judicial Council sees nothing wrong with that.

3.) The assistant to the bishop can claim to have misplaced a crucial e-mail which references my remorse while later telling the trial court that I was not remorseful, but the Judicial Council sees nothing wrong with that.

4.) The church counsel can help to hold back that same e-mail and then also claim to the trial court that he never heard me express remorse, but the Judicial Council sees nothing wrong with that.

5.) The presiding officer can help ensure that the e-mail is hidden from the jury, but the Judicial Council sees nothing wrong with that.

6.) The church counsel in tandem with the presiding officer can withhold the original complaint which set off all the proceedings and which contained exaggerated and character damaging information about the defendant from the trial court but the Judicial Council sees nothing wrong with that.

7.) The Florida Conference can wrestle and fight to hold on to a judicial process which belonged to another annual conference, but the Judicial Council sees nothing wrong with that.

8.) The presiding officer as well as the counsel for the church can lie about when the request was first made to have the matter adjudicated in the annual conference where it belonged, but the Judicial Council sees nothing wrong with that.

9.) The Committee on Appeals and the Judicial Council can clearly ignore the laws of the church and an established ruling (JC ruling number 580), but there is nothing wrong with that, and that is okay and acceptable.

10.) The district superintendent and the assistant to the bishop can share information from the supervisory session with the counsel for the church and then turn around and witness against the defendant, but the Judicial Council sees nothing wrong with that.

11.) The bishop in Florida in tandem with his cabinet can illegally place the defendant on involuntary leave of absence without following the correct process and then pretend that it was an error on their part, but the Judicial Council sees nothing wrong with that.

12.) The counsel for the church in tandem with the presiding officer can prevent witnesses called by the defense and who could share pertinent information with the trial court from witnessing, but that is okay with the JC.

13.) The counsel for the church in tandem with the presiding officer can leave out relevant material that would be helpful to the defense but harmful to the church out of the documentary evidence, but the Judicial Council sees nothing wrong with that.

14.) The Committee on Appeals as well as the Judicial Council can totally ignore and dance-round decision number 580 established in 1987 by a precedent body, and they can all go home and sleep with a pure and clear conscience.

History has taught us that for a very long time, there have been countries where corruption has been prevalent. This has been shown in many and varied forms. Sometimes elections have been rigged to produce a planned or desired result. The impasse over impeachment at the time of writing is one very clear indicator that grown, educated, and intelligent men and women are not always willing to look at facts objectively and then draw a rational conclusion. Instead persons determine the end they want to accomplish, and then try to force a path to get to that end even if the thoughts are irrational.

In the first impeachment trial of the US president, many persons saw the process as a sham, a cover-up, and a routine exercise or demonstration of going through the motions. There was a vote mostly along party lines in the House of Representatives, and when one senator dared to vote his conscience, he was attacked by many persons who were members of the same party. Several diplomats in the US government testified against the president, and they were immediately fired for honoring their oath "to speak the truth, the whole truth, and nothing but the truth." It is very sad that even at the highest level of government, there does not seem to be a willingness among officials to be fair and honest in their judgment. One therefore has to wonder what are youngsters supposed to learn from this kind of behavior? Where should kids look for examples as to how to live honorable lives? To whom should youngsters look for the mentors which most of them seek? It is truly unfathomable and mystifying that in the year 2020 and at the high level of government, one can have a trial where documents are withheld from the court; informed witnesses are ordered not to testify such that pertinent information is withheld from the jurors who will make an analysis of the facts and a judgment on the case. It is truly unfathomable and mystifying that people who took an oath to protect and defend the laws and constitution of a country can intentionally where blinders and go into a trial with their mind already made up as to how they are going to vote before they hear the facts relative to the case. There was also another recent case of an ex-national security adviser—Michel Flynn—who was indicted for multiple violations by special counsel Bob Mueller and placed under investigation for crimes to which he admitted. Then out of nowhere, the Justice Department determines that the charges were inappropriate and has been on a mission to drop the charges. This action has been interpreted as another sign of the corruption at even high levels in the secular world.

Within the last six years, several innocent Black young men have been killed by white police officers, and regardless of the circumstances, the police officers would claim self-defense as their reason for pulling the trigger. The sad and frustrating thing is that almost always the officers are acquitted. Many persons would remember the Rodney King beatings from the early 1990s. The beatings were caught on camera, but the defense attorneys were able to get the police officers all acquitted. Something is wrong as some persons would interpret the acquittal of the respective police officers to be a sign of a corrupt justice system. The most recent example of this abuse by police officers was seen through the death of George Floyd when an officer knelt on his neck for nearly nine minutes. There seemed to have been quite a bit of support for the many protestors who came out to show their disapproval of excessive use of force by the police. However, and unfortunately, there were several persons in high office who did not seem to acknowledge that anything was wrong with what happened, and as such they deemed the protests to be unnecessary. In one instance, there was even a threat to let vicious dogs loose on the protestors. Now young Black men are afraid to walk on the road because they fear that they may be targeted by the police and as such may be wrongfully arrested.

There have been many dictators and tyrants who have ruled countries with an iron hand, and this they have done proudly and unapologetically. The unfortunate piece of this news is that because of the imbalance of power, these dictators have mostly gotten away with leading a brutal regime. At other times, we have seen a form of tribalism in politics where the color red is determined to be green and the color green is determined to be red depending on one's perspective. As this memoir is being written, there is a political situation in America which is very unhealthy and does not augur well for the next generation. In fact, all over the world, we have sometimes seen blatant wrongdoing which is being covered up in order to protect one person or a group of persons who are in power.

History has also taught us that there have been some very corrupt judges and lawyers in the judicial system. As such, many innocent persons have spent time behind bars or even sentenced to death because those who held the power to be fair and let justice prevail have chosen to ignore fairness and punish people who do not deserve to be punished. History has taught us that corruption can be prevalent in the workplace as managers at varying levels can do and have done outrageous things in order to get one or more employees dismissed. This is usually done out of malice or vindictiveness.

The Bible records many stories in the Old Testament where there were corrupt kings and leaders who cheated people who were weak and poor. It was into this kind of environment that the prophet Amos came and prophesied. I have taught a few times on the subject of prophets and prophecy in the Old Testament. Amos was one of those prophets who prophesied doom and was never intimidated by kings or priests or other rulers. One of his signature statements came about in his confrontation with Amaziah who thought that this Amos was just another false prophet. When Amos prophesied doom on Jeroboam, Amaziah, the high priest, asked him to flee from their company and prophesy elsewhere. It was to this that Amos responded, "I am neither a prophet nor a prophet's son." Amos then went on to establish the authenticity of his call to prophesy. Several other prophets would confront kings and other rulers who practiced injustice as a part of their way of life. After all, this is what the people of God were called to do. They were to let the others know when they were doing wrong; they were supposed to show them the path to righteousness and justice. Where are the prophets in the United Methodist Church who are willing to stand up to and confront signs of corruption and injustice within the wider body of the church? I can imagine what Amos would say now to some district superintendents and bishops. He would probably remind them that the same Decalogue which says, "Thou shalt not commit adultery," also says, "Thou shalt not bear false witness against thy neighbor." He would then utter the notable and often used quotation recorded in Amos 5:24.

BUT LET JUSTICE ROLL DOWN LIKE WATERS AND RIGHTEOUSNESS LIKE AN EVER FLOWING STREAM.

I can imagine what Jesus would say to these same bishops and district superintendents. If Jesus Himself was to address the leaders and officers of the church who were directly involved with my case, He would probably remind them that the same Bible, which speaks out against sexual immorality, is also plastered with teachings against lying and deceitfulness. He would then say:

> Why do you look at the speck of sawdust in your brother's eye and pay no attention to the plank in your own eye? How can you say to your brother, "Let me take the speck out of your eye," when all the time there is a plank in your own eye? You hypocrite, first take the plank out of your own eye, and then you will see clearly to remove the speck from your brother's eye.

In the year 2007, I wrote a song which was born partially out of what some persons deemed to have been an unjustified war in Iraq. Here are some of the lyrics below.

We want a revival

1) Many problems in the world are found;
greed and lust and hatred all around;
Stubborn are the people in this land;
Dear Lord come down and take us in your hand

Cho
We want a revival here on earth;
send us a revival and rebirth
come down and heal us Lord we pray;
We need Your presence to show us the way

2) Dishonest business people here and there;
corrupt politicians everywhere.
Injustice and oppression so unfair;
yet are practiced by people who don't care.

3) The poor; the sick and lonely need a break;
Inflations, wars, deception they can't take;
They face an uphill battle and heartache;
Oh save them from their woes for your name's sake.

I would never have thought that the message from those lyrics could be applicable to some persons in the church today.

This next statement is not meant to be an indictment on the FBI or on the Justice Department of the United States, but at the time of writing, there have been several allegations made against both these arms of the government. In the popular case of investigating the investigators, the inspector general's report suggested that the FBI made errors in the process even though there were no clear signs of a political bias. It is one thing for a body with power to make genuine mistakes when carrying out investigations; it is a completely different thing to knowingly and intentionally approach any such investigations with a bias that will lead to a pre-determined end.

When Jesus preached on earth, He often made reference to the expected very sharp difference between those who sought to follow Him and those who would remain "in and of the world." Very often this same Jesus who we all serve would make a comment about the behavioral pattern of people in the world and would then follow it up by saying…"But it must not be so among you," referring of course to the followers with whom Jesus was communicating.

In spite of this very clear and frequently referenced distinction made by Jesus, we had a situation in the sixteenth century where the church was so corrupt that Martin Luther in Tandem with Zwingli, Calvin, and others broke away from the Catholic Church and established what has now come to be known as the Protestant Movement. As most of us know, there were many hitches and hurdles which the original reformers faced, but they pressed on to the point where things smoothed themselves out. As I have stated in previous pages, I do not consider myself to be innocent in relation to the charges which were brought against me. However, equally, I would not want to think that I am the only pastor in history that has succumbed to the imbalance of power which has been so prevalent in the church. But therein lies the problem—that I am not the only one. I am hoping that the publishing of this memoir will be as much a wakeup call to the "higher-ups" in the church as the trials which I faced turned out to be a wake-up call for me. Whether it is the woman caught in the act of adultery or the Samaritan woman at the well or Zaccheus at whose house Jesus had a meal, Jesus always seemed to be compassionate to those whose sinfulness was often called out and in so doing defied the Pharisees around him who continuously complained that Jesus mixed, mingled, and ate with publicans and sinners. In relation to the bishop and other leaders in the United Methodist Church, at no time did anyone reach out to me with a view to determining what personal negative emotions that I was experiencing in my life and then offer a hand like the Good Samaritan who took care of the man who traveled from Jerusalem to Jericho and was beaten by thugs. That which I described in the opening of this memoir was real. The invitation to come to the altar and pray given by the person who shared the message that night helped to ease the heavy burden I was carrying at the time. I had issues with my physical health; I had issues with my emotional health; and by extension, I had issues with my spiritual health. However, no one in the leadership of the church cared enough to offer any kind of comfort or healing. It was bad enough that they did not offer any kind of healing and, depending on one's perspective, bad enough that they sought to punish me in the ways described above. Even worse was the fact that the church at every judiciary level used underhand, unethical, corrupt, and blatantly inhumane ways to get me out.

My defense counsel got an official calculation as to what would be the long-term financial impact if I were to be excluded from the church's pastoral ministry just one or two years shy of the actual qualifying date for my retirement. This piece of information was submitted to both the counsel for the church as well as the presiding officer for their consideration as they moved forward, but the document was callously ignored and dismissed. Here is the document below.

January 8, 2016
Rev. Errol E. Leslie
156 King Street
East Hartford, CT 06108

Dear Rev. Leslie:

At the request of Rev. Scott Campbell, I have reviewed a variety of documents related to the benefits afforded to you through the United Methodist Church, and would offer the following assessments based on my 16 years of employment as a financial planner (1986–1999) prior to ordination in the United Methodist Church.

A. If you were to lose your credentials in 2016, and be forced to take early retirement from the United Methodist Church at age 62, as opposed to working until age 66 (the age at which you are eligible for full Social Security retirement benefits), you will lose the following benefit amounts:

1.) You indicated that your current salary is $43,000. Assuming that the churches you might have served in the years 2016–2020 would increase your salary by 3% a year, you would lose approximately $ 183,494 in salary.

2.) Another key benefit for United Methodist clergy is health and dental insurance for you and your family which is provided through the conference. This year, your church is paying $ 14,940 towards the total cost for this coverage. Assuming that the cost of this insurance program would increase by 5% per year, you would lose approximately $ 67,613 of funds available to pay for health insurance if you were to take early retirement at age 62.

3.) Your church also makes contributions into your denominational pension plan on your behalf. Your church is currently paying approximately $ 7,213 per year into your pension accounts. Again assuming that your salary will increase by 3% a year: if your years of active service in the United Methodist Church were to end in 2016, you would be losing approximately $ 27,905 of additional contributions into your pension plan.

4.) For the record, it should finally be noted that ending your active service in the United

Methodist Church this year, as opposed to 2020, would also mean losing the benefits of the long-term disability and life insurance plans provided to you through the Clergy Protection Plan program offered by the denomination. While the annual cost paid on your behalf by the local church for this program is nominal, the loss of the benefits themselves could be significant if you were to be disabled or pass away between now and July 1, 2020.

B. Your benefits available after retirement will also be adversely affected by losing your credentials in 2016 and taking early retirement.

1.) Your Social Security projections clearly demonstrate that retiring early will have a negative impact on the income available from this program. The Social Security Administration's website offers a "life expectancy calculator." This indicates that a person born on April 16,1954 has a life expectancy (at age 62) of 21.9 more years. Since your Social Security projections indicate that you will lose $193 per month if you retire early, this would mean the loss of approximately $50,720 of Social Security benefits over your remaining lifetime.

2.) Your benefits available through the denominational pension plan will also be adversely impacted by the proposed required retirement. With regards to the guaranteed monthly benefits from your plan, beginning benefits in 2016, as opposed to 2021, would translate into a difference of $625 per month, or a total of $ 164,250 in guaranteed income over your projected lifetime. In addition, the projections from the General Board of Pensions indicate that the account balance in your defined contribution portion of the plan would generate an estimated $ 448 less per month (valued in today's dollars) if retirement began in 2016. Over your proposed lifetime, this would mean receiving $117, 344 less in retirement benefits from your defined contribution plan.

3.) According to Section 107 of the Internal Revenue Code, ministers in retirement are eligible to exclude from income some (or all) of the pension benefits received from a denominational pension program. Based on the estimates received from the General Board of Pensions, you will receive approximately $20,568 per year if you begin receiving retirement benefits at age 62. However, losing your ministerial credentials will also mean the loss of access to the housing allowance exclusion described in Section 107 of the IRS Code. Assuming that you and your wife earn less than $ 74,900 per year (based on the 2015 tax tables), you will be in the 15% Federal tax bracket. It would be reasonable to assume that you would have actual housing expenses each year totaling more than $ 20,568, and that the fair market rental value of your home would be greater than $20,568. Therefore, 100% of your annual United Methodist pension could be excluded from Federal taxation if you still held your credentials in retirement. Losing such will mean paying at least $ 2,163 more a year in Federal taxes starting with tax year 2016. Assuming that number stays constant through life expectancy, you would end up paying at least $ 47,370 more in Federal taxes.

4.) The New England Annual Conference offers its retired clergy (and their spouses) a benefit to assist in paying the cost of health and dental insurance in retirement. This program is available to all pastors serving the New England Annual Conference who have a minimum of 10 years of service with the conference. According to the 2015 Journal of the New England Annual Conference, you will have 17 years of service in this conference at the end of this conference year. If you were allowed to retain your credentials and retire at age 62, you would be eligible for a retiree health insurance benefit of $350 per person prorated by the number of years of service. Multiplying 17 years of service by a factor of 3.3% per year equals 56.1%. This means that you and your wife would be eligible for a monthly benefit of $ 196.35 each if allowed to retain your ministerial credentials. Over your life expectancy, that would translate into a total benefit of at least $ 51,601 for you. For your wife (her birthdate of February 10, 1960 translates into a life expectancy of 30 more years), this would mean a benefit of at least $ 70,686. However, this benefit will not be available to either of you if you are required to surrender your ministerial credentials.

I hope these projections will help provide a clear understanding of the financial impact you will face if required to surrender your credentials within the United Methodist Church. Please feel free to contact me at xxx xxx xxxx, if I can answer any questions on these projections or the underlying assumptions.

Sincerely,
Billy Paul (not his real name)
Methodist Church

When the prophet Nathan confronted David, he used a parable suggesting that the rich man who had all the wealth and power robbed, abused, and bullied the poor man who had just one sheep. In a backhanded way, this is the same message which Nathan would give to the church now. With all your power and a battery of professionally trained attorneys, you pushed out one of God's chosen servants who was not granted the privilege of hiring legal counsel.

There have been several known instances when clergy men and women have crossed the same moral lines I crossed in the church, but they are still serving. In many of these instances, the administration of the church would offer counseling and other remedial help to get that person back on their feet. In many such instances, there would be a concern for the negative financial impact which the ultimate punishment could have on the defendant, but in this one instance the church chose to be merciless in responding to that bad choice on my part. It would have been one thing if the church had followed its own laws and operated with strong Christian ethics and then determined that they wanted to have the same punishment meted out. However, it is a completely different thing when the church employed all the unethical, deceptive, and unfair principles which I described above to not only deprive a pastor who had served nearly forty years of his desire to continue pastoral ministry but also knowingly deprived him of monetary benefits as indicated in the document above. The irony in all this is that Bishop Carter has a quotation from the prophet Micah 6:8 on his letterhead which reads like this:

> He has told you O man what is good and what does
> the Lord require of you but to do justice and to love
> kindness and to walk humbly with your God?

Similarly, Reverend Therrell has a quotation from the book of Proverbs 3:5–6.

> Trust in the Lord with all your heart; don't rely on your
> own intelligence. Know him in all your paths, and he
> will keep your ways straight.

Did Bishop Carter really consider the reference to justice in that quotation from the book of Micah when he was overseeing the many acts of injustice on the part of the church from the top? Did Reverend Therrell rely on his own intelligence, or did he seek God's path so his own ways could be kept straight? He really did not allow the process to be played out fairly. Instead, he played the roles of prosecutor, judge, jury, and executioner. All other persons seemed to have been mere figureheads.

In his brief, my defense counsel made several references to the imbalance of power as he also did in relation to how emphatically the Book of Discipline stressed fairness when it comes to the conference relationship of any of its clergy. While Dr. Larry Lake agreed that my transgressions needed to have been called out, he was also able to recognize that the church had far more blatantly egregious activities and just stopped short of using the word *corrupt*.

However, between the Committee on Appeals and the Judicial Council, there was no effort to examine the arguments presented by the defense in its briefs. Whatever points they could not counter, they totally ignored or they declared it moot or waived. One example relates to the very sound and valid argument suggesting that the Florida Conference did not have the constitutional authority to even have the trial. When we got to the stage of the Judicial Council, Judicial Council ruling number 580 (referenced earlier) was cited as the precedent to confirm that by the church's own law, any such trial should have taken place in the New England Conference. Because that was such a slam-dunk "case closed" or "game over" situation, the Judicial Council totally ignored that reference in the brief presented by my defense. The Judicial Council ruling number 580 made in 1987 is as clear as day, yet the same corresponding body of 2016 found a way to get around it. Of course, they did not consider that argument because they claimed it was moot since (according to them) it was not mentioned in my counsel's initial arguments. In an effort to force the hands of the Judicial Council to look at that argument, my defense counsel was able to obtain a ruling of law from the bishop of the New England Conference so that the issue could be discussed at the appeals hearing. Instead of owning up to the church's error, the Judicial Council initially ruled that bishops are not allowed to take part in trial issues.

Notwithstanding the fact that Bishop Carter attended part of the opening day of the trial. Then a little later on, they stated another reason why they were reversing the bishop's decision of law, and in that second effort, they danced around the subject. Well, dance as much as they wanted to, an earlier Judicial Council placed before them ruling number 580, which was made in 1987. It was the exact same situation, and therefore that Judicial Council of 1987 made the very same argument as did my defense. The ruling in its entirety with the emphasis placed on the established law and constitution of the United Methodist Church is referenced above on pages 203–205.

My defense counsel was a gentleman, and his Christian principles came out through his actions. Honesty, fairness, respect were just some of the traits which emanated from his style. On the other hand, Reverend Therrell played the game well. He spared no tactic and omitted no strategy from his professional legal training. A very effective one was for him to pretend that he was offended by the several times when his dishonesty was called out by my defense. The examination of documents included in this narrative will speak for themselves and speak otherwise. Then ironically, when he commented to the church's press reporter following the case and in reference to the penalty imposed on me, he had the nerve to say, *"Justice has been done."*

Generally speaking, there are some kinds of unethical behavioral patterns which are so blatant that even the proverbial blind can see through an action. Very often the intent of such behavioral pattern is obvious. So he uses this approach where he claims to be offended when the truth hits him in the face. This style of fake and pretend anger and deception was clearly effective and must have been impressive at least from the perspective of Bishop Carter. Bishop Carter chose to reward Reverend Therrell for all his hard work of deception and unethical behavior by appointing him to become a district superintendent. Bishop Carter also rewarded assistant counsel for the church (Rev. Dionne Hammond) with the same prize. The Reverend Gary Spencer had told me that I had to sign the document agreeing to have the case heard in Florida within three days or I would lose the opportunity to choose. Now both Reverend Therrell and Reverend Hammond were going to be elevated to the same level. They were going to become district superintendents like Reverend Spencer. They were both going to be added to the list of great statesmen and stateswomen of the church who are above reproach and whose ethics should never be questioned even if the most blatantly dishonest practices are evident day after day. Really ironic!

On the other hand, and contrary to the perceived justice which Reverend Therrell claimed, as I have reflected on the whole process, I have been able to match the main "players" with several biblical characters. Rev. Jay Therrell, the counsel for the church, is likened unto the pharaoh of Egypt, whose heart was hardened and would not let "God's people go" in spite of the pleas and negotiations from Moses. I have likened Rev. Gary Spencer (working in tandem with the complainant) to King Saul who remained in hot pursuit of David and wanted to destroy him. Saul had determined that he was going to kill David by whatever means he could and with no regard for David's call by and potential to serve God. I have likened Bishops Devadhar and Carter to the priest and the Levite referenced in the parable of Jesus both of whom passed by on the other side. They were both more interested in carrying out their "priestly" duties instead of helping the wounded man. I have likened Bishop Gwinn to Pilate who "felt that Jesus should have been released" yet he "washed his hands" when Jesus was on trial and was just swayed by the pressure and demands of the crowd. In this instance, Bishop Gwinn was swayed and pressured by the crowd comprising Therrell, Spencer, Carter, Dodge, Hammond, and a few more. I have likened Rev. Scott Campbell and Rev. Larry Lake to the Good Samaritan. Neither of them had met or known of me before. They just saw a wounded man beaten up and lying by the side of road and decided to do all they could to take care of him by bandaging his wounds. They both put countless hours in trying to rescue me. I have likened Rev. Sydney Sadio to Moses, who started off doing battle for me against the pharaoh, and after his hands got tired, they were held up by Reverends Campbell and Lake.

At no time did either the Committee on Appeals or the Judicial Council consider fairness and integrity as part of the appeals process when this was such a big part of the concerns which my defense team had. If fairness was even remotely considered, I would not be writing this memoir. On the other hand, both appellant bodies dealt with the appeal as if it was a retrial of the facts related to the case. If this is a correct approach, it means that precious time, words and pages were wasted in both the Book of Discipline as well as the constitution where due process and fairness were spelt out very clearly.

As is the case in the secular courts, the Methodist Book of Discipline makes a reference to the possibility of double jeopardy coming into play in certain circumstances. One would have to assume that that must have been the factor which played into the minds of the Judicial Council as they handed down their decision. I had experienced humiliation at its height from Bishop Carter, District Superintendent Spencer, the counsel for the church, Rev. Jay Therrell, and to a lesser extent, Bishop Devadhar. I could not handle any more, so it was apparent that if the Judicial Council ruled—as they should have—that the judicial process was supposed to have taken place in the New England Conference, the clear call of double jeopardy would have come into play, and supposedly I would have been automatically reinstated. However, rather than doing the correct thing and stick with its own laws, the Judicial Council ignored their conscience and the laws of the United Methodist Church. So we find that those who are supposed to uphold the law end up breaking it.

I will now put God's restorative work into perspective.

1.) When I received the first letter that my salary was going to be totally cut, I began to panic as at that time I had a daughter who was in her junior year in college and a second daughter who was in her junior year in high school. I immediately put in several applications for office jobs but never received much by way of response and was only called to one interview. I seemed to have done well in that one interview because they invited me to go and do my drugs test and also asked for details on the names I had submitted for referrals. I went to do the drug test full of hope and enthusiasm. However, as the weeks ensued, I did not hear back from that organization. One evening I went back to the old parsonage to collect my mail and received a letter from them. They told me the exact opposite of what I expected to hear. They had identified someone who was more suitable for the position for which I had interviewed. I was, of course, very devastated as by that time I was about halfway through the total amount which I had taken out of my pension plan. I had withdrawn every cent that was available to me. Shortly after as the funds ran low, and as I have put it, I started to run on "financial fumes," I got the letter from the Florida Conference office saying that they had made a mistake and would be paying me a salary and other benefits up until the end of June. My God had come through for me as He has always promised—just when I needed the funds.

2.) After the trial was over, it took me a little while to start packing for the second time. This one from the parsonage in East Hartford, Connecticut. I just could not process the reality especially that I had gone through the pain of packing and moving just about one year before. At some point during that period after the trial, I called the pension office of the United Methodist Church and was told that because I was nearing sixty-two years of age at that time, I would have some more funds available to me, which I could either take in a lump sum or draw down incrementally as needed. I chose to go the latter route and hoped that it would last until I got myself a job. More importantly, my God had come through for me again. For twice when I was looking at having no fixed income to take care of my family and associated bills, finances appeared from sources that I never planned on. Once more I applied for several office jobs, but just like the first time, I got little or no response. It was at about that time when the Panic button was once more activated, that someone from the church in New England suggested that I enroll in a Certified Nursing Assistant (CNA) course. The rationale was that while it did not pay a ton of money, it was a pretty marketable vocation. I surprised myself in that I did not hesitate nor even stop to think about it much. Almost as soon as I returned to Florida, I registered for the next available course and prepared myself for this new vocation. On my first day in the class, I observed that all my fellow students could easily have been my grandkids, but even then, we all interacted well, and they all seemed to show some respect for the fact that I was a pastor and much older than they were. They would curb the average "young people talk" because I would glare at them with that fatherly stare, and they would get the message. However, it was when I finished the course and started applying for jobs that I found that my pride was really being hurt, and I had to swallow my pride from time to time. The offers for compensation that I was being given were far from being appealing, and it was very humbling to hear offensive comments from persons who were not only much younger than I was but who were also far less qualified academically. It was just as humbling once I started working in the system.

3.) While my pastoral status was in limbo, and for a long while, the only health insurance which we were able to get was the Affordable Care Act. While I served at the Methodist church in Palm Bay, my wife, Kaye, had worked very effectively as the administrative assistant for the church. However, from day 1 of the process, the district superintendent had tried to get her out of that position. However, she decided to hold on to it, and rightly so, for she had not "committed any crimes." In order to try and force her out, he worked with my successor and the staff parish relations committee to reduce her hours to a point where she would only be making thirty-two dollars ($32) per week. Especially because we knew that this was a way to try and force her to resign voluntarily, she decided that she was not going to give them the pleasure of forcing her out, so she continued working for the small amount of $128 per month. Then after another few weeks, she was summoned into the office of the pastor, and without any explanations, she was told to pack up her personal things from the office and leave the campus. The most humiliating thing for my wife as she reported the incident to me was that he sat down and watched her pack everything and kept ordering her around like she was a criminal. Unfortunately, my wife had received the same kind of humiliation from the new pastor at the local level as I received from the district superintendent, counsel for the church, and the bishop at the conference level. In her case, she had done nothing wrong. With all that, she successfully applied and received a job (in which she is still working at the time of writing) in the call center for a bank. This job came with benefits, including health insurance. In fact, it came with some benefits which the church did not offer. So even when we lost our health insurance and other benefits because of what the church had done to me, God provided a means—through my wife's job for us to get these benefits back.

4.) Even though both the complainant as well as the church made every effort to destroy my life as well as my family's, my daughter who was a junior in college when the process began graduated as an industrial engineer and is enjoying a promising career in Seattle with a very well-known and reputable company. She has had the benefits of two promotions since she started and is awaiting a third. She continues to get great reviews from her superiors. My second daughter who was a junior in high school when the process started is now less than one year from graduating from a prestigious arts college in Chicago. She has also done well academically and has also enjoyed serving in some important administrative positions at the student level.

5.) This last reference may appear to be insignificant, but for me it was another big demonstration of the hand of God working. The dates for the trial were January 16 and 17 (Monday and Tuesday). This meant that I had worked up until January 15 when I preached my last two sermons in the New England Conference to which I had been reappointed. When I returned to New England following the trial, the treasurer of both churches were told that I should be paid for only half of that month. So now I was going to be packing and moving back to Florida at my own expense, but I was only going to be paid half my salary since I had only worked "half of the month." There were, however, a few persons from the church who recalled that I was human, so they offered a little financial help, which was of huge significance. These were all unsolicited gifts. One person drove by the parsonage and gave me an envelope with three hundred dollars ($300). Another one who helped me to pack also gave me an envelope with two hundred dollars ($200). Still a third friend who helped me to pack also gave me an envelope with $200. This last referenced friend had actually driven from Maine in order to help me. I was so touched that he drove out of Connecticut at 11:30 p.m. on a Sunday night to drive back to Maine as he had to work the following day. Having shared all that, I must state that the one leader in the church who showed some kind of humane action and treated me with some dignity was Rev. David Calhoun, who was the district superintendent under whom I worked for the six months in Connecticut. Not only did he fly down to Florida to show some support by being a witness to my work in the New England Conference, but he also arranged to help me with some funds, which I was able to use to put some belongings in storage when I was kicked out of the parsonage for a second time. My cousin who lived close to one of the churches which I served there was also able to help me with storage for my more delicate electronic equipment and musical instruments. In so dong, she also saved me quite a bit of money, which I would have had to pay in a regular storage facility. My cousin also allowed me to stay at her house, without a cost, until it was practical to start the drive back to Florida.

In relation to number two (2) above, after a short while I realized that I was really carrying out a ministry. I was enjoying giving the service to residents in assisted living facilities or being a caregiver in the home situation. While it turned out to be a specialized ministry, I was getting some amount of satisfaction from serving. It was especially fulfilling when I was asked by relatives to officiate at funeral services for persons whom I had cared for or to officiate at weddings for friends, sons, daughters, etc. There was one instance when one of the persons for whom I had cared attended the church services for my nondenominational congregation whenever her physical energy allowed her to do so. In another situation, when I was taking care of a gentleman, I was literally giving pastoral counseling to him, and his wife as they continued to have arguments over domestic issues and would do that right in my hearing. It is not that I was being nosey, but they would invite me to intervene, for they too recognized that I was a pastor. It felt good and was very fulfilling to be carrying out a pastoral role even in that setting. From all appearances, it seemed that the ultimate intent of the church working through its counsel was not only to get rid of me but also to send me into obscurity and oblivion. Fortunately, while they were planning and scheming, God had some other plans. The fact of the matter is that my call to ministry came from God and not from them. My ordination was of God and not of man. My ministry, which continues to be restored by God, continues to show evidence that no one on earth can take it away from me. As such, when the presiding officer and some members of the Judicial Council hastily dropped the "Reverend" from my name, while it did not go unnoticed, it really did not bother me. I was going to continue to be a pastor anyway, and that is evidenced by the connections which I have with my present parishioners to this day. My pastoral responsibilities are not based on a title in a name but on a deep-rooted call from God and is demonstrated in action. The United Methodist Church attempted to steal the grace, which was lavished upon me through the death of Christ who had already paid the price for my sin. However, what they deemed to be stolen was restored to me by God and the restoration continues. Thank God for His amazing grace that saved a wretch like me. *Hallelujah* for the cross. Christ looked beyond my fault and saw my need. And just as God raised Him from the dead, my God has raised and restored me again. I have so many reasons to praise God. They are too many to mention in this story. With this great rescue from God, like Charles Wesley, I wish I had one thousand tongues to sing my great Redeemer's praise. I wish I had a thousand tongues to sing the glories of my God and King. I wish I had one thousand tongues to sing the triumphs of his grace! King David also had many reasons to praise God, so I can truly join him in saying from Psalm 18.

I love you, Lord, my strength.

> The Lord is my rock, my fortress and my deliverer; my God is my rock, in whom I take refuge, my shield and the horn of my salvation, my stronghold. I called to the Lord, who is worthy of praise, and I have been saved from my enemies. The cords of death entangled me;

the torrents of destruction overwhelmed me. The cords of the grave coiled around me; the snares of death confronted me. In my distress I called to the Lord; I cried to my God for help. From his temple he heard my voice; my cry came before him, into his ears… He reached down from on high and took hold of me; he drew me out of deep waters. He rescued me from my powerful enemy, from my foes, who were too strong for me. They confronted me in the day of my disaster, but the Lord was my support. He brought me out into a spacious place; he rescued me because he delighted in me.

I still have flashbacks to the days when I was younger and growing up in the church. I remember several old songs which speak to God's readiness to seek out and find any of His children who had gone astray. One of them used to be the favorite of my father. This one song is universally known.

This song is based on the parable which Jesus told regarding the lost sheep. I pray that we can all relive the message from this parable as we read the words of this song.

There were ninety and nine

1) There were ninety and nine that safely lay
In the shelter of the fold
But one was out on the hills away
Far off from the gates of gold
Away on the mountains, wild and bare
Away from the tender shepherd's care
Away from the tender shepherd's care

2) "Lord, Thou hast here Thy ninety and nine
Are they not enough for Thee"
But the shepherd made answer" This of mine
 has wandered far from me
 And though the road be rough and steep
I go to the desert to find my sheep
 I go to the desert to find my sheep"

3) But none of the ransomed ever knew
How deep were the waters crossed
Nor how dark was the night that the Lord passed through
Ere He found His sheep that was lost
Out in the desert He heard its cry
Sick and helpless and ready to die
Sick and helpless and ready to die

This next verse has a very meaningful message as it speaks to the efforts which God will make to rescue us.

4) But all through the mountains, thunder riven
And up from the rocky steep
There rose a glad cry at the gates of Heaven
"Rejoice, I have found my sheep!"
And the angels echoed around the throne
"Rejoice for the Lord brings back His own!
Rejoice for the Lord brings back His own!"

The message from the last verse is even more profound where it describes the shepherd as having completed his search.

5) And up though the mountain, thunder riven
and up from the rocky steep
 and made the glad cry from the gates of heaven,
behold I have found my sheep.

Then the angels echoed around the throne
rejoice for the Lord brings back his own;
rejoice for the Lord brings back His own.

God found me after I went astray and the
bible tells me that angels in heaven do rejoice over
one sinner that repenteth. Through this medium
and with joy, I announce to my friends, family,
colleagues and to the rest of the world that I WAS THAT SHEEP

About the Author

Rev. Dr. Errol E. Leslie is the founding pastor of Grace and Mercy Ministries Inc. in Palm Bay, Florida. Along with his family, he immigrated to the USA from Jamaica in August of 1995. Prior to that, he had worked as a Methodist minister in the Caribbean. He continued his ministry at five separate congregations within the United Methodist Church in Massachusetts, Connecticut, and Florida. As a pastor, Reverend Leslie has been strong on evangelism, Bible study, youth work, missions, and Christian outreach. For every congregation which he served, he either started a food-sharing ministry or helped to enhance any existing ones. He also believed strongly in visiting and praying with his parishioners so that he could get to know them and their situation better.

He has a natural and innate love for music and drama. Over the duration of his ministry, he wrote several plays and skits with a Christian message. Among his productions are two full-length Christmas musicals which are based on the Christmas narrative as we know it from the Bible but added some imaginary scenes and characters which are not detailed in the biblical narrative. He is also a singer and a self-taught musician with the gift of being able to play several musical instruments. For a long time, he and his family participated in a reggae gospel music ministry where they were able to minister in song to several audiences all over Jamaica and in several states within the USA. In tandem with his wife and family, he has released three separate musical CDS. Very recently, he also released what he describes as a solo a capella album comprising older gospel songs. For this project, he used his gift of creating harmony to lay several separate vocal tracks using only his voice. The net effect is that he created the feel of an all-male a capella group. This latest a capella CD is titled *The Old Time Religion* and is available on all the major musical platforms including Spotify, iTunes, Apple, and Amazon.

Reverend Leslie received his BA in theology from the University of the West Indies, Mona Campus, Kingston, Jamaica, in 1978 and his DMin from Columbia Theological Seminary, Decatur, Georgia, in 1991.

www.ingramcontent.com/pod-product-compliance
Lightning Source LLC
Chambersburg PA
CBHW021602120626
46545CB00001B/24